Jornadas Iberoamericanas de Ingenieria de Software e Ingenieria del Conocimiento (JIISIC 2018)

Copiapo, Chile
13-15 June 2018

Editors:

John W. Castro
Omar S. Gomez
Dante Carrizo

ISBN: 978-1-5108-6325-5

Printed from e-media with permission by:

Curran Associates, Inc.
57 Morehouse Lane
Red Hook, NY 12571

proceedings.com

Some format issues inherent in the e-media version may also appear in this print version.

Printed by Curran Associates, Inc. (2018)

For permission requests, please contact Escuela Superior Politecnica de Chimborazo, ESPOCH and Universidad de Atacama at the address below.

Escuela Superior Politecnica de Chimborazo
Panamericana Sur km 1 1/2
Riobamba - Ecuador
Postal Code: EC060155

Phone: 593 (03) 2 998-200
Fax: (03) 2 317-001

http://www.espoch.edu.ec/

Universidad de Atacama
Copiapo, Chile
Copayapu 485, Copiapo
Region de Atacama, Chile

Phone: + 56 52 225 5000

http://www.uda.cl/

Additional copies of this publication are available from:

Curran Associates, Inc.
57 Morehouse Lane
Red Hook, NY 12571 USA
Phone: 845-758-0400
Fax: 845-758-2633
Email: curran@proceedings.com
Web: www.proceedings.com

Preface

The Ibero-American Conference on Software Engineering and Knowledge Engineering, known as JIISIC, represents a forum for the international meeting of scientists and professionals dedicated to the study and research of Software Engineering and Knowledge Engineering. Its fundamental purpose is to foster scientific and professional cooperation, as well as the transfer of technology in the Ibero-American context.

Since the first one in 2001, held in Buenos Aires, Argentina, an increasing number of attendees have convened at JIISIC. Previous conferences have been held in Salvador de Bahía (Brazil), Valdivia (Chile), Madrid (Spain), Puebla (Mexico), Lima (Peru), Guayaquil (Ecuador), Merida (Mexico), Lima (Peru), Medellin (Colombia), Riobamba (Ecuador), Latacunga (Ecuador). In this 2018 edition, JIISIC is held in the city of Copiapo Chile.

In this edition, 41 manuscripts were received, and based on the reviews made by the members of the program committee and the successful registration, 21 manuscripts have been accepted; thus, having an acceptance rate of 51%.

The editors of this book of proceedings wish to thank those who chose JIISIC 2018 for their participation and the dissemination of their research work. We would also like to thank the members of the program committee for their valuable collaboration in the reviewing process. We are sure that their recommendations were positively valued by the authors of the accepted papers, as well as being positively valued by those authors whose works were not selected for this edition.

June 2018, Copiapo, Chile

John W. Castro
Universidad de Atacama (Chile)

Dante Carrizo
Universidad de Atacama (Chile)

Omar S. Gómez
Escuela Superior Politécnica de Chimborazo (Ecuador)

Steering Committee

Silvia Teresita Acuña. *Universidad Autónoma de Madrid* (Spain)
José Antonio Pow-Sang. *Pontificia Universidad Católica del Perú* (Peru)
Raúl Antonio Aguilar Vera. *Universidad Autónoma de Yucatán* (Mexico)
Mónica Villavicencio. *Escuela Superior Politécnica del Litoral* (Ecuador)
Omar S. Gómez. *Escuela Superior Politécnica de Chimborazo* (Ecuador)

Local Committee

John W. Castro. *Universidad de Atacama* (Chile)
Dante Carrizo. *Universidad de Atacama* (Chile)

Program Committee

Adrian Santos. *University of Oulu* (Finland)
Alicia Mon. *Universidad Nacional de la Matanza* (Argentina)
Ania Cravero. *Universidad de la Frontera* (Chile)
Beatriz Marín. *Universidad Diego Portales* (Chile)
César Pardo. *Universidad del Cauca* (Colombia)
Claudia Zapata. *Pontificia Universidad Católica del Perú* (Peru)
Claudio Meneses. *Universidad Católica del Norte* (Chile)
Dante Carrizo. *Universidad de Atacama* (Chile)
Efraín R. Fonseca C. *Universidad de las Fuerzas Armadas ESPE* (Ecuador)
Enrique Chavarriaga. *B2T Concept I+D+i S.L.* (Spain)
Francisco José García Peñalvo. *Universidad de Salamanca* (Spain)
Francy Rodríguez. *IMDEA Software Institute* (Spain)
Freddy Paz. *Pontificia Universidad Católica del Perú* (Peru)
Gloria Gasca. *Universidad de Medellín* (Colombia)
Isidro Ramos. *Universidad Politécnica de Valencia* (Spain)
Javier Gonzalez-Sanchez. *Arizona State University* (USA)
Jorge Triñanes. *Universidad de la República* (Uruguay)
José Antonio Macias Iglesias. *Universidad Autónoma de Madrid* (Spain)
José Antonio Pow-Sang. *Pontificia Universidad Católica del Perú* (Peru)
José Gallardo. *Universidad Católica del Norte* (Chile)
Jose Ignacio Panach Navarrete. *Universidad Politécnica de Valencia* (Spain)
Juan M. Ferreira. *Cámara de Senadores, Poder Legislativo de Paraguay* (Paraguay)
Juan Manuel Vara. *Universidad Rey Juan Carlos* (Spain)
Juan Pablo Ucán Pech. *Universidad Autónoma de Yucatán* (Mexico)
Luis Flores. *Pontificia Universidad Católica del Perú* (Peru)
Luis Rojas. *Universidad Andrés Bello* (Chile)
Karen Cortes. *Universidad Veracruzana* (Mexico)
Karina Carvajal. *Universidad de Atacama* (Chile)
Manuel Tupia. *Pontificia Universidad Católica del Perú* (Peru)

María V. De Castro Martínez. *Universidad Rey Juan Carlos* (Spain)
Marianella Aveledo. *Universidad Simón Bolivar* (Venezuela)
Martin Solari. *Universidad ORT Uruguay* (Uruguay)
Mirna Muñoz. *Centro de Investigación en Matemáticas – Unidad Zacatecas* (Mexico)
Mónica Villavicencio. *Escuela Superior Politécnica del Litoral* (Ecuador)
Nelly Condori-Fernández. *Vrije Universiteit Amsterdam* (Netherlands)
Omar S. Gómez. *Escuela Superior Politécnica de Chimborazo* (Ecuador)
Oscar Dieste. *Universidad Politécnica de Madrid* (Spain)
Pedro O. Rossel. *Universidad Católica de la Santísima Concepción* (Chile)
Raúl Antonio Aguilar Vera. *Universidad Autónoma de Yucatán* (Mexico)
Raul Hernán Rosero. *Escuela Superior Politécnica de Chimborazo* (Ecuador)
Reyes Juárez Ramírez. *Universidad de Baja California* (Mexico)
Rodolfo Villarroel Acevedo. *Pontificia Universidad Católica de Valparaiso* (Chile)
Romina Torres. *Universidad Andres Bello* (Chile)
Silvana Moreno. *Universidad de la República* (Uruguay)
Vianca Vega. *Universidad Católica del Norte* (Chile)
Vladimir Riffo. *Universidad de Atacama* (Chile)
Wilson A. Castillo R. *Universidad de Atacama* (Chile)

Table of Contents

PSP: How well it matches the skill set sought by the software industry in Latin America? A proposal to incorporate PSP into undergraduate SE education.......... 1
Brian Pando, and Glen Rodríguez

The scientific landscape of agile software development and methodologies: A social network analysis perspective.......... 15
Brian Keith-Norambuena, and Vianca Vega-Zepeda

Methodology for the development of VR immersive virtual reality applications that comply with universal design principles. Case study: Uniagustiniana immersive virtual tour.......... 27
Martha Yaneth Segura Ruiz, and Ricardo Fonseca

Determination and prioritization of requirements for software projects: SIMEER case study.......... 37
Manuel Ibarra, Mario Aquino, Hesmeralda Rojas, Ebert Gomez, Lintol Contreras, and Ronald Rentería

An exploratory study of the role of product owner in industrial practice.......... 49
Gerardo Matturro, Felipe Cordovés, and Martin Solari

Enhancing spherical photography with videogame visual effects in virtual reality experiences for users with limited mobility.......... 61
Gabriel de Ioannes Becker, Exequiel Plaza, and Felipe Besoain

Reusing and creating OERs for software engineering training.......... 73
Mónica Villavicencio, Jhonny Pincay, Kattya Desiderio, and Stephany Quimba

Factors influencing the adoption of agile practices in very small software development companies.......... 85
Shirley Coque, and Mónica Villavicencio

Helping novice architects to manage architectural technical debt in microservices architecture.......... 97
Gastón Márquez, and Hernán Astudillo

Web Information system for the consignment and routing of vehicles.......... 109
Néstor Díaz Escobar, Marion Riquelme, Rodrigo Linfati, Sebastián Gutiérrez, and Gustavo Gatica

Modeling of the Teniente converter through artificial neural networks.. 125
Alejandro Pulgar Sandoval, and Karina Carvajal Cuello

SMMicro: A methodological proposal for migrating from monolithic architecture to microservices.. 137
Carlos Arboleda, Pamela Flores, and Jenny Torres

MoProPEI-MP an adaptation in the selection of process mining tools for software processes.. 151
Silvia Jaqueline Urrea-Contreras, Brenda Leticia Flores-Rios, María Angélica Astorga-Vargas, Jorge Eduardo Ibarra Esquer, and Felix Fernando González-Navarro

Cyberbullying in developing countries: Uncovering the profiles of the aggressors, victims, manifestations and dynamics.. 163
Javier Aliaga, Diego Fuentealba, Cherie Flores-Fernández, Katherina Kuschel, Raúl Carrasco, and Marcelo Pizarro

Digital catalogue of software acquisition patterns 177
Ítalo Donoso-Barraza, Vianca Vega-Zepeda, and Diego Bravo-Rojas

Evaluating the impact of training software engineers using the R&G methodology.. 185
Mauricio Diéguez, Ricardo Gacitúa, and Elizabeth Vidal

Traceability of requirements in agile methodologies: A systematic mapping.. 197
Héctor Cornide, and Rodolfo Villaroel

Guide for the selection of software development methodologies for small projects and small equipment.. 209
Nahur M. Meléndez Araya, and Claudio Salazar Cortes

Gaps regarding requirements engineering protocol: A preliminary empirical study.. 221
Richard Esparza, Paola Peláez, John W. Castro, and Efraín R. Fonseca C.

Adding sensitivity analysis to component selection reduced effort yet increased difficulty, hurting acceptance 233
Fabián Villarroel, Hernán Astudillo, and Bernhard Hitpass

Continuous integration in Chile: Knowledge, perception, and interest 247
Tomás Vargas, Henrique Chevreux, Valeria Henríquez, and Harlley Lima

Sponsors

- Universidad de Atacama
- Escuela Superior Politécnica de Chimborazo

PSP: How well it matches the skill set sought by the Software Industry in Latin America? A proposal to incorporate PSP into undergraduate SE education

Brian Pando[1,2], Glen Rodríguez[1]

[1] Universidad Nacional Mayor de San Marcos, Perú
brian.pando@unmsm.edu.pe, grodriguezr@unmsm.edu.pe
[2] Universidad Nacional Agraria de la Selva, Perú
brian.pando@unas.edu.pe

Abstract. Software engineering (SE) practitioners must follow mature and quality processes, so that they can compete in an industry that demands quality products. In order to address this need, SEI proposed a personal methodology called PSP to improve the SE skill set of practitioners. In Latin American, there are more than 1200 professionals certified in this methodology, but the number should be higher if indeed PSP helps improving SE skills. This work uses data from job advertisements portals and survey to recruiters to find out what are the soft skills requested by companies in the Latin American software industry and compare them with the responses of PSP professionals regarding what are the strengths of PSP formation. The comparison brought favorable results. Then, a proposal of integration of PSP into the Curriculum of a Software Engineering career is presented.

Keywords: PSP, Skills, Industry, Academy, Improvement Software Process.

1 Introducción

Existen varios modelos, marcos de trabajo, entre otros artefactos para mejorar la calidad del proceso de software, los cuales trabajan a nivel de toda la organización a nivel de un equipo o a nivel individual, como es el caso de PSP [1]; el cual establece un conjunto de buenas prácticas orientadas a mejorar la calidad del proceso de software a nivel individual [2] a partir de la medición de tiempos, defectos, productos del trabajo, desempeño, entre otros elementos del proceso individual. Sin embargo, la aplicación de PSP en la industria en Latinoamérica no es muy frecuente, pese a que en países como México[3], Taiwán[4], entre otros([5], [6], [7]), se han realizado propuestas para integrar PSP en el proceso de formación profesional con las necesidades de la industria. Para PSP es clave la recolección de datos durante todo el proceso de desarrollo, así poder analizar y mejorar el desempeño evolutivamente, basado en un flujo de proceso que va desde los requisitos hasta la entrega del producto final, pasando por el diseño, la codificación y las pruebas, recolectando datos de tiempo y defectos.

Esta investigación presenta primero el estado del arte de PSP y su relación con la industria en Latinoamérica y hace notar la brecha entre las habilidades de los recién egresados y las habilidades que la industria solicita. Luego se encuesta a empresas y profesionales PSP de Latinoamérica y se comparan los resultados. Por último, se presenta una propuesta de integración de los principios y artefactos de PSP a la malla curricular de pregrado y se valida por expertos. Se concluye que las prácticas y principios de PSP debería integrarse desde la academia para complementar las habilidades no técnicas del ingeniero.

2 Estado del Arte

Basado en una revisión exploratorio de la literatura en la tabla 1 se resumen el estado del arte en 4 categorías definidas para esta investigación.

Tabla 1. Matriz del Estado de Arte PSP y la Industria del Software

Categoría	Investigaciones
Evaluación de PSP	[8], [9], [10], [11], [12].
PSP + Otros Métodos	[13], [14], [15], [16], [17], [18].
Industria y Habilidades	[19], [20], [21], [22], [23], [24], [25], [26], [27], [28], [29], [30], [31], [32], [33].
Mejora Académica	[34], [5], [4], [6], [35], [7], [3], [36].

2.1 Evaluación de PSP

En las investigaciones de [8], [10], [11], se evalúan los resultados de aplicación de PSP en un curso, con resultados favorables mayormente en la densidad de defectos. En [9], al aplicar PSP se ayuda a descubrir el tiempo perdido en interrupciones a un equipo de desarrolladores. Por otro lado, quizás exista resistencia al cambio al momento de implementar un método de desarrollo en el equipo, por ello [12] identifica factores de resistencia al implementar PSP.

2.2 PSP integrado a otros métodos

PSP por naturaleza se integra con TSP [13], sin embargo, también puede integrarse a métodos como XP [14], BDD [15], SCRUM [17], estas investigaciones demuestran que los métodos ágiles son compatibles con PSP; inclusive [18], fortalece la idea de integrar de PSP los métodos agiles.

También PSP puede integrarse a las pequeñas empresas, es la propuesta de [16], en el que presenta un marco de trabajo integrado de PSP, SCRUM y la ISO 25000.

2.3 Industria y habilidades

La industria solicita habilidades esenciales en un ingeniero de software ([19], [20], [22], [23], [24], [25], [33], [27], [28]). En [21], se explica las áreas de trabajo solicitados para los egresados; estas habilidades solicitadas son tanto técnicas como blandas, y los profesionales que recién egresan de las carreras no satisfacen en su totalidad estas necesidades en la industria.

Algunas investigaciones han logrado diferenciar estas habilidades por roles ([30], [26]), mostrando que no todos los perfiles del desarrollo de software debieran cumplir las mismas habilidades blandas. Por su parte, en [31], se sugieren cuáles deberían ser los atributos de grandes ingenieros.

2.4 Mejora académica con PSP

En muchos lugares del mundo se viene impulsando la aplicación de PSP para mejorar la formación académica ([34], [5]) ante la brecha de habilidades entre los egresados y la industria ([29], [32]).

Un trabajo a resaltar es el de [4], en el que se crea un organismo en Taiwán para mejorar las habilidades de los egresados involucrando PSP. Así como otras propuestas en otros países([6], [7], [3]).

Destacar también que en Latinoamérica se propone mejorar esta diferencia según los trabajos presentados por [35], [36].

2.5 Síntesis del estado del arte

Las investigaciones que evaluaron PSP, dejan claro que PSP mejora la productividad, pero podría haber resistencia a la implementación, entonces se debe buscar una manera en la que estos cambios no sean tan pesados y bruscos.

Las investigaciones que buscaron integrar PSP con otros métodos los han logrado satisfactoriamente, demostrando que PSP no solo se puede integrar con TSP sino con método agiles.

Las investigaciones que estudian las habilidades y su relación con la industria hacen notar la necesidad de habilidades blandas en los profesionales del software.

Las investigaciones que buscaron mejorar la academia con PSP reflejan la existencia de una brecha, y que en muchas partes del mundo intentan resolverlo desde la academia usando PSP como parte del proceso de mejora.

Por lo que todas estas investigaciones sugieren que los esfuerzos por llevar PSP a la academia siguen latente y debe seguirse buscando ideas de concretar esta tarea de manera conjunta para el beneficio tanto de los profesionales y de la industria del software.

3 Determinando la necesidad de PSP en la industria

Para determinar en qué medida la industria requiere de las habilidades obtenidas producto de la formación en PSP, se buscó y organizó las habilidades solicitadas en los anuncios de los portales de trabajo; con ello se realizó una encuesta, aplicada a los profesionales PSP en Latinoamérica y otra encuesta a los reclutadores de empresas para luego procesar y comparar resultados.

3.1 Identificación de habilidades

Un paso previo a las encuestas fue explorar solicitudes en los portales web de trabajo, entre ellas aptitus.pe y computrabajo.com (en sus distintos países de Latino América); se analizó un aproximado de 100 solicitudes, similar al proceso en [28], y se detecta que hay muchas formas de pedir la misma habilidad, por lo que se homologan algunas palabras para describir habilidades, así diseñar las encuestas, revisando sugerencias de [37] y [38]. En la tabla 2 se agrupan las habilidades por las fases del software.

Tabla 2. Habilidades categorizadas para las encuestas.

Habilidades para Requerimientos	Habilidades para Diseñar Software
Tratar con usuarios (H1); tratar con miembros del equipo (H2); frecuente comunicación de avances (H3); extrovertido(H4).	Habilidades en análisis y resolución de problemas (H5); separar los problemas en componentes (H6); innovador por naturaleza (H7).
Habilidades para Construcción	**Habilidades para Testing**
De mente abierta (H8); introvertido (H9); pensante, capaz de analizar y encontrar soluciones (H10); receptivo, capaz de escuchar ideas distintas (H11).	Receptivo y de buen juicio para escuchar ideas distintas (H12), conocer procesos desde pruebas unitarias hasta de integración (H13).
Habilidades Integrales	
Habilidades para gestión de la configuración de software (H14), enfocado en la calidad del software (H15), habilidades para gestión de la ingeniería de software (H16), conocimiento de herramientas y métodos para la ingeniería de software (H17), conocimientos de procesos de la ingeniería de software (H18), medir y organizar sus tiempos para terminar según lo planeado (H19), certeza para pronosticar la duración de las tareas (H20).	

Las habilidades son agrupadas por fases por temas de organización y para detectar en la etapa de resultados si es que hay diferencias de valoración según estas fases.

3.2 Resultado de las encuestas a los profesionales y empresas

Las mismas preguntas se hicieron a los profesionales y empresas, solo debía cambiar la perspectiva de valoración, el profesional valora su destreza en la habilidad y la empresa valora la necesidad de esa habilidad en sus trabajadores. La muestra para las encuestas fueron 49 empresas de todo Latino América de un total de 144 según [39], y 14 profesionales PSP, estas empresas fueron contactadas de asociaciones como CESSI, CBTI, ACTI, CHILETEC, FEDESOFT, AESOFT, AMITI, CANIETI, CISOFT, APESOFT, CUTI, CAVEDATOS, y los profesionales de redes sociales como Linkedin, Upwork, Workana, blogs, foros, etc, además de la base de datos de certificados PSP del SEI [40]. Los resultados son analizados comparando las medias independientemente por habilidad.

La tabla 3 muestra los resultados estadísticos de cada habilidad, la mayoría con una media superior a 4 (valoración de 1 a 5), que coinciden con la valoración del profesional, determinando a la habilidad como muy importante, para ambos.

Tabla 3. Resultado de valoración de habilidades entre industria y profesionales PSP.

Ref.	Habilidad	X_E	(Error Típ.)$_E$	X_P	(Error Típ.)$_P$	Aceptado
RQ	H1.	4	,152	4.41	,225	Si
RQ	H2.	4.22	,114	4.47	,173	Si
RQ	H3.	4.06	,128	4.35	,244	Si
RQ	H4.	2.83	,139	3.76	,304	No
DI	H5.	4.33	,125	4.67	,169	Si
DI	H6.	4.22	,121	4.53	,173	Si
DI	H7.	3.78	,158	4.14	,245	Si
CT	H8.	4.00	,127	4.76	,163	Si
CT	H9.	2.39	,133	3.04	,331	No
CT	H10.	4.37	,126	4.63	,227	Si
CT	H11.	4.35	,115	4.76	,163	Si
TS	H12.	3.9	,134	4.65	,132	Si
TS	H13.	3.76	,153	4.24	,238	Si
IN	H14.	3.51	,134	4.1	,314	Si
IN	H15.	4.08	,148	4.55	,228	Si
IN	H16.	3.73	,130	4.47	,172	Si
IN	H17.	3.76	,126	4.27	,214	Si
IN	H18.	3.59	,140	4.47	,172	Si
IN	H19.	4.18	,136	4.53	,228	Si
IN	H20.	3.88	,112	4.61	,172	Si

3.3 Análisis de resultados de encuestas

Por una comparación de medias se aceptan las habilidades con valoraciones superiores a 3 para las empresas y los profesionales, confirmando que 18 de 20 habilidades son necesarias en la industria y que con PSP es posible conseguirlas. Además se hace notar que los profesionales PSP superarían levemente el manejo de estas habilidades.

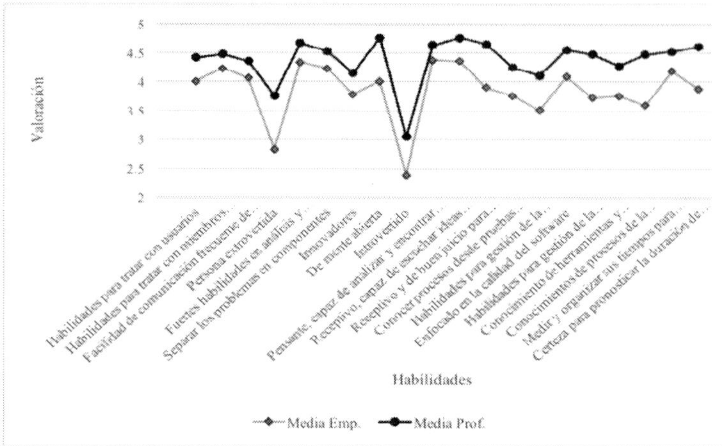

Fig. 1. Comparación de medias entre empresas y profesionales PSP.

En la figura 1 se distinguen las 2 habilidades que son descartadas, la de ser una persona introvertida y la de ser extrovertido, Además, los resultados de la prueba t-student basados en la aplicación estadística de [41], indican que hay diferencia significativa (<0.05) en estas 2 habilidades, en la figura 2 se detalla la evaluación, indicando también que para las empresas no son muy importantes estas 2 habilidades, con media inferior a 3.

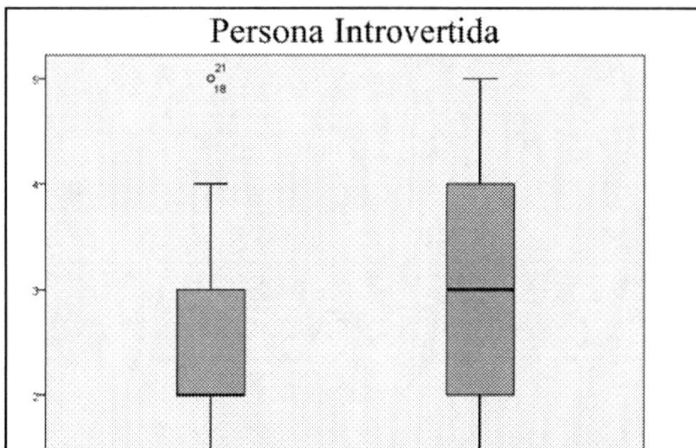

Par	Media	E. típ.	Sig.
Em - Prof	-,939	,197	,000

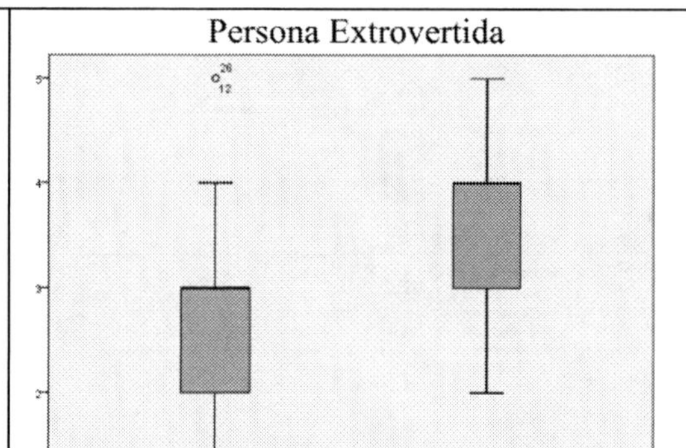

Par	Media	E. típ.	Sig.
Em - Prof.	-,653	,217	,004

Fig. 2. Resultados independientes de habilidades de introvertido y extrovertido.

Según los datos recolectados, en Latinoamérica la cantidad de personas certificadas en PSP son pocas respecto al total de profesionales dedicados al software en cada país, en la figura 3 se aprecia que PSP aporta habilidades en todas las fases del software (requisitos, diseño, construcción y testing, integrales), y en cada fase están al nivel que exige la industria. Esto implica también que PSP podría aportar en el proceso de formación del ingeniero de software como componentes complementarios a los tópicos de formación actuales de su carrera.

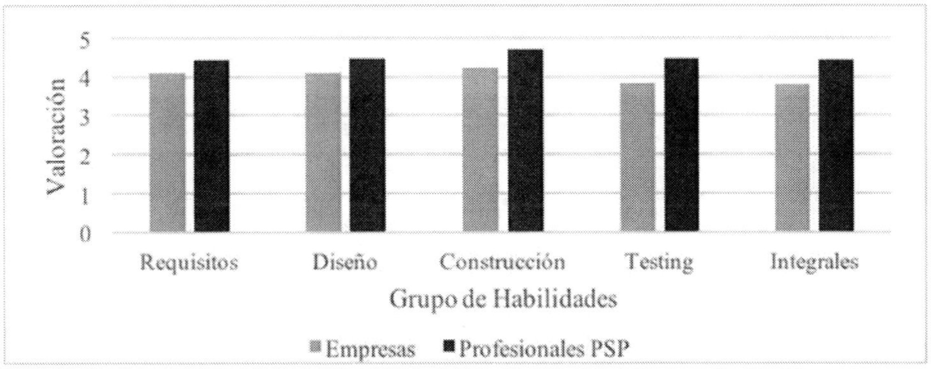

Fig. 3. Comparación de medias entre empresas y profesionales PSP por grupo.

4 Propuesta para incluir PSP en el currículo de pregrado

La propuesta considera sugerencias y resultados de [5], [35], [42] y [36], e implementa los artefactos y principios del PSP en el marco de toda la carrera, así no se percibiría la carga extra que este indica. Otro criterio resultado de las otras investigaciones es que no es efectiva la inserción de PSP si lo consideran como trabajo opcional. En la figura 4 se muestra esta implementación gradual.

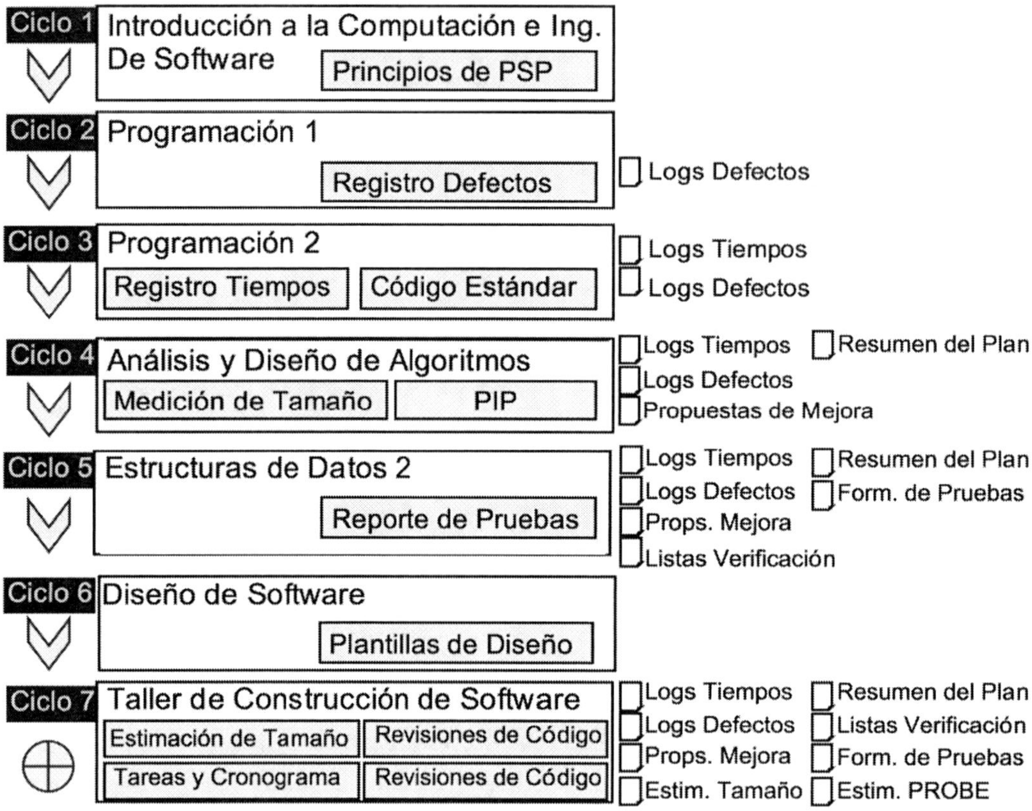

Fig. 4. Modelo propuesto PSP en la malla curricular.

Se toma como objeto de estudio la malla curricular 2014 de la carrera de Ingeniería de Software de la Facultad de Ingeniería de Sistemas e Informática de la UNMSM [43] mostrado en la figura 5. Se analiza y seleccionan 7 cursos secuenciales para la implementación gradual de PSP, y estos deben calificarse como parte de la documentación del proyecto final de curso.

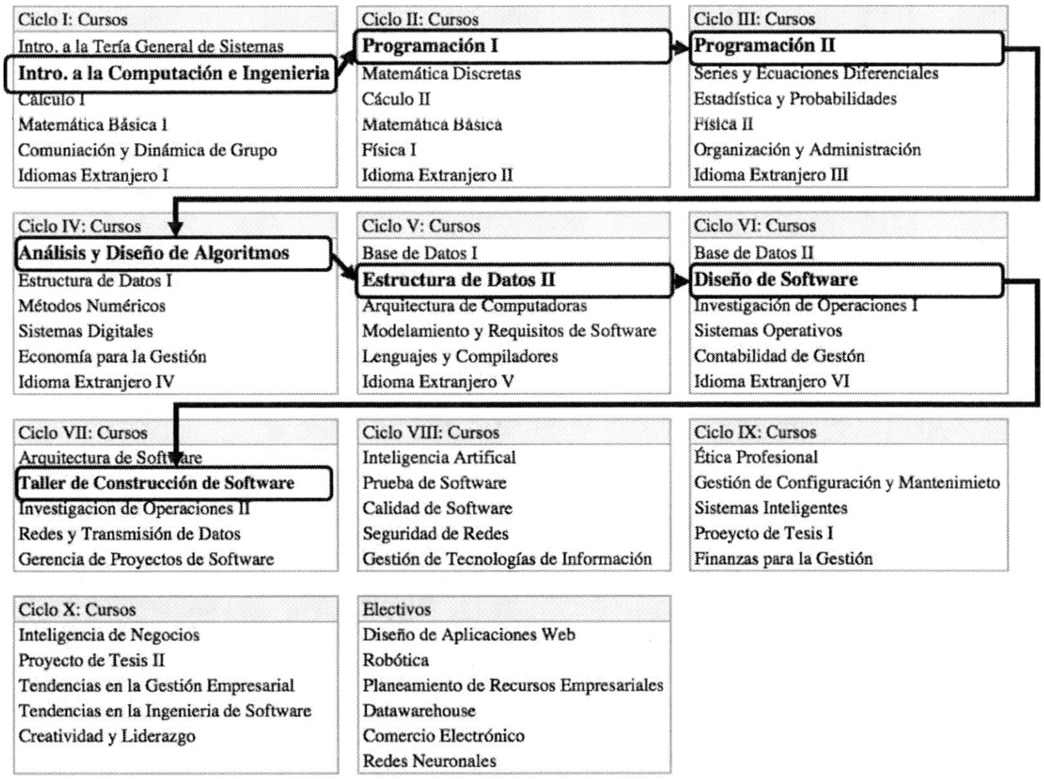

Fig. 5. Flujo de PSP en la malla curricular de la UNMSM.

En la tabla 4 se presenta los artefactos de PSP usados como propuesta; también se pone a disposición una hoja de cálculo con artefactos adaptados de las investigaciones revisadas en el estado del arte y algunos conceptos de la herramienta PSP Studio, https://drive.google.com/open?id=1EwWJdCdbW38JknEyaCxx8y2JB9MG2BJa.

Tabla 4. Artefactos usados para la propuesta PSP.

Actividad	Artefactos de PSP
Registro de tiempos.	Formulario de registro de tiempos e interrupciones.
Registro de defectos.	Formulario de registro de tiempos e interrupciones.
Uso de estándares de código.	Elección del profesional.
Medición del tamaño	Formulario del resumen de plan.
PIP	Formulario de registro de propuestas de mejora.
Estimación del tamaño	Formulario de estimación del tamaño. Formulario de mediciones de tamaño relativo. Método PROBE.
Reporte de Pruebas	Formulario de Pruebas Unitarias.
Planeación de Tareas	Formulario de lista de tareas.
Planeación de Calendario	Elección del profesional.
Revisión de código	Lista de Verificación
Revisión de diseño	Lista de Verificación
Plantillas de Diseño	Elección del profesional.

La propuesta se valida mediante juicio de expertos según [44], con 3 expertos con perfiles de ser profesional PSP y/o estar activo en la academia. Los resultados de la figura 6 demuestra que el modelo propuesto es acertado basado en la media de valoraciones de los expertos.

Fig. 6. Validación de la propuesta por expertos.

5 Discusiones

La exploración de sitios web de anuncios de trabajo en Latinoamérica se utilizó teniendo en cuenta a [28], y fue para hacer un acercamiento a las palabras claves de como la industria pide habilidades en los profesionales. Según lo encontrado, todos los países de la región en general solicitan habilidades parecidas y mismos roles en sus proyectos, confirmando también que la misma habilidad puede ser llamada con distintos nombres pero que refieren a lo mismo.

Los resultados de las encuestas indican que las empresas están interesadas en 18 de las 20 habilidades que proporciona PSP. Las investigaciones revisadas también confirman el alto grado de habilidades no técnicas solicitadas por la industria y la brecha que a nivel mundial debe resolver academia ([32], [25], [31], [26], [23], [20], [19] y [24]), considerando inclusive personalidad y roles [30].

La efectividad de PSP ha sido evaluado en distintos momentos y lugares del mundo ([8], [9], [10], [11], [12]) con resultado favorable sobre todo en la densidad de defectos, pero considerar a PSP como herramienta para cubrir la brecha de la industria no significa que esta sea una solución absoluta ya que se puede complementar con métodos ágiles([14], [15], [16], [17]), inclusive integrarse en pequeñas empresas [18].

El modelo propuesto se alinea a la academia debido a que las investigaciones que preceden sugieren que los graduados deberían contar con habilidades que la empresa las considera dentro de la brecha [7], [6], [4], [3].

El modelo implica que cuando los estudiantes lleguen a los cursos superiores de Ingeniería de Software ya habrán conocido y experimentado con ciertos artefactos de PSP, permitiendo así, reducir la curva de aprendizaje comparado con ensayar el método completo en un solo curso, superando los inconvenientes de [5]. El modelo recoge sugerencias y resultados de [5], [35], [42] y [36].

6 Conclusiones

El estado del arte manifiesta que en Latinoamérica, las empresas de software requieren habilidades y competencias de acuerdo al perfil al que se dedican, y al puesto laboral a cubrir ([26], [30]). Las técnicas, herramientas y metodologías son impartidas desde la etapa de formación, pero existen habilidades blandas importantes que la empresa requiere en el profesional y que no están siendo cubiertas ([29], [32]), pero las investigaciones revisadas y el resultado de las encuestas de este trabajo indica que PSP cubren habilidades importantes en todas las fases del software, reduciendo así la brecha existente.

Se realizó una encuesta a profesionales PSP para determinar las habilidades blandas conseguidas a través del proceso de formación en PSP, corroborando que los profesionales en su mayoría cuentan con las habilidades que teóricamente PSP desarrolla.

Se realizó una encuesta a representantes de empresas de software en Latinoamérica para determinar las necesidades de la industria respecto a las habilidades que propone PSP, encontrándose que la mayoría de éstas son requeridas, indicando que cumpliría un valor importante si es integrada desde los procesos de formación de pregrado en los profesionales.

Habiéndose determinado la necesidad de PSP en la industria en Latinoamérica, Se propuso un modelo que incorpora PSP en el proceso de formación profesional en el currículo de pregrado de forma transversal e incremental de manera que al final de la carrera el estudiante haya adquirido la mayoría de habilidades propuestas por PSP; obteniéndose una validación favorable mediante juicio de expertos, dando oportunidad a las universidades Latinoamericanas a iniciar la adaptación del método en sus mallas curriculares y promover la calidad del proceso personal del software.

7 Trabajos Futuros

Para reforzar la propuesta se debe validar el modelo implementando y revisando los resultados en otras universidades. También proponer herramientas de software de ayuda para documentar los artefactos de PSP de forma automatizada, de manera que PSP sea un componente de ayuda y que no quite mucho tiempo en la documentación de lo solicitado por el método, estos pueden tomar sugerencias de [45], [46] y [47].

Referencias

[1] W. S. Humphrey, "The Personal Software Process SM (PSP SM)", Software Engineering Institute, Pittsburgh, PA, 2000.

[2] M. Pomeroy-Huff y T. A. Chick, "The Personal Software Process SM (PSP SM) Body of Knowledge , Version 2 . 0", Boston, MA, 2010.

[3] I. García, C. Pacheco, y J. Calvo-Manzano, "Changing the Software Engineering Education: A Report from Current Situation in Mexico", Springer International Publishing, 2015, pp. 43–58.

[4] J. Lee y Y. C. Cheng, "Change the face of software engineering education: A field report from Taiwan", *Inf. Softw. Technol.*, vol. 53, núm. 1, pp. 51–57, 2011.

[5] J. Borstler, D. Carrington, G. W. Hislop, S. Lisack, K. Olson, y L. Williams, "Teaching PSP: challenges and lessons learned", *IEEE Softw.*, vol. 19, núm. 5, pp. 42–48, sep. 2002.

[6] A. K. Khan, "Assimilation of Software Process Management in Software Engineering Undergraduate Curriculum", *Softw. Eng. an Int. J.*, vol. 2, núm. 2, 2012.

[7] S. Hanna, H. Jaber, A. Almasalmeh, y F. A. Jaber, "Reducing the Gap between Software Engineering Curricula and Software Industry in Jordan", *J. Softw. Eng. Appl.*, vol. 7, núm. 7, pp. 602–616, 2014.

[8] C. F. Kemerer y M. C. Paulk, "The Impact of Design and Code Reviews on Software Quality: An Empirical Study Based on PSP Data", *IEEE Trans. Softw. Eng.*, vol. 35, núm. 4, pp. 534–550, jul. 2009.

[9] H. K. Elminir, E. A. Khereba, M. Abu, y I. El-Hennawy, "Application and Evaluation of The Personal Software Process", *Int. J. Basic Appl. Sci. IJBAS-IJENS*, vol. 9, núm. 33, pp. 96010–1212, 2012.

[10] S. Ramingwong y L. Ramingwong, "Implementing a Personal Software Process (PSP SM) Course: A Case Study", *J. Softw. Eng. Appl.*, vol. 5, pp. 639–644, 2012.

[11] F. Grazioli, U. De La República, y W. Nichols, "7 A Cross Course Analysis of Product Quality Improvement with PSP", *TSP Symp.*, pp. 76–89, 2012.

[12] M. H. N. M. Nasir, R. Ahmad, y N. H. Hassan, "Resistance Factors in the Implementation of Software Process Improvement Project in Malaysia", *J. Comput.*

Sci., vol. 4, núm. 3, pp. 211–219, mar. 2008.

[13] B. Maharrey, "An Exploration of the Personal Software Process (PSP)", Auburn, Alabama, 2011.

[14] N. Iqbal, M. ul Hassan, A. Rehman Osman, y M. Ahmad, "A framework for partial implementation of PSP in Extreme programming", *Int. J. Eng. Res. Appl. www.ijera.com*, vol. 3, núm. 2, 2013.

[15] G. B. Gerbaldo y J. M. dos Santos, "Aplicação do PSP (Personal Software Process) integrado ao BDD (Behavior-Driven Development) no desenvolvimento de um aplicativo Android", *An. do Comput. Beach*, vol. 0, núm. 0, pp. 424–426, 2014.

[16] J. A. H. Barrera, "Integración de marcos de trabajo para desarrollo de software: Scrum, PSP e ISO 25000 [Integrating software development frameworks: Scrum, PSP and ISO25000]", *Vent. Informática*, núm. 32, pp. 151–164, 2015.

[17] M. L. Urbina Delgadillo, M. A. Abud Figueroa, G. Peláez Camarena, G. Alor Hernández, y A. I. Sánchez García, "Propuesta de un modelo de integración de PSP y Scrum para mejorar la calidad del proceso de desarrollo en una MiPyME", *Res. Comput. Sci. 120*, vol. 120, núm. 2016, pp. 147–157, 2016.

[18] M. Shen, G. Rong, y D. Shao, "Integrating PSP with agile process:a systematic review", *Proc. 2nd Int. Conf. Syst. Eng. Model.*, pp. 805–811, 2013.

[19] R. T. Turley y J. M. Bieman, "Identifying essential competencies of software engineers", en *Proceedings of the 22nd annual ACM computer science conference on Scaling up : meeting the challenge of complexity in real-world computing applications - CSC '94*, 1994, pp. 271–278.

[20] P. J. Kovacs y G. A. Davis, "Determining Critical Skills and Knowledge Requerements of IT Professionals by Analyzing Keywords in Job Postings", *Issues Inf. Syst. IACIS*, vol. IX, núm. 1, 2008.

[21] C. L. Aasheim, S. R. Williams, y S. Williams, "Knowledge and Skill Requirements for Entry-Level Information Technology Workers: Do Employers in the IT Industry View These Differently than Employers in Other Industries?", en *Information Technology Faculty Publications*, 2009, pp. 1–5.

[22] R. Colomo-Palacios, E. Tovar-Caro, y J. M. Gómez-Berbís, "Identifying Technical Competences of IT Professionals. The Case of Software Engineers", *Int. J. Hum. Cap. Inf. Technol. Prof.*, vol. 1, núm. 1, pp. 31–43, 2012.

[23] F. Ahmed, "Software Requirements Engineer: An Empirical Study about Non-Technical Skills", *J. Softw.*, vol. 7, núm. 2, pp. 389–397, 2012.

[24] A. Suhaimi y A. Safura, "Skills Needed by IT Graduates as Perceived by Malaysian IT Professionals", en *International Conference on Management, Economics and Finance (ICMEF 2012) Proceeding*, 2012, pp. 224–230.

[25] A. M. Moreno, M.-I. Sanchez-Segura, F. Medina-Dominguez, y L. Carvajal, "Balancing software engineering education and industrial needs", *J. Syst. Softw.*, vol. 85, núm. 7, pp. 1607–1620, 2012.

[26] M. Rehman, A. K. Mahmood, R. Salleh, y A. Amin, "Mapping job requirements of software engineers to Big Five Personality Traits", en *2012 International Conference on Computer & Information Science (ICCIS)*, 2012, pp. 1115–1122.

[27] V. Garousi, A. Coşkunçay, A. Betin-Can, y O. Demirörs, "A survey of software engineering practices in Turkey", *J. Syst. Softw.*, vol. 108, pp. 148–177, 2015.

[28] G. Matturro, "Soft skills in software engineering: A study of its demand by software companies in Uruguay", en *2013 6th International Workshop on Cooperative and Human Aspects of Software Engineering (CHASE)*, 2013, pp. 133–136.

[29] A. Radermacher y G. Walia, "Gaps between industry expectations and the abilities of graduates", en *Proceeding of the 44th ACM technical symposium on Computer science education - SIGCSE '13*, 2013, p. 525.

[30] F. Ahmed, L. F. Capretz, S. Bouktif, y P. Campbell, "Soft Skills and Software Development: A Reflection from the Software Industry", *Int. J. Inf. Process. Manag.*, vol. 4, núm. 3, pp. 171–191, 2013.

[31] P. Luo, A. J., y J. Zhu, "What makes a great software engineer?", en *Proceedings of the 37th International Conference on Software Engineering - Volume 1*, 2015, pp. 700–710.

[32] S. Naiem, M. M. Abdellatif, y S. S. E, "Evaluation of Computer Science and Software Engineering Undergraduate's Soft Skills in Egypt from Student's Perspective", *Comput. Inf. Sci.*, vol. 8, núm. 1, p. 36, ene. 2015.

[33] Global Knowledge Training LLC, "2016 IT Skills and Salary Report A Comprehensive Study from Global Knowledge", Atlanta, GA, 2016.

[34] M. Towhidnejad y T. Hilburn, "Integrating the Personal Software Process (PSP) across the undergraduate curriculum", en *Proceedings Frontiers in Education 1997 27th Annual Conference. Teaching and Learning in an Era of Change*, 2002, vol. 1, pp. 162–168.

[35] R. Salazar, "Lessons Learned in Seven Years of Teaching PSP to University Students", en *TSP Symposium*, 2013.

[36] O. S. . Gomez, A. A. Aguiletae, G. E. Gómez, y R. A. Aguilar, "Estudio del Proceso Software Personal (PSP) en un entorno académico", *ReCIBE*, vol. 3, núm. 2, 2014.

[37] Fernando Belfo, "A Web Survey Implementation Framework: Evidence-Based Design Practices", 2012. [En línea]. Disponible en: http://www.academia.edu/953111/A_Web_Survey_Implementation_Framework_Evidence-Based_Design_Practices. [Consultado: 04-may-2017].

[38] M. Kasunic, "Designing an Effective Survey", Pittsburgh, PA, USA, 2005.

[39] MINTIC Colombia, "Colombia líder en la región en la producción de software de calidad", 2015. [En línea]. Disponible en: http://www.mintic.gov.co/portal/604/w3-article-8571.html. [Consultado: 04-may-2017].

[40] Software Engineering Institute, "SEI Certification | Certified Professionals", 2017. [En línea]. Disponible en: http://www.sei.cmu.edu/certification/professionals/index.cfm. [Consultado: 04-may-2017].

[41] A. A. Juan y A. Vila, "Introduccion al diseño y analisis de encuestas. Aplicaciones estadísticas a la selección de muestras y al análisis de cuestionarios", *Universitat Oberta de Catalunya*, Catalunya, 2010.

[42] Y. López Trujillo, M. André Ampuero, y A. L. Infante Abreu, "Training of roles and good practice for quality work of a computer engineer", *Ingeniare. Rev. Chil. Ing.*, vol. 19, núm. 3, pp. 382–395, dic. 2011.

[43] UNMSM, "Plan de Estudios 2014 | Sistemas | Facultad de Ingeniería de Sistemas e Informática | FISI". [En línea]. Disponible en: http://sistemas.unmsm.edu.pe/sistemas/eap/plan-2014. [Consultado: 06-may-2017].

[44] J. Escobar-Pérez y Á. Cuervo-Martínez, "Validez de Contenido y Juicio de Expertos: Una Aproximacón a su Utilización", *Av. en Medición*, vol. 6, núm. 1, pp. 27–36, 2008.

[45] C. B. Duarte, J. P. Faria, y M. Raza, "PSP PAIR: Automated Personal Software Process Performance Analysis and Improvement Recommendation", en *2012 Eighth International Conference on the Quality of Information and Communications Technology*, 2012, pp. 131–136.

[46] E. Salinas, N. Cerpa, y P. Rojas, "Arquitectura orientada a servicios para software de apoyo para el proceso personal de software", *Ingeniare*, vol. 19, núm. 1, pp. 40–52, 2011.

[47] P. Puello, S. D. Oviedo, y D. A. Franco, "Metodología para el Diagnostico de Prácticas del Modelo PSP", *Inf. tecnológica*, vol. 25, núm. 2, pp. 57–66, 2014.

The Scientific Landscape of Agile Software Development and Methodologies: A Social Network Analysis Perspective

Brian Keith-Norambuena[1] and Vianca Vega-Zepeda[1]

[1] Departamento de Ingeniería de Sistemas y Computación, Universidad Católica del Norte, Av. Angamos 0610, Antofagasta, Chile
{brian.keith, vvega}@ucn.cl

Abstract. Since the publication of the Agile Manifesto at the beginning of the 2000s, the influence of agile methods in the scientific literature of software development and the industry has grown in a considerable manner. Considering the importance of these approaches in software engineering, the purpose of this work is to provide a bibliometric analysis of the publications on agile methods in Web of Science since the beginning of the millennium. In order to accomplish this, several analyses are performed on the co-citation networks of documents and keyword. In particular, this article provides a list of emerging topics and trends using burst analysis and a list of relevant works in the field of agile software development. These results provide a high-level overview of the main topics in current agile software development research.

Keywords: Software engineering, Agile methodologies, Social network analysis, Bibliometric analysis.

1 Introduction

Agile software development is an approach to software development that arises as a reaction to the traditional ways of developing software. Agile methods provide an alternative to the heavy and documentation-driven development processes [1] [2]. While agile methods have existed for a long time, there are still several key challenges that must be addressed by both academia and industry practitioners.

In the past years there have been several systematic literature reviews focusing on different areas of agile software development research, ranging from early adoption issues to newer applications such as product line engineering. Also, significant progress has been made with regards to better connecting agile software development with established domains such a usability, CMMI, and global software engineering [3].

On the other hand, using agile methods as defined in the literature does not work very well and requires further adaptation by practitioners, where both the domain and the process influence the adaptation [4]. However, practitioners are less concerned about adopting agile and more concerned about sustaining agile [5].

The scientific literature on agile software development has struggled to reach a consensus towards Critical Success Factors [6, 7]. An understanding of these factors is vital towards leading agile projects into a successful outcome.

While agile software development is often associated with improved decision making, there are some failings of decision making in an agile setting that must be tackled [8]. One of the main challenges in agile projects is the lack of knowledge of agile practices [9]. In this context, the purpose of this article is to provide a starting point in terms an overview of the relevant literature and terminology for researchers and practitioners who want to tackle such challenges. Also, we provide a list of emerging topics in the field obtained through burst analysis.

Social Network Analysis (SNA) techniques are used to study the contents and interaction of the scholar networks [10]. These techniques seek to analyze the relationships within communities through structured and systematic means by mapping and analyzing relationships among its basic constituents, such as people, groups or organizations [11]. This approach provides a way to find non-trivial network patterns in a social network. It is also capable of handling large volumes of data [12] and identifying critical knowledge gaps in a domain [13]. These analyses also provide a guideline for new research lines. SNA techniques can find regularities in the work of academics and can reveal the underlying structure of knowledge within a research field. Also, it provides a way to identify communities of researches in a network [14] [15]. These techniques can also be applied to perform citation analyses [16] [17].

Bibliometric analysis is regularly applied to understand the landscape of research and innovation in emerging domains [18] [19]. One way of enhancing our understanding of a field is through the identification of emerging and fading trends in the field. To do this, one can perform a popularity-based analysis or a network-based analysis [20]. The works by Ord et al. [21] and Huang [22] study are examples of popularity-based approach. Text mining approaches can be used to analyze keywords as well, this has been applied to patents to identify new technological opportunities [23].

Some examples of network-based approach are: Whitley and Galliers [24] who analyze the citation network formed by research papers on information systems, providing insight into emerging trends; Meyer et al. [25] create a citation network to analyze the different structures in the fields of strategic management, accounting and social simulation; and Khan and Wood [13] provide an emerging themes study through a social network approach in the field of information technology management, our work takes their approach as a general guideline.

Given the relevance of agile methods to the development of software engineering and the relative lack of analyses using social network techniques in this field; this study seeks to fill the extant void of empirical social network analysis in the field of agile software development. Thus, the aim of this work is to apply such techniques and provide a detailed analysis of the corresponding results.

The rest of the paper is organized as follows: first, the methodology applied in this study is presented. Then, the keyword and document networks are presented alongside the emerging trends obtained from the application of burst analysis. Finally, we present a series of relevant conclusions.

2 Materials and methods

In order to retrieve all the studies related to agile development methods a search was performed on the Web of Science (WoS) database on the 27th of February. In order to do this, the following research query was entered into the WoS search engine:

Searched for topic: ((agile OR scrum OR "extreme programming" OR "lean development" OR "lean software development") AND ("software engineer" OR "software engineering" OR "software development" OR "software methodology" OR "software process" OR "requirements engineering" OR "software design" OR "software construction" OR "software integration" OR "software operation" OR "software metrics" OR "software evaluation" OR "software process improvement" OR "agile software" OR "software project" OR "software project management" OR "software engineering education" OR "software developer" OR "software developing")); Years: 2000 – 2018. Coverage: Web of Science Core Collection.
Scrum, XP and Lean were selected due to them being the most prominent and known agile methodologies. The other parts of the string cover a myriad of different parts of the software development process.

The search retrieved 977 documents which had appeared in 326 journals from 2000 to 2017. The h-index as provided by WoS for this set of documents was 47 and the average citations per element was 10.63. The total number of citations was 10387. These documents were authored by 1006 institutions, 79 countries, and 2325 total authors.

VOSviewer [26] was utilized to construct and visualize the different networks used in this work. The main networks used in this work correspond to the keyword co-occurrence network, which are created either from the author supplied keywords or the title keywords appearing in the publications. These networks provide a way to study the knowledge created in a domain [20] [23].

The identification of emerging and fading themes on keywords was done using the burst detection algorithm provided by the Science of Science Tool [27]. Author supplied keywords and the titles of publications are the best place to look for new and fading trends in a research domain [28]. Burst detection has been used in similar studies for trend identification in several research domains [29] [30] [31] [32] [33] [34] [13]. Standard preprocessing was applied before using the algorithm indicated.

3 Results and discussion

3.1 Author supplied keywords

The network of the top 80 keywords that co-occurred at least 5 times is shown in Figure 1. The keywords are grouped into six clusters as indicated by the colors of the nodes.

Cluster 1 (Red) consists of 19 nodes; its most prominent keywords are "agile" and "software engineering", both with 76 occurrences, followed by "case study" (29) and "software process improvement" (21). This cluster seems to be associated with works that center on the incorporation of agile methods as a software process improvement strategy. Cluster 2 (Green) consists of 18 nodes; its most prominent keyword is "agile software development" itself with 140 occurrences. Other interesting keywords in this cluster are "lean software development" (22), "requirements engineering" (18), "grounded theory" (17) and "continuous integration" (12). There does not seem to be any explicit relationship between these terms. Cluster 3 (Blue) consists of 16 nodes; its most prominent keyword is "software development" (48), followed by "agile development" (43) and "project management" (33). This cluster seems to be generated by keywords from works relating to software project management with an agile approach.

Figure 1: Top 80 author supplied keyword that occurred at least 5 times.

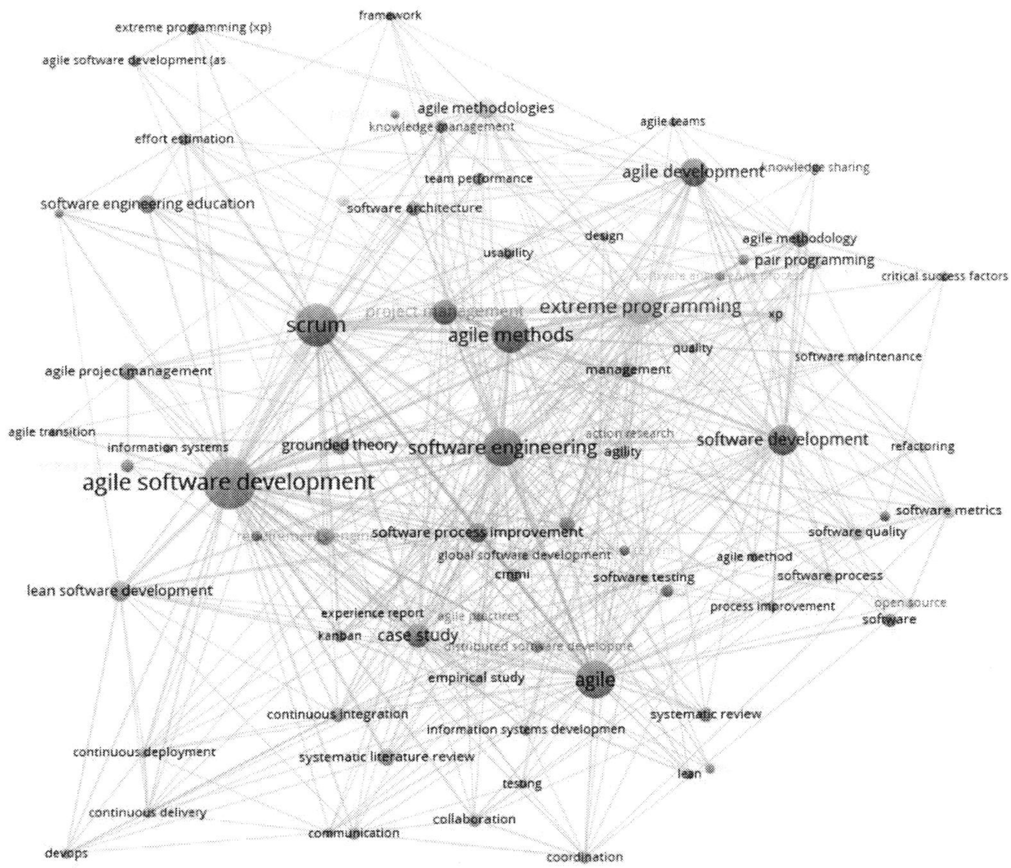

Cluster 4 (Yellow) consists of 16 nodes; its most prominent keyword is "extreme programming" (67), followed by "agile methodologies" (21) and "pair programming" (18). This cluster is centered on extreme programming and in particular it is interesting to note that its most prominent practice appears here. Cluster 5 (Purple) consists of only 11 nodes; its most prominent keyword is "SCRUM" with 94 occurrences, followed by "agile methods" (71) and "software engineering education" far behind with 17 occurrences. This could be related to the interest in using SCRUM for software project management in software engineering courses. Some additional keywords that might be of interest in this cluster are "agile project management" (15) and "effort estimation" (8). This part could be related to complexity of estimating the required efforts with agile methods, which are inherently prone to accepting changes, which would impact the original estimations.

As part of our keyword analysis we present a list of emerging topics, some of which are still relevant today and others which lie in a state of dormancy in terms of publications (see Table 1). These topics were obtained using the burst detection algorithm, which generates a list of the word bursts ranked according to their burst weight. The burst weight corresponds to the intensity of the burst. In terms of author supplied keywords we can see that most of the active topics shown in Table 1 is mostly composed by topics that have emerged this year. It is important to note that some of these terms are trivial or empty for the purposes of this work (e.g. they might be general agile development synonyms or are simply too general).

The currently active terms highlight potential areas of research that are currently the focus of deep learning research. While the inactive terms show which areas are not as popular or significant as they were before. It is important to note that while these topics might be currently not as popular since they have only been inactive since recent times they might yet be useful for new research. The words have been stemmed due to preprocessing, thus some terms might refer to different instances of the same root (e.g. program and programming would both have "program" as root).

Table 1: The bursting and disappearing topics extracted from author supplied keywords (words are stemmed due to preprocessing).

Word	Weight	Length	Start	End
object	3.02	8	2001	2008
program	21.87	8	2002	2009
extrem	20.61	6	2002	2007
method	4.02	6	2002	2007
metric	3.56	10	2003	2012
xp	4.95	9	2003	2011
open	3.76	4	2004	2007
sourc	3.38	4	2004	2007
empir	3.02	6	2005	2010
pair	3.81	4	2006	2009
methodolog	4.74	4	2006	2009
adapt	3.18	6	2008	2013
manufactur	3.49	3	2009	2011
theori	3.5	4	2009	2012
framework	3.16	2	2017	-
analyt	3.03	2	2017	-
effort	3.29	2	2017	-
continu	3.82	2	2017	-
devop	3.03	2	2017	-

For the purposes of this work, even though there are several words that can be associated with many software engineering concepts (e.g. framework), we assume that in the context of this work they are used in the context of agile methods. Although the idea of software development frameworks has a long history, the results show that in the agile software development community they are currently in vogue. Other keywords that are currently trending according to the burst detection algorithm corresponds to "analyt" (possibly referring to analytics), "effort", which possibly reflects the inherent difficulty of effort estimation with methods that embrace change, "continuous" (probably referring to continuous integration or a similar topic) and "DevOps". Note that all such active trends started in 2017.

On the other hand, there are terms such as "XP" and "extreme" are not currently in vogue with researchers according to the findings of burst detection, with its prime period ending between 2007 and 2011.

3.2 Title supplied keywords

For the purposes of our graphical analysis, the top 80 terms that occurred at least 5 times are included in Figure 2. Node size represents the number of occurrences and the links represent the co-occurrence relationship between the different title keywords. Based on co-occurrence relationships, words are grouped into seven clusters.

Figure 2: Top 80 title keywords that occurred at least 5 times.

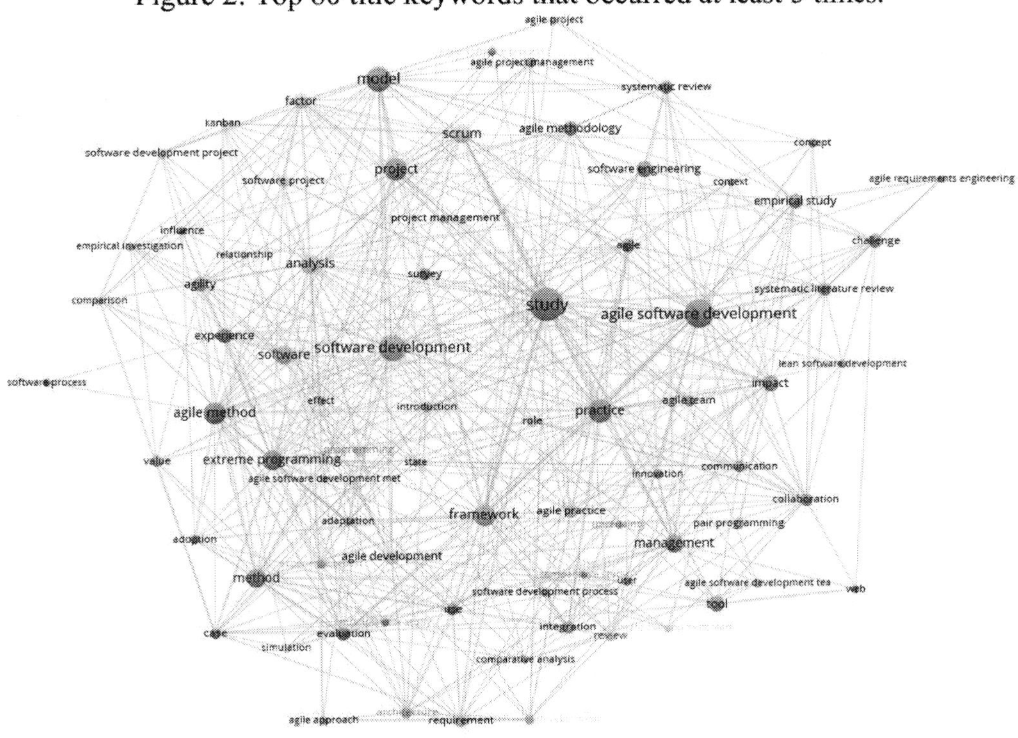

Cluster 1 (Red) consists of 22 nodes; its most prominent keyword is "study" with 93 occurrences, followed by "agile software development" (71) and "model" (55). There seems to be no further relationship among these concepts. Other notable keywords in this node relate to "practice" (47) and "project" (44). Cluster 2 (Green) consists of 16 nodes; its most prominent keyword is "software development" itself with 61 occurrences, followed by "framework" (41) and "software" (31). Perhaps the source of the importance of "framework" comes from the fact that the software engineering community is searching for a more detailed guide on how to apply agile methods. Cluster 3 (Blue) consists of 12 nodes; its most prominent keyword is "agile method" with 41 occurrences, followed by "extreme programming" (34) and "method" (30).

These relationships are trivial, since XP is an agile method. Cluster 4 (Yellow) consists of 14 nodes; its most prominent keyword is "analysis" (34), followed by "SCRUM" (31) and "factor" (21). There seems to be no direct relationship between these terms.

The last three cluster seem to be less relevant compared to the previous clusters, taking as a metric for relevance the total occurrences of its constituents. Cluster 5 (Purple) consists of only 6 nodes; its most prominent keywords are "management" (26), "tool" (21) and "innovation" (9). This cluster could be related to the difficulty of managing a project where the scope is subject to change due to the nature of agile methods. Cluster 6 (Cyan) consists of only 6 nodes; its most prominent keywords are "agile practice" (16), "requirement" (15) and "architecture" (13). This cluster could be related to the recent search of a methodology for the application of an agile approach for requirements engineering. Since requirements are so important for software development, it is relevant to clarify them without losing agility. Cluster 7 (Beige) consists of only 6 nodes and its most prominent keywords are "agile development" (25), "programming" (14) and "review" (13). There seems to be no apparent unifying theme in this cluster.

Table 2 shows the emerging and disappearing themes extracted from the titles of the documents, in terms of currently active words the results are quite similar to those found in Table 1 with respect to original keywords, however, the term "estim" (estimation) appears as a bursting topic since 2017.

Table 2: The bursting and disappearing topics extracted from title keywords (words are stemmed due to preprocessing).

Word	Weight	Length	Start	End
program	16.59	9	2001	2009
extrem	16.57	6	2001	2006
xp	4.92	3	2003	2005
pair	4.41	4	2006	2009
driven	3.28	4	2010	2013
improve	3.28	1	2010	2010
distribut	3.44	4	2012	2015
systemat	4.49	2	2015	2016
literature	4.58	2	2015	2016
review	5.21	1	2015	2015
challeng	3.19	1	2016	2016
effort	3.07	2	2017	-
continu	3.61	2	2017	-
estim	3.15	2	2017	-

Note that framework does not appear as a bursting nor disappearing topic when using title keywords. Inactive terms show more variation compared to the case of the original author keywords. Some interesting inactive terms are "driven" (2010-2013), possibly referring to test-driven development and of course "XP" and "extreme" referring to extreme programming again as in the case of author keywords. Another interesting example is "pair" and "program", possibly referring to the practice of "pair programming", which according to this stopped being in vogue by 2009.

3.3 Relevant document analysis

Finally, we present an analysis of the most relevant documents in terms of citations. First, we show the relation between documents in a graph constructed using the bibliographical coupling among the publications (See Figure 3). Only the top 330 documents are shown in the graph, due to forming the largest connected component. Based on this graph and using the bibliographical coupling of the documents we can identify a total of four main clusters (See Table 3). The publications presented in Table 3 provide a starting point for researchers that are interested in learning about the most influential topics in this area of research.

Table 3: Top 3 publications (number of citations) in each cluster of Figure 3.

Cluster	Title	Authors	Year	Citations
1 (Red)	Empirical studies of agile software development: A systematic review	Tore Dybå & Torgeir Dingsøyr	2008	504
	The Scrum software development process for small teams	Linda Rising & Norman Janoff	2000	127
	Chaste: A test-driven approach to software development for biological modelling	Joe Pitt-Francis et al.	2009	119
2 (Blue)	A survey study of critical success factors in agile software projects	Tsun Chow & Dac-Buu Cao	2008	178
	Get ready for agile methods, with care	Barry Boehm	2002	172
	Identifying some important success factors in adopting agile software development practices	Subhas Chandra Misra, Vinod Kumar & Uma Kumar	2009	72
3 (Green)	A decade of agile methodologies: Towards explaining agile software development	Torgeir Dingsøyr, Sridhar Nerur, VenuGopal Balijepally & Nils Brede Moe	2012	163
	Empirical evidence in global software engineering: a systematic review	Darja Šmite, Claes Wohlin, Tony Gorschek & Robert Feldt	2009	100
	Toward agile: an integrated analysis of Quantitative and qualitative field data on software development agility	Gwanhoo Lee & Weidong Xia	2010	95
4 (Yellow)	Management challenges to implementing agile processes in traditional development organizations	Barry Boehm & Richard Turner	2005	104
	The situational factors that affect the software development process: Towards a comprehensive reference framework	Paul Clarke & Rory V.O'Connor	2011	91
	Agile Modeling, Agile Software Development, and Extreme Programming: The State of Research	John Erickson, Kalle Lyytinen & Keng Siau	2005	88

Figure 3: Bibliographical coupling network formed by the top 330 documents.

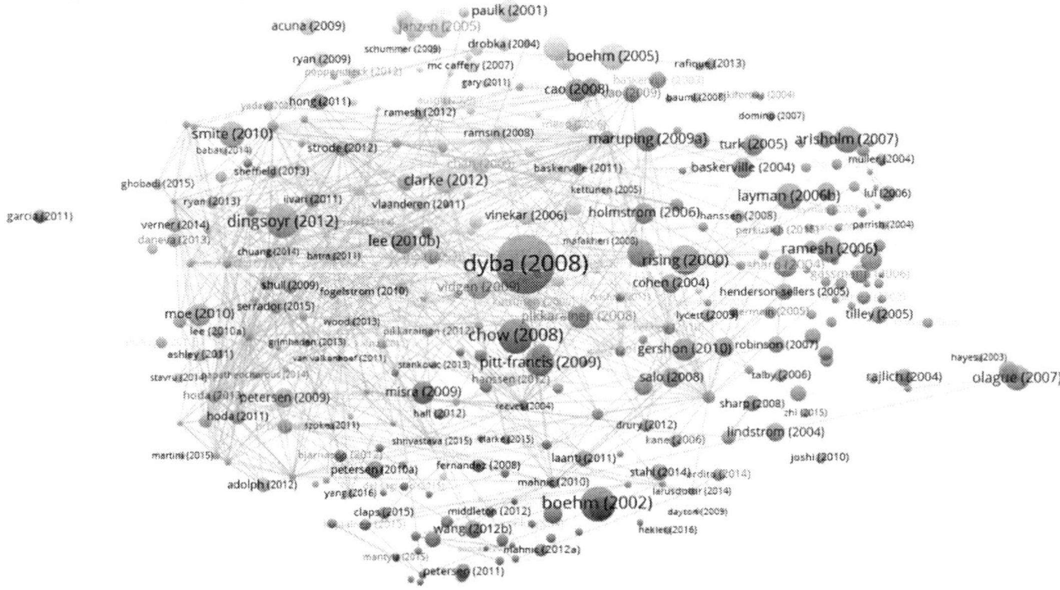

4 Conclusions

This article has presented a detailed bibliometric analysis of the agile software development field by querying the Web of Science database. The retrieved document set has been analyzed through SNA techniques. The results of this analysis have provided several insights on the nature of research in the agile software development field. Finally, an overview of some of the most relevant works in scientific landscape of agile software development has been presented.

Through SNA techniques this study has analyzed the keyword networks in the agile software development domain. Also, important documents from the field and the most relevant countries were analyzed by their contribution. The analysis also included the application of the burst detection algorithm to identify emerging and fading themes in academic research published in WoS. In particular, several emerging and disappearing topics were identified, in this context the potential importance of the topics emergent in the previous year (2017) must be highlighted. Topics such as "effort estimation" (or perhaps other kinds of estimation) seem to be in vogue in current research. Other emergent themes that must be considered are frameworks for agile methodologies, analytics and continuous integration and similar topics.

The limitations of the study must be addressed. This work has only considered the main WoS database. Thus, several other sources that publish research on agile software development or its applications are not included in this research. Also, it is important to note that recently, agile scaled approaches or new frameworks based on Scrum and Lean have been proposed. These topics were not included in this analysis. Therefore, it is necessary to be cautious when generalizing the results from this work.

References

1. Cohen, D., Lindvall, M., & Costa, P. Agile software development. DACS SOAR Report, 11, 38 (2003).
2. Beck, K., Beedle, M., Van Bennekum, A., Cockburn, A., Cunningham, W., Fowler, M., ... & Kern, J. Manifesto for agile software development (2001).
3. Hoda, R., Salleh, N., Grundy, J., & Tee, H. M. Systematic literature reviews in agile software development: A tertiary study. Information and Software Technology, 85, 60-70 (2017).
4. Diebold, P., & Dahlem, M. Agile practices in practice: a mapping study. In Proceedings of the 18th International Conference on Evaluation and Assessment in Software Engineering (p. 30). ACM (2014).
5. Gregory, P., Barroca, L., Sharp, H., Deshpande, A., & Taylor, K. The challenges that challenge: Engaging with agile practitioners' concerns. Information and Software Technology, 77, 92-104 (2016).
6. Aldahmash, A., Gravell, A. M., & Howard, Y. A Review on the Critical Success Factors of Agile Software Development. In European Conference on Software Process Improvement (pp. 504-512). Springer, Cham (2017).
7. Senapathi, M., & Srinivasan, A. Sustained agile usage: a systematic literature review. In Proceedings of the 17th International Conference on Evaluation and Assessment in Software Engineering (pp. 119-124). ACM (2013).
8. Drury-Grogan, M. L., Conboy, K., & Acton, T. Examining decision characteristics & challenges for agile software development. Journal of Systems and Software, 131, 248-265 (2017).
9. Fortunato, C. A., Furtado, F., Selleri, F., de Farias Junior, I., & Júnior, N. L. Quality Assurance in Agile Software Development: A Systematic Review. In Brazilian Workshop on Agile Methods (pp. 142-148). Springer, Cham (2016).
10. Wasserman, S., & Faust, K. Social network analysis: Methods and applications (Vol. 8). Cambridge university press (1994).
11. Cross, R., Parker, A., Prusak, L., & Borgatti, S. P. Knowing what we know. Networks in the knowledge economy, 208 (2003).
12. Khan, G. F., & Park, H. W. The e-government research domain: A triple helix network analysis of collaboration at the regional, country, and institutional levels. Government Information Quarterly, 30(2), 182-193 (2013).
13. Khan, G. F., & Wood, J. Information technology management domain: emerging themes and keyword analysis. Scientometrics, 105(2), 959-972 (2015).
14. Vidgen, R., Henneberg, S., & Naudé, P. What sort of community is the European Conference on Information Systems? A social network analysis 1993–2005. European Journal of Information Systems, 16(1), 5-19 (2007).
15. Krystallis, A., Ormond, R., & Christensen, K. V. Patterns and regularities in the European marketing academic community: A social network analysis of the EMAC annual conferences 2000–2010. In European marketing academy: Conference Proceedings of the 2011 EMAC Conference (2011).
16. Zinkhan, G. M., Roth, M. S., & Saxton, M. J. Knowledge development and scientific status in consumer-behavior research: A social exchange perspective. Journal of Consumer Research, 19(2), 282-291 (1992).

17. Carter, C. R., Leuschner, R., & Rogers, D. S. (2007). A social network analysis of the Journal of Supply Chain Management: knowledge generation, knowledge diffusion and thought leadership. Journal of Supply Chain Management, 43(2), 15-28.
18. Small, H., Boyack, K. W., & Klavans, R. Identifying emerging topics in science and technology. Research Policy, 43(8), 1450-1467 (2014).
19. Shapira, P., Kwon, S., & Youtie, J. Tracking the emergence of synthetic biology. Scientometrics, 112(3), 1439-1469 (2017).
20. Choi, J., Yi, S., & Lee, K. C. Analysis of keyword networks in MIS research and implications for predicting knowledge evolution. Information & Management, 48(8), 371-381 (2011).
21. Ord, T. J., Martins, E. P., Thakur, S., Mane, K. K., & Börner, K. Trends in animal behaviour research (1968–2002): ethoinformatics and the mining of library databases. Animal Behaviour, 69(6), 1399-1413 (2005).
22. Huang, C. P. Bibliometric analysis of obstructive sleep apnea research trends. Journal of the Chinese Medical Association, 72(3), 117-123 (2009).
23. Yoon, B., & Park, Y. A systematic approach for identifying technology opportunities: Keyword-based morphology analysis. Technological Forecasting and Social Change, 72(2), 145-160 (2005).
24. Whitley, E. A., & Galliers, R. D. An alternative perspective on citation classics: Evidence from the first 10 years of the European Conference on Information Systems. Information & Management, 44(5), 441-455 (2007).
25. Meyer, M., Lorscheid, I., & Troitzsch, K. G. The development of social simulation as reflected in the first ten years of JASSS: a citation and co-citation analysis. Journal of Artificial Societies and Social Simulation, 12(4), 12 (2009).
26. Van Eck, N. J., & Waltman, L. Software survey: VOSviewer, a computer program for bibliometric mapping. Scientometrics, 84(2), 523-538 (2010).
27. Team, S. Science of science (Sci2) tool. Indiana University and SciTech Strategies (2009).
28. Leydesdorff, L. The knowledge-based economy: Modeled, measured, simulated. Universal-Publishers (2006).
29. Kleinberg, J. Bursty and hierarchical structure in streams. Data Mining and Knowledge Discovery, 7(4), 373-397 (2003).
30. Mane, K. K., & Börner, K. Mapping topics and topic bursts in PNAS. Proceedings of the National Academy of Sciences, 101(suppl 1), 5287-5290 (2004).
31. Chen, C. CiteSpace II: Detecting and visualizing emerging trends and transient patterns in scientific literature. Journal of the Association for Information Science and Technology, 57(3), 359-377 (2006).
32. Chen, C., Chen, Y., Horowitz, M., Hou, H., Liu, Z., & Pellegrino, D. Towards an explanatory and computational theory of scientific discovery. Journal of Informetrics, 3(3), 191-209 (2009).
33. Guo, H., Weingart, S., & Börner, K. Mixed-indicators model for identifying emerging research areas. Scientometrics, 89(1), 421-435 (2011).
34. Swar, B., & Khan, G. F. Mapping ICT knowledge infrastructure in South Asia. Scientometrics, 99(1), 117-137 (2014).

Methodology for the development of VR immersive virtual reality applications that comply with universal design principles. Case study: Uniagustiniana immersive virtual tour

Martha Yaneth Segura Ruiz[1], Ricardo Fonseca[2],

[1] Ingeniera de Sistemas, Universitaria Agustiniana, Colombia, Cundinamarca, Bogotá,
martha.segurar@uniagustiniana.edu.co

[2] Licenciado en Electrónica, Universitaria Agustiniana, Colombia, Cundinamarca, Bogotá,
ricardo.fonseca@uniagustiniana.edu.co

Abstract. This project starts from the need to plan and control the development process of immersive virtual reality applications that are accessible to the greatest number of people. According to Cantone (2006) "The methodology for software development is a systematic way to make, manage and manage a project to take it to out with high chances of success. So, a methodology for the development of software are the principles to follow systematically, to devise, implement and maintain a software product since the need for the product arises that the objective for which it was created is fulfilled". Therefore, the project intends to be innovative, because it seeks to adopt, adapt or create a new methodology of software development for immersive virtual reality applications, if none of existing ones is adapted to the accessibility requirements and the principles of universal design promulgated by the United Nations Convention on the Rights of persons with disabilities, improving their interaction and usability in this type of applications and their inclusion in ICT. It seeks to analyze the current models or methods of software development and the formal tools of software modeling, as well as studies on the application of methodologies in virtual reality.

Uniagustiniana software developers are required to recognize this type of requirements and are aligned to the fulfillment of them. As a consequence of the use of this methodology, a practical case will be presented in which develops a multi-platform, multi-platform immersive virtual reality application language and dynamically adaptable to user requirements (Perlman, 2000), and evaluated by real users through usability test.

Keywords: Virtual reality, immersive virtual reality, universal design, software engineering.

1 Introducción

La investigación parte de la necesidad de planear y controlar el proceso de desarrollo de aplicaciones de realidad virtual inmersiva que sean accesibles para el mayor número de personas. Según Cantone (2006) "La metodología para el desarrollo de software es un modo sistemático de realizar, gestionar y administrar un proyecto para llevarlo a cabo con altas posibilidades de éxito. Entonces, una metodología para el desarrollo de software son los principios a seguir sistemáticamente, para idear, implementar y mantener un producto de software desde que surge la necesidad del producto hasta que se cumple el objetivo por el cual fue creado". Por tanto, la investigación pretende ser innovadora, porque se busca adoptar, adaptar o crear una nueva metodología de desarrollo de software para aplicaciones de realidad virtual inmersiva, si ninguna de las existentes se adecua a los requerimientos de accesibilidad y los principios de diseño universal promulgados por la Convención de las Naciones Unidas sobre los Derechos de las personas con discapacidad, mejorando su interacción y usabilidad en este tipo de aplicaciones y su inclusión en las tecnologías de la información y las comunicaciones (TIC). Se busca analizar los actuales modelos o métodos de desarrollo de software y las herramientas formales de modelado de software, así como estudios sobre la aplicación de metodologías en realidad virtual.

Se requiere que los desarrolladores de software de Uniagustiniana reconozcan este tipo de requerimientos y estén alineados al cumplimiento de los mismos. Una vez establecida la metodología de desarrollo, el paso futuro a emprender será la aplicación de la misma en un caso práctico multiplataforma, multi-idioma y adaptable dinámicamente a los requerimientos del usuario (Perlman, 2000) y el mismo será sometido a evaluaciones de usabilidad utilizando para ello usuarios reales.

2 Marco de referencia

El principio rector o filosofía de la metodología, es la norma o idea fundamental que rige el pensamiento o la conducta, y orienta el análisis, diseño y desarrollo del software. Es el principio, el que ordena y estructura las herramientas que son aplicables en la metodología, así como los procedimientos con los que se aplica (Pressman, 2015).

El desarrollo de software ha cambiado a través del tiempo, nuevas aplicaciones surgen debido al auge de nuevos dispositivos y elementos de hardware, es imperiosa la necesidad de utilizar metodologías de desarrollo de software acordes a los nuevos requerimientos de usuario y especificaciones de software.

Aunque hay un aumento en proyectos de investigación y artículos tanto en países desarrollados como países en desarrollo relacionados el desarrollo de aplicaciones de realidad virtual en diferentes áreas, son menores las investigaciones relacionadas con la aplicación de una metodología de desarrollo que cumpla los requerimientos del diseño universal. No se han encontrado investigaciones que correlacionen metodologías de desarrollo, la realidad virtual inmersiva y el diseño universal.

Los estudios de investigación aplicados a la problemática generan que la estructura del estado del arte se organice en dos apartados, uno dedicado las Metodologías de diseño o desarrollo de software de realidad virtual, y el otro al Diseño universal o diseño para todos y accesibilidad en las tecnologías de la información y las comunicaciones TIC.

A continuación, se proponen los trabajos realizados en el contexto internacional y nacional para presentar las problemáticas afines a la descrita en el presente proceso de investigación:

1) Metodologías de diseño o desarrollo de software de realidad virtual:

En el mundo se han desarrollado diversos libros, proyectos de investigación, artículos y tesis relacionadas.

La investigación realizada por Quiroz, J. D. C. (2010) en su proyecto de tesis doctoral UP4VED Método de Desarrollo basado en el Proceso Unificado y en Buenas Prácticas para la Construcción de Entornos Virtuales, presenta una metodología de desarrollo que se fundamenta en el RUP (sigla del inglés Rational Unified Process) y en buenas prácticas para la construcción de EV (Entornos Virtuales); la metodología recoge las mejores propuestas planteadas en las metodologías existentes para el desarrollo de EV, las consideraciones especiales para su modelado, los pilares del proceso unificado, así como las sugerencias del estándar SPEM (sigla del inglés Software & Systems Process Engineering Metamodel) 2.0 de OMG (sigla del inglés Object Management Group).

Con el objetivo de validar y aplicar las propuestas realizadas en la metodología UP4VED, realizaron dos desarrollos para contextos de aplicación distintos, que permitiesen revisar elementos relacionados con las consideraciones específicas de modelado para entornos virtuales. Un primer caso, se concentró en el desarrollo de un recorrido virtual del campus de la Universidad Autónoma de Occidente, Cali, Colombia; el segundo caso, se trató de un entorno virtual para la simulación de procesos de mecanizado en un torno CNC sobre Internet. (Quiroz, J. D. C, 2010).

La generación de estos dos EVs (Entornos Virtuales Simulados), permitió utilizar tanto los elementos base del contenido del método (roles, tareas y productos de trabajo), así como orientar el proceso a través del ciclo vital definido por UP4VED en un contexto real de desarrollo. (Quiroz, J. D. C, 2010).

Así mismo, (Molina, J. P., García, A. S., López Jaquero, V., & González, P., 2005) realizaron el artículo Developing VR applications: the TRES-D methodology que presenta la metodología TRES-D para el desarrollo de la aplicación de realidad virtual, e identifica oportunidades para crear herramientas que no sean amigas de la realidad virtual. Esta metodología se basa en enfoques en la creación de mundos virtuales, tanto en la práctica observada como en los métodos propuestos, métodos y técnicas forman la ingeniería de software y los dominios de interacción humano-computador.

La Escuela Superior Politécnica del Chimborazo en Ecuador tiene como fortaleza el desarrollo de trabajos de grado enfocados a metodologías en el área de videojuegos y realidad virtual, como se presenta a continuación: El proyecto de tesis de grado para optar al título de ingenieros informáticos, (Barreno, A., Alexander, G., Guaraca, S., & Gonzalo, M., 2013), Adaptación de las metodologías ágiles Scrum y XGD (sigla del inglés Extreme Game Development) en una metodología para el desarrollo de videojuegos en Android. Caso práctico: Desarrollo de un videojuego, es una aproximación en conocimiento para el desarrollo de la investigación, pues aplica un método analítico e investigativo en cada metodología, obteniéndose resultados de los parámetros de cada criterio de acuerdo a pruebas realizadas en el desarrollo del prototipo de videojuego.

Para la demostración de hipótesis no se utilizó ningún método estadístico debido a que no se posee una población. Se concluye que Scrum se enfoca en la gestión del proyecto, no posee prácticas de ingeniería a diferencia de XGD que es una metodología de ingeniería que contiene prácticas que aseguran la calidad focalizándose en el código.

Por lo tanto, combinar Scrum con Extreme Game Development en la nueva metodología incrementa la calidad y productividad de código desarrollado, la gestión del proyecto con un seguimiento estricto en la planificación, tareas, iteraciones y tiempos; planteando fases y actividades muy prácticas, fuertemente ligadas, ayudando a desarrollar de manera rápida. Se recomienda a los desarrolladores de videojuegos que al utilizar la nueva metodología adaptada se siga el proceso en su totalidad debido a que facilita su creación.

Otro proyecto de tesis de los autores (Noboa, C., Carlos, J., & Maggi Murillo, B. G., 2016) para optar al título como ingenieros en diseño gráfico, referente al Desarrollo de una metodología para diseñar paseos virtuales; caso práctico acerca de los personajes más emblemáticos de Riobamba, la investigación proporciona las características y directrices a seguir para la creación de una nueva metodología para la creación de visitas virtuales en 3D, fundamentada en la historia de Riobamba.

Como aporte al desarrollo de la investigación (Gallardo, S., Barrero, F., & Toral, S. L., 2005) crean el articulo Building a Web-based virtual laboratory with VRML (Virtual Reality Modeling Language). A case study: An electronic instrumentation subject que analiza la creación de un ambiente virtual de un laboratorio real empleando el lenguaje llamado VRML.

Rambli, D. R. A., & Muhaiyuddin, N. D. M. (2013) presentan el articulo Design Methodology for IBVR (sigla del inglés Image-based Virtual Reality Application), que describe una metodología para IBVR que podría generar una gran experiencia de presencia espacial entre los usuarios, se estructura la metodología de diseño basada en su experiencia práctica creando aplicaciones de IBVR y también basado en el resultado de su estudio comprensivo en características de IBVR. Se deriva y se propone la metodología de cuatro etapas basada en el resultado del estudio: Planificación y Refinamiento de Proyectos, Especificación de Requisitos de Usuario, IBVR, Desarrollo e Implementación, Verificación y Validación IBVR.

En Colombia (Londoño, F., Alvarez, M. L., Chiappe, A., & Ramirez, M. E., 2002), en la Universidad Católica de Manizales realizan el artículo Metodología de desarrollo de producciones educativas hipermediales personalizantes que presenta un método que contribuye a clarificar el complejo proceso de desarrollo de software educativo hipermedial partiendo de la perspectiva personalizante de la educación, articulada con elementos de orden comunicativo del modelo de interlocución que permitan enriquecer la construcción informática de un producto educativo intencionado en el criterio formativo del estudiante. En él se plantean tres componentes para el modelo desde lo educativo, lo comunicacional y lo informático, articuladas a la luz del modelo personalizante en proceso de institucionalización por parte de la Universidad Católica de Manizales, en el que se describen las etapas asociadas con cada fase.

2) Diseño universal o diseño para todos y accesibilidad en las TIC (Tecnologías de la Información y las Comunicaciones).

El artículo, An Introduction to 3D User Interface Design (Bowman, D. A., Kruijff, E., LaViola Jr, J. J., & Poupyrev, I. ,2001) que describe como el diseño de interfaz de usuario 3D es un componente crítico de cualquier aplicación en un EV (Entorno Virtual), el panorama de la interacción tridimensional (3D) y las interfaces de usuario, el documento se centra en presentar no sólo las técnicas disponibles, sino también directrices prácticas para el diseño de la interacción 3D, se discuten dos enfoques de este diseño y algunas aplicaciones de ejemplo con complejos requerimientos de interacción 3D.

En Japón, Watanuki, K. (2010) presenta el artículo Development of virtual reality-based universal design review system, en el cual expone el desarrollo de un sistema de revisión de diseño tangible que hace uso de la tecnología de realidad virtual para mostrar un modelo cercano del producto real, haciendo fácilmente disponible no sólo la información visual, sino también la percepción de volumen y peso a través de la fusión de la información kinestésica, permitiendo que mucha gente se comunique fácilmente mientras experimenta esta realidad virtual.

Barzabal, L. T. (2004) en su artículo Accesibilidad al contenido web para todas las personas, pretende recapacitar sobre un problema que afecta a muchas personas en los entornos educativos y en la sociedad en general: la imposibilidad de acceso a la red, pues existen diversas barreras en el medio virtual que impiden llegar adecuadamente a la información alojada en las páginas web.

Los motivos por los cuales se limita el acceso a la red pueden ser diversos, pero de cualquier forma se plantean una serie de barreras que dejan al margen de la información y comunicación a un grupo considerable de usuarios. Estas dificultades podrían disminuirse si se comienza a apreciar la importancia de las normas o pautas establecidas para que los diseños de los contenidos alojados en una página web sean accesibles a todos los usuarios o al menos a la mayor cantidad de ellos. Investigación que puede aportar desde los requerimientos de accesibilidad a las TIC.

Kamieth, F., Dähne, P., Wichert, R., Villalar, J. L., Jimenez-Mixco, V., Arca, A., & Arredondo, M. T. (2010) en la investigación Exploring the potential of virtual reality for the elderly and people with disabilities, dos grupos de investigación responsables del capítulo del libro - Fh-IGD y LST-UPM- han avanzado en el potencial de las TIC para superar las limitaciones de ambientes y servicios, en particular abordando la convergencia de RV (Realidad Virtual), domótica y accesibilidad. Ambos grupos están explorando la aplicación práctica de las tecnologías realidad virtual en el proceso de diseño y desarrollo de soluciones accesibles para el E&D (sigla del inglés Elderly and people with Disabilities).

Como avance en el desarrollo de software inclusivo y accesible (Sánchez, J., Guerrero, L., Sáenz, M., & Flores, H., 2009) desarrollan el Modelo de desarrollo de aplicaciones móviles basadas en videojuegos para la navegación de personas ciegas, este trabajo presenta un modelo de desarrollo, con sus principales características, que considera distintos niveles de abstracción y distintas etapas en el diseño y desarrollo de sistemas que permitan mejorar habilidades de movilidad y orientación para personas con discapacidad visual.

3 Metodología

En esta investigación se utilizará la Metodología "UP4VED: Método de Desarrollo basado en el Proceso Unificado y en Buenas Prácticas para la Construcción de Entornos Virtuales" (Quiroz, J. D. C, 2010). Esta es una metodología de desarrollo fundamentada en RUP y en buenas prácticas para la construcción de entornos virtuales (3D, interactividad y tiempo real); donde se recogen las mejores propuestas planteadas en las metodologías existentes para el desarrollo de Entornos Virtuales, las consideraciones especiales para su modelado, así como los pilares del proceso unificado (Quiroz, J. D. C, 2010).

El contenido de UP4VED está organizado mediante una jerarquía de paquetes, cada uno de los cuales incluye disciplinas, roles, tareas, productos de trabajo y guías. Por su parte, el ciclo vital de UP4VED está compuesto por la descripción de las actividades que conforman sus fases de desarrollo: inicio, elaboración, construcción y transición (Quiroz, J. D. C, 2010).

Esta metodología puede ser de gran utilidad en el desarrollo de la investigación ya que se aplica a entornos virtuales incluida la realidad virtual, aunque no hace énfasis en la realidad virtual inmersiva, razón por la cual se realiza una adaptación de la metodología citada. Al utilizar la metodología UP4VED se asegura la calidad en el proceso de desarrollo de aplicaciones virtuales. Se deben incluir los siete principios del diseño universal adaptados a especificaciones del software de realidad virtual inmersiva, para obtener un producto software inclusivo y accesible.

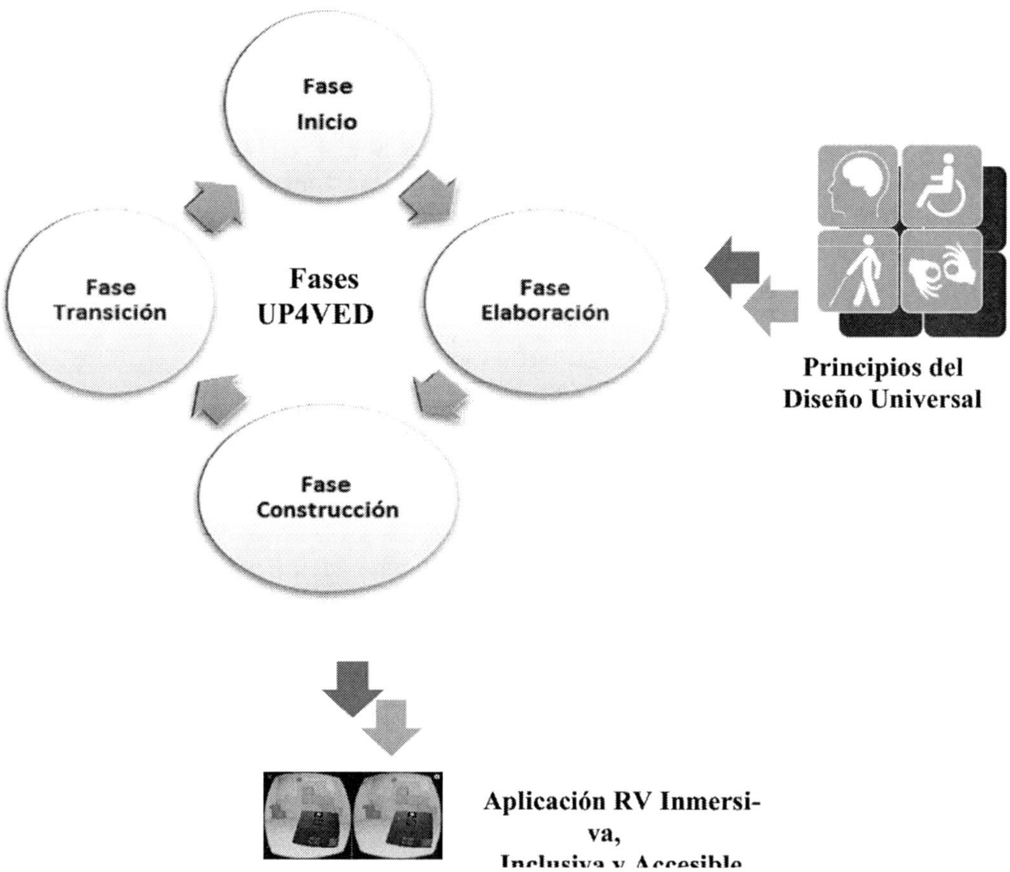

Fig 1. Adaptación metodología UP4VED (Quiroz, 2010)

La Fig. 1, representa las fases de la Metodología UP4VED, metodología que inspira a la Metodología para el desarrollo de aplicaciones de realidad virtual inmersiva que cumpla los principios del diseño universal.

La Convención de las Naciones Unidas sobre los Derechos de las personas con discapacidad, define el "diseño universal", como el "diseño de productos, entornos, programas y servicios que puedan utilizar todas las personas, en la mayor medida posible, sin necesidad de adaptación ni diseño especializado". Así mismo, la Convención en su se refiere a la Accesibilidad, y es de resaltar para el diseño de la metodología, el apartado "h) Promover el diseño, el desarrollo, la producción y la distribución de sistemas y tecnologías de la información y las comunicaciones accesibles en una etapa temprana, a fin de que estos sistemas y tecnologías sean accesibles al menor costo" (ONU, 2006, artículo 9°).

Se busca aplicar los siete principios del diseño universal al desarrollo de software de realidad virtual inmersiva, los cuales son: 1) Uso equiparable, 2) Uso flexible, 3) Simple e intuitivo, 4) Información perceptible, 5) Con tolerancia al error, 6) Que exija poco esfuerzo físico, 7) Tamaño y espacio para el acceso y uso (Design, U, 1997).
Los principios del diseño universal se deben incluir como requerimientos funcionales y no funcionales en el desarrollo del software de realidad virtual inmersiva que deben ser modelados utilizando el VRLM (sigla del inglés Virtual Reality Modeling Language), lenguaje que debe ser adaptado a un ambiente de realidad virtual.

Durante cada una de las fases de la metodología UP4VED se debe reflejar la accesibilidad y la inclusión para la mayoría de personas. Se describe cada una de las fases proyectadas:

Fase de inicio: Se realiza el reconocimiento del entorno u organización, se definen los objetivos, identifican las necesidades para realizar el análisis de requerimientos, el diseño de especificaciones de software y el modelado de casos de uso utilizando el VRML, teniendo como fundamento los principios del diseño universal. Artefactos a entregar en esta fase, documento visión, especificación de requerimientos, casos de uso.

Fase de elaboración: Se describe la arquitectura del ciclo de vida del software de realidad virtual inmersiva, se realiza el diseño del entorno virtual inmersivo mediante guiones gráficos y técnicos. Artefactos a entregar, documento de la arquitectura del software.

Fase de construcción: Se realiza la integración de los componentes multimedia del entorno virtual inmersivo 2D y 3D, se publica un prototipo del software de realidad virtual inmersiva. Para el desarrollo del software se utilizan herramientas tecnológicas actuales. El artefacto a entregar se fundamenta en el diseño y desarrollo de los casos de uso.

Fase de transición: Se incluyen pruebas de usabilidad a usuarios reales, usuarios que pueden presentar algún tipo de discapacidad. Se entrega la versión final del software de realidad virtual inmersiva operativa y funcional. Se concluye la documentación del proceso de desarrollo de software y el producto. Como artefactos de la fase, se incluyen las pruebas de usabilidad y pruebas finales de aceptación.

Las pruebas de usabilidad están proyectadas para realizarse a personas con alguna discapacidad temporal o permanente, definida esta como las "deficiencias físicas, mentales, intelectuales o sensoriales" (ONU, 2006a, artículo 1°). A partir del diseño de un estudio piloto se define el número de participantes y los espacios físicos adecuados para la realización de las pruebas, se realiza la selección de los participantes y se aplican las pruebas.

Con las pruebas de usabilidad se busca obtener datos cualitativos y cuantitativos relacionados con la metodología aplicada al software de realidad virtual inmersiva y resolver problemas del diseño, así como documentar la investigación.

4 Resultados esperados

Presentar una metodología de desarrollo de software que incluya al mayor número de personas en aplicaciones de realidad virtual inmersiva, asegurando la aplicación de los principios del diseño universal.

Realizar un aporte de la metodología propuesta en el desarrollo de aplicaciones de realidad virtual inmersiva mediante un estudio comparativo de aplicaciones que cumplan y no cumplan con los requerimientos del diseño universal.

Generar apropiación de buenas prácticas relacionadas con accesibilidad en el desarrollo de aplicaciones de realidad virtual inmersiva en ingenieros de sistemas y tecnólogos de desarrollo de software.

Contribuir en la definición de pautas para promover el acceso a las TIC para personas con discapacidad o limitación, en aplicaciones de realidad virtual inmersiva permitiendo su inclusión a este tipo de software.

Aplicación de la metodología a un software de realidad virtual inmersiva, innovador, que sea accesible utilizando herramientas tecnológicas que aseguren la portabilidad en dispositivos móviles, entornos web y computadores de escritorio ajustándose a los requisitos para desarrollo del motor de videojuegos de Unity.

Generar un espacio de interés para la comunidad Agustiniana y el público general, que será implementado por medio de un tour virtual de la universidad dando la posibilidad de mostrar sus sitios de interés a los futuros aspirantes, otorgándoles así una posibilidad de conocer su próxima institución educativa y se sientan a gusto en las instalaciones.

5 Hipótesis

En la actualidad, se está viviendo un avance de las nuevas tecnologías aplicadas a la Realidad Virtual, lo que hace más atrayente la visión de este nuevo reto; es conveniente desarrollar proyectos que vayan de la mano con los últimos descubrimientos tecnológicos.

Es así que nace la idea de organizar escenarios virtuales inmersivos asignados de tridimensionalidad y de inmersión en tiempo real, que accedan representar lugares geográficos remotos 360° mediante la presentación de contenidos en formato estereoscópico, unas gafas y sensores de movimiento; permitiendo así, que el usuario se sienta inmerso en un ambiente nuevo, diferente del que se localiza (Cañellas, 2017).

Para desarrollar una aplicación de realidad virtual inmersiva que es una tecnología nueva e inexplorada, será necesaria la participación de dos niveles de conocimiento:

- Un primer nivel es diseñar una metodología para el desarrollo de aplicaciones de realidad virtual inmersiva. Es una metodología muy distinta dependiendo del proyecto a realizar, ya que algunas metodologías existentes no tienen todas las fases y profundización que necesita y requiere la aplicación. Se toman diferentes metodologías de software para el desarrollo de la aplicación virtual inmersiva para cumplir este nivel.
- Un segundo nivel de investigación de lo que forma parte y se requiere para la creación de aplicaciones virtuales, pues resulta intrínseco al tema de Realidad Virtual, y para ello se debe contener previamente el conocimiento y recursos para la conceptualización, diseño y construcción de escenarios virtuales inmersivos.

Se plantea entonces la pregunta de investigación:

¿Qué metodologías de desarrollo de software cumplen con los requerimientos del diseño universal en aplicaciones de realidad virtual inmersiva que permitan la accesibilidad de personas con alguna discapacidad o limitación?

6 Conclusiones

Se puede concluir que, aunque existe diversidad de investigaciones en las áreas cercanas a la problemática y que aportan a la investigación, existen pocos referentes internacionales y nacionales que aborden directamente la problemática planteada, es decir, metodologías de desarrollo de software que incluyan los principios del diseño universal en software de realidad virtual inmersiva.

El desarrollo de la metodología proporcionará buenas prácticas para la construcción de software de realidad virtual inmersiva de calidad cumpliendo con estándares internacionales, generando un impacto en la población con algún tipo de discapacidad.

Referencias

1. Barreno, A., Alexander, G., Guaraca, S., & Gonzalo, M. (2013). Adaptación de las metodologías ágiles Scrum y Extreme Game Development en una metodología para el desarrollo de videojuegos en Android. Caso práctico: Desarrollo de un videojuego (Bachelor's thesis).
2. Barzabal, L. T. (2004). Accesibilidad al contenido web para todas las personas. Comunicación y pedagogía, 194, 13-19.
3. Bowman, D. A., Kruijff, E., Laviola JR, J. J., & Poupyrev, I. (2001). An introduction to 3-D user interface design. Presence: Teleoperators and virtual environments, 10(1), 96-108.
4. Cantone, D (2006). Implementation y Debugging. USER.CODE. [online] Available at: https://ingsw.pbworks.com/f/Ciclo+de+Vida+del+Software.pdf
5. Cañellas Mayor, A. (2017). Apuntes docentes posibilidades educativas de la realidad virtual inmersiva. [online] Centrocp.com. Available at: http://www.centrocp.com/apuntes-docentes-posibilidades-educativas-la-realidad-virtual-inmersiva/ Correa Pintado, J. A.

(2016). Análisis, diseño y desarrollo de un paseo virtual en 3D para la carrera de informática educativa, de la Universidad Nacional de Loja, enfocado como una herramienta de difusión de los espacios que conforman la carrera de informática educativa (Bachelor's thesis).
6. Design, U. (1997). The Principles of universal design. NC State University, The Center for Universal Design, an initiative of the College of Design
7. Gallardo, S., Barrero, F., & TORAL, S. L. (2005). Building a Web-based virtual laboratory with VRML. A case study: An electronic instrumentation subject. In ICECE: International Conference On Engineering and Computer Education.
8. Kamieth, F., Dähne, P., Wichert, R., Villalar, J. L., Jimenez-Mixco, V., Arca, A., & Arredondo, M. T. (2010). Exploring the potential of virtual reality for the elderly and people with disabilities. In Virtual Reality. InTech.
9. Londoño, F., Alvarez, M. L., Chiappe, A., & Ramirez, M. E. (2002). Metodología de desarrollo de producciones educativas hipermediales personalizantes. In Memorias del VI Congreso Colombiano de Informática Educativa RIBIE-Col, Medellín, Colombia. Extraído el (Vol. 10).
10. Molina, J. P., García, A. S., López Jaquero, V., & González, P. (2005, October). Developing VR applications: the TRES-D methodology. In First International Workshop on Methods and Tools for Designing VR applications (MeTo-VR), in conjuntion with 11th International Conference on Virtual Systems and Multimedia (VSMM'05), Ghent, Belgium.
11. Monroy Univio, C. C., & Pachón Cumbe, M. A. (2016). Diseño de una aplicación basada en realidad virtual inmersiva que permita evidenciar infracciones cometidas al momento de conducir.
12. Noboa, C., Carlos, J., & Maggi Murillo, B. G. (2016). Desarrollo de una metodología para diseñar paseos virtuales; caso práctico acerca de los personajes más emblemáticos de Riobamba (Bachelor's thesis, Escuela Superior Politécnica de Chimborazo).
13. ONU Organización de las Naciones Unidas, 2006a. Convención sobre los Derechos de las Personas con Discapacidad. Doc. A/61/611, Nueva York, 13 diciembre.
14. Pressman, Roger (2005). Ingeniería de Software, un enfoque práctico. Editorial Mc Graw Hill.
15. Quiroz, J. D. C. (2010). UP4VED: Método de Desarrollo basado en el Proceso Unificado y en Buenas Prácticas para la Construcción de Entornos Virtuales (Doctoral dissertation, Universidad Pontificia de Salamanca).
16. Rambli, D. R. A., & Muhaiyuddin, N. D. M. (2013). Design Methodology for Image-based Virtual Reality Application. International Journal of Interactive Digital Media, 1 (3).
17. Sánchez, J., Guerrero, L., Sáenz, M., & Flores, H. (2009). Modelo de desarrollo de aplicaciones móviles basadas en videojuegos para la navegación de personas ciegas. Nuevas Ideas en Informática Educativa, 5, 177-187.
18. Watanuki, K. (2010). Development of virtual reality-based universal design review system. Journal of mechanical science and technology, 24(1), 257-262.

Determination and prioritization of requirements for software projects: SIMEER case study

Manuel Ibarra[1], Mario Aquino[1], Hesmeralda Rojas[1], Ebert Gomez[1], Lintol Contreras[1] and Ronald Rentería[2]

[1] Micaela Bastidas National University of Apurimac, Academic Engineering Department, Garcilazo Avenue S/N, Apurimac, Peru
{manuelibarra, mario.ac23, marianhre, gomezintimpa, lintol.contreras}@gmail.com

[2] Andean Technological University, Academic Engineering Department, Apurimac, Peru
rrenteriaa@utea.edu.pe

Abstract. Defining and prioritizing software requirements according to user's neediness is a complex and crucial task in software development process. The purpose of this research is to define a strategy for the prioritization of software requirements for projects related to the qualification of exams. In this study we used the observation methodology, Requirements Determination Meeting and Nominal Group Meeting. The results show that the proposed strategy, allows to define requirements more quickly, adequately and without ambiguities; in this experiment, 18 users participated in the Requirements Determination Meeting and 4 users in the Prioritization of Requirements Meeting; in addition, the proposed strategy was applied in the development of the Integral System for Monitoring the Evaluation of Regional Students (SIMEER) in Cusco-2017, in which 1805 Schools and 119847 students participated. The prioritization of software requirements has been widely discussed by the researchers; however, this proposal defines a strategy based on a prioritization matrix, to define and prioritize software requirements for Education field.

Keywords. Requirements engineering, exam qualification, requirements analysis, requirements prioritization, requirements determination.

1 Introducción

Según menciona Pressman [1] "La Ingeniería de Requerimientos (IR) ayuda a los ingenieros de software a entender mejor el problema en cuya solución trabajarán. Incluye el conjunto de tareas que conducen a comprender cuál será el impacto del software sobre el negocio, qué es lo que el cliente quiere y cómo interactuarán los usuarios finales con el software". Por otro lado, Sommerville [2] manifiesta que "Un requerimiento es simplemente una declaración abstracta de alto nivel de un servicio que debe proporcionar el sistema o una restricción de éste".

Obtener los requisitos adecuadamente y acorde con lo que el usuario requiere depende mucho de las habilidades y experiencia de los analistas. Una de las principales causas de los fallos de software es definir inadecuadamente los requisitos. Se estima que el 50% de los fallos de software se deben a los requerimientos insuficientemente comprendidos, el 30% se deben a que se realizan incorrectamente la transformación de los requerimientos al diseño del software [3], esto muestra claramente que definir con precisión los requisitos y priorizarlos es un proceso muy importante para que el software sea de calidad y se cumplan con los plazos establecidos en un proyecto de software.

Según Arias [4], en la etapa de determinación de requerimientos se presentan muchos inconvenientes, dentro de los más comunes están: los requerimientos no son obvios y vienen de muchas fuentes; son difíciles de expresar en palabras (el lenguaje es ambiguo); la cantidad de requerimientos en un proyecto puede ser difícil de manejar; un requerimiento puede cambiar a lo largo del ciclo de desarrollo; el usuario no puede explicar con claridad lo que requiere; tiende a recordar lo excepcional y olvidar lo rutinario; habla de lo que no funciona; los usuarios tienen vocabulario distinto al de los desarrolladores; los usuarios usan el mismo término con distinto significado.

Por otro lado, una vez especificado los requerimientos del usuario en forma completa, correcta y sin ambigüedades, se presenta un segundo problema: ¿cómo priorizar los requerimientos?. Normalmente el jefe de proyecto, en base a su experiencia o en consenso con los miembros del equipo de desarrollo, prioriza los requisitos para que sean diseñados y posteriormente implementados. Esta etapa es crucial para que el producto de software tenga éxito. Existen varias formas de abordar la priorización de requisitos y que han sido abordados por los investigadores del área[5]–[9]

Priorizar los requerimientos es una tarea compleja, porque el usuario no tiene mucha noción de qué requisitos son más importantes que otros, o qué requisitos son más complejos que otros; mientras que por el lado del equipo de desarrollo, conoce la complejidad de los requisitos, pero no sabe la prioridad de cada uno ellos para el cliente.

Este trabajo de investigación propone una estrategia para priorizar los requisitos en base a un conjunto de variables que son ponderadas entre el equipo de desarrollo y el usuario, de tal forma que los requerimientos quedan priorizados en forma conjunta y consensuada, evitando de esta manera ambigüedades y contradicciones. Para poner en prueba los conceptos teóricos planteados de esta propuesta, se ha aplicado esta estrategia con un caso real en el desarrollo de un proyecto de software denominado: Sistema Integral de Monitoreo de Evaluación de Estudiantes Regional (SIMEER) en la ciudad del Cusco en el año 2017, considerando que en la Región Cusco el 63.7% de las Instituciones Educativas están ubicadas en zona rural [10] y no tiene acceso a Internet, por tanto se debe utilizar una hoja electrónica de cálculo para llenar los resultados marcados por los alumnos en cada pregunta y área evaluada y luego esos datos se debe centralizar en la una base de datos cuando haya conexión a Internet (en la Unidad de Gestión Educativa Local-UGEL).

2 Marco teórico

2.1 Ingeniería de requisitos

La Ingeniería de Requerimientos (IR) tiene varias técnicas para capturar u obtener las necesidades de los usuarios o clientes y así poder definir las características que debe satisfacer un determinado producto de software [11]–[13]. Posteriormente, estas características son plasmadas en el documento formal que se denomina "Especificación de Requisitos". De la variedad de técnicas existentes para la obtención de requisitos, hay algunas que se destacan porque han tenido éxito o popularidad en la construcción de software [14]–[16], así por ejemplo, tiene la entrevista, el cuestionario, la observación, el análisis de protocolos, clasificación de conceptos, lluvia de ideas, entre otros.

Por otro lado, hoy en día, en la industria del software, se ha intensificado la tendencia por el uso de aplicaciones web para dar solución a los problemas que requieren manejo de datos. Las razones porque las aplicaciones web son más utilizadas son: la portabilidad, facilidad de instalación, entre otras. Por otro lado, se ha cuestionado la calidad de los desarrollos web, así por ejemplo, Cutter Consortium está enfocada en el desarrollo aplicaciones web de gran envergadura, y realizó una encuesta en la cual encontró que entre los principales problemas que tienen las aplicaciones web se encuentran: fallas en satisfacer las necesidades de negocio (84%), falta de funcionalidad (53%) y baja calidad de los entregables (52%) [17].

Esto nos hace visualizar que uno de los mayores problemas de la ingeniería de software proviene de la imprecisión en la especificación de requerimientos. Un diseñador de software a veces da interpretaciones de un requerimiento ambiguo, con el fin de simplificar su implementación; sin embargo, al finalizar el proyecto, el cliente se da cuenta que eso no es lo que deseaba del producto de software; por tanto, se tiene que modificar el requerimiento y hacer cambios sustanciales al sistema, lo cual disminuye la calidad del producto, retrasa la entrega del producto, incrementando el costo y finalmente crea malestar en el cliente.

Priorizar y determinar los requisitos es una tarea muy compleja que requiere de técnicas adecuadas para que el proyecto de software tenga éxito. En la investigación realizada por Carrizo, Dieste y Juristo [18], propusieron un marco de trabajo para apoyar a los analistas en la determinación y priorización de los requisitos, analizaron la "elicitación" en forma teórica y empírica, luego validaron su propuesta y finalmente concluyeron que el marco de trabajo desarrollado es extensible y modificable.

Algunos aspectos importantes se deben considerar para la priorización de requisitos. Berander y Andrews [19] mencionan que, un aspecto es una propiedad, criterio o característica del proyecto que deberán ser priorizados. Los autores mencionan que existen aspectos o características que ayudan a priorizar los requisitos, así por ejemplo: importancia, penalidad, costo, tiempo y riesgo.

2.2 Tipos de requerimientos

Existen dos tipos de requerimientos: los requerimientos funcionales (RF) y los requerimientos no funcionales (RNF).

Los RF definen las funciones que el sistema será capaz de realizar, es decir describen los procesos y actividades que el sistema requiere [20]; por ejemplo, Gestión de usuarios de un sistema web, en la cual se pueden agregar, eliminar o modificar usuarios y sus accesos al menú.

Por otro lado, los RNF son aquellos que no están directamente relacionados con los procesos ni actividades que definen el sistema, sino más bien están vinculados con las características adicionales como: robustez, mantenimiento, portabilidad, restricciones, etc. [20]; por ejemplo, un RNF podría ser que el usuario desee que el sistema utilice gestor de base de datos "Sql Server 2008 R2", porque ya tiene las licencias adquiridas para su área de trabajo.

3 Trabajos relacionados

Existen varios trabajos relacionados a la priorización de requisitos, así por ejemplo Salas y Hernández [21] realizaron un trabajo de investigación denominado "La priorización de requisitos de software en proyectos de entorno interactivos 3D", el principal objetivo de este trabajo fue definir un procedimiento de priorización de requisitos de software en proyectos interactivos 3D. El procedimiento consta de 4 pasos, y considera 4 variables para la priorización: dependencias con otros requisitos, factibilidad de implementación del requisito, cantidad de objetos 3D y necesidad del requisito para el cliente. Este trabajo está orientado netamente a entornos interactivos 3D y depende de la cantidad de objetos 3D, lo cual hace complicado aplicar al campo educativo.

Por otro lado, Hadad y su equipo de investigación [22] hicieron un trabajo de investigación denominado "Facilitando la Asignación de Prioridades a los Requisitos", este trabajo se realizó en Argentina y aplicaron en un caso de estudio de producción y acopio de papas de alta calidad. Aquí se presenta un mecanismo para la compatibilización de prioridades de requisitos basados en la descomposición de objetivos en subobjetivos del sistema de software, para que luego estos sean transformados en requisitos.

Similarmente, Wiegers [23] realizó una investigación intitulada "First Things First: Prioritizing Requirements", este trabajo presenta los conceptos básicos relacionados a la priorización de Requerimientos. Asimismo, propone hacer la priorización en base a la asignación de escalas en 3 categorías, las escalas son asignadas de manera subjetiva y a veces de una manera no muy precisa. La priorización está basada en enfoque semi-cuantitativo en la que se considera el valor, costo y riesgo; además, considera 8 pasos para realizar el proceso de priorización. Para probar los conceptos planteados crearon un sistema denominado "seguimiento de productos químicos". Los resultados muestran que el enfoque funciona adecuadamente para este tipo de proyectos, sin embargo, no se han realizado pruebas para sistemas relacionados con educación.

4 Metodología para para la determinación y priorización de requisitos

4.1 Usuarios del sistema que participan en la priorización de requisitos

En proyectos educativos relacionados con la preparación y calificación de exámenes, por lo general existe un conjunto de personas que participan utilizando un protocolo establecido: acciones que se deben desarrollar antes, durante y después de la prueba, en cada una de estas fases existen responsables y tiempos que se deben cumplir en forma estricta. A las personas que participan en el sistema les denominaremos "usuarios del sistema". La Tabla 1 muestra los usuarios y sus respectivos roles, la columna "Ítem" indica un número correlativo, la columna "Usuario" describe el nombre del usuario y una descripción corta y finalmente la columna "Rol" describe en forma breve el rol que cumple el usuario en el sistema.

Table 1. Usuarios y roles del sistema

Ítem	Usuario	Rol
1	***Admin***: Administrador del sistema	Crear usuarios y dar permisos
2	***Dir-DRE***: Director de la Dirección Regional de Educación	Planificar las evaluaciones regionales y ver reportes a nivel regional
3	***Dir-UGEL***: Director de Unidad de Gestión Educativa Local	Planificar y ejecutar las evaluaciones en su UGEL y ver reportes de su UGEL
4	***Esp-DRE***: Especialista DRE en Gestión Pedagógica	Preparar indicadores, preguntas y claves de respuesta y ver los reportes a nivel regional
5	***Esp-UGEL***: Especialista UGEL en Gestión Pedagógica	Capacitar a Directores y docentes en el proceso de Evaluación y ver los reportes de su UGEL
6	***Dir-IE***: Director de Institución Educativa	Coordinar con docentes la ejecución del examen, marcar las respuestas de los alumnos y ver los reportes de su Institución
7	***Doc***: Docente de Institución Educativa	Llevar a cabo el examen
8	***Alu***: Alumno de Institución Educativa	Es el que rinde el examen

Los usuarios que participan con mayor importancia en la determinación y priorización de los requisitos del sistema son: ***Admin***(Ítem 1), ***Esp-DRE*** (Ítem 4), ***Esp-UGEL*** (Ítem 5) y ***Dir-IE*** (Ítem 6).

4.2 Sesiones para la Determinación de los Requisitos (SDR)

Para determinar los requisitos se realizaron tres reuniones de trabajo con la Dirección Regional de Educación Cusco, en las cuales participaron 18 personas entre Analistas, Jefe de Proyecto, Especialista de la DRE, Especialista de la UGEL, Director de la DRE, Director de UGEL, Director de Institución Educativa, entre otros; todos ellos se reunieron para determinar los requisitos, el esquema gráfico se muestra en la Figura 1.

Fig. 1. Reunión para determinar los requisitos

Los pasos para recabar los requisitos fueron los siguientes:

Paso 1.- En las reuniones SDR, el Jefe de Proyecto inicia las reuniones indicando el propósito de la reunión y determina el contexto del problema a resolver: hacer un sistema que permita recabar las respuestas marcadas por cada alumno en un examen y luego centralizar todos los resultados en una base de datos para que luego se pueda visualizar los resultados mediante reportes.

Paso 2.- El analista empieza a hacer preguntas, por ejemplo, cómo realizaban antes esta evaluación, calificación y centralización de la información, a lo cual los Especialistas de UGEL y DRE responden indicando que, el trabajo se hacía manualmente y que en total se tenía que calificar cerca de 100 000 pruebas en cada UGEL y luego reportar a la DRE, y consolidar toda la información demoraba más de 6 meses por varias razones, así por ejemplo: Instituciones Educativas muy alejadas de la UGEL, demora en la calificación de las pruebas, entre otras.

Paso 3.- Luego hay una lluvia de ideas de parte de los usuario participantes, en la cual plantean toda la problemática de los procesos anteriores y que los resultados de la consolidación se obtiene al finalizar el año, lo cual no permite tomar decisiones para los alumnos que tienen bajo rendimiento académico en los exámenes. Un aspecto adicional para este sistema es que es que un 63.7% de las Instituciones Educativas están ubicadas en zona rural y en la mayoría de dichas Instituciones Educativas no hay conexión a Internet, lo cual imposibilita hacer los exámenes en línea. Finalmente, los Directores y Profesores de las zonas rurales están familiarizados con el manejo de un procesador de textos, una hoja electrónica y el uso básico de correo electrónico y páginas web.

Paso 4.- Luego el Analista empieza a redactar los requisitos en la pizarra indicando básicamente los siguientes campos: identificador del requisito, descripción del requisito, la persona que indica el requisito, la fecha y otros datos necesarios. Estos requisitos son planteados en base a las opiniones de los usuarios. Debemos aclarar que a veces existen contradicciones entre los usuarios, que después de un debate se llega a acuerdos por opinión mayoritaria.

Paso 5.- Luego el Analista se reúne con el equipo de desarrollo de software y analizan detalladamente cada uno de los requisitos y su determinan su *factibilidad* de realización, su *complejidad* y el *tiempo* que podría demorar cada uno de los requisitos.

Paso 6.- En las siguientes reuniones, el Analista realiza un finamiento de los requisitos y desambigua los requisitos que no están claros y aclara con los Especialistas aquellos que no estaban completamente entendidos.

Paso 7.- En las siguientes reuniones se tuvo que afinar los requisitos que serán muy complejos, el Analista tuvo que realizar entrevistas individuales a los especialistas, para afinar y entender de mejor manera el requisito.

Paso 8. Finalmente, el analista concluye con la lista completa de los requisitos, y todos firman en señal de conformidad.

4.3 Determinación de las variables y los pesos asignados para priorizar requisitos

Para realizar la priorización de requisitos se han considerado algunas variables o criterios que son preponderantes para definir aquellos requisitos que son más prioritarios que otros. La tabla 2 muestra la "Variable a medir", la "Descripción" y la "Puntuación" asignada a cada nivel de la variable. Se asigna el puntaje de 3, cuando el nivel es calificado como "Alta"; se asigna el puntaje de 2 cuando el nivel es calificado como "Media" y finalmente, se asigna el puntaje de 1 cuando el nivel es calificado como "Baja".

Table 2. Variables y pesos asignados para la priorización de requisitos

Variable a medir	Descripción	Puntuación
Prioridad	Nivel de prioridad del requisito	Alta[3], Media[2], Baja [1]
Granularidad	Nivel de detalle de datos que necesita el requisito	Alta[3], Media[2], Baja [1]
Importancia	Nivel de importancia o necesidad del requisito para que el usuario	Alta[3], Media[2], Baja [1]
Complejidad	Nivel de dificultad en el diseño e implementación del requisito	Alta[3], Media[2], Baja [1]
Cohesión	Nivel de relación con otros requisitos	Alta[3], Media[2], Baja [1]
Frecuencia de uso	Nivel de uso del requisito por parte de los usuarios	Alta[3], Media[2], Baja [1]
Tiempo desarrollo	Nivel del tiempo necesario para cumplir con el requisito.	Alta[3], Media[2], Baja [1]

4.4 Matriz de priorización de requisitos para SIMEER

Grupo Nominal para la Priorización de Requisitos (GNPR)

Para priorizar los requisitos, se realizaron reuniones de grupo nominal (técnica que se aplica a grupos heterogéneos, no requiere consenso, toma menos tiempo en decidir y se establecen prioridades) con los usuarios y/o clientes involucrados y el equipo de desarrollo; estas reuniones permitieron definir los requisitos y sus ponderaciones.

La Tabla 3 muestra los requisitos y su priorización. La columna "Nro" indica el número de requisito, la columna "Descripción" describe brevemente el requisito, luego la columna "Prioridad usuario" mide la prioridad que tiene el usuario, "Granularidad" mide el nivel de granularidad del requisito, "Importancia" mide la importancia del requisito para el usuario, "Complejidad" mide la complejidad del requisito desde el punto de vista del desarrollador, "Cohesión" mide relación del requisito con otros requisitos, "Frecuencia de uso" mide las veces que el usuario usará el requisito, la columna "Tiempo desarrollo" que mide el tiempo necesario para desarrollar el requisito y finalmente, la columna "Suma" acumula el puntaje total adquirido para un requisito. Las 7 variables o criterios se han considerado después de haber hecho un análisis con el cliente y/o usuario y de acuerdo a la naturaleza del sistema a desarrollar. Para este caso de estudio se han registrado un total de 17 requisitos funcionales (RF).

Table 3. Lista de requisitos y su priorización

Nro.	Descripción	Prioridad usuario	Granularidad	Importancia	Complejidad	Cohesión	Frecuencia de uso	Tiempo desarrollo	Suma
R01	Acceder al sistema mediante usuario y contraseña	2	1	2	2	1	2	3	13
R02	Gestión de Archivos con extensión *.csv (Agregar, Quitar, Modificar)	2	2	2	2	1	2	3	14
R03	Buscar archivos subidos, por nombre, por fecha, por estado	1	2	1	1	1	1	1	8
R04	Gestión de Usuarios (Agregar, Quitar, Modificar)	2	1	2	2	1	1	2	11
R05	Buscar usuarios, por DNI, por nombre, por fecha de registro, por tipo, por estatus	1	1	1	1	1	2	2	9
R06	Gestión de Instituciones Educativas (Agregar, Quitar, Modificar)	1	1	2	1	2	1	2	10
R07	Buscar Instituciones Educativas por DNI, por código modular, Nombre, Provincia, Distrito, Nivel, UGEL	1	2	2	3	1	2	2	13
R08	Reporte de Instituciones Educativas que subieron y no subieron resultados, por Año, por Número de Evaluación, por UGEL, por Nivel, por Idioma	3	3	2	3	2	3	3	19
R09	Reporte de las Estadísticas: por Año, por Número de Evaluación, Región, por Nivel, por Area, por Ugel, por Distrito, Por Institución Educativa, por Grado, por Idioma; con la opción de ver los resultados en pantalla y exportar a Excel.	3	3	3	3	3	3	3	21
R10	Reporte de las Estadísticas del porcentaje de aciertos y desaciertos de cada pregunta; con la opción de ver los resultados en pantalla y exportar a Excel	3	3	2	3	3	3	3	20
R11	Crear una hoja de configuración en Excel, que permita definir la cantidad de alumnos por grado y sección,	3	3	2	2	1	2	3	16

	indicando los totales								
R12	Calificar cada una de las preguntas de cada área de acuerdo a la clave de respuestas y el puntaje asignado	3	1	2	2	1	2	3	14
R13	Generar una plantilla e Excel que permita registrar datos del alumno y las calificaciones obtenidas, para cada grado, sección y área	3	3	3	3	2	2	3	19
R14	Generar un gráfico en Excel en barras que muestre las estadísticas de cada alumno y por cada área, indicando si el alumno se encuentra en Inicio, Proceso o Satisfactorio	3	1	3	2	2	3	3	17
R15	Generar un gráfico en Excel en barras que muestre las estadísticas de cada pregunta con el número de aciertos y desaciertos	3	1	3	2	2	3	3	17
R16	Exportar los resultados a un formato ligero *.csv	3	3	2	2	3	2	3	18
R17	Guardar los resultados *.csv en una base de datos centralizada	2	3	2	1	2	2	3	15

Después de asignar los puntajes, se ordenaron los resultados en forma descendente respecto al campo "Suma" de tal forma que los primeros requisitos tendrán los puntajes más altos (requisitos con mayor prioridad) y los últimos requisitos tendrán los puntajes más bajos (requisitos con menor prioridad), los resultados se muestran en la Figura 2.

Este trabajo se ha experimentado con 17 requisitos, en caso de tener muchos requisitos (por ejemplo para el caso de un software de control de viajes para trenes y/o aviones), esta propuesta se podría expandir utilizando un pequeño aplicativo web de tal forma que se podría trabajar en forma colaborativa.

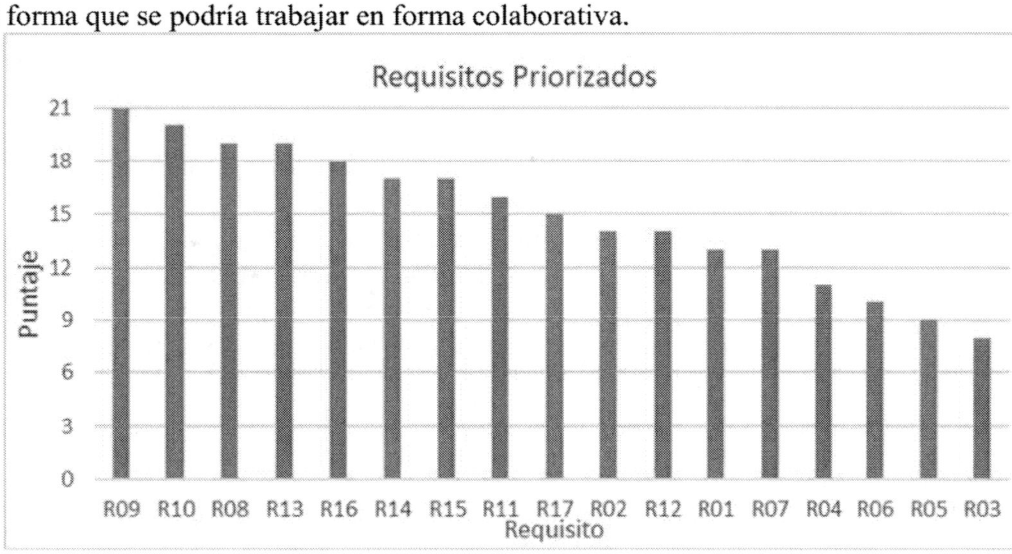

Fig. 2. Requisitos ordenados por puntaje en forma descendente

En la Figura 2 se puede observar que el puntaje máximo obtenido es de 21, que pertenece al Requisito R09, le sigue el puntaje de 20 que pertenece al requisito R10; por otro lado, el puntaje mínimo obtenido es de 8 que pertenece al Requisito R03. Finalmente el valor promedio obtenido es de 14.94 puntos.

En caso de que hubiese un empate en el puntaje final, entonces se consulta directamente al cliente para decidir por requisito con mayor prioridad.

Matriz de priorización de requisitos

Matricialmente, la priorización de requisitos podemos representar de la siguiente manera:

$$MP_{(mXn)} = \begin{array}{c} \begin{array}{cccccc} v_1 & v_2 & v_3 & \dots & v_n & \end{array} \\ \left[\begin{array}{cccccc} 2 & 1 & 2 & \dots & 3 \\ 2 & 2 & 2 & \dots & 3 \\ 1 & 2 & 1 & \dots & 1 \\ 2 & 1 & 2 & \dots & 2 \\ \vdots & \vdots & \vdots & \vdots & \vdots \\ 2 & 3 & 2 & 1 & 3 \end{array}\right. \end{array} \begin{array}{c} \sum v_i \\ \left.\begin{array}{c} 13 \\ 14 \\ 8 \\ 11 \\ \vdots \\ 15 \end{array}\right] \end{array} \begin{array}{c} \\ R_1 \\ R_2 \\ R_3 \\ R_4 \\ \vdots \\ R_m \end{array} \quad (1)$$

La ecuación (1) nos muestra la representación matricial para la priorización de requisitos en proyectos de software. Donde: "MP" es la matriz de priorización; "mXn" representa el número de Requisitos (m) y número de criterios de priorización (n) respectivamente; "v_i", $\forall i = 1 \dots n$ representa las variables o criterios de priorización; "R_j" $\forall j = 1 \dots m$ representa los Requisitos del proyecto; "$\sum_{n}^{i=1} v_i$" $\forall i = 1 \dots n$ representa la sumatoria del puntaje obtenido.

5 Resultados obtenidos

Para obtener los resultados primero se realizaron 3 Sesiones de Determinación de Requisitos, en la cual participaron 18 personas entre Especialistas y Directores que dieron sus puntos de vista para determinar los requisitos del sistema, ésta se realizó con la metodología lluvia de ideas y en algunos casos se tuvieron reuniones individuales para el caso de requisitos complejos que requerían mayor análisis. El producto final de esas reuniones fue el "Documento de Requisitos".

Por otro lado, se han realizado reuniones del tipo Grupo Nominal para priorizar los requisitos, en la cual participaron 4 personas: Director de UGEL, Director de Institución Educativa y dos Especialistas. En dichas reuniones se analizaron las 7 variables o criterios para cada uno de los 17 requisitos del sistema. El producto final de estas reuniones fue la matriz de priorización de requisitos.

Finalmente, en la última reunión del Grupo Nominal, se ha podido obtener la opinión de los usuarios sobre la forma de determinar y priorizar los requisitos; en esta parte se les hizo algunas preguntas como por ejemplo: ¿Crees que esta forma de determinar y priorizar los requisitos a ayudado a cumplir con los plazos establecidos para el sistema SIMEER?, a lo cual ellos respondieron diciendo *"Esta forma de colaborar directamente en la implementación de la aplicación nos ha permitido tener el sistema en el tiempo establecido y sobre todo sin errores"*, luego se les preguntó ¿sientes que todo lo que quisiste o pensaste al inicio de este proyecto ahora lo ves implementado en el software?, la respuesta fue *"El hecho de reunirnos con el analista y los programadores, hizo que nos involucremos con el desarrollo del software y nuestras sugerencias fueron consideradas en el producto final".*

6 Conclusiones y trabajo futuro

Este artículo presenta una estrategia para determinar y priorizar los requerimientos de un producto de software para el área de educación, específicamente para la calificación de pruebas a alumnos de primaria y secundaria en la Región Cusco-Perú en la cual más del 63.7% de Instituciones Educativas pertenecen a la zona rural y no tienen conexión a internet.

Después de realizar las reuniones entre los usuarios (Especialistas y Directores) y el equipo de desarrollo, se ha podido determinar y priorizar los requisitos para el proyecto de software denominado SIMEER. La priorización se ha realizado mediante la valoración de siete características o indicadores que son: *Prioridad*, *Granularidad*, *Importancia*, *Complejidad*, *Cohesión*, *Tiempo de desarrollo* y *Frecuencia de uso*. Los Especialistas y Directores opinan que, participar en la priorización de los requisitos hizo que el producto de software implementado sea muy similar a lo que ellos se imaginaban al a inicio y sienten el software es de calidad, y lo más importante es que se cumplieron con los plazos establecidos.

Como parte del trabajo a futuro es necesario crear una herramienta colaborativa que permita definir y priorizar los requisitos de manera virtual y en base a los indicadores propuestos en este artículo, es decir que funcione en la Web, para que los usuarios puedan dar su opinión llenando un formulario (a veces los Especialistas están de viaje de monitoreo y no disponen de tiempo para reuniones presenciales); además, para que el usuario y el equipo de desarrollo puedan tener visibilidad de los cambios y/o avances de cada requisito. Por otro lado, para dar mayor validez a esta propuesta de investigación, se realizará pruebas en otros contextos de proyectos de software.

7 Referencias Bibliográficas

[1] R. Pressman, *Ingeniería de software un enfoque práctico*, Quinta. Mc Graw Hill, 2001.

[2] I. Sommerville, *Ingeniería del software*, Sétima. Pearson Addison Wesley, 2005.

[3] G. Lomprey and S. Hernandez, "La importancia de la calidad en el desarrollo de productos de software," 2008.

[4] M. Arias Chaves, "La ingeniería de requerimientos y su importancia en el desarrollo de proyectos de software," *InterSedes Rev. las Sedes Reg.*, vol. 6, no. 10, 2005.

[5] D. Greer, "Prioritisation for Incremental and Iterative Development," *Requir. Eng. Sociotechnical Syst.*, p. 100, 2005.

[6] D. Leffingwell and D. Widrig, *Managing software requirements: a unified approach*. Addison-Wesley Professional, 2000.

[7] R. E. Zultner, "Quality function deployment (QFD) for software: Structured requirements exploration," *Total Qual. Manag. Software, New York Van Nostrand Reinhold*, pp. 297–317, 1992.

[8] J. Karlsson and K. Ryan, "A cost-value approach for prioritizing

requirements," *IEEE Softw.*, vol. 14, no. 5, pp. 67–74, 1997.

[9] F. Moisiadis, "Prioritising scenario evolution," in *Requirements engineering, 2000. Proceedings. 4th International Conference on*, 2000, pp. 85–94.

[10] ESCALE, "Estadísticas Instituciones Educativas," 2017. [Online]. Available: http://escale.minedu.gob.pe/.

[11] N. Maiden, A. Gizikis, and S. Robertson, "Provoking creativity: Imagine what your requirements could be like," *IEEE Softw.*, vol. 21, no. 5, pp. 68–75, 2004.

[12] H. Solheim, F. Lillehagen, S. A. Petersen, H. Jorgensen, and M. Anastasiou, "Model-driven visual requirements engineering," in *Requirements Engineering, 2005. Proceedings. 13th IEEE International Conference on*, 2005, pp. 421–425.

[13] P. Pytel *et al.*, "Ingeniería de requisitos basada en técnicas de ingeniería del conocimiento," in *XIII Workshop de Investigadores en Ciencias de la Computación*, 2011.

[14] P. Britos, B. Rossi, and R. García Martínez, "Notas sobre didáctica de las etapas de formalización y análisis de resultados de la técnica de emparrillado. Un Ejemplo," in *Proceedings del V Congreso Internacional de Ingeniería Informática*, 1999, pp. 200–209.

[15] R. Winter and B. Strauch, "A method for demand-driven information requirements analysis in data warehousing projects," in *System Sciences, 2003. Proceedings of the 36th Annual Hawaii International Conference on*, 2003, p. 9--pp.

[16] L. Jiang and A. Eberlein, "Selecting Requirements Engineering Techniques Based on Project Attributes--A Case Study," in *Engineering of Computer-Based Systems, 2007. ECBS'07. 14th Annual IEEE International Conference and Workshops on the*, 2007, pp. 269–278.

[17] M. J. Escalona and N. Koch, "Requirements engineering for web applications-a comparative study," *J. Web Eng.*, vol. 2, no. 3, pp. 193–212, 2004.

[18] D. Carrizo, O. Dieste, and N. Juristo, "Systematizing requirements elicitation technique selection," *Inf. Softw. Technol.*, vol. 56, no. 6, pp. 644–669, 2014.

[19] P. Berander and A. Andrews, "Requirements prioritization," in *Engineering and managing software requirements*, Springer, 2005, pp. 69–94.

[20] J. M. Bahamonde and R. Rossel, "Un Acercamiento a la Ingeniería de Requerimientos," 2003.

[21] S. Salas and A. Hernández, "La priorización de requisitos de software en proyectos de entorno interactivos 3D," in *CIBSE*, 2015.

[22] G. D. S. Hadad, J. H. Doorn, M. Ridao, and G. N. Kaplan, "Facilitando la Asignación de Prioridades a los Requisitos.," in *WER*, 2009.

[23] K. Wiegers, "First things first: prioritizing requirements," *Softw. Dev.*, vol. 7, no. 9, pp. 48–53, 1999.

An exploratory study of the role of Product Owner in industrial practice

Gerardo Matturro, Felipe Cordovés, Martín Solari

Universidad ORT Uruguay

matturro@uni.ort.edu.uy, felipecordoves@gmail.com, martin.solari@ort.edu.uy

Abstract. The role of Product Owner of the Scrum methodology is clearly defined in the literature in terms of the responsibilities it entails and the personal characteristics of the person who performs it. However, in professional practice, the understanding of the role and its responsibilities is quite different among organizations, and rarely in perfect conformity with the official method. This article reports the process and results of an exploratory study oriented to know how some aspects of this role is performed in the reality of the industrial practice. Through semi-structured interviews to a group of product owners, the aspects of the process and criteria for choosing the PO for a project, the ceremonies in which they participate, and their personal characteristics in the form of desirable soft skills in a good PO were investigated.

Keywords: Scrum, Product Owner, Soft Skills

1 Introducción

En la metodología ágil Scrum, el de Product Owner (en adelante, PO) es uno de los tres roles definidos con características y responsabilidades bien establecidas. Aún así, este rol suele ser asimilado a otros más tradicionales en ingeniería de software, tales como el de Gerente de producto (*Product Manager*) o Analista de negocios (*Business Analyst*).

Según sostiene Pichler [1], puesto que el PO es un rol relativamente nuevo, las personas a menudo necesitan tiempo y apoyo para la transición al rol y para adquirir las habilidades necesarias para desempeñarlo adecuadamente. Según este autor, además, un desafío común en las organizaciones es encontrar empleados con la amplitud y profundidad de conocimientos, experiencia, y habilidades personales necesarios para hacer bien el trabajo.

Por otra parte, Sverrisdottira y colegas [2] mencionan que la comprensión del rol y de las responsabilidades del PO es bastante diferente entre las organizaciones, y rara vez en perfecta conformidad con el método oficial de Scrum.

El propósito de este artículo es reportar el proceso seguido y los resultados obtenidos de un estudio exploratorio orientado a conocer cómo se desempeñan, en la realidad de la práctica industrial, algunos aspectos del rol de PO.

Este estudio presenta una síntesis de la caracterización del rol de PO obtenida de la literatura aceptada por la comunidad, para establecer similitudes y diferencias con lo observado en la práctica profesional.

El resto de este artículo está organizado de la siguiente manera. En la sección 2 se hace un repaso de los principales conceptos y definiciones relativos al rol del PO, y se exponen algunos trabajos relacionados con el tema de investigación. La sección 3 explica el diseño metodológico del estudio, donde se exponen las preguntas de investigación y los procedimientos de recolección y preparación de datos. En la sección 4 se presentan los principales resultados obtenidos, mientras que en la sección 5 se expone la discusión de estos resultados. La sección 6 aborda las amenazas a la validez de este estudio y en la sección 7 se presentan las conclusiones y se esbozan los trabajos futuros.

2 Antecedentes

En esta sección se presenta una revisión de los elementos conceptuales relacionados con los aspectos de son el foco de este trabajo, obtenidos a partir de la literatura.

2.1 Definición del rol de PO

El rol de PO en un equipo de Scrum está bien documentado en la literatura técnica, y es claramente coincidente en cuanto a su función y sus principales responsabilidades.

Así, Schwaber y Sutherland [3] lo describen como responsable de maximizar el valor del producto y el trabajo del equipo de desarrollo, y como la única persona responsable de administrar el *product backlog* del producto a desarrollar.

Layton [4], por su parte, caracteriza este rol indicando que su principal trabajo es ocuparse del lado comercial del proyecto. Es responsable de maximizar el valor del producto entregando el retorno de la inversión (ROI) a la organización. El PO es una persona sola, no un comité, y es un miembro dedicado y de tiempo completo del equipo de Scrum.

2.2 La elección del PO

En opinión de Rubin [5], el rol del PO es una combinación de autoridad y responsabilidades que históricamente se han encontrado en varios roles tradicionales. En su expresión más abarcadora, el PO incorpora elementos de los roles de gerente de producto, comercializador de producto, gerente de proyecto, analista de negocios y evaluador de aceptación.

Para este autor, así como para Larman y Voode [6], exactamente quién debería ser el PO depende del tipo de esfuerzo de desarrollo y de la organización específica, y distinguen tres situaciones: desarrollo interno, desarrollo comercial, y desarrollo tercerizado (o subcontratado):

- Desarrollo interno: el PO debe ser una persona empoderada del grupo que se beneficiará del desarrollo del producto.
- Desarrollo comercial: el PO debe ser un miembro de la organización que actúe como la voz de los clientes reales. Con frecuencia, esta persona proviene de las áreas de gestión de productos o marketing de productos.
- Desarrollo subcontratado: el PO debe ser de la compañía que está pagando por la solución (la que recibe el sistema en desarrollo) y recibiendo los beneficios.

Moreira [7], por su parte, considera que, en general, cualquiera que haya desempeñado un papel en el que ha trabajado con los clientes/usuarios para recopilar las necesidades y luego trabaje con los equipos para crear productos o soluciones que satisfagan esas necesidades puede convertirse en un PO eficaz.

2.3 Responsabilidades del PO

En la literatura sobre Scrum son múltiples las actividades en las que debe participar y las responsabilidades asignadas al rol de PO.

Así, Rubin [8] menciona las siguientes: participar en la planificación, "acicalar" (grooming) el *product backlog*, definir criterios de aceptación para cada elemento del *product backlog* así como verificar que esos criterios se cumplan, y colaborar con el equipo de desarrollo y con los interesados ("stakeholders") del proyecto.

Por su parte, Green [9] considera que algunos de los deberes más importantes del PO son aclarar las necesidades del cliente, desarrollar un *backlog* en las características (*features*) del producto en las cuales trabajar, y escribir historias de usuario claras que comuniquen las expectativas completas del producto a desarrollar. El PO también es responsable de comunicarse regularmente con el cliente para asegurarse de que las historias que escriben y que la acumulación de tareas pendientes cumpla con las expectativas actuales.

También Layton [10] aborda las responsabilidades de un PO y menciona, entre otras, las siguientes: establecer los objetivos y la visión del producto, incluida la redacción de la declaración de la visión, crear y mantener la hoja de ruta del producto, que es una visión amplia del alcance del producto y del *product backlog* inicial, establecer los objetivos de lanzamiento (*release*) y de cada *sprint*, determinar qué elementos del *product backlog* entran en el siguiente *sprint*, y estar disponible durante todo el día para trabajar directamente con los miembros del equipo de desarrollo, aumentando así la eficiencia a través de una comunicación clara e inmediata

2.4 Características personales del PO

En relación con las características personales de quien desempeñe el rol de PO Rubin [8], comenta que, aunque hay muchas características que se deben buscar en un buen

PO, éstas se pueden agrupar en cuatro categorías: habilidades de dominio, habilidades personales, toma de decisiones y responsabilidad (*accountability*).

Por su parte, Resnick, Bjork y de la Masa [11] mencionan las siguientes cuatro características de un buen PO: conocimiento profundo del dominio, fuertes habilidades de comunicación verbal y escrita, presencia, empoderamiento.

Para Pichler [1], las principales características que debe tener un buen PO son las siguientes: visionario y hacedor, líder y jugador de equipo, comunicador y negociador, empoderado y comprometido, y disponible y calificado.

Las características y habilidades mencionadas por los autores precedentes, con la excepción de las habilidades o conocimiento profundo del dominio, suelen mencionarse en la literatura como ejemplos de "soft skills" o habilidades blandas. En un estudio reportado por Matturro y colegas [12], las habilidades de comunicación, la orientación al cliente y el trabajo en equipo son las tres habilidades blandas que aparecen como las más valoradas para un PO, desde las perspectivas particulares de los Scrum Masters, los miembros de equipos, y los PO entrevistados para el estudio referido.

3 Diseño Metodológico

El diseño metodológico consistió en la definición de las preguntas de investigación, la selección de los informantes claves, la elaboración de los instrumentos de recolección de datos, su aplicación en entrevistas personales semi-estructuradas, la lectura crítica y codificación de las respuestas obtenidas, y el análisis y la interpretación de los datos obtenidos.

3.1 Preguntas de investigación

El rol de PO es clave en un equipo Scrum y la elección de la persona adecuada tiene un impacto relevante en el funcionamiento del equipo y en la correcta aplicación de la metodología. Por esto, en relación con la elección del PO la primera pregunta de investigación planteada fue:

- RQ1: ¿Cuáles son los procedimientos y los criterios utilizados para seleccionar la persona que se desempeñará como PO, y quienes participan en su elección?

De las múltiples responsabilidades asociadas al rol de PO reseñadas arriba, para este estudio el interés se centró particularmente en el grado de participación del PO en las diferentes ceremonias de Scrum. Así, la segunda pregunta de investigación planteada fue:

- RQ2: ¿En cuales ceremonias de Scrum suele participar el PO, y con qué frecuencia?

En cuanto a las características personales deseadas para un buen PO, este estudio se enfocó en las denominadas habilidades blandas y, sobre esto, la tercera pregunta de investigación planteada fue:

- RQ3: ¿Cuáles son las habilidades blandas consideradas más valiosas en un PO?

3.2 Selección de los informantes claves

Según sostienen Hernández Sampieri y colegas [13], el muestreo cualitativo (como es el caso de este estudio) es propositivo, y las primeras acciones para elegir la muestra ocurren desde el planteamiento mismo del problema de investigación y cuando se selecciona el contexto, en el cual se esperan encontrar los casos que interesan. Para estos autores, en los estudios cualitativos el tamaño de la muestra no es importante desde una perspectiva probabilística pues lo que se busca en la indagación cualitativa es profundidad. Lo que interesa son casos o unidades (participantes, organizaciones, eventos, hechos, etc.) que ayuden a entender el fenómeno de estudio y a responder a las preguntas de investigación.

De este modo, para contactar informantes claves que pudieran dar su visión sobre los aspectos del rol de PO que son el foco de este trabajo, se contactaron seis empresas de desarrollo de software basadas en Montevideo que utilizan Scrum como metodología para gestionar sus proyectos de desarrollo.

De estas empresas, tres accedieron a participar en el estudio, facilitando el contacto con miembros de la organización o con personas externas que estén desempeñando o hayan desempeñado el rol de PO en algún proyecto software.

3.3 Recolección de datos

La recolección de datos fue realizada mediante entrevistas semi-estructuradas a los informantes claves, siguiendo las pautas establecidas en los cuestionarios.

El proceso de recolección de los datos fue el siguiente:

- Coordinar entrevistas a los informantes claves de las empresas participantes, poniendo especial cuidado en que cumplan con el criterio de estar desempeñando, o haber desempeñado, el rol de PO.
- Durante cada entrevista se utilizó un cuestionario para ir preguntando sobre los aspectos a relevar, y se solicita aclaración o ampliación en caso necesario.
- Cada entrevista fue grabada, con la autorización del entrevistado, de modo de tener una referencia posterior para extraer las respuestas a las preguntas formuladas.

Las preguntas formuladas durante las entrevistas estuvieron directamente vinculadas a la obtención de información para dar respuesta a las preguntas de investigación planteadas.

Así, para la pregunta de investigación RQ1 las preguntas del cuestionario fueron: 1A *¿De qué tipo es el proyecto de desarrollo en el que participa o ha participado como PO?*; 1B *¿Por qué fue elegido para desempeñar el rol de Product Owner?*; 1C

¿Quién o quienes participaron en el proceso de decisión para elegirlo?; 1D *¿Pertenece al área de negocio que se benefició o se beneficiará del sistema en desarrollo?*

Para la pregunta de investigación RQ2, se les propuso a los entrevistados la lista de eventos o "ceremonias" de Scrum para que indicaran su grado de participación durante el desarrollo del proyecto, tal como se muestra en la Tabla 1.

Tabla 1. Lista de ceremonias Scrum y opciones de grado de participación

Ceremonia	Nunca	Pocas veces	Algunas veces	Muchas veces	Siempre
Daily stand up meeting					
Planificación del sprint					
Revisión del sprint (demo)					
Retrospectiva del sprint					
Refinamiento (Grooming)					

Finalmente, para la pregunta de investigación RQ3 se les propuso a los entrevistados una lista cerrada de 15 habilidades blandas tomadas de un trabajo previo de uno de los autores [12], para que indicaran cuales consideran que son las más relevantes en un buen PO.

3.4 Codificación de las respuestas

Luego de cada entrevista, se procedió a la transcripción de lo declarado por el entrevistado, al tiempo que se verificó si las respuestas brindadas aseguraban que se haya obtenido la información necesaria para responder las preguntas de investigación planteadas.

En caso de detectarse alguna inconsistencia entre preguntas o ausencia de respuesta adecuada, se procedió a entrevistar nuevamente al informante clave correspondiente para completar la información necesaria.

El procedimiento para extraer y clasificar las respuestas se hizo en base al proceso de codificación de preguntas abiertas que se propone en [13]. La codificación de preguntas abiertas es una técnica para realizar el análisis de respuestas en entrevistas con preguntas abiertas. Las preguntas abiertas fueron codificadas luego de conocer todas las respuestas de los encuestados. Los códigos son etiquetas para identificar categorías, es decir, describen un segmento de texto donde, en este caso, los textos corresponden a las transcripciones de lo declarado en las entrevistas.

Por ejemplo, en relación con la elección del PO para un nuevo proyecto, un entrevistado declaró "*Yo era desarrollador en <la empresa> y cuando salió este proyecto me eligieron a mí, creo porque yo en proyectos anteriores definía historias y hacia algunas tareas que serían de product owner.*" En este caso, el código asignado como motivo principal de elección fue "Experiencia en el rol". En cambio, otro entrevistado dijo "*Yo había trabajado en un proyecto para un banco; entonces creo que por unidad de negocio les debe haber parecido que yo podía aprovechar esos conocimientos* *del área financiera para este nuevo proyecto.*" En este otro caso, el código asignado fue "Conocimiento del negocio".

4 Resultados obtenidos

En total se entrevistaron seis informantes claves de las empresas participantes que han desempeñado o estaban desempeñando el rol de PO en el momento del relevamiento. Las entrevistas tuvieron una duración promedio de 50 minutos y, cuando hubo necesidad de volver a entrevistar, estas segundas partes promediaron los 25 minutos.

Con las declaraciones obtenidas en las entrevistas a los informantes claves, en las siguientes sub-secciones se presentan las respuestas a las preguntas de investigación planteadas para este estudio.

4.1 Sobre la elección del PO

En relación con los procedimientos para la elección del PO (pregunta de investigación RQ1) los entrevistados encontraron difícil responder a esta cuestión de manera concreta, pues ninguno dijo haber participado de un proceso formal, más allá alguna entrevista personal a la interna de su organización.

Sin embargo, destacaron que, en sus casos personales, se buscaba personas con experiencia previa en el desempeño del rol (tres de seis casos) o con conocimiento del negocio (dos de seis casos), como motivos principales para la designación.

La Tabla 2 muestra un compendio de las respuestas obtenidas respecto a los aspectos indagados para la elección del PO de un proyecto.

Tabla 2. Aspectos relativos a la elección del PO

Entrevistado	Tipo de proyecto	Pertenece al área de negocio	Motivo principal de elección	Participación del cliente
Andrés	Subcontratado	No	Experiencia en el rol	No
Juan	Subcontratado	No	Experiencia en el rol	No
Julieta	Subcontratado	No	Conocimiento del negocio	Si
Mateo	Subcontratado	No	Solicitud personal	Si
Nicolás	Interno	Si	Experiencia en el rol	Si
Martin	Interno	Si	Conocimiento del negocio	Si

Por otra parte, de lo obtenido en las entrevistas se observa que, en los casos de proyectos subcontratados, la evidencia indica que no se suele seguir la recomendación de que el PO sea alguien que pertenezca al área de negocio del cliente que se beneficiará con el producto desarrollado, tal como se comentó en la Sección 2.

Con respecto a quienes intervienen en la elección del PO, en todos los casos se mencionó que un participante habitual es el gerente o responsable del área en la que el candidato a PO trabaja.

Además, tanto en los casos de proyectos de desarrollo interno, como en la mitad de los del tipo subcontratados, "el cliente" (entendido como el área de negocio que se beneficiará de producto desarrollado) también tiene participación directa en la elección del PO.

4.2 Sobre las responsabilidades del PO

La pregunta de investigación RQ2 refiere a la participación de los PO en las diversas ceremonias de Scrum a lo largo de la ejecución de un proyecto.

De acuerdo con las respuestas brindadas por los entrevistados en cuanto a su participación en las ceremonias y la frecuencia con la que asisten (Tabla 3), hay dos ceremonias en las que se muestran "infaltables". Estas son las reuniones de planificación del sprint, (*sprint planning meeting*), las reuniones de revisión del sprint (*sprint review meeting*).

Un tercer tipo de reunión, las denominadas de refinamiento del *product backlog* (*grooming*), aparece como de asistencia "casi unánime".

Por lo general, el PO es el encargado de guiar estas ceremonias, especialmente las reuniones de planificación del sprint que, según la literatura, resulta ser la ceremonia más importante para el PO y para el proyecto en sí puesto que es la instancia donde se utiliza el artefacto primordial que gestiona el PO – el *product backlog* – y donde el equipo y el PO negocian qué trabajo se extraerá para el próximo *sprint*.

Tabla 3. Grado de participación de los PO en las ceremonias de Scrum

Ceremonia	Nunca	Pocas veces	Algunas veces	Muchas veces	Siempre
Daily stand up meeting		2	1	1	2
Planificación del sprint					6
Revisión del sprint (demo)					6
Retrospectiva del sprint		2	1	1	2
Refinamiento (grooming)		1			5

En cuanto a las reuniones de refinamiento (del *product backlog*) o "*grooming meetings*", si bien no están definidas en la propuesta metodológica canónica como una ceremonia típica de Scrum, en la práctica los PO suelen realizarla cuando el entorno lo requiere, ya sea como respuesta a necesidades del equipo por mayor claridad en las historias de usuario y sus estimaciones, como cuando lo requiere el cliente al crear nuevas historias de usuario o refinar las existentes.

4.3 Sobre las características del PO

En cuanto a las características personales valoradas en quienes desempeñen el rol de PO, la pregunta de investigación RQ3 apunta particularmente a las denominadas habilidades blandas o *soft skills*.

De las respuestas de los entrevistados se observa la unanimidad de opiniones en cuanto a que las habilidades de comunicación, el trabajo en equipo y la orientación al cliente son las tres habilidades blandas que debe exhibir un buen PO.

La Tabla 4 muestra las habilidades blandas que fueron mencionadas por al menos la mitad de los entrevistados.

Tabla 4. Habilidades blandas más valoradas en los PO

Habilidades blandas	Menciones
Habilidades de comunicación, Trabajo en equipo, Orientación al cliente	6
Compromiso y responsabilidad, Habilidades de planificación, Liderazgo, Analítico y resolutor de problemas	5
Habilidades interpersonales, Iniciativa y proactividad, Motivación	4
Orientación a resultados	3

Las habilidades de comunicación, tanto oral como escrita, son fundamentales en un PO pues su rol implica dialogar y estar en contacto permanente tanto con los interesados como con el equipo, así como, por ejemplo, escribir las historias de usuario que alimentan el *product backlog* del proyecto.

5 Discusión

Aunque se trata de un estudio exploratorio para un grupo reducido de escenarios, los resultados obtenidos establecen ciertos puntos para una discusión más profunda sobre cómo se desempeña el rol del PO en la práctica.

La ingeniería de requerimientos es una de las áreas críticas en el desarrollo de software y la metodología Scrum propone el rol de PO como puente para resolver muchos de los desafíos relacionados a los requerimientos y la interacción con los interesados. Dada la importancia del rol de PO en el contexto de la metodología Scrum, llama la atención que las organizaciones no tienen un mecanismo formal de selección de la persona que ha de desempeñar el rol. Por otro lado, no existe un consenso en el motivo principal para la selección del PO. La mayor parte de las respuestas se orientan a la experiencia de la persona en el rol y, en menor medida, el conocimiento del negocio. Esto nos hace plantear la hipótesis de que la asignación del PO puede estar más influida por motivos de experiencia interna o jerárquicos (el gerente de proyecto lo asigna por confianza en su desempeño).

En un contexto ágil, la especificación y validación del producto no se realiza de una sola vez, sino en pequeños ciclos y con interacción continua presencial entre el PO y el equipo. Se podría decir que los requerimientos de software surgen de una conversación y descubrimiento continuo de todo el equipo facilitada por el PO, más que únicamente de instancias de validación formal. Los resultados del estudio muestran un consenso en que el PO participa siempre en las ceremonias de planificación y revisión del sprint. Sin embargo, en la ceremonia de interacción diaria del equipo (*daily stand up meeting*), observamos menor participación de este rol. En la ceremonia de retrospectiva del *spint*, donde el equipo reflexiona sobre su trabajo y propone mejoras, también observamos baja participación del PO. Estos resultados plantean la hipótesis de que el PO sea visto como una figura de enlace, pero no efectivamente parte del núcleo del equipo. Esto podría ser una diferencia sustancial en cuanto al planteo del rol que se realiza en la metodología Scrum, donde el PO colabora continuamente con el equipo y es parte integral de su actividad diaria.

Con respecto a las habilidades blandas requeridas para el PO, del estudio surgen resultados claros que priorizan las habilidades de comunicación, el trabajo en equipo y la orientación al cliente. Esos resultados confirman aspectos clave mencionados en la literatura sobre el rol del PO en Scrum. También observamos que los entrevistados identifican explícitamente estas habilidades como necesarias en el perfil de la persona que desempeña el rol. Este énfasis en el perfil de habilidades de la persona podría ser un mecanismo indirecto para minimizar el impacto de otras carencias en el proceso.

Por ejemplo, la no participación diaria en las ceremonias se puede compensar con habilidades de comunicación o un menor conocimiento específico del negocio aumentado con la orientación al cliente.

6 Amenazas a la validez

Según Merriam y Tisdell [14], debido a que la investigación cualitativa se basa en supuestos sobre la realidad diferentes de los de la investigación cuantitativa, los estándares para el rigor en la investigación cualitativa difieren necesariamente de los de la investigación cuantitativa.

Por su parte, Hernández Sampieri y colegas [13] mencionan que los principales autores en la materia han formulado una serie de criterios para establecer cierto "paralelo" con la confiabilidad, validez (interna y externa) y objetividad cuantitativa, que han sido aceptados por la mayoría de los investigadores (aunque reconocen que son rechazados por otros). Estos criterios sustitutivos se denominan dependencia, credibilidad, y transferencia.

El criterio de dependencia se define como el grado en que diferentes investigadores que recolecten datos similares en el campo y efectúen los mismos análisis, generen resultados equivalentes. Hernández Sampieri y colegas, citando a Franklin y Ballau, mencionan dos clases de dependencia: a) interna (grado en el cual distintos investigadores, al menos dos, generan categorías similares con los mismos datos) y b) externa (grado en que diferentes investigadores generan categorías similares en el mismo ambiente y periodo, pero cada uno recaba sus propios datos).

Para cumplir con el criterio de dependencia interna, el análisis de los datos recolectados se hizo en forma independiente por los tres autores, de modo de identificar y discutir las diferencias que pudieran surgir y arribar a resultados unificados.

El criterio de dependencia externa no se pudo verificar pues no hay otros investigadores (más allá de los tres autores de este estudio) que hayan recolectado datos de los mismos entrevistados y en circunstancias similares (mismo ambiente y período).

El criterio de credibilidad refiere a si el investigador ha captado el significado completo y profundo de las experiencias de los participantes, particularmente de aquellas vinculadas con el planteamiento del problema.

En este sentido, el haber grabado las entrevistas y disponer de los audios ha permitido volver a escuchar lo declarado por cada entrevistado, de modo de asegurar no haber omitido nada importante. Además, se procuró evitar los sesgos del investigador en cuanto a ignorar o minimizar datos que no apoyen sus creencias y conclusiones.

Finalmente, en cuanto al criterio de transferencia (o aplicabilidad de los resultados), éste no se refiere a generalizar los resultados a una población más amplia, ya que ésta no es una finalidad de un estudio cualitativo, sino que parte de esos resultados o su esencia puedan aplicarse en otros contextos.

En relación con este criterio, de los seis informantes claves entrevistados, cuatro son o fueron POs de proyectos subcontratados, por lo que estos resultados de la investigación, en principio, no pueden aplicarse a los casos de POs de proyectos de desarrollo interno o comercial.

7 Conclusiones y trabajos futuros

Se realizó un estudio exploratorio sobre el rol del PO en la práctica industrial. En primer lugar, se recogieron de la literatura aceptada por la comunidad de Scrum características consideradas clave para el desempeño del rol. En segundo lugar, recogimos información mediante entrevistas semi-estructuradas a seis informantes clave que desempeñaron el rol de PO en distintas empresas. Las transcripciones de las entrevistas fueron codificadas mediante la técnica de codificación abierta para responder a 3 preguntas de investigación principales.

A partir de los resultados obtenidos en este estudio se evidencian ciertas diferencias entre la propuesta canónica de la metodología Scrum en cuanto al desempeño del rol de PO y de sus responsabilidades, y lo que ocurre en la práctica industrial.

Así, la recomendación metodológica de que el PO sea un representante del área de negocio que se beneficiará del producto en desarrollo mayoritariamente no se cumple, al menos en los casos de los entrevistados. Tampoco el conocimiento del negocio es usado como criterio de selección del PO en la mayoría de los casos, en cambio, la experiencia en el rol es frecuentemente mencionada como criterio principal.

Por otra parte, siendo el PO un miembro más del equipo, debería participar en todas las ceremonias. Sin embargo, la evidencia obtenida indica que solo hay unanimidad de participación en las de planificación y de revisión del cada *sprint* dejando, en el otro extremo, las *daily stand up meeting* y las reuniones de retrospectiva con participación esporádica.

En cuanto a las habilidades blandas buscadas en la persona que desempeña el rol de PO hay un consenso significativo sobre la capacidad de comunicación, trabajo en equipo y orientación al cliente. Esto hace pensar que una forma de compensar las carencias mencionadas de conocimiento del negocio y participación en ceremonias pueda ser mediante la búsqueda explícita de personas con estas habilidades blandas.

Estos hallazgos plantean nuevas interrogantes, que serán motivo de indagación y profundización en futuros trabajos.

Para el caso de los PO de proyectos subcontratados que no pertenecen al área de negocio beneficiaria del desarrollo, es interesante indagar de qué manera adquieren los conocimientos del negocio para poder actuar como "la voz del cliente".

En cuanto a las ceremonias en las que se denota escasa participación por parte de los PO, se considera interesante conocer los motivos; por ejemplo, si no encuentran valor en esas ceremonias, o si es por falta de tiempo por estar los PO participando en simultáneamente otros proyectos.

Referencias

[1] R. Pichler, *Agile product management with Scrum. Creating products that customers love*. Boston, MA: Pearson Education, 2010.

[2] H. Sverrisdottira, H. Ingasonb, y H. Jonassonc, "The role of the product owner in scrum. Comparison between theory and practices", *Procedia Soc. Behav. Sci.*, n° 119, pp. 257–267, 2014.

[3] Ken Schwaber y Jeff Sutherland, *The Scrum guide*. Scrum Inc., 2017.

[4] Mark C. Layton, *Scrum for Dummies*. Hoboken, NJ: John Wiley & Sons, 2015.

[5] Kenneth Rubin, *Essential Scrum. A practical guide to the most popular agile process*. Upper Saddle River, NJ: Pearson, 2013.

[6] Craig Larman y Bas Vodde, *Large-Scale Scrum. More with LeSS*. Boston, MA: Addison-Wesley, 2017.

[7] Mario Moreira, *Being Agile. Your roadmap to successful adoption of Agile*. New York: NY: Apress, 2013.

[8] K. Rubin, *Essential Scrum. A practical guide to the most popular agile process*. Upper Saddle River, NJ: Pearson, 2013.

[9] D. Green, *Scrum. Novice to Ninja*. Collingwood: Sitepoint, 2016.

[10] M. C. Layton, *Scrum for Dummies*. Hoboken, NJ: John Wiley & Sons, 2015.

[11] S. Resnick, A. Bjork, y M. de la Maza, *Professional Scrum with Team Foundation Server 2010*. Indianapolis, IN: Wiley Publishing, 2011.

[12] G. Matturro, C. Fontán, y F. Raschetti, "Soft Skills in Scrum Teams. A survey of the most valued to have by Product Owners and Scrum Masters", 27th International Conference on Software Engineering and Knowledge Engineering (SEKE), Pittsburgh, 2015, pp. 42–45.

[13] R. Hernández Sampieri, C. Fernández, y P. Baptista, *Metodología de la investigación*, 6ª ed. México: McGraw Hill, 2014.

[14] S. B. Merriam y E. J. Tisdell, *Qualitative research: a guide to design and implementation*, 4ª ed. Hoboken: NJ: John Wiley & Sons, 2016.

Enhancing spherical photography with videogame visual effects in virtual reality experiences for users with limited mobility

Gabriel de Ioannes Becker[1], Exequiel Plaza[2], and Felipe Besoain[1,3,*]

[1] Escuela de Ingeniería en Desarrollo de Videojuegos y Realidad Virtual, Universidad de Talca, Avenida Lircay s/n, Talca, Chile

[2] Escuela de Fonoaudilogía, Universidad de Talca, Avenida Lircay s/n, Talca, Chile

{fbesoain,gdeioannes,eplaza}@utalca.cl

[3] Internet Interdisciplinary Institute (IN3), Universitat Oberta de Catalunya, Av.Carl Friedrich Gauss, 5, Castelldefels, Barcelona, Spain

{fbesoain}@uoc.edu

Abstract. For people with a condition of disability, including those with limited mobility, accessing places of interest can be a challenge, affected by factors such as transportation distances, costs, and available infrastructure, among others. Inclusion is a current topic, as there is a need to provide and develop universal access. How can a virtual reality experience be developed to help disabled people experience public or private places of interest? To answer this question, we developed and tested an application for smartphones with virtual reality concepts. The application allows users to explore a sculpture museum, taking into consideration the con- text of the target group and the quality of a virtual reality experience. To test the application, we conducted a feasibility test with eleven patients with Parkinson's disease, who then responded to a survey with 57 questions. The test showed that users liked and found the application useful for bridging the gap for disabled persons in accessing culture through an enhanced photospheres virtual reality experience. The main contribution of this work is the design of an immersive user experience at low cost, with spherical pictures and effects inspired by game development.

Keywords: spherical immersive images, Virtual Reality, assistive technology, mobile devices, mhealth.

1. Introduction

When people's health is affected by their body structure and functioning, and this condition becomes chronic, they may be seen as disabled. Infrastructure must be adapted or created to provide universal access to places of work, recreation and culture for people with a condition of disability, including those with limited mobility.

In central Chile, there is a total of 2,068,062 disabled people, about 12.9 % of the total population [1]. Maule Region, which is located in this geographical area, shows the highest prevalence rate of disability across the country at 17.8 %. Social awareness of these people, including those with sensory, mobility or mental disabilities, has occurred in Chile only since the eighties [2]. In fact, the condition of disability was only recognized legally ten years ago [3].

Despite the concern of health professionals, educators, and other social actors, the issues of disability persist and are strongly associated with vulnerability factors such as poverty, rurality, low educational instruction and old age [4]. This concurrence of dimensions is not unique to this region. It can also be seen in other areas of the country, such as the Araucanía Region (17.5 % rate of disability) and O'Higgins Region (15.1 % rate of disability) that are inaccessible to professionals and managers of the Ministries of Health and Social Development, which are the entities that preferably address this issue in Chile [1].

As recently enforced laws recognize, people with disabilities are entitled to the same rights and responsibilities as any other citizen, thus closing gaps and promoting social integration and social inclusion. However, some of the main challenges for disabled people when accessing public or private places for free time are: 1) distance between their comfort zone and a place of interest; 2) poor infrastructure for people with a condition of disability; 3) expensive transportation costs for people living in rural areas or cities far from the capital; and 4) timing and planning involved in a particular visit. These issues have an adverse impact on the quality of life for people with a condition of disability.

In the present paper, we took into consideration the complex local context of disabled people, in order to provide a technological solution with a positive impact on people's lives. This solution is based on the principles of virtual reality (VR) to provide and contextualize an immersive visit to places of interest using mobile devices and their potential communication technologies at low cost. Although other studies have been conducted using VR applications for improving the quality of life of disabled people [18, 19], those applications were not necessarily developed using the new hardware available, such as commercial 360 cameras and VR device headsets. In contrast, the current project seeks to provide an immersive experience at a low cost through spherical photographs and effects inspired by video game development.

Our goal is to use these technologies to create a natural, non-invasive entry point to provide universal access to places of interest for people with a condition of disability. With this in mind, we developed an application that provides a virtual visit to the National Sculpture Museum located in Talca, Chile. This application is called the Museum App.

We developed the Museum App to create a VR experience. The common terms used to determine the quality of a VR experience are: *immersion* and *presence*.

Immersion is a widely used term in the analysis of VR experiences because it is objective. It points to the quality of specific parameters established in a VR. In summary, immersion" refers to the objective level of sensory fidelity a VR system provides" [5].

Presence, on the other hand, is difficult to measure since it is subjective. It is described as a "user's physiological response to a VR system," or more specifically, a "sense of being there in a VR" [6, 16].

It is considered important to study as objectively as possible the extent to which the VR evokes a sensation of presence in the user.

Taking into account these factors, we worked with specific requirements and functionalities such as particles, visual effects (VFXs), 3D sound, environmental effects and specific transition effects between virtual environments (VEs). These aspects allowed us to create an immersive experience for the users.

There is a broad range of products that exist for developing VR experiences. In this project, we use Unity 3D Game development software in order to develop scalable, modular, robust and portable software [7].

This document is structured as follows: the second section describes the motivation of the project as well as the Museum App; the third section presents our findings from the test carried out with a volunteer group; finally, the document closes with concluding remarks and an outlook towards further work.

2. Motivation of the Project

The main question to be addressed in this project is how to develop a VR experience that could help disabled people to experience public or private places of interest. To answer this question, we developed and tested the Museum App with VR concepts, taking into consideration the context of the target group and the quality of a VR experience.

Since creating an immersive VR experience is a challenge, how we define the VE is very important. For defining the environment, we considered the weather and the light of the pictures that we used to create the experience. In this project, the photos were taken on a cloudy and rainy day. Therefore, in order to provide an engrossing total environment, it is necessary to work with VFXs and 3D Sound to enhance the user's sensations [17]. For instance, VFX helps create a totally immersive environment by adding rain and lightning. At the same time, 3D sound helps intensify stimuli related to the weather by including the sound of rain drops and thunder. Furthermore, both VFX and 3D sound is used to create transitions when users move from exterior to interior spaces.

It is important to work with the sensation of the environment because our main goal is to evoke and promote the perception of being physically present in a virtual world.

2.1. General Use Case

To understand how the software behaves, we present a general use case (see Table 1). This use case briefly explains each process and its interaction with the various solution components, which will also be outlined in thissection.

Table 1. General use case of the Museum App

Actor:	User.
Purpose:	To give an immersive walk-through experience of places of interest.
Summary:	This use case begins when the user starts the application. The application places users outside the museum, where they can walk freely to the museum following different markers. In contrast to a tour that has been previously programmed, the application allows users to decide where to go. The user has the chance to interact with the environment and predetermined sounds, walking between scenes in an open area.
Preconditions:	(1) The smartphone should be connected to headphones. (2) The users should focus the VR device so that the image is clear.

Based on the general use case, we took into consideration the following aspects:

- Mapping of the museum on spherical images.
- Applying concepts of videogames such as: VFXs, 3D sound and transitions.
- Integrating scenes and modules in a VR application.

2.2. Software Description

The application was developed following the System Development methodology as a Design and Creation research strategy [10], integrating a strong focus on the design of a user experience according to the need and experience that we wanted to transmit through the VR experience to the target group.

2.3. User Experience (UX)

The goal of the application is to give the opportunity to experience a location through VR to people that have low income, movement difficulties and that are far away from places of interest, reducing transportation and logistics costs. The place that was chosen for the development of the application was a sculpture museum in Talca, Chile (see Fig. 1). The application allows the user to explore the outer and inner parts of the building, including: the exterior gardens and sculptures, and the interior space with two different auditoriums.

The technique used to register the space was spherical panoramic photo- graphs connected together through markers in each VE. A soundscape was added to the VE to enhance the experience. To interact, the users must look around and direct their view to a specific marker inside each VE. Then, they must tap the VR device's touch panel to move to the next location. To explore the whole scene, users must turn their head and body in a full range of movement, providing a 360 degree experience. If their movement is limited, then their experience of the scene will be restricted to that range.

Fig. 1. Area of the sculpture museum located in Talca, Chile

The hardware used for the development and test of this experience were:
1) Samsung VR: has 96 degrees of FOV with 20ms photon movement latency, sensors (accelerometer, gyroscope, magnetic and proximity), as well as a touch panel, back button and volume button for physical interaction; 2) Reko Theta Camera: has 14MP of resolution to register the environment; and 3) Samsung Galaxy 6: a smartphone used to develop and run the program in the Samsung VR.

Since the cameras used were not professional, image quality was a challenge. The use of spherical panoramas with these cameras negatively affects the quality of the VEs. Also, the use of images instead of 3D models further diminishes the quality of immersion in terms of the representation of physical space. As a result, it was necessary to use other techniques to enhance the experience, including sound, particle systems and VFXs.

Besides the issue of image capture, current VR visualization devices have some additional constraints in achieving the best immersion quality. For example, frames per second (FPS), movement tracking, field of view (FOV) and field of regard (FOR) are common problems in new VR devices [18]. Products like Google Cardboard extend the reach of this technology at a low cost, but they reduce quality levels to achieve it.

2.4. VE Development

There is a large amount of software available to implement VR experiences. 3D Game development software was the most appropriate choice due to the specific requirements and the necessity to add functionalities such as Particles, VFXs, 3D sound, environmental effects and specific transition effects between VEs. There is a wide range of products that suit the development of VR tours. The software considered for the task were Unreal [8], Unity3D [7] and Ogre3D [9] (Rendering Engine). Among these, Unity3D was the final choice due to its multiport capabilities, VR libraries for Samsung and Google Cardboard, and its large community with wide support. Also, the engine has a license for free use with limited functionalities, but which were sufficient for our project's requirements, thus lowering the cost of development.

- **Environment Setup:** The VEs were composed with spherical panorama pictures used as a texture in a sphere shape object imported in the Unity Editor, with Skybox material attached. The views allow us to control the specific position of every VE and create a distribution similar to the real distribution of the museum. This was necessary for placing the markers and connecting every VE to each other with the correct physical direction. The correct direction of the marker was critical in terms of achieving continuity of movement in the overall experience. When the user jumps from one VE to another, the application maintains the specific point of interest between places (the users don't lose their spatial orientation). In previous tests without this feature, users got lost in the spaces, which lowered their level of immersion. Another big issue in the mapping was distribution and dispersion; there is a maximum distance between VEs that is required to maintain continuity. Also, to reach places that are hidden in corners, an extra map point is needed to avoid the ghost effect of passing through walls, which also diminishes the sense of immersion (see Fig. 2).

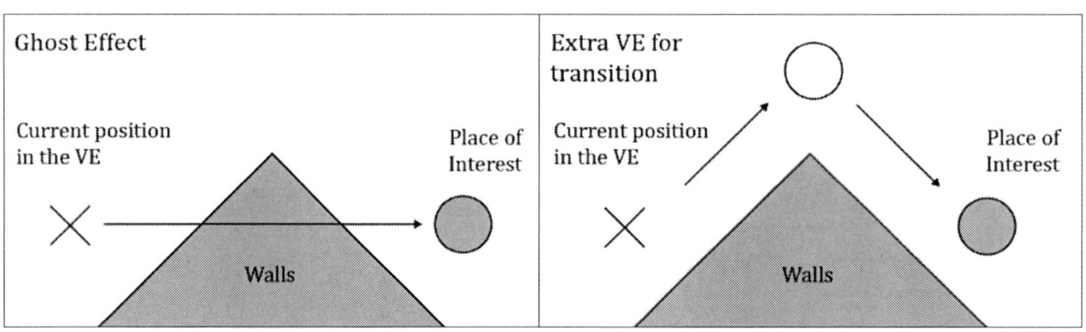

Fig. 2. Ghost effect versus adding an extra VE for transition

- **Navigation:** Each VE has markers, and every marker has a specific environment indexed to it. When the user taps the touch panel of the device, a raycast is shot through the center of the camera. If the raycast collides with the marker bounding box, it triggers the event of moving to the next VE. The colliders of the marker were made to be very wide, so there is no need for a graphic target in the VR, which avoids information cluttering [15]. The main camera of the scene is moved to the next VE, maintaining the orientation of the camera in each transition.

The graphic aspect of the marker is important, because it needs to show direction to maintain the user orientation in the spatial aspect of the VE. Also, in terms of graphics, the marker needed to work with different background settings (see Fig. 3), in case of low or high brightness.
A transition was added for moving between scenes (a fade to black animation and a delay between transitions) to avoid the notion of tele-transportation between spaces. Also, this was complemented by the sound effect of steps, which gives extra feedback to the user. The connection of each VE was critical to achieve a better level of immersion and increase the sensation of presence.

Fig. 3. Markers and VFX in different scenes.

- **VFXs**: Due to the use of low cost 360 camera pictures and static images, the immersion level had to be increased using VFX added to the VEs.

There are two main visual effects:

  - **Rain**: Particle Effect, added to the exterior areas with no roof. The soundscape of the effect blends with the particles and the context of the environment, constructing a dynamic exterior scene. The particles and sound were looped with a specific time range, so loops detection is not a problem. The particles can be set at different places depending on the environment, which allows a second layer of customization.
  - **Lightning**: Texture exposure effect with specific audio feedback of the thunder sound. The trigger for this effect is random with a specific threshold control range, avoiding predictability for the user to enhance immersion in the environment. The effect is used outdoors and indoors, close to the windows of the building.

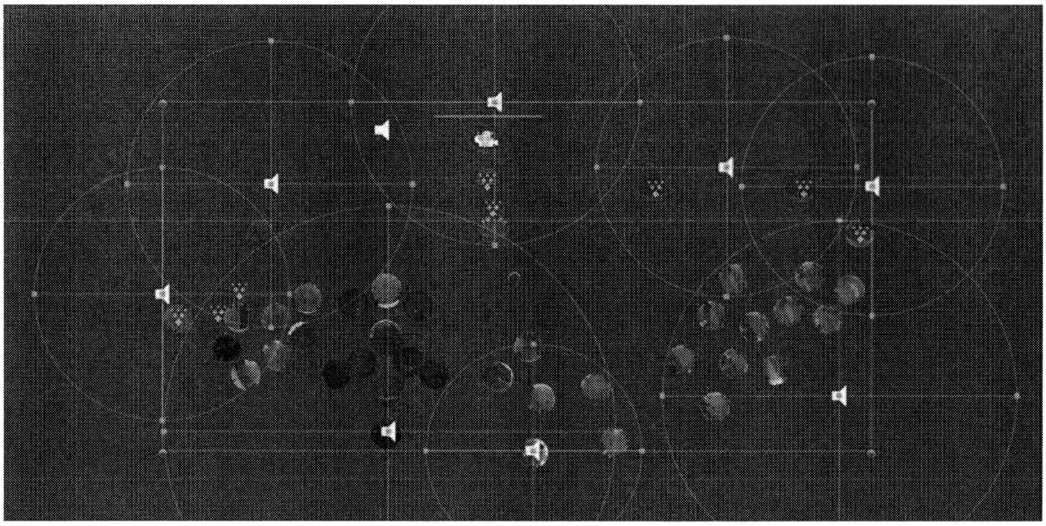

Fig. 4. Graphical representation of the walkable area, the VEs and sound positions.

- **3D sound**: Sounds are added to a specific cluster of VEs with the built- in functionality Audio Source. The component allows us to add sound and parameters of minimum and maximum range, with the specific volume control according to distance. Thanks to the natural distribution of the VEs in the editor, adding the proper sounds and matching the changes in volume according to their placement happens naturally. 3D sound was critical to enhance the immersion in the movement and spatial reference. Three main soundscapes where defined: 1) the gardens with a storm background sound; 2) inside the sculpture space with a mix of outer and inner sounds; and 3) the main auditorium with a piano concert background sound. When the user moves across the different VE, the proximity of the sound source makes the sound louder, giving a second and important feedback for physical space and movement awareness (see Fig. 4).

3. Results

After the development of the application, the second objective of the present work is to test the effectiveness and experience of the application and VE with a target group. The test was carried out with the Museum App and Samsung VR device. The study was designed according to the recommendations suggested by several reports for medical or therapeutic-like interventions as in [11, 12]. Eleven patients with Parkinson's disease (PD) volunteered to participate in the feasibility evaluation of the VR System (four woman and seven men, with an average age of 71).

PD is a chronic and progressive process caused by neuronal degeneration in the substantia nigra, leading to a decrease in dopamine levels. Its etiology is unknown and probably multifactorial. It shows an incidence of 16/100000 people and an estimated prevalence of 1000/100000. The average age of onset is around 55 years and most patients are between 50 and 80 years old, although there are early forms of the disease (5-10 % of patients are under 40 years) [13, 14].

The primary PD lesion strikes the compact area of the substantia nigra (SN), which is part of the basal ganglia (GB). Despite significant advances in the possible mechanisms of neuronal degeneration, based on the anatomy and function of the basal ganglia and some studies on experimental models of Parkinsonism, *the limitation of personal functioning remains a major issue for those patients who have PD*. This comprises body function and structure as well as affects daily activities and social participation. Mobility is a major factor that limits PD patients' access to work, recreation and culture. For this reason, the PD patients' participation in this study was considered ideal.

The evaluation was done in three phases. First, the patients with PD were taken to see the sculpture museum, where they visited and viewed the permanent art exhibition. Second, under controlled conditions six months later, the Museum App was presented individually to each member of the group. The application's VR experience showed the same facility and all the pieces of art that were previously seen in person. Third, a survey with 57 questions that were di- vided into four dimensions (Immersion, Presence, Relevance and Hardware) was applied to each of the volunteers. After each patient lived the experience, they were asked to rate several aspects with a Likert scale ranging from 1 to 5, 5 being the most positive value.

In the third phase, the survey was used to identify participants' perceptions of the VR, sounds, VFX, features, and potential use in the context of the main objective. The results of the surveys suggest that participants have a positive perception and value the technological proposal. This takes into consideration the age of the target group, which is sometimes associated with technological illiteracy.

In Table 2, it is possible to see that there is a wide acceptance of the technology and the experience. The section of the survey targeting *relevance* shows that the participants were interested in sharing and using the Museum App in other places and contexts. It is interesting that the questions corresponding to *immersion* and image quality were highly scored. We believe that this result is due to the specific group chosen, including factors such as: age and geographic location. These participants did not have access to professional resolution images or others quality mediums, so the immersion level of the project was sufficient for them. With regards to the *presence* section, the survey results were positive. Participants indicated that they actually felt that they were present in the museum during the experience.

Based on the feedback from users, three points of interest were identified: 1) the user experience (UX), 2) the user's perception of the VR and 3) the user's feelings about the VR device during and posttest.

We designed the application considering the user experience, a feature that was highly valued by the users. They felt that they were present in the application's scenes. The timing of the VFX and the 3D sounds make walking through different scenes feel more real. This is very important, since we worked with static images and we did not add any virtual assets to the scenes, other than the VFX related to the context of the situation. Markers on the ground make the interactions friendlier between the user and the scenes.

Table 2. Findings of highlighted post intervention survey questions, divided into sections based on immersion, presence, relevance and hardware

Section	Question	Average scoring by the users
Immersion	Do you feel that the virtual environment is similar to reality?	4,9
Immersion	Can you hear sounds while you look at the images?	4,5
Immersion	The image seemed clear to me.	4,5
Presence	Do you feel present, that you are inside the projected scene?	4,9
Presence	The device helps me to experience the sensation of visiting other places (far away).	4,8
Relevance	I would recommend seeing the art gallery on the device to people who haven't been there.	4,6
Relevance	Experiencing other places using the device seems interesting to me.	4,5
Relevance	I would show the device to someone who has difficulty going out or walking.	4,3
Relevance	I believe that with the device I can visit places more safely.	4,7
Relevance	The experience with the device was fun.	4,6
Hardware	After using the device, I felt discomfort.	1,4
Hardware	I felt nervous using the device.	2,5

An interesting point to mention is that one user was anxious and nervous to use the application. This was attributed principally to the user's age group. In addition, a second user became dizzy at the end of the virtual tour. This issue has been reported in other VR experiences, and might happen to some users. Nevertheless, one form of mitigating these effects is shortening the length of the experience and avoiding situations that could cause vertigo due to heights or other related factors. Given the nature of our goal, these drawbacks were taken into account in the design and development of the user experience in order to minimize their effects.

4. Conclusion and Future Work

The aim of this research was to develop and investigate how VR could be used as a tool for providing universal access to places of interest. We developed the Museum App with Unity3D for the Samsung VR device. This application runs on an Android Operating System. The application was developed taking into consideration the context of the users and the use of a low cost camera to take 360 photographs. In order to enhance immersion, we used and applied game VFX and 3D sounds in certain scenes to provide a rich and unique experience. The interaction with the devices was simple in order to avoid complex instructions or problems associated with the usability of the application. In this way, the users were able to walk-through the system by simply pointing to a place and clicking an action interface to walk smoothly, avoiding the ghost effect and loss of orientation in the VE.

From the developed test, it can be concluded that users liked and found it useful for bridging the gap for disabled persons in accessing to culture. They considered the experience as a contribution to promoting an inclusive environment and also manifested that they will be able to share the application with their peers. Additionally, participants agreed that the Museum App has the capability of replicating aspects of reality to convince users that they are living a parallel situation. Another relevant aspect that was highly valued was that the VR experience puts the user in a context where they have control over their movement and interaction with the world. It was not automatized or previously programmed, as a traditional virtual tour might be, which would have limited their freedom in the VR.

Further work will address three directions: first, development of an algorithm that will help people with limited movement of their head to have 180 degree movement; second, the design of an automatic information system that will allow users or institutions to map virtually a specific area with the aim of producing VR experiences with standard VFX and sounds for disabled people; and third, the design and implementation of a user friendly protocol for creating VR material with the automatic information system.

The source code and others assets of the present work are available at [20].

References

1. Chilean Ministry of Social Development. Endisc 2004. National Survey for Disability. Web, 14 june 2016. http://www.ine.cl/canales/chile_estadistico/encuestas_discapacidad/pdf/estudionacionaldeladiscapacidad(ingles).pdf
2. Pamela Gutirrez. Cuerpo, discapacidad y prcticas institucionales: Una visión crítica de su evolucion histórica en chile. *Revista Chilena de Terapia Ocupacional*, 14(2), 2014.
3. Lucy Series. The development of disability rights under international law: from charity to human rights. *Disability & Society*, 30(10):1590–1593, 2015.
4. Juan Cabas Monje, Rosana Vallejos Cartes, and Hector Manuel Garrido Henriquez. Reconfiguracion de la pobreza en Chile: un análisis comparativo entre los espacios rurales y urbanos. *Cuadernos de Desarrollo Rural*, 12:99 – 122, 06 2015.
5. Michael Meehan, Brent Insko, Mary Whitton, and Frederick P. Brooks, Jr. Physiological measures of presence in stressful virtual environments. *ACM Trans. Graph.*, 21(3):645–652, July 2002.
6. Mel Slater. A note on presence terminology. *Presence Connect*, 3(3), 2003.
7. Unity - Game Engine http://unity3d.com.
8. Unreal Engine http://www.unrealengine.com.

9. Ogre - Open Source 3D Graphics Engine http://www.ogre3d.org.
10. Oates, B.J.: Researching Information Systems and Computing, SAGE Publications Ltd; 1 edition (November 23, 2005).
11. Bowen, D.J., Kreuter, M., Spring, B., Cofta-Woerpel, L., Linnan, L., Weiner, D., Bakken, S., Kaplan, C.P., Squiers, L., Fabrizio, C., Fernandez, M.: How We Design Feasibility Studies (2009)
12. Leon, A.C., Davis, L.L., Kraemer, H.C.: The role and interpretation of pilot studies in clinical research. Journal of Psychiatric Research 45, 626–629 (2011)
13. Mark Guttman, Stephen J. Kish, and Yoshiaki Furukawa. Current concepts in the diagnosis and management of parkinson's disease. *Canadian Medical Association Journal*, 168(3):293–301, 2003.
14. Levine CB, Fahrbach KR, Siderowf AD, et al. Diagnosis and Treatment of Parkinson's Disease: A Systematic Review of the Literature: Summary. 2003 May. In: AHRQ Evidence Report Summaries. Rockville (MD): Agency for Healthcare Research and Quality (US); 1998-2005. 57. http://www.ncbi.nlm.nih.gov/books/NBK11895/
15. Nicholas F. Polys, Seonho Kim, and Doug A. Bowman. Effects of information layout, screen size, and field of view on user performance in information-rich virtual environments. *Computer Animation and Virtual Worlds*, 18(1):19–38, 2007.
16. D. A. Bowman and R. P. McMahan. Virtual reality: How much immersion is enough? *Computer*, 40(7):36–43, July 2007.
17. S. Serafin, G. ; Serafin. Sound design to enhance presence in photorealistic vir- tual reality. *Presented at the 10th International Conference on Auditory Display (ICAD2004)*, 2004.
18. Pallavi Halarnkar, Sahil Shah, Harsh Shah, Hardik Shah, and Anuj Shah. A re- view on virtual reality. *International Journal of Computer Science Issues (IJCSI)*, 9(6):325–330, 2012.
19. T. Kuhlen and C. Dohle. Virtual reality for physically disabled people. *Computers in Biology and Medicine*, 25(2):205–211, 1995.
20. Website of the Museum App project. Accessed 4 may 2018. https://goo.gl/rjZESz

Reusing and Creating OERs for Software Engineering training

Mónica Villavicencio, Jhonny Pincay, Kattya Desiderio, and Stephany Quimba

Facultad de Ingeniería en Electricidad y Computación (FIEC)
Escuela Superior Politécnica del Litoral (ESPOL)
Campus Gustavo Galindo, Km 30.5 vía Perimetral, Guayaquil-Ecuador
{mvillavi, jvpincay, desideri, struquim} @espol.edu.ec

Abstract. There is a considerable variety of freely available Open Educational Resources (OERs) that can be used for training purposes. However, they are not always suitable for specific needs or ready for been used immediately, which demands a personalization process. In this article, we present a five-phases methodology used to create or personalize OERs as well as to choose an e-learning platform where to make the resources available for learners. The phases of the methodology consider a set of criteria that can help educators to choose whether to use or personalize an OER rather to create it. As a result of following the proposed methodology, ten OERs were selected to be used -without modification-, one was personalized and fourteen created for training purposes.

Keywords: OER, Open Educational Resources, Software engineering, Software testing, Software training

1 Introducción

Como consecuencia de la creciente aparición de material pedagógico ofrecido de manera libre al público por parte de un número de instituciones educativas, en el año 2002 la UNESCO acuñó el concepto de Recurso Educacional Abierto REA (en inglés conocidos como Open Educational Resource - OER) dentro del marco del primer foro mundial sobre recursos educativos de libre acceso [5]. En los últimos años el uso de los REAs se ha popularizado tanto en la academia como en la industria, pues constituyen una alternativa de aprendizaje de fácil acceso y gratuita [2].

El tipo de REA que se encuentra disponible en repositorios a través internet es muy variado, pues existen desde ejercicios y lecturas hasta colecciones de videos y cursos MOOC (Massive Open Online Course). Además, al ser material cuya licencia es abierta, estos pueden ser editados, ampliados, personalizados y combinados con otros recursos existentes [12].

La Ingeniería de Software es un campo que no es ajeno a la utilización de REAs. Muchos estudiantes universitarios y profesionales en el área optan por emplear este tipo de recursos educativos para reforzar conocimientos previos o adquirir nuevas habilidades [9]. Sin embargo, a pesar de existir una gran cantidad de recursos disponibles en la red, no todos son efectivos y no se ajustan a las necesidades de los aprendices. Aspectos como el idioma, calidad del contenido y cantidad de ejemplos son algunos de los factores que influyen en la utilidad percibida de un REA [10]. Por esta razón, nuestro equipo de investigación emprendió un estudio para identificar las necesidades de formación de los desarrolladores de software ecuatorianos, y -a partir de éstas- desarrollar REAs que satisfagan sus expectativas, tanto en contenido como en duración. El estudio consta de cinco fases: 1) Identificación de necesidades de formación de profesionales de software; 2) Desarrollo de REA, 3) Preparación del entorno de aprendizaje en línea, 4) Uso y evaluación de REAs, y 5) Mantenimiento de REAs. En este artículo se presentan en detalle las fases 2 y 3.

El resto del documento se organiza de la siguiente manera: la Sección 2 resume los trabajos relacionados en torno a la creación y evaluación de REAs; la Sección 3 explica la metodología sobre la que se basa este estudio; la Sección 4 expone los resultados obtenidos de las fases 2 y 3; y la Sección 5 presenta las conclusiones de este trabajo.

2 Trabajos Relacionados

Para que los aprendices experimenten buenas experiencias educativas, es necesario que dispongan de recursos educativos adecuados. Crear REAs no es una tarea trivial; varios autores han propuesto metodologías y marcos de trabajo para la creación de recursos educativos que respondan a las necesidades de educandos y educadores. Los autores Khanna y Basak, proponen un marco de trabajo para la creación de recursos educativos correctamente estructurados y de fácil acceso. De acuerdo a su propuesta, un REA debe ser articulado considerando seis dimensiones: pedagógica, tecnológica, administrativa, académica, financiera y ética. Adicionalmente, los investigadores consideran que se deben tomar en cuenta otros aspectos relevantes al momento de publicar los REAs, tales como: la infraestructura informática, el sistema de soporte a usuarios, el mantenimiento del contenido, el sistema de evaluación de los aprendices y la asistencia en línea [11].

Masaru *et al.* [1] proponen un procedimiento inspirado en las metodologías ágiles de ingeniería de software para el desarrollo de REAs. Los investigadores identificaron que uno de los principales problemas al que se enfrentan los desarrolladores de recursos educativos es producir material educacional que pueda ser reusado y adaptado a diferentes situaciones y contextos que surgen durante su desarrollo. Por tanto, sugieren que el proceso de creación y estructuración de los REAs incorpore las siguientes prácticas ágiles: participación activa de usuarios; desarrollo colaborativo e iterativo; refactorización; y evaluación temprana y continua. Los investigadores afirman que al aplicar estas prácticas se obtienen REAs que se ajustan a las necesidades específicas de los usuarios.

Por otra parte, la UNESCO y la Commonwealth of Learning proponen un conjunto de lineamientos para el desarrollo de REAs para educación superior [14]. Este documento señala cuáles son los principales problemas que se presentan al momento de integrar REAs en la enseñanza superior y cómo enfrentarlos. En cuanto a las recomendaciones dirigidas al personal académico que desarrolla recursos educativos, se sugiere que empiecen explorando repositorios de REAs, analicen los recursos existentes en las temáticas de interés, determinen su utilidad, y de acuerdo a ello, decidan reutilizar los recursos existentes, mejorarlos o, en el peor de los casos, crear REAs completamente nuevos.

Con respecto a los recursos educativos dirigidos a entrenamiento de profesionales, en la literatura consultada no se encontraron estudios enfocados en proveer lineamientos a tener en cuenta al momento de crear REAs para ellos. Sin embargo, las personas que cuentan con títulos profesionales constituyen el grupo que más consume cursos masivos -MOOCs- de distinta índole, pues buscan actualizar sus conocimientos o adquirir nuevas habilidades, ya que éstos constituyen una alternativa fácilmente accesible y económica de capacitación [3] [6] [8].

La carencia de esquemas a seguir al momento de crear REAs orientados a entrenar a profesionales es la principal motivación del presente trabajo, el cual se enfoca en el desarrollo, publicación, evaluación y mantenimiento de REAs para profesionales del área de Ingeniería de Software.

3 Metodología

La metodología de nuestro estudio incluye cinco fases: 1) Identificación de necesidades de formación de profesionales de software; 2) Desarrollo de REAs, 3) Preparación del entorno de aprendizaje en línea, 4) Uso y evaluación de REAs, y 5) Mantenimiento de REAs (ver Figura 1). La primera fase identifica las necesidades y expectativas de los profesionales de software en Ecuador mediante la formulación de las siguientes preguntas de investigación: ¿Qué tipo de REAs prefieren los profesionales? ¿Cuáles son los temas que a los profesionales de software les gustaría aprender mediante el uso de REAs? ¿Cuáles son las características que los profesionales esperan de los REAs?. Los resultados de esta fase están en proceso de publicación; sin embargo, podemos indicar que uno de los temas que los profesionales desean aprender es pruebas de software. La segunda fase (desarrollo de REAs) amplía el trabajo expuesto en [15], en donde sugerimos acciones para buscar, seleccionar y evaluar REAs. La tercera fase considera la selección de una plataforma e-learning para alojar los REAs y gestionar el aprendizaje en un entorno virtual. La cuarta fase incluye la puesta en práctica de los REAs desarrollados; y la quinta considera la mejora continua de los mismos. En este artículo presentamos como se llevaron a cabo las fases 2 y 3; las fases 4 y 5 están aún en proceso de ejecución.

3.1 Desarrollo de REAs (Fase 2)

El desarrollo de REAs considera varias actividades, las cuales permiten decidir entre crear un REA o personalizarlo para adaptarlo a una necesidad de aprendizaje específica (ver Figura 1).

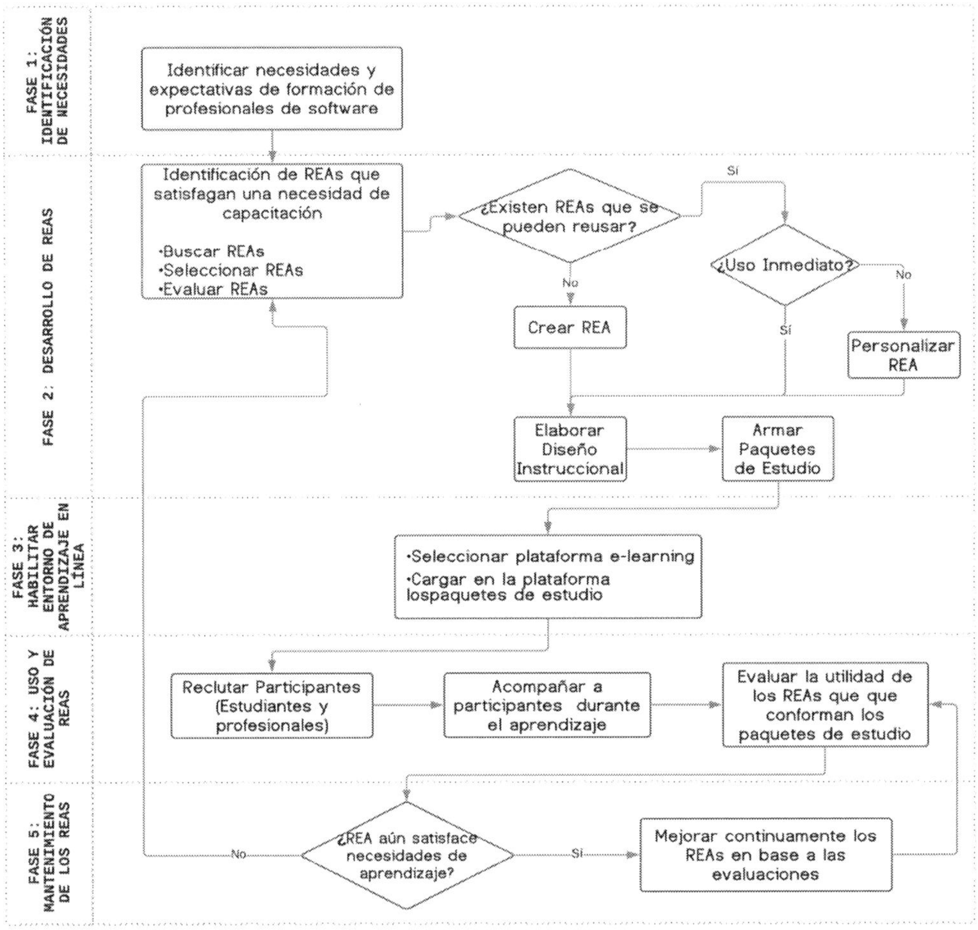

Figura 1: Visión general de la metodología aplicada.

Para realizar la búsqueda de REAs de pruebas de software (tema sobre el cual nos enfocamos en este artículo) recurrimos a Audacity, EdX, Coursera, YouTube, Google y bases de datos científicas como Scopus y Science Direct. En ellas utilizamos combinaciones de palabras claves, en inglés y español, como son: software; pruebas/testing; caja negra/black box; caja blanca/white box; integración/integration; educación superior/higher education; MOOC; REA/OER; material educativo/teaching material. La búsqueda generó un listado de recursos de todo tipo (videos V, material de lectura L, ejercicios para talleres T, MOOC), los cuales se sometieron a un proceso de selección, proceso para el cual se definieron un conjunto de criterios, algunos de los cuales ya fueron explicados en [15], y otros nuevos que fueron identificados en este estudio (ver Tabla 1).

Tabla 1: Criterios para seleccionar REAs. Adaptado de [15].

Código	Criterio de Selección	Descripción
CS1	Tiempo transcurrido desde su publicación	5 años o menos.
CS2	Gratuidad	Disponibilidad del recurso sin costo [5].
CS3	Área de conocimiento	Pruebas de Software: Pruebas de Caja negra, Caja Blanca e Integración.
CS4	Tipo de recurso	Materiales completos o tópicos específicos de un contenido en forma de cursos, videos, lecturas, ejercicios [4].
CS5	Idioma	Español o Inglés
CS6	Aval académico	El recurso tiene el aval de una institución educativa o de un profesor o investigador de Ingeniería de Software [12].
CS7	Derechos de autor	Poseer libre autorización para su utilización y adaptación (recombinación, traducción, etc.)

Posteriormente, los recursos seleccionados fueron evaluados utilizando algunos de los criterios expuestos en [15], así como nuevos criterios. La Tabla 2 resume los criterios de evaluación utilizados. Luego de la evaluación, identificamos recursos que podían ser reusados sin necesidad de ser modificados, otros que requerían modificaciones (por ejemplo: edición de videos, redacción de instrucciones, reescritura de partes del texto) y otros que no cumplían con los criterios de evaluación (por ejemplo: recursos puramente teóricos y sin ejemplos, difíciles de comprender, o de larga duración). Para las personalizaciones de los videos, tomamos en consideración su duración, la cual debe ser corta y no exceder los 6 minutos [13]; en nuestro caso, la duración máxima es de 5 minutos.

Para la creación de REAs, consideramos tanto su duración como la inclusión de ejemplos que faciliten la comprensión de un tema en particular. Hacemos mucho énfasis en la duración de los videos y tiempo de dedicación a otro tipo de recursos educacionales (lecturas, talleres), porque en un estudio previo realizado por nuestro grupo de investigación, identificamos que el 51% de una muestra de 85 profesionales de software dedicaría menos de 5 horas a la semana para auto capacitación, y el 45% entre 5 y 10 horas [1]. Por lo tanto, nuestra finalidad es construir paquetes de estudio que requieran hasta 5 horas de dedicación.

Luego de tener el conjunto de REAs, elaboramos el diseño instruccional de cada temática a abordar y armamos los paquetes de estudio (pruebas de caja negra, pruebas de caja blanca y pruebas de integración) para subirlos a la plataforma de aprendizaje en línea. El diseño instruccional permite organizar los recursos educacionales, y consta de: el tema a cubrir, el objetivo, el contenido, el tiempo de dedicación requerido y la forma de evaluación.

[1] El documento que contiene dicha información ha sido enviada para evaluación a una conferencia

Tabla 2: Criterios para evaluar REAs. Adaptado de [15].

Código	Criterio de Evaluación	Descripción
CE1	Calidad de Contenido	Contenido actualizado. Detalla el tema que aborda. Proporciona ejemplos de la vida real. Presenta de forma precisa cómo el recurso soporta o contribuye al proceso de desarrollo de software.
CE2	Usabilidad	Intuitivo, fácil de usar, con instrucciones claras de lo que el usuario debe realizar. Fácil de aprender y recordar (el usuario no necesitará invertir mucho tiempo en entender la mecánica del recurso, ni esforzarse en memorizar demasiadas reglas o instrucciones)
CE3	Valor Educativo	Estimula el aprendizaje del estudiante por medio del uso de ilustraciones, tareas y actividades de corta duración basadas e ejemplos concretos e ilustrativos.
CE4	Duración	El uso del recuso no debe exceder los 5 minutos.

3.2 Habilitar el Entorno de Aprendizaje en Línea (Fase 3)

En esta fase, seleccionamos una plataforma de e-learning para facilitar el acceso de los profesionales a los paquetes de estudios. Los criterios utilizados para la selección de la plataforma están basados en las propuestas y recomendaciones de [7][11][16] ideadas para escoger plataformas para la publicación de REAs y cursos MOOC (ver Tabla 3).

4 Resultados

4.1 Desarrollo de REAs: Evaluación, Modificación y Creación

La búsqueda de REAs dio como resultado 28 recursos, de los cuales 14 fueron seleccionados y posteriormente evaluados. La Tabla 4 muestra los resultados de la evaluación. La columna *Uso* de esta tabla denota: 1) uso inmediato (**I**) -el REA está listo para ser usado; 2) requiere personalización (**P**) -el REA necesita cambios; 3) no es lo que buscamos (**N**). Los REAs que aparecen con N fueron descartados por una o varias de las siguientes razones: muy teórico, difícil comprensión, carece de ejemplos o muy extenso.

Tabla 3: Criterios para selección de plaforma e-learning

Criterio de Evaluación	Descripción
Accesibilidad	CEP1: Visible y accesible a través de computador y dispositivos móviles. CEP2: Es posible cambiar el idioma desde la interfaz.
Usabilidad	CEP3: Intuitivo, fácil de usar con instrucciones claras de lo que se debe realizar. CEP4: Proporciona un camino claro de navegación a través de los recursos.
Herramientas de Interacción y Colaboración	CPE5: Existen herramientas que facilitan la interacción entre participantes CPE6: La plataforma facilita que el profesor interactué y provea retroalimentación al estudiante.
Costos	CP7: Acceso gratuito para participantes con rol de estudiante y profesor. CP8: Número ilimitado de usuarios en plan gratuito.

Las Tablas 5 y 6 muestran información de los videos, material de lectura y talleres que fueron creados para complementar los paquetes de estudio.

Videos. Se crearon videos de corta duración utilizando Icecream Screen Recorder, el cual permite realizar capturas de pantalla del ordenador y grabar audio al mismo tiempo. Los temas abordados incluyen la creación de un proyecto en Github, el uso de Travis como herramienta de Integración continua y de Coveralls para realizar pruebas de cobertura de código

Lecturas. El material de lectura consta de máximo 13 diapositivas en español, las cuales permiten complementar la teoría que se presenta en los videos. El texto de las diapositivas está acompañado de uno o dos ejemplos basados en una situación real, junto con tablas, imágenes y diagramas.

Tabla 4: Recursos Evaluados

			Criterios					
Código	Recurso	Tipo	CE1	CE2	CE3	CE4	Uso	URL
R01	*Pruebas Funcionales*	V	✓	✓	✓	✓	I	goo.gl/JXQ64u
R02	*Clases de Equivalencia*	V	✓	✓	✓	X	P	goo.gl/kJ5Y3g
R03	*How to write a test case? Software Testing Tutorial 13*	V	✓	✓	✓	✓	I	goo.gl/6qPn9E
R04	*What is white box testing?*	V	✓	✓	✓	✓	I	goo.gl/Ami2CW
R05	*Statement coverage*	V	✓	✓	✓	✓	I	goo.gl/dBBGv9
R06	*Branch coverage*	V	✓	✓	✓	✓	I	goo.gl/o3kscW
R07	*Path Coverage*	V	✓	✓	✓	✓	I	goo.gl/F9iUsx
R08	*Condition coverage*	V	✓	✓	✓	✓	I	goo.gl/RHczZ7
R09	*Curso Git - Introducción a Git*	V	✓	✓	X	✓	N	goo.gl/8vqKp8
R10	*Te enseño GIT en 30 minutos*	V	✓	✓	✓	X	N	goo.gl/8vqKp8
R11	*Monopolio*	T	✓	✓	✓	✓	I	goo.gl/wXzv28
R12	*What is Integration Testing?*	V	✓	✓	✓	✓	I	goo.gl/PkDgbR
R13	*What is Integration Testing? Software Testing Tutorial*	V	✓	✓	✓	✓	I	goo.gl/6aSr3c
R14	*ISTQB Certification: Chapter 2.1 - Test Types*	V	✓	✓	X	X	N	goo.gl/n9Jj72

Tabla 5: Recursos creados (Parte 1)

Tipo	Recurso	Contenido	Tiempo
V	*Descripción y ejemplo de cómo usar Git – parte 1*	¿Qué es Git? Importancia sobre su uso	3m 8s
	Descripción y ejemplo de cómo usar Git – parte 2	¿Cómo descargarlo? Configuración de Git con una cuenta	3m 16s
	Descripción y ejemplo de cómo usar Git – parte 3	Ejemplo de cómo crear un proyecto en Github	5m
	Descripción y ejemplo de cómo usar Travis	¿Qué es Travis? ¿Para qué sirve? Ejemplo	4m 44s
	Descripción y ejemplo de cómo usar Coveralls	¿Qué es Coveralls? ¿Para qué sirve? Ejemplo	3m 39s
L	*Descripción y características de pruebas funcionales*	¿Qué son pruebas funcionales? Características	3m
	Ejercicio de una aplicación bancaria	Contexto del ejemplo Datos sobre el ejercicio Análisis de las Clases de equivalencia	5m
	Descripción de Casos de Prueba	¿Qué son casos de prueba? Ejemplo	3m
	Valores de Frontera	¿Cómo identificarlos? Ejemplo	3m
	Clases de equivalencia que no poseen valores frontera	Ejemplo de clases de equivalencia que no tienen valores de frontera	3m
	Intersección de clases de equivalencia para Casos de Pruebas	Ejemplo de intersecciones entre las clases de equivalencia Casos de pruebas con las intersecciones encontradas	3m
	Ejemplos sobre Cobertura de sentencias y ramas	Contexto del ejemplo Desarrollo del ejemplo para la cobertura de sentencias y ramas	3m

Tabla 6: Recursos creados (Parte 2)

Tipo	Recurso	Contenido	Tiempo
	App Pharmacys - parte 1	Identificar clases de equivalencia Escribir casos de prueba de una variable específica	30m
T	*App Pharmacys - parte 2*	Realización de pruebas de integración Clonar el proyecto con Git Ver los casos de pruebas desarrollados en el proyecto Desarrollar el Caso de Prueba faltante Probar el caso de Prueba con Travis	60m

Talleres. Para los talleres se elaboraron casos de estudio de corta duración, los cuales se basan en situaciones cotidianas (p.e. pedido a domicilio de medicamentos). Cada taller consta de instrucciones para su realización acorde al tiempo asignado (30 o 60 minutos). Fue necesario elaborar actividades muy precisas, concatenadas y acompañadas de instrucciones que les permitan concentrarse en lo que se desea aprender (pruebas de software). Por ello, los talleres cuentan con código fuente disponible en Github, el cual puede integrarse y probarse utilizando Travis.io y Coveralls.io respectivamente. La Tabla 6 presenta detalles de los talleres desarrollados.

4.2 Desarrollo de REAs: Paquetes de Estudio

Los paquetes de estudio fueron elaborados utilizando tanto los REAs creados como los que aparecen con I y P en la tabla 4. Los paquetes se encuentran disponibles en los siguientes URLs:

- Caja Negra: www.braincert.com/course/10541-Pruebas-de-Software#
- Caja Blanca: www.braincert.com/course/11400-Pruebas-de-Caja-Blanca-Cobertura#
- Introducción a las Pruebas de Integración: www.braincert.com/course/11112-Testing#

Al realizar una búsqueda en Google, estos REAs pueden ser encontrados rápidamente usando las palabras: Braincert + caja negra (o caja blanca o pruebas de integración).

A continuación presentamos, a manera de ejemplo, la estructura del paquete Pruebas de caja negra: 1. Prueba de conocimientos iniciales; 2. Qué son las pruebas funcionales? (video); 3. Descripción y características de las pruebas funcionales (diapositivas); 4. Clases de equivalencias (video); Casos de prueba (video); 6. Valores de Frontera (diapositivas); 7. Taller; 8. Prueba de conocimientos; 9. Evaluación del paquete de estudio.

4.3 Selección de Plataforma e-learning

Para la selección de la plataforma e-learning, revisamos las plataformas recomendadas en la literatura consultada [7] [16] y que, además, sean de acceso libre y gratuito. Esta restricción se debe a las limitaciones de presupuesto en nuestra universidad (entidad pública). La Tabla 7 presenta el resultado de la evaluación de las plataformas aplicando los criterios definidos en la Tabla 3. Braincert fue escogido como la plataforma de publicación de los paquetes de estudio elaborados, puesto que fue la herramienta que cumplió con las características que buscábamos. BrainCert es una plataforma e-learning basada en la nube, permite a sus usuarios crear y vender cursos ilimitados en línea, brinda herramientas de personalización, no tiene restricciones en cuanto al número de estudiantes accediendo al contenido, y para usarla sólo se requiere registrarse con un email.

Tabla 7: Comparación de plataformas e-learining para la publicación de REAs

Criterio	Moodle	OpenEdX	Xerte	Braincert
Accesibilidad CEP1	✓	✓	X	✓
Accesibilidad CEP2	✓	✓	✓	✓
Usabilidad CEP3	✓	✓	X	✓
Usabilidad CEP4	X	X	X	✓
Herramientas de Interacción y Colaboración CEP5	✓	✓	✓	✓
Herramientas de Interacción y Colaboración CEP6	✓	✓	✓	✓
Costos CEP7	✓	X	X	✓
Costos CEP8	✓	X	X	✓

5 Conclusiones

Si bien es cierto existe una gran variedad de recursos educativos disponibles a través del internet, no todos ellos se ajustan a necesidades de capacitación específica de los profesionales; por lo cual, es necesario personalizarlos o enriquecerlos con información relevante, a fin de cubrir las necesidades de formación de los usuarios. Aspectos que a groso modo parecen ser poco significativos, como el idioma, la duración, o la cantidad de ejemplos, son determinantes al momento de diagnosticar la utilidad de un REA. Convertir un REA existente en un recurso útil para una audiencia específica, requiere seguir un esquema estructurado, que permita obtener REAs adecuados a sus necesidades.

En el presente artículo, reportamos como efectuamos el desarrollo de paquetes de estudio -conformados por REAs de diversos tipos- para satisfacer requerimientos y expectativas de profesionales de ingeniería de software. Proponemos un conjunto de criterios para seleccionar y evaluar REAs y un esquema de trabajo conformado por cinco fases. Consideramos que, siguiendo este esquema es posible obtener recursos que se ajusten a las necesidades de los aprendices y que puedan ser mejorados continuamente. Consideramos, además, que la metodología de este estudio puede ser extendida y aplicada a otras disciplinas que buscan generar REAs para formar continuamente a sus profesionales.

Referencias

1. Arimoto, M.M., Barbosa, E.F., Barroca, L.: An agile learning design method for open educational resources. In: Frontiers in Education Conference (FIE), 2015 IEEE. pp. 1–9. IEEE (2015)
2. Atkins, D.E., Brown, J.S., Hammond, A.L.: A review of the open educational resources (OER) movement: Achievements, challenges, and new opportunities. Creative common (2007)
3. Bayeck, R.Y.: Exploratory study of mooc learners' demographics and motivation: The case of students involved in groups. Open Praxis 8(3), 223–233 (2016)
4. Brasil, C.R.: Preguntas frecuentes sobre recursos educacionales abiertos (2018), http://www.rea.net.br/es/preguntas-frecuentes
5. Butcher, N.: A Basic Guide to Open Educational Resources (OER) (2015), http://unesdoc.unesco.org/images/0021/002136/213605e.pdf
6. Christensen, G., Steinmetz, A., Alcorn, B., Bennett, A., Woods, D., Emanuel, E.J.: The mooc phenomenon: who takes massive open online courses and why? (2013)
7. Colace, F., De Santo, M.: Evaluation models for e-learning platforms and the ahp approach: a case study. The IPSI BGD Transactions on Internet Research 7(1), 31–43 (2011)
8. Despujol, I.M., Turró, C., Busquéis, J., Cañero, A.: Analysis of demographics and results of student's opinion survey of a large scale mooc deployment for the spanish speaking community. In: Frontiers in Education Conference (FIE), 2014 IEEE. pp. 1–8. IEEE (2014)
9. Dichev, C., Dicheva, D.: Open educational resources in computer science teaching. In: Proceedings of the 43rd ACM technical symposium on Computer Science Education. pp. 619–624. ACM (2012)
10. D'Antoni, S.: Open educational resources: Reviewing initiatives and issues (2009)
11. Khanna, P., Basak, P.: An oer architecture framework: need and design. The International Review of Research in Open and Distributed Learning 14(1), 65–83 (2013)
12. McGreal, R.: Creating, using and sharing open educational resources (2013), https://www.fosteropenscience.eu/sites/default/files/pdf/514.pdf
13. Monedero-Moya, J.J., Cebrián-Robles, D., Desenne, P.: Usabilidad y satisfacción en herramientas de anotaciones multimedia para mooc. Comunicar 22(44) (2015)
14. UNESCO, C.o.L.: Guidelines for Open Educational Resources (OER) in Higher Education (2015), http://unesdoc.unesco.org/images/0021/002136/213605e.pdf
15. Villavicencio, M., Revelo, H.V., Pincay, J.: Towards the evaluation of open educational resources for learning software engineering. In: Computing Conference (CLEI), 2016 XLII Latin American. pp. 1–9. IEEE (2016)
16. Zancanaro, A., Nunes, C.S., de Souza DOMINGUES, M.J.C.: Evaluation of free platforms for delivery of massive open online courses (moocs). Turkish Online Journal of Distance Education 18(1), 166–181 (2017)

Factors influencing the adoption of agile practices in very small software development companies

Shirley Coque[1], Mónica Villavicencio[2]

[1] Universidad Politécnica Salesiana (UPS)
Campus Centenario, Robles 107 y Chambers, Guayaquil - Ecuador
scoque@ups.edu.ec
[2] Facultad de Ingeniería en Electricidad y Computación (FIEC)
Escuela Superior Politécnica del Litoral (ESPOL)
Campus Gustavo Galindo, Km 30.5 vía Perimetral, Guayaquil - Ecuador
mvillavi@espol.edu.ec

Abstract

Agile software development is a trend that is gaining more adepts. However, moving from traditional ways to develop software to agile practices could be a challenge for developers. In this article, we analyze five technology adoption models to identify the factors that may influence software developers to adopt agile methodologies. With those factors, a model was designed and evaluated with 62 software developers. As a result, it was found that the behavioral intention for adopting agile methodologies is related to the perceived ease of use, of the methodology and the voluntariness of software developers. Such intention that is neither influenced by the subjective norm exerted by the organization nor the perceived usefulness of the methodology.

Keywords: Agile software development, software engineering, adoption models, VSE

1 Introducción

Las micros, pequeñas y medianas empresas son fundamentales en el desarrollo de la economía global, debido al impacto social que tienen generando empleo [1]; dentro de ese grupo se encuentran mayoritariamente las empresas desarrolladoras de software [2].

El desarrollo de software ha sufrido cambios a través del tiempo, esto se debe a que los cambios de los productos son más dinámicos, debiendo realizarlos en menor tiempo y costo. Existen dos grandes corrientes en el desarrollo de software; por un lado, están las metodologías tradicionales, que han sido utilizadas por muchas décadas y, por otro lado, las metodologías ágiles que nacieron a principios del año 2000.

Las metodologías tradicionales se enfocan en la documentación, planificación y proceso; mientras que las metodologías ágiles se caracterizan por la planificación adaptativa. [3]

Las metodologías ágiles han tenido gran acogida en los últimos años por los principios que estas siguen, lo que ha generado -para las empresas que las utilizan- obtener mayor productividad en los equipos de trabajo [4]. Sin embargo, las micro y pequeñas empresas (miPymes) tienen dificultades para adoptarlas, más aún porque carecen de recursos para invertir en capacitación y cambios organizacionales.

De acuerdo a Sihuay, la adopción de estas metodologías depende de los siguientes factores: personas, procesos, organización y el proyecto [5]. Cada factor contiene un número de variables que pueden afectar el proceso de desarrollo del producto.

Los estudios realizados sobre metodologías ágiles, generalmente se basan en experiencias positivas de adopción, tanto en organizaciones como en proyectos, por lo que resulta muy difícil llegar a una generalización [6]. La aplicación de metodologías ágiles viene con sus problemas, así como riesgos y amenazas; algunas iniciativas propuestas para dar solución a este problema se encuentran en [7]; sin embargo, se debe considerar la realidad de cada empresa y los factores que pueden influir en el camino a un desarrollo de software ágil.

Este artículo presenta un análisis de los factores que intervienen en los modelos de adopción de tecnologías de información y las relaciones de dependencia que existen entre ellos. La contribución del presente trabajo es la creación de un modelo de adopción de metodologías ágiles, basado en factores de adopción de tecnologías de información bajo la perspectiva actitudinal es decir, considera los resultados de la creencia de la percepción de la adopción de una metodología.

Este artículo está distribuido de la siguiente manera: la sección 2 resume y analiza los modelos de adopción de tecnologías, la sección 3 presenta el modelo propuesto de adopción de metodologías ágiles, la sección 4 evalúa el modelo, y la sección 5 concluye el artículo.

2 Modelos de adopción de tecnologías

En esta sección, presentamos los modelos de adopción de tecnologías, los cuales fueron concebidos para ser aplicados al ámbito de los sistemas de información [8]; sin embargo, su fundamentación teórica ha permitido: desarrollar una metodología de aprendizaje [9], crear un modelo unificado de adopción del comercio electrónico [10], y un modelo unificado de adopción de teletrabajo [11]. Con estos antecedentes, integramos los factores de los modelos de adopción para crear un modelo de adopción de metodologías ágiles.

Los modelos de adopción de tecnologías se basan en un conjunto de factores que pueden ser de naturaleza motivacional, de control o socio normativo [10]. La tabla 1 muestra los modelos acompañados de una breve descripción y los factores que lo constituyen. La explicación de dichos factores se presenta a continuación:

Utilidad percibida (UP), es la convicción que tiene una persona acerca de la utilización de un sistema, considerando que el uso puede ayudar a mejorar su rendimiento profesional, la perspectiva de la utilidad puede verse afectada de forma positiva o negativa dependiendo del producto que este en proceso de adopción [10].

Facilidad de uso percibida (FU), se define como la presunción que tiene una persona en relación a que el uso de una tecnología, sistema o innovación se realiza sin esfuerzo. Se establece como el grado en que los usuarios esperan que la utilización de un sistema requiera de esfuerzos menores [10].

Tabla 1. *Modelos de adopción de tecnologías y factores que lo constituyen*

MODELO	DESCRIPCION	FACTORES								
		UP	FU	AU	IC	UR	PN	V	PIC	RD
Modelo de aceptación de la tecnología (TAM)	Basado en la teoría razonada de Icek Ajzen, este modelo sugiere que la aceptación de tecnología está basada en su uso; la actitud hacia el uso de un sistema depende de la utilidad y la facilidad que se perciba.[12]	X	X	X	X	X				
Modelo de Adopción y Uso de la Tecnología (TAU)	Desarrolla el "rango medio" que busca vencer las dificultades que ha tenido la aplicación de teorías generalizadas; este modelo indica que no solo la motivación es un factor influyente en la adopción, sino también la influencia social que se puede tener al momento de adoptar un sistema. [8]					X	X		X	
Modelo de Utilización de las Tecnologías de la Información (UIT)	El modelo incorpora la teoría de difusión de innovaciones de Rogers con la teoría de la acción razonada de Icek Ajzen, aplicando escalas que evalúan las características de una innovación [13]. De la innovación se toma la percepción como un factor determinante para adoptar; mientras que la acción razonada se centra en el uso real de un bien o servicio; este modelo agrega el factor voluntariedad [8].	X	X	X		X	X	X		X
Modelo de Adopción de las Tecnologías de la Información (AIT)	Es una modificación del modelo UIT, incluye seis de sus factores y agrega el factor Voluntariedad Percibida, que fue utilizada en las investigaciones acerca de las creencias antes y después de una adopción [14]. Con este modelo se analiza la intención de realizar el comportamiento y la intención de continuar usando alguna tecnología [8].	X	X	X	X	X	X	X		X
Modelo de usuario perezoso (LUM)	Este modelo considera al usuario como el centro de atención. Destaca las singularidades que denota el usuario durante el proceso de selección de una solución tecnológica. El modelo indica que el usuario llega a una adopción basado en una necesidad, la que posee un rango de soluciones [14]. El usuario basará su elección en la solución que signifique realizar el esfuerzo mínimo, debido a que el modelo plantea que el usuario es perezoso [15].		X					X		

Actitud hacia el uso (AU), se describe como la reacción emocional de una persona sobre algún determinado sistema o producto (me gusta o no), que deriva o está condicionada por la utilidad percibida y de la facilidad de uso que este tenga [10].

Intención conductual (IC), este factor trata de explicar la construcción mental que realiza una persona acerca de un comportamiento voluntario que tiene intención de realizar, esa construcción mental puede cambiar o puede no corresponder al comportamiento en términos de acción [10].

Presión Normativa Social (PN), es la presión que realiza la organización o las entidades externas como el gobierno, colegios profesionales, asociaciones, entre otros. Las fuerzas sociales suelen afectar en la construcción de ideas que inciden en la toma de decisiones, creencias y evaluaciones con respecto a la adopción de sistemas o productos tecnológicos [8].

Voluntariedad (V), este factor se describe como el estado consciente en que un individuo sabe que su accionar no es una obligación, por tanto incide en su construcción mental y en su intención [8].

Uso real (UR), describe el actuar de una persona en relación a la adopción de un sistema o de un producto tecnológico; se puede identificar como los actos ejecutados que se consiguen a través de una valoración formal acerca de lo que se va a realizar [10].

Planificación, iniciación y control de actos (PIC), consiste en el proceso controlado que conlleva a una adopción; corresponde al conjunto de pasos necesarios para convertir una decisión en una acción; en la mayoría de los casos las decisiones no se ejecutan de manera rápida o inmediata, sino a través de un proceso [8].

Resultados demostrables (RD), se define como la certeza de los beneficios obtenidos al aceptar un cambio, una innovación, o una adaptación [8].

2. 1. Análisis de los Modelos

Para el análisis de los modelos presentados en la sección 2, identificamos los factores que cada uno de ellos considera (e.g. utilidad percibida, facilidad de uso percibida, actitud hacia el uso real, intención conductual, uso real, presión normativa social, voluntariedad, etc). La tabla 1 sintetiza los factores que cada modelo posee; como se observa, existen factores que son comunes en varios modelos debido a su relevancia.

Cada modelo tiene factores que pueden influir en otros factores. La tabla 2 muestra la interrelación entre los factores que más se utilizan en los modelos de adopción; indicando si el factor afecta o es afectado por otro. El símbolo (↓) indica que el factor influye sobre otro. Por ejemplo, se puede observar que la utilidad percibida (UP) afecta a la actitud hacia el uso (AU), a la intención conductual (IC) y al uso real (UR). El símbolo (↑) indica que la utilidad percibida está influenciada o afectada por la facilidad de uso (FU), la presión normativa (PN) y los resultados demostrables (RD).

Tabla 2. *Relación entre factores de adopción*. Tomada de [16]

Factores	UP	FU	AU	IC	UR	PN	V	PIC	RD
Utilidad Percibida (UP)		↑	↓	↓	↓	↑			↑
Facilidad de uso percibida (FU)	↓		↓	↓					
Actitud hacia el uso (AU)	↑	↑		↓		↑	↑		↑
Intención conductual (IC)	↑	↑	↑		↓	↑	↑		
Uso real (UR)	↑			↑			↑	↑	
Presión Normativa (PN)	↓		↓	↓				↓	
Voluntariedad (V)			↓	↓	↓				
Planificación, iniciación y control (PIC)					↓	↑			
Resultados demostrables (RD)	↓		↓						

3 Modelo propuesto

A partir del análisis de modelos y de la interrelación de los factores que los conforman, generamos una propuesta de modelo de adopción de metodologías ágiles, que se muestra en la Figura 1.

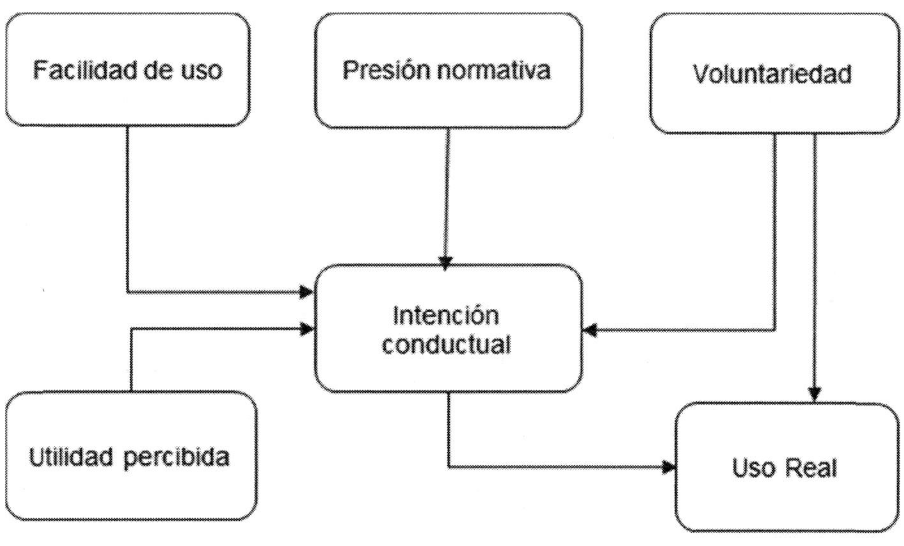

Fig. 1. Modelo de adopción de metodologías ágiles. Adaptado de [16]

El modelo propuesto, está compuesto de los siguientes factores:

Los factores utilidad percibida, la presión normativa, la facilidad de uso y la voluntariedad influyen sobre el factor intención conductual; es decir que, la construcción mental de la intención acerca de la adopción, depende de la combinación de dichos factores. Para iniciar un proceso de asimilación para la adopción de metodologías ágiles, es fundamental establecer cuán fácil es su uso (facilidad de uso), pero también la adopción debe ir acompañada de la decisión de la organización, lo cual se refleja en las normas que priorizan el cambio que se desea aplicar (presión normativa). Además, se requiere la voluntad del individuo inmerso en el proceso de cambio, el cual debe percibir alguna utilidad del cambio [8] [10].

De acuerdo al modelo propuesto, para lograr el alcance del objetivo, es decir el uso real de las metodologías ágiles, se requiere tanto la intención y la voluntad de los individuos que conforman el equipo de desarrollo de software.

Para cada factor del modelo propuesto, elaboramos un conjunto de afirmaciones que establecen su relación con respecto a las metodologías ágiles; dichas afirmaciones aparecen en la Tabla 3.

Tabla 3. *Afirmaciones asociadas a cada factor del modelo propuesto.* Adaptado de [16]

Utilidad Percibida (UP)
• El uso o la incorporación de una metodología ágil mejora la administración de un proyecto de software. • El tiempo de desarrollo de un producto software disminuye cuando se aplican metodologías ágiles
Facilidad de uso percibida (FU)
• En las metodologías ágiles, los tiempos de entrega son cortos y flexibles, ya que se acoplan al alcance de cada entregable y a la estimación del equipo de desarrollo. • En las metodologías ágiles, existen roles bien definidos; lo que facilita la organización del equipo de trabajo.
Presión normativa (PN)
• Cuando la organización impone el uso de una metodología ágil, su adopción se hace efectiva. • Cuando en una organización prevalece el criterio de adoptar una metodología ágil, ésta se pone en práctica.
Voluntariedad (V)
• Los individuos adoptan una metodología ágil porque les gusta poner en práctica cosas que sirvan para su trabajo. • Los individuos adoptan voluntariamente una metodología ágil cuando ésta favorece la realización de su trabajo.
Intención conductual (IC)
• La intención de cambiar a una metodología ágil requiere verificar si el personal de desarrollo muestra predisposición de hacerlo. • La intención de cambiar a una metodología ágil requiere analizar si hay poca resistencia al cambio del equipo de desarrollo.
Uso Real (UR)
• La disminución de documentación en el proceso de desarrollo del producto software refleja que se está usando una metodología ágil • Uno de los resultados visibles de implementar una metodología ágil es la comunicación constante y efectiva con el dueño del producto

4 Evaluación del modelo

Para evaluar el modelo diseñamos un instrumento de medición a manera de cuestionario, el cual contiene dos secciones: información general del encuestado y adopción de metodologías ágiles. La primera sección contiene la formación académica del participante, sus años de experiencia en desarrollo de software, rol que desempeña en la organización que trabaja, tipos de metodologías de desarrollo de software que conoce y que utiliza, años de experiencia aplicando metodologías ágiles. La segunda sección contiene el conjunto de afirmaciones mostradas en forma aleatoria y no en orden como se muestran en la tabla 3. Por cada afirmación, el participante debía manifestar su nivel de acuerdo o desacuerdo, por medio de una escala ordinal de 5 puntos que va desde Totalmente en desacuerdo (1) a Totalmente de acuerdo (5).

El cuestionario fue piloteado con 11 personas para determinar su fiabilidad. Como resultado del piloto, identificamos que varias afirmaciones eran confusas, lo que llevó a obtener un nivel de confiabilidad bajo para los factores presión normativa, facilidad de uso y uso real. Esto nos obligó a reescribir algunas afirmaciones, para lo cual fue necesario la participación de dos académicos externos que contribuyeron a mejorar la redacción de las afirmaciones. Posteriormente, realizamos un segundo piloto, con el cual obtuvimos un nivel de confiabilidad de 0.88.

Para este estudio, invitamos a participar a profesionales que tuvieran el siguiente perfil: ser empleados de miPymes desarrolladoras de software o profesionales en libre ejercicio de su profesión; tener estudios de pregrado o posgrado en áreas afines al desarrollo de software; estar dedicados al desarrollo de software y que cuenten con conocimientos de metodologías ágiles. La invitación fue realizada por medio de correo electrónico y les fue enviado un recordatorio 7 días después, los participantes pertenecen a una comunidad ágil y son parte de un listado de 10 empresas desarrolladoras de software que están registradas en la Superintendencia de Compañías.

El cuestionario fue contestado por 62 individuos entre 16 de junio de 2017 y 16 de julio de 2017; la mayoría de ellos hombres (77.8%). El grupo de participantes tiene edades que fluctúan entre 18 años y 50 años, siendo predominante el grupo de 26 -35 años (49.2%). El 92% de participantes, manifestaron que tienen más de dos años de experiencia en metodologías ágiles para desarrollar software, siendo Scrum la metodología ágil más utilizada (77%).

Tabla 4. *Matriz de Correlación.* Tomado de [16]

	Mediana	s	alfa	UP	FU	PN	V	IC
UP	4,00	0,770	0,721					
FU	4,00	0,821	0,778	,530**				
PN	4,00	0,806	0,691	,494**	,566**			
V	4,00	0,778	0,847	,572**	,519**	,572**		
IC	4,00	0,831	0,804	,410**	,592**	,558**	,577**	
UR	4,00	0,823	0,834	,607**	,589**	,536**	,502**	,617**

**. La correlación es significativa al nivel 0,01 (bilateral).

La confiabilidad del instrumento, incluyendo todas las afirmaciones utilizadas como descriptores de los factores que intervienen en el modelo, es de 0,949.

La tabla 4 muestra la media, la desviación estándar, el alfa de Cronbach y la correlación entre los factores del modelo propuesto, la cual fue analizada con la prueba Tau-b de Kendall, que según [17] es la más apropiada para aplicar en una escala ordinal.

La aplicación del instrumento en 62 individuos dio como resultado una alta consistencia en las afirmaciones de cada factor, ya que según [18] un valor aceptable es 0,70. En el caso del factor presión normativa (PN), el valor de 0,69 está muy cercano al aceptado.

Sólo dos afirmaciones deben ser revisadas, una en el factor Presión Normativa y otra en Uso Real. La primera afirmación a revisar es "Cuando la organización impone el uso de una metodología ágil, su adopción se hace efectiva", ya que obtuvo una mediana baja, considerando el conjunto de afirmaciones de este factor, lo que indica que ésta no tuvo el impacto esperado. La segunda afirmación a revisar es "La disminución de documentación en el proceso de desarrollo del producto software refleja que se está usando una metodología ágil"; los resultados reflejan que no es relevante para los encuestados, a pesar de que en [19] se describe como una evidencia de la aplicación de una metodología ágil.

El análisis de correlación aplicado a las variables para determinar la relación existente, indica una fuerte relación entre todas ellas, debido al valor del coeficiente de significancia que fue de 0,000 (1 x 10 -4) y solo en un caso fue de 0,001; lo que indica que la relación es bastante significativa.

Para determinar la relación de dependencia de las variables Intención Conductual (IC) y Uso Real (UR) se aplicó un análisis de regresión lineal. En el modelo propuesto la variable IC es dependiente de las variables: Utilidad Percibida (UP), Facilidad de Uso (FU), Presión Normativa (PN) y Voluntariedad (V). Los resultados del grado de significancia de estas variables sobre IC se encuentran en la figura 2.

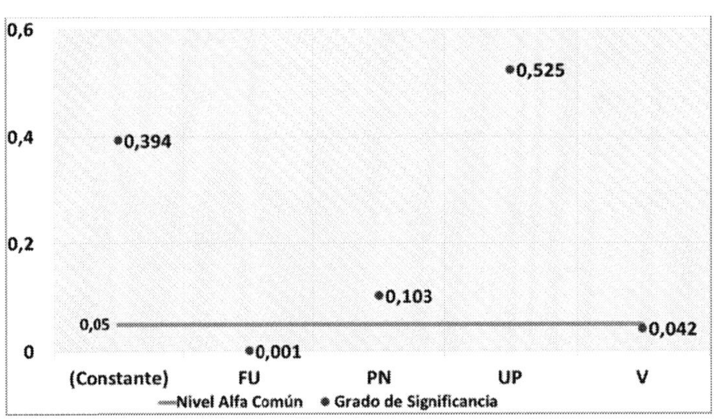

Fig. 2. *Dependencia de la variable Intención Conductual*

En la figura 2 se muestra que la Intención Conductual (IC) depende de la Facilidad de Uso (FU) y de la Voluntariedad (V) ya que ambas variables mantienen un valor por debajo del nivel alfa común que es 0.05. Las variables Utilidad Percibida (UP) y Presión Normativa (PN) de acuerdo al análisis de regresión no influyen sobre la Intención Conductual.

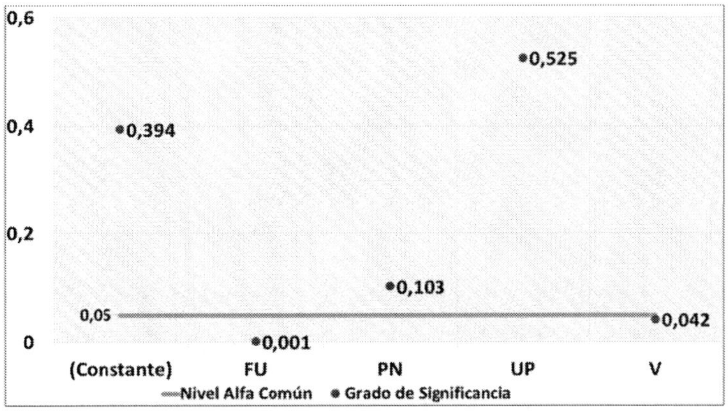

Fig. 3. *Dependencia de la variable Uso Real*

El nivel de dependencia del factor Uso Real (UR) se presenta en la figura 3; de acuerdo al modelo, este factor está influenciado por la Intención Conductual (IC) y la Voluntariedad (V). La prueba de regresión demuestra que los dos factores son significativos para el Uso Real (UR).

Según lo observado, se evidencia que la Intención Conductual (IC) depende de la Facilidad de Uso (FU) y de la Voluntariedad (V), pero no de la Utilidad Percibida (UP) ni de la Presión Normativa (PN), como se había propuesto en el modelo. Esto nos indica que los individuos crean su Intención Conductual con respecto a un cambio metodológico, pensando –sobretodo- en la facilidad de realizar dicho cambio, sumado a la voluntad que le pongan. Por otro lado, se evidencia también que la Intención Conductual no se ve influenciada por la presión que ejerce la organización sobre los desarrolladores de software, ni a la utilidad que pueda generar el cambio.

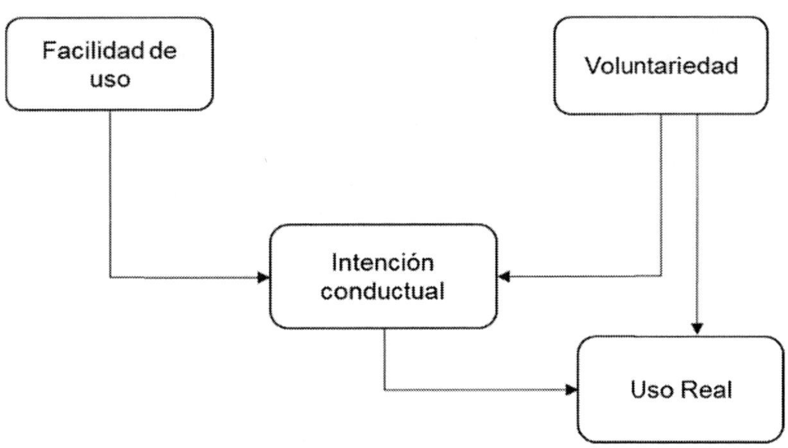

Fig. 4. *Factores con dependencia*

El modelo propuesto también suponía la dependencia del factor Uso Real (UR) de los factores Intención Conductual (IC) y Voluntariedad (V); los resultados indican que si existe tal dependencia. Es decir, la voluntad propia y la intención de cambio de los miembros del equipo de desarrollo son necesarias para adoptar una metodología ágil.

El modelo obtenido en base al análisis de resultados se muestra en la Figura 4. Como se pude observar, éste difiere del inicialmente propuesto, pues dos relaciones entre los factores no existen (PN – IC y UP – IC).

5 Conclusiones

En este artículo presentamos un modelo de adopción para metodologías ágiles para miPymes basado en el análisis de cinco modelos de adopción de tecnologías y de los nueve factores que los conforman.

La propuesta inicial del modelo de adopción consta de 6 factores que se asocian mediante 6 relaciones. Las relaciones fueron evaluadas por desarrolladores de software por medio de un instrumento de medición, el cual obtuvo una confiabilidad de 0,949.

El análisis de las variables del modelo demostró que el factor Intención Conductual IC no es dependiente de la Utilidad Percibida UP de adoptar metodologías ágiles ni de la Presión Normativa PN que se ejerza en una organización para conseguir tal adopción. Por tanto, el análisis de los resultados identificó variaciones al modelo propuesto, generando –en su lugar- un modelo de 6 factores y 4 relaciones.

El modelo identificado permite a los directivos de las miPymes desarrolladoras de software, tomar en cuenta un conjunto de variables que son determinantes para pasar de un modelo de desarrollo tradicional a uno ágil. Adoptar una metodología ágil depende fuertemente del componente humano; es decir, del equipo de trabajo encargado de asumir el nuevo reto.

Referencias

1. S. Y. T. Cabello, "Importancia de la micro, pequeñas y medianas empresas en el desarrollo del país", *Lex*, 2014.
2. Instituto Nacional de Estadísticas y Censos (INEC), "Directorio de Empresas y Establecimientos", 2013.
3. S. A. Hossain, "Comparative Study on Agile software development methodologies", *Glob. J. Comput. Sci. Technol.*, 2013.
4. J. G. Manzaba, "Aumento de la productividad en la gestión de proyectos, utilizando una metodología ágil aplicada en una fábrica de software en la ciudad de Guayaquil", *Rev. Tecnológica ESPOL – RTE*, 2014.
5. A. D. y M. P. M. Sihuay, "Factores en la Adopción de Métodos Ágiles en el Proceso de Desarrollo de Software: Revisión Sistemática de la Literatura", in *Conference: 12 Workshop en Ingeniería del Software Experimental (ESELAW 2015) en XVIII Congreso Iberoamericano en Ingeniería de Software (CIBSE2015)*, 2015.
6. P. Rodríguez *et al.*, "Adopción de metodologías ágiles: un estudio comparativo entre España y Europa", *Rev. Española Innovación, Calid. e Ing. del Softw.*, 2010.
7. G. Kaberwal, "An Agile Adoption Model", 2013. [Online]. Available: https://www.scrumalliance.org/community/articles/2013/july/an-agile-adoption-model.
8. L. M. López-Bonilla and J. M. López-Bonilla, "Los modelos de adopción de tecnologías de la información desde el paradigma actitudinal", *Cad. EBAPE.BR*, vol. 9, no. 1, pp. 176–196, Mar. 2011.
9. A. V. Martín García, Á. García del Dujo, and J. M. Muñoz Rodríguez, "Factores determinantes de adopción de blended learning en educación superior. Adaptación del modelo UTAUT*", *Educ. XX1*, 2014.

10. A. Hernández, "Desarrollo de un modelo unificado de adopción del comercio electrónico entre empresas y consumidores finales. Aplicación al mercado Español", 2011.
11. M. Pérez Pérez, Á. M. Sánchez, P. de Luis Carnicer, and M. J. V. Jiménez, "Un modelo de adopción de innovaciones: el caso del teletrabajo", *ICADE.Revista de las Facultades de Derecho y Ciencias Económicas y Empresariales*. 2005.
12. Z. Y. Liu, "An Analysis of Technology Acceptance Model", *An Anal. Technol. Accept. Model*, 2014.
13. S. Alwahaishi, V. Snásel, Saleh al-Wahaishi, and V. Snásel, "Consumers' acceptance and use of information and communications technology: A UTAUT and flow based theoretical model", *J. Technol. Manag. Innov.*, 2013.
14. M. de León Sigg, J. L. Villa Cisneros, S. Vázquez Reyes, and J. A. R. Salcedo, "Explicación de la adopción de tecnologías de información en pequeñas empresas usando el modelo del usuario perezoso: Un caso de estudio", *RISTI - Rev. Iber. Sist. e Tecnol. Inf.*, 2014.
15. J. Hayes, "LAZY USER THEORY AND INTERPERSONAL COMMUNICATION NETWORKS," 2012.
16. S. G. COQUE VILLEGAS, "Modelo de adopción de metodologías ágiles en mi PYME desarrolladora de software", ESPOL, 2017.
17. R. J. A. Guale and F. V. Beltrán, "La interacción personal y su efecto en la decisión de compra", *Retos*, 2017.
18. H. Oviedo Celina and a Campo-Arias, "Aproximación al uso Coeficiente Alfa de Cronbach", *Rev. Colomb. Psquiatría*, 2005.
19. Ian Sommerville, "Ingenieria De Software", *Informática Ind.*, 1997.

Helping Novice Architects to Manage Architectural Technical Debt in Microservices Architecture

Gastón Márquez and Hernán Astudillo

Toeska research group
Universidad Técnica Federico Santa María
Valparaíso, Chile
gaston.marquez@sansano.usm.cl, hernan@inf.utfsm.cl

Abstract. Microservices architectural styles consist in the development of applications as a set of small services, where the design of decisions of microservices architecture is the first and the fundamental step to address quality goals surrounding attributes. However, there is not enough evidence on how to evaluate if architectural decisions (AD) taken in microservices architectures produce architectural technical debt (ATD) when is necessary satisfy new system requirements, for example, high availability. To face this challenge, this article describes preliminary research about a content-based recommender system (CBRS) composed by microservices architecture patterns and architectural tactics as a basis for obtaining a recommendation of ADs in microservices architectures to make more robust decisions to manage ATD. With the purpose to observe the preliminary results of the CBRS, we conduct a case study to evaluate ADs in an open source project. The results reveal that the ADs generated by the CBRS serve as a basis for discovering preliminary problems in the microservice architecture and provides initial visualization of ATD interest. Finally, future work focuses on improving the CBRS and refining ATD evaluation metrics.

Keywords: Microservices architecture, architecture patterns, architectural tac- tics, architectural technical debt, content-based recommender system

1 Introduction

Cloud computing is gaining popularity among business allowing the emergence of new trends in software development, such as *microservices*. A microservice architectural style is an approach to developing a single application as a suite of small services, each running in its process and communicating with lightweight mechanisms. These services are built around business capabilities and independently deployable by fully automated deployment machinery [9]. But, these properties tend to fail when the development teams need to implement and maintain a microservices architecture.

According to [20], different views within the team on the benefits of a microservice architecture versus a more traditional mono- lithic stack together with encouraged democratic decision-making caused a lot of needless and time-consuming debate, conducting to *technical debt* (TD)through the system development cycle. This concept (introduced by Ward Cunningham) describe immature work in coding that can yield short-term benefit (e.g., fast delivery), but will lead to high maintenance and evolution cost in the long term [2]. TD can be reflected in the software architecture through architectural technical debt (ATD) [11], which affects quality attributes (QAs), like maintainability and evolvability, when architectural decisions (ADs) are capable of compromising system-wide QAs.

Industrial experiences reveal that it is unclear what ADs should be analyzed in the microservices architecture. This questioning may involve taking inappropriate decisions, increasing ATD in the architecture. To address this issue, we propose a preliminary technique based on a content-based recommendation sys- tem (CBRS) that uses sources of knowledge regarding design decisions (tactics) [1] and recurring solutions (patterns) to recommend to the architect a set of solutions that support new system requirements with the purpose of helping the architect in the identification of ATD. The remainder of this paper is organized as follows: in Section 2 we describe the related work. In Section 3 we describe the technique, and in Section 4, we apply the technique in a high availability case study. In section 5 we discuss the analysis of the case study. Finally, in Section 6, we detail our conclusions, and we reveal the future work.

2 Related work

The evaluation of microservices architectures has been examined in the literature in different aspects. Kecskemeti et al. [7] proposes a methodology for decomposing monolithic services into microservices. The authors see the monolithic application as the ancestor of a microservice family. The basic techniques used by the authors are virtual machine synthesis and analysis. Levcovitz et al. [8] describes a technique to identify and define microservices in a monolithic system. The proposal considers that a monolithic application has three main parts: client interface, server application, and a database. Escobar et al. [4] propose a model- centered process to analyze and visualize the current structure and dependencies between the business layer and the data layer in microservices architectures. Furthermore, they suggest a modularization into clusters and microservices using four different diagrams. Finally, Sampaio et al. [19] discuss an approach based on service evolution modeling in which combine static and dynamic information to generate an accurate representation of the evolving microservice-based system.

Although there is evidence that addresses the study of decisions in microservices architectures, we do not find enough evidence that evaluates ATD in this kind of architectures. Therefore, this lack of information motivates us to propose our preliminary research.

3 Explanation of the technique

The technique consists of three phases aimed at reusing tacit knowledge and pre-packaged solutions (tactics and patterns) to recommend solutions to the architect to make more informed decisions. The basis of the technique is the interaction between patterns and tactics. Tactics are "architectural building blocks" from which architecture patterns are created [1][6]. According to this composition, while patterns may be largely composed of tactics, also provide the starting point for incorporation of tactics. Our experiences in previous research [13][14][5] reveal that tactics serve as a reference to select patterns to solve specific problems. Next, we proceed to describe the phases that support the CBRS (See Figure 1).

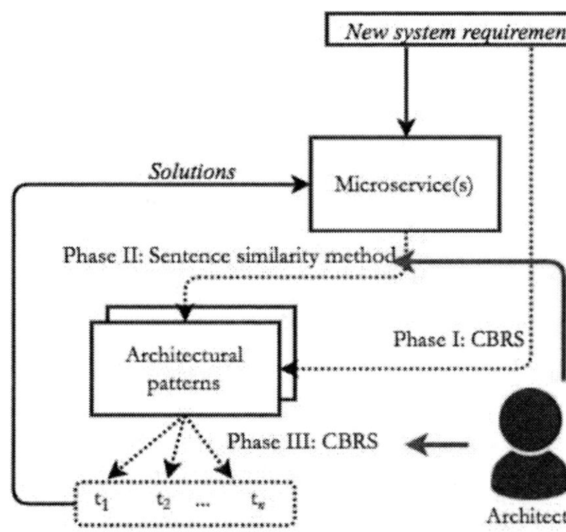

Fig. 1. Detail of the phases of the technique

3.1 Phase I

In the first phase, the technique recommends patterns based on the description of the new system requirement. Since we consider the new requirement and the patterns as a set of sentences, we use Information Retrieval (IR) techniques in the CBRS [16], which are: Term frequency - Inverse document frequency (TF- IDF weight) [17] and cosine similarity [21]. The inputs of the CBRS are (1) the description of the new system requirement and (2) a catalog of patterns in microservices (created from a literature revision in the academy and industry [15]). The output of the CBRS is a recommendation of five patterns (arbitrary number) that are related to the description of the new system requirement.

3.2 Phase II

The objective of phase II is to make sense of the results obtained in Phase I. Although the techniques used in the previous phase (TF-IDF and cosine similarity) help to achieve a preliminary set of patterns, it is necessary to associate these patterns to the context of the microservice(s) that the architect is interested in modifying in the architecture, given the new system requirement. Therefore, in this phase, we propose a high-level catalog (based on the proposal of Levcovitz et al. [8]) to describe a microservice that compose an architecture. The high-level catalog has the next fields:

- *Name*: name of the microservice
- *Domain*: subject area on which the microservice is intended to apply
- *Context* : The setting in which a word or statement appears that determines the microservice meaning
- *Input*: data set, systems or ports that are introduced
- *Output*: information that a microservice provides after processing a given set of data
- *Database*: Source of information related to the microservice

To find a relationship between the patterns and the catalog of microservices, we decide to use similarity techniques between sentences. There are proposals to study the semantic relationship based on a set of documents and the terms they contain, such as Latent Semantic Analysis (LSA [3]). But we decide to use the proposal of Li et al. [10], which is an algorithm that takes account of semantic information and word order information implied in the sentences. The semantic similarity of two sentences is calculated using data from a structured lexical database (WordNet) and corpus statistics (Brown Corpus). The advantage using this algorithm is (1) can be used in a variety of applications that involve text knowledge representation and discovery, and (2) reduce common problems in sentence similarities like high dimensionality/sparsity. Finally, this phase has as output three patterns willing to be selected by the architect.

3.3 Phase III

This phase uses the pattern(s) selected by the architect to recommend those tactics(s) that are closest to the definition of the pattern(s). To achieve this goal, we use the same IR techniques described in phase I, and we have refined the description of tactics [1] to make the recommendation more accurate. Each tactic has the following fields: name, purpose, mechanism, mechanism detail and result. For example, one of the availability tactics is *Heartbeat* and its corresponding description is detailed in Table 1.

Table 1. Example: heartbeat tactic definition

Name	*Heartbeat*
Purpose	Detect fault
Mechanism	Periodic message
Mechanism detail	Periodic message exchange between a system monitor and a process being monitored
Result	Check if the watchdog timer is reset to reduce piggybacking

Finally, the output of this phase is a set of tentative solutions (tactics) recommended by our technique with the aim that the architect can evaluate and perform the relevant trade-offs before making a design decision to satisfy the new requirement in the microservices architecture.

3.4 Architectural Technical Debt

The output of our CBRS serves as a basis for managing ATD. To carry this out, we use the approach proposed by Li et al. [12], which identify ATD using architecture decision and change scenarios. The approach is composed of the following two guidelines and their corresponding steps (see Table 2):

Table 2. Steps of the approach of Li et al.

Decision-based	Scenario-based
1.1 Analyze an AD	2.1 Analyze a change scenario
1.2 Add new potential ATD item(s)	2.2 Identify which QA is compromised
1.3 Come up with impacted change scenario(s)	2.3 AD incurring the ATD item
1.4 Record the ATD item(s)	2.4 Assign change scenario(s) to the ATD item
	2.5 Record the ATD item(s)

The approach proposes to identify ATD based on architecture decisions made during the architecting process and change scenarios for software maintenance and evolution, taking ADs and change scenarios as input, and then comes up with ATD items that are caused by the architecture decisions or negatively impact the change scenarios. Our goal is expand the approach described in the paper using our output (recommended design decisions selected by the architect) the help novice architect to take decisions on ATD.

4 Case study

To evaluate our technique, we will use as reference the guidelines to conduct case studies proposed in [18]. Next, we break down the topics that compose in this case study.

4.1 Objective

The primary objective of this study is to evaluate if our technique allows a novice architect to evaluate ATD more efficiently, through the generation of ATD item that illustrates a catalog where can be made decisions.

4.2 The case

The case study based on an open source project called Sock Shop[1,2,3] (see Table 3), an open source application built using microservice architecture for buying and selling socks from a fictitious company.

Table 3. Specifications of the project under study

Project name	Sock Shop
URL	https://github.com/microservices-demo/microservices-demo
Technology	Java, NodeJS
# Services	14
# Contributors	39
# Commits	1,600
#Last commit	January 29, 2018
# Releases	13

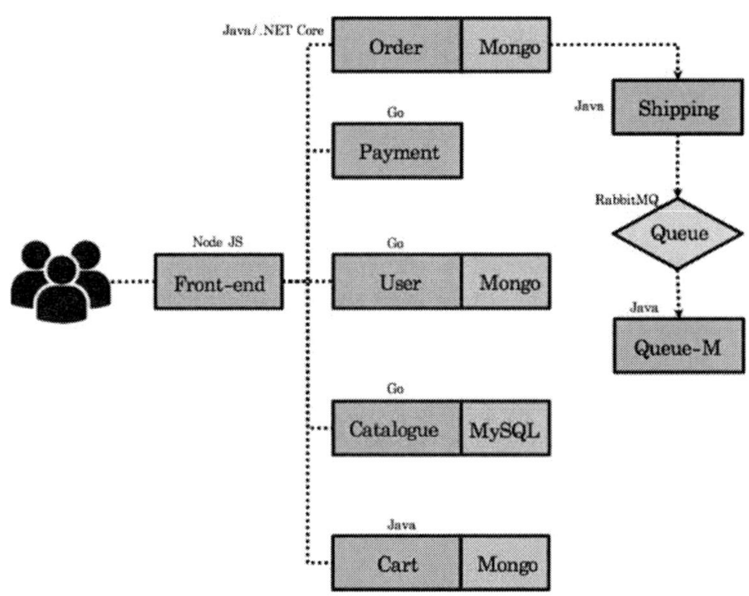

Fig. 2. High-level architecture of the project

On the other hand, we define the new system requirement that will affect the architecture of Sock Shop. This requirement will be oriented to high avail- ability. The description of the requirement is: *The microservices "payment" and "shipping" must be 98% available for use whenever needed in the three months before the Black*

[1] https://microservices-demo.github.io/
[2] https://www.weave.works/
[3] https://container-solutions.com/

Friday. The system may not go down these microservices or be inaccessible, as the sale of socks is dependent on the real-time updates of these microservices.

The architect who participates in this study has experience of three years in the development of software projects with java technology.

4.3 Research questions

The research questions (RQs) proposed for this case study are the following: **RQ1**: *Can a CBRS complement the proposal of Li et al. [12] to help the management of ATD?* ; and **RQ2**: *Are useful architectural tactics and patterns to help in the management of ATD?*

4.4 Methodology

Phase I. Taking as input the specification of the new system requirement and the description of the *payment* and *shipping* microservices, the 5 patterns generated by the CBRS were: REST Integration, Correlation ID, Service Registry, Replication State, and Change Code Dependency to Service Call.

Phase II. The Table 4 represents the high-level catalog for microservices proposed in this paper. Following, we will describe one of the catalogs that are input for the semantic algorithm:

Table 4. *Payment* microservice catalog

Name	payment-svc
Domain	Sales
Context	Generate the procedure to pay products
Input	port: 80
Output	targetPort: 80
Database	No database

Once the algorithm of sentence similarity is executed, the more similar pat- terns regarding the context of the *payment* microservice are: Service Registry, Replication State, and Change Code Dependency to Service Call (The detailed description of these patterns is in [15]). The architect who is evaluating the tar- get architecture decides to select the Change Code Dependency to Service Call pattern, which is described in the Table 5. For the *shipping* microservice, the selected pattern was Service registry.

Phase III. Since the new requirement is related to high availability, the CBRS uses the catalog of availability tactics proposed in [1]. This catalog describes design decisions and pre-packaged solutions for availability that solve three types recover from fault,

Table 5. Change Code Dependency to Service Call microservice architectural pattern

ID	AMSP22
Name	*Change Code Dependency to Service Call*
Context	A software system has been decomposed to a set of small services to use microservices architectural style. There is a component in the system that is acting as a dependency to another services or components.
Problem	When it is appropriate to change this code-level dependency to service-level dependency? And when it is not?
Solution	Try to keep the services code as separate as possible. When services shares code as a dependency there is a high chance that a service.

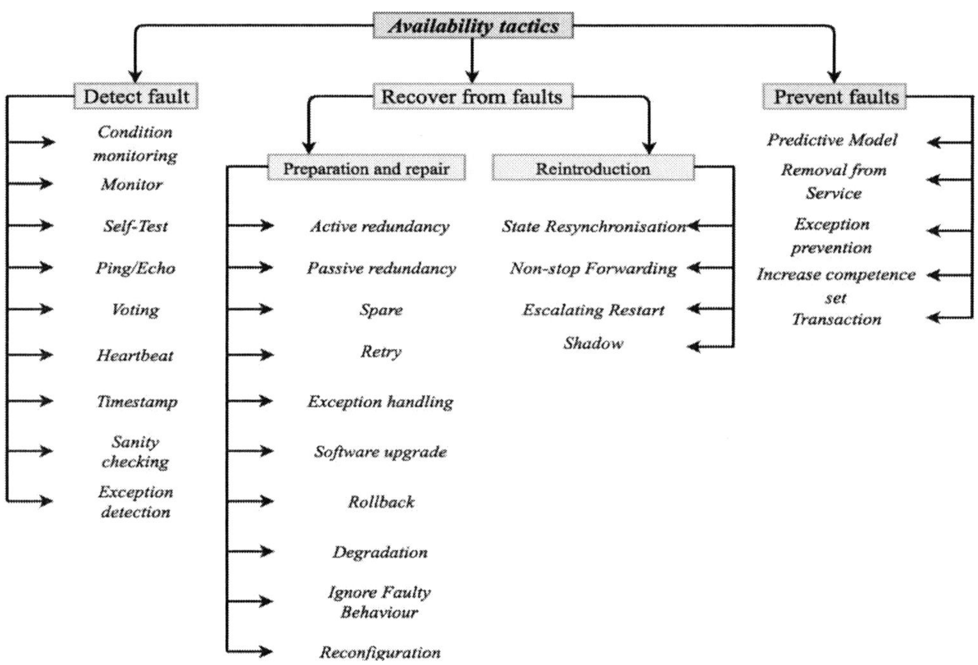

Fig. 3. Availability tactics [1]

and prevent fault. Each type of problem has its own set of tactics (see Figure 3).

For the *payment* microservice, the tactics recommended by the CBRS were: Software upgrade, Escalating restart, Monitor, State resynchronization, and Pas-sive redundancy. For the *shipping* microservice, the tactics recommended are: Software upgrade, State Resynchronization, Monitor, Retry, and Spare. As a final result of this phase, from the list of tactics recommended by the CBRS, the architect selected four: **Passive redundancy**, **Monitor**, **Escalating restart**, and **Retry**. One of them was Passive redundancy and the output of this tactic (adapted from [12]) is described in the Table 6.

Table 6. Passive redundancy AD list

ID	AD1
Name	Passive Redundancy
Description	One component (the primary) responds to events and informs the other components (the standbys) of state updates they must make
Intention	Recover from faults
Rationale	When a fault occurs, the system must first ensure that the backup state is sufficiently fresh before resuming services
Microservice affected	payment-svc
Pros	Save important financial and credit card data of payment service
Contra	It will time-consuming to add a backup state
Architecture diagram	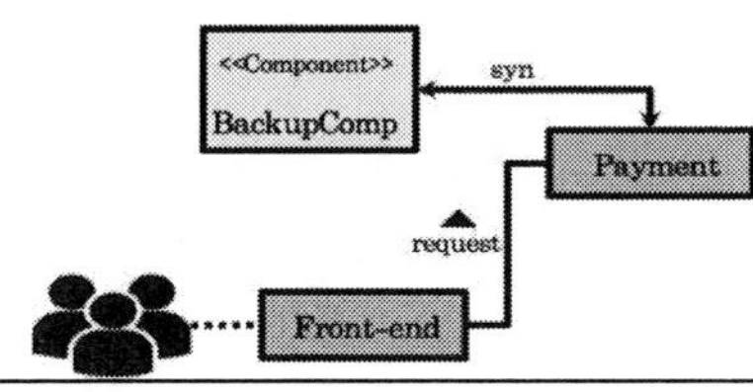

Result. The result is a final set of items that are generated from the tactics recommended by the CBRS. With this set, the novice architect not only obtains a set of first ATD items but may also have an early approximation of the interest generated by each DTA (the interest calculation was not part of this investigation.) For now, the estimate was manual). Is described one of the ATD items in the following Table 7.

4.5 Analysis

To answer **RQ1**, the contributions of our CBRS for the management of ATD in the illustrative example are described in the following points (we also consider the feedback of the architect):

- The CBRS recommends tactics, so the analysis and discussion of the ADs are contextualized.
- Since our refining of tactics involves the purpose, mechanism, and result, the analysis of the ADs was simpler and took less time.
- It was helpful to analyze the pattern that is related to the tactics selected by the architect, because the implementation of tactics is done within the architectural structure of the system, including the compositions of the pat- terns.
- We realize that the tactic implemented may or may not be quickly developed, depending on what the pattern participants are, and how they depend on each other.
- Patterns can impact individual tactics by making it easier or more challenging to implement them, due to tactics are performed in the code.

Table 7. One of the ATD item for AD1

<table>
<tr><th>ID</th><th>ATD1</th></tr>
<tr><td>Name</td><td>Redundant transmitters: one transmitter (who is ready to be used) doesn't know if an other transmitter stops working</td></tr>
<tr><td>Date</td><td>16-01-2018</td></tr>
<tr><td>Intentionality</td><td>Intentional</td></tr>
<tr><td>Incurred by</td><td>AD1</td></tr>
<tr><td>Compromised QA</td><td>Maintainability</td></tr>
<tr><td>Rationale</td><td>There must be a control unit that detects that payment microservice has a problem, then shuts the microservice down, and switches the inputs and outputs and tells BackupComp to start</td></tr>
<tr><td>Benefit</td><td>3 person-day</td></tr>
<tr><td>Cost</td><td>8 person-day</td></tr>
<tr><td>Principal</td><td>5 person-day</td></tr>
<tr><td>Interest</td><td>$3 \times 0.7 + 3 \times 0.8 = 4.5$ person-day</td></tr>
<tr><td>Change scenarios</td><td><table><tr><th>SD</th><th>C</th><th>SI</th><th>Proba.</th></tr><tr><td>SD_1</td><td>C_1</td><td>3 person-day</td><td>0.7</td></tr><tr><td>SD_2</td><td>C_2</td><td>3 person-day</td><td>0.8</td></tr></table></td></tr>
<tr><td>Architecture diagram</td><td>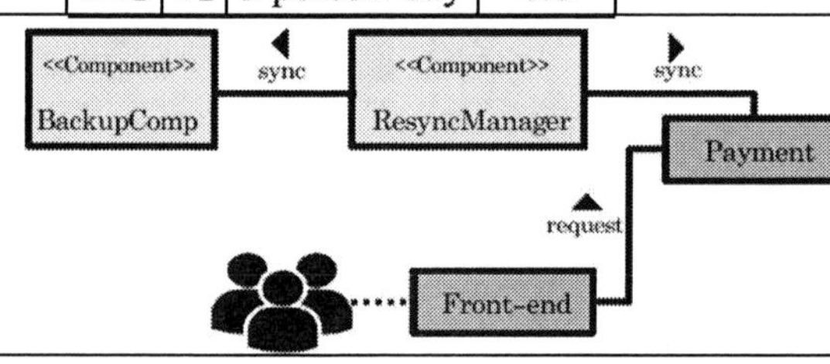
</td></tr>
</table>

- The implementation of the tactics and the suggestion of the pattern allow us to quickly identify ATD, which helps the architect to fill more informed the ATD item template.
- About steps 1.3 and 2.1, the identification of ADs and ATDs in steps 1.1 and 1.2, allows the expeditious association to scenarios. This discovery implies that the identification of the ATD interest can be taken at an early stage. Since availability tactics are widely covered in the literature [1], it was accessible to obtain the data to calculate interest in the ATD (see Table 7).

Regarding **RQ2**, our observations are directed to (a) the effectiveness and (b) the ease of use of the approach [12]. Regarding (a), the tactics obtained from the CBRS reveal guidelines that allowed to evaluate possible problems in the implementation of the selected ADs in the established scenarios. We find more ATDs in maintainability than in evolvability since the selected ADs necessarily involve manipulating extensions in frameworks, such as Go framework. On the other hand, we realize that this approach is quite useful to identify problems in early architectural analysis. Listing the ATDs not only implies having a description of possible problems in the target architecture but also identifying other ADs, can serve to complement the CBRS. From ADs, the tactics recommendations shown by the CBRS were useful, but the CBRS is limited only to availability requirements. Although the requirement of availability may merit the use of tactics of other quality attributes (for example, security), the success of CBRS, for now, is related to availability solutions. Therefore, the four ADs selected from the CBRS only helped identify a part of the ATDs in the change scenarios.

Concerning (b), the approach was easy to use. Although it is an open source project, applying all the steps of the approach did not involve a more considerable effort on the part of the architect.

5 Conclusions

This paper presents a work in progress related to obtaining ADs through a CBRS using microservices architecture patterns and architectural tactics as a basis to identify ATDs to satisfy new system requirements. In turn, is described a case study where we explain the use of the CBRS in an open source project. The preliminary results of this case study reveal that the contribution of the tactics and patterns is that both elements allow the identification of ATDs more expeditiously. The tactics help identify ADs, and the patterns contextualize what type of ATD can be identified. In the illustrative example, the identification of ATDs in the change scenarios was directed through the information provided by the tactics and was complemented by the context of the pattern associated with tactics, reducing the time of ADs analyzing.

The future work that emerges based on from our preliminary study is the improvement of the CBRS. In this paper, we have described the first version of our CBRS. However, we are exploring new techniques to improve the recommendation that help to obtain a list of more robust tactics and evaluate what kind of impact the tactics have on the associated pattern. At the same time, we are studying the inclusion of trade-offs information between tactics in the recommendation.

Acknowledgments

This work has been financially supported by Comisión Nacional de Investigación Cient'ıfica (CONICYT) CONICYT-PCHA/Doctorado Nacional/2016-21161005

References

1. Bass, L., Clements, P., Kazman, R.: Software Architecture in Practice (3rd Edition). SEI Series in Software Engineering (2013)
2. Cunningham, W.: The wycash portfolio management system. Proceedings of the Addendum to the proceedings on Object-oriented programming systems, languages, and applications (Addendum) pp. 29–30 (1992)
3. Dumais, S.T.: Latent semantic analysis. Annual review of information science and technology 38(1), 188–230 (2004)
4. Escobar, D., Crdenas, D., Amarillo, R., Castro, E., Garcs, K., Parra, C., Casallas, R.: Towards the understanding and evolution of monolithic applications as microservices. Computing Conference (CLEI), 2016 XLII Latin American pp. 1–11 (2016)

5. Gatica, D., Márquez, G., Astudillo, H.: Systematic selection of software components through architectural tactics. Is a relationship between tactics and NFRs possible? XX Ibero-American Conference on Software Engineering (CIbSE) (2017)
6. Harrison, N.B., Avgeriou, P.: How do architecture patterns and tactics interact? A model and annotation. Journal of Systems and Software 83(10), 1735–1758 (2010), http://dx.doi.org/10.1016/j.jss.2010.04.067
7. Kecskemeti, G., Marosi, A.C., Kertesz, A.: The entice approach to decompose monolithic services into microservices. International Conference on High Performance Computing Simulation (HPCS) p. High Performance Computing Simulation (HPCS) (2016)
8. Levcovitz, A., Terra, R., .V., T., M.: Towards a technique for extracting microservices from monolithic enterprise systems. arXiv preprint arXiv:1605.03175 (2016)
9. Lewis, J., Fowler, M.: Microservices-a definition of this new architectural term. https://martinfowler.com/articles/microservices.html (2014)
10. Li, Y., McLean, D., Bandar, Z.A., O'shea, J.D., Crockett, K.: Sentence similarity based on semantic nets and corpus statistics. EEE transactions on knowledge and data engineering 18(8), 1138–1150 (2006)
11. Li, Z., Avgeriou, P., Liang, P.: A systematic mapping study on technical debt and its management. Journal of Systems and Software 101, 193–220 (2015)
12. Li, Z., Liang, P., Avgeriou, P.: Architectural technical debt identification based on architecture decisions and change scenarios. 12th Working IEEE/IFIP Conference on Software Architecture (WICSA) pp. 65–74 (2015)
13. Márquez, G., Astudillo, G.: Selecting components assemblies from non-functional requirements through tactics and scenarios. 35th International Conference of the Chilean Computer Science Society, SCCC pp. 1–11 (2016)
14. Márquez, G., Astudillo, G.: Selection of software components from business objectives scenarios through architectural tactics. Proceedings of the 39th International Conference on Software Engineering Companion pp. 441–444 (2017)
15. Márquez, G., Osses, F., Astudillo, H.: Review of architectural patterns and tactics for microservices in academic and industrial literature. IEEE Latin America Transactions ((In press)) (2018)
16. Pazzani, M.J., Billsus, D.: Content-based recommendation systems. The adaptive web pp. 325–341 (2007), http://dl.acm.org/citation.cfm?id=1768197.1768209
17. Ramos, J.: Using tf-idf to determine word relevance in document queries. Proceedings of the first instructional conference on machine learning (242) (2003)
18. Runeson, P., Host, M.: Guidelines for conducting and reporting case study research in software engineering. Empirical software engineering 14(2), 131 (2009)
19. Sampaio, A.R., Kadiyala, H., Hu, B., Steinbacher, J., Erwin, T., Rosa, N., Beschastnikh, I., Rubin, J.: Supporting microservice evolution. In: 2017 IEEE International Conference on Software Maintenance and Evolution (ICSME). pp. 539–543 (Sept 2017)
20. Stenberg, J.: Experiences from failing with microservices. InfoQ (2014)
21. Tata, S., Patel, J.M.: Estimating the selectivity of tf-idf based cosine similarity predicates. ACM Sigmod Record 36(2), 7–12 (2007)

Web Information System for the Consignment and Routing of Vehicles

Néstor Díaz Escobar[1], Marion Riquelme[2], Rodrigo Linfati[2], Sebastián Gutiérrez[3,4], and Gustavo Gatica[1]

[1]Universidad Andrés Bello, Facultad de Ingeniería, ggatica@unab.cl

[2]Universidad del Bío-Bío, Chile, rlinfati@ubiobio.cl

[3]Universidad Central de Chile, Facultad de Economía y Negocios

[4]Universidad de Santiago de Chile, Facultad de Administración y Economía.

Abstract.
The collection, transfer and final disposal of hospital waste is a public health problem. An information system with web deployment is presented, for the assignment and routing of vehicles, which uses mixed integer linear programming, for programming and assigning the different clients within a month horizon by frequency. In addition, it assigns the fleet, according to its geographical location and capacity, to subsequently incorporating those clients into the transport routes of the system. To improve the service, the number of scheduled customers is normalized and, thus, balancing the vehicle loads by routes and month. The development of the application has a service-oriented architecture model implementing Rest API as a central request orchestrator, to ensure scalability and extensibility, and thus, parametrize any geographical area, given the existing integration with applications such as Google Maps ® and a set of good software quality practices present in ISO9126.

Keywords: service oriented architecture, trips programming and assignment, vehicle routing

1 Introducción

El Ministerio de Salud del Gobierno de Chile, en el Decreto Supremo n° 6 publicado el año 2009, define la necesidad de prevenir y controlar los riesgos provenientes respecto a la recolección y acopio transitorio de residuos hospitalarios generados en los establecimientos de atención de salud como hospitales, centros de salud familiar, diálisis, postas y particulares de la salud, por su eventual riesgo a la salud del personal y a los usuarios de estos establecimientos [1]. Es así que disponer de un servicio que contribuya en la recolección, traslado y disposición final de los residuos, especialmente hospitalarios, es un tema de salud pública y ambiental.

Uno de los mayores problemas presentes en la administración de operaciones de cualquier empresa, ya sea en el área de manufactura como de servicios, es la programación de actividades de los trabajos propuestos por los clientes, debido a la existencia de dificultades o restricciones en la asignación de los recursos, tanto de máquinas, instalaciones, personal o insumos [2]. Desarrollar estrategias en paralelo, logística verde en una implementación sustentable requiere del esfuerzo gubernamental y de empresa [3] [4]. En este sentido, el gerenciamiento de hoteles y hospitales estaría ampliamente relacionado [5] [6]. Reporte de sustentabilidad se han generado empleando diversas técnicas, ejemplo de ello es lo realizado por Pérez [7] , con un acercamiento del tipo SD-SAM.

Existen estrategias como los descritos por Argón [8] para el desarrollo Buenas Prácticas de sustentabilidad en hospitales. Sin embargo, otros incorporan el factor de satisfacción del cliente en sus lineamientos [9] [10] [11] [12]. Por otra parte la literatura propone marcos de trabajo para un manejo integral de los residuos tanto de hospitales como hoteles [13] [14] [15] [16] [5] [17] [18] [19]. Por ello, para su resolución se emplean técnicas heurística, metaheurísticas, métodos exactos si son instancias reducidas y software especializado [20]. El estudio abarca los clientes del servicio de recolección de residuos hospitalarios especiales [21]. El cual hasta el término del proyecto hacían asignación y programación con planillas Excel y manualmente.

Se presenta un sistema de información con despliegue web, para asignación y ruteo de vehículo con data determinística, basado en un modelo matemático de programación lineal entera [22]. Se programaron y asignaron a los distintos clientes dentro de un horizonte temporal correspondiente a un mes calendario, según su frecuencia: diaria, bisemanal, trisemanal, semanal, quincenal y mensual, además de asignar a los vehículos recolectores, según su ubicación geográfica y respetando la capacidad de éstos, para posteriormente agregar a dichos clientes a las rutas de transporte del sistema computacional de la empresa. Con el fin de mejorar el cumplimiento de visitas se balancea la cantidad de clientes programados diarios y las cargas de los vehículos durante cada día del mes [23].

La aplicación, se ha definido bajo un modelo de arquitectura orientada a servicios [24], que permite la escalabilidad y extensibilidad, para parametrizar cualquier zona geográfica, dado la integración existente con aplicaciones como Google Maps ®. Es así que, para el éxito del desarrollo, fue determinante la inclusión de buenas prácticas de calidad de software presentes en la ISO9126 [25].

Como herramienta de construcción, se utilizó el entorno de desarrollo LAMP (Linux, Apache, MariaDB y PHP) [26], el lenguaje de programación matemática AMPL (A Mathematical Programming Language) [27], y para resolver las instancias se utilizó el software solver SCIP 4.0 [28].

Al ser un problema de la clase NP-Hard, se define un umbral de tiempo de 35.000 segundos (9,7 horas) para ejecutar el modelo, tiempo que se estima adecuado para obtener una solución factible. Dicho modelo se aplica dos veces, una vez por cada región.

El artículo, en la segunda sección presenta el modelo empleado, en la tercera la arquitectura empleada con sus respectivos atributos de calidad. Se presentan los resultados preliminares del Caso de Estudio en la cuarta sección y se finaliza con un conjunto de conclusiones tanto a nivel de proyecto como del problema de optimización.

2 Materiales y métodos

Las rutas de transporte actuales están basadas en un archivo Excel confeccionado a partir de la experiencia de los conductores y en base a la periodicidad de los clientes. El horizonte es de lunes a viernes con los clientes semanales, diarios y los que se visitan dos o tres veces a la semana, posteriormente se asignan los clientes quincenales y mensuales dentro de las rutas ya establecidas de manera manual. Las problemáticas presentadas por el uso de este método, se identificaron de manera visual y en conjunto con los involucrados, destacando la falta de coordinación de las rutas de transporte, sobre todo con aquellos clientes que tienen una periodicidad superior a una semana, falta de segmentación de los clientes en las rutas según tamaño, frecuencia, ubicación geográfica (priorización por distancia) y kilos transportados, criterios que son relevantes para la empresa, pero que no están incorporadas en el proceso de transporte, previo al desarrollo de la solución. Para finalizar, el incumplimiento global de visita, el cual se calcula a partir de los clientes programados diariamente que bordea el 90%, es inferior al establecido por la empresa de un 97 por ciento a nivel nacional [22].

2.1 Formalización matemática del problema

El modelo matemático de programación lineal entera que busca resolver la programación y asignación de clientes en un calendario mensual, programa según su frecuencia: diaria, bisemanal, trisemanal, semanal, quincenal y mensual, además de asignar a los clientes programados a los distintos camiones recolectores según la ubicación de éstos, respecto a una planta ubicada en Talcahuano para los clientes de la Región del Biobío y otra ubicada en la Región del Maule, desde ahora llamada depósito, con el objetivo de balancear las cargas de los camiones diariamente y además, clusterizar por zonas geográficas [22].

2.2 Conjuntos

D: Conjunto de clientes con frecuencia diaria.

TS: Conjunto de clientes con frecuencia trisemanal, se visitan los días lunes, miércoles y viernes.

DS: Conjunto de clientes con frecuencia bisemanales, pueden ser visitados los días lunes y miércoles o martes y jueves.

S: Conjunto de clientes con frecuencia semanal, pueden ser visitados días lunes, martes, miércoles, jueves o viernes siempre el mismo día todas las semanas.

Q: Conjunto de clientes con frecuencia quincenal, se visitan cada diez días.

M: Conjunto de clientes con frecuencia mensual, se visitan cada veinte días.

I: Conjunto de clientes $(D \cup TS \cup DS \cup S \cup Q \cup M)$

J: Conjunto de días del mes, correspondiente a veinte días de lunes a viernes por cuatro semanas.

V: Conjunto de camiones diarios disponibles para la recolección de los residuos hospitalarios.

2.3 Índices

$i = clientes$

$j = día$

$k = Camión$

2.4 Parámetros

F_i: Frecuencia de visita del cliente i.

K_i: Demanda del cliente i en contenedores.

C_k: Capacidad del camión k en contenedores diario.

θ_i: Ángulo asociado al cliente i con respecto al depósito.

ϵ : Sector de la región que se desea tomar para cada clúster diariamente.

M : Ángulo máximo, que abarca la región completa.

c : Cantidad de clientes que atiende cada camión recolector diariamente

2.5 Variables de decisión

$$x_{ij} = \begin{cases} 1 & si\ el\ cliente\ i\ es\ asignado\ al\ día\ j \\ 0 & en\ otro\ caso \end{cases}$$

$$y_{ijk} = \begin{cases} 1 & si\ el\ cliente\ i\ es\ asignado\ al\ día\ j\ en\ el\ camión\ k \\ 0 & en\ otro\ caso \end{cases}$$

cap = Capacidad en contenedores del día j.

$capmax$ = Capacidad máxima en contenedores diario.

θm_{jk}= Ángulo mínimo del clúster que minimiza la dispersión del día j del camión k.

θp_{jk} =Ángulo máximo del clúster que minimiza la dispersión del día j del camión k.

θd_{jk} = Ángulo de dispersión del día j del camión k.

Cam_{jk} = Camión k más cargado de clientes el día j.

2.6 Función Objetivo

$$Minimizar : capmax \tag{5.1}$$

2.7 Restricciones

$$\sum_j x_{ij} = F_i \qquad \forall i \in C \quad \forall j \in J$$

(5.2)

$$x_{ij} = x_{i(j+10)} \qquad \forall i \in Q \quad \forall j \in \{1..10\} \tag{5.3}$$

$$x_{ij} = x_{i(j+5)} = x_{i(j+10)} = x_{i(j+15)} \qquad \forall i \in S \quad \forall j \in \{1..5\}$$

(5.4)

$x_{ij} = x_{i(j+2)} = x_{i(j+5)} = x_{i(j+7)} = x_{i(j+10)}$ $\forall i \in DS \;\; \forall j \in \{1,2\}$
(5.5)
$= x_{i(j+12)} = x_{i(j+15)} = x_{i(j+17)}$
$x_{i5} = x_{i10} = x_{i15} = x_{i20} = 0$ $\forall i \in DS$ (5.6)
$x_{ij} = 0$ $\forall i \in TS \; \forall j \in \{2,4,7,9,12,17,19$
(5.7)
$\sum_i x_{ij} * K_i = cap_j$ $\forall i \in C \;\; \forall j \in J$
(5.8)
$cap_j \leq capmax$ $\forall j \in J$
(5.9)
$x_{ij} = \sum_k y_{ijk}$ $\forall i \in C \;\; \forall j \in J \; \forall k \in V$
(5.10)
$\sum_i K_i * y_{ijk} \leq C_k$ $\forall i \in C \;\; \forall j \in J \; \forall k \in V$
(5.11)
$-M(1-y_{ijk}) + \theta m_{jk} \leq \theta_i \leq \theta p_{jk} + M(1-y_{ijk})$ $\forall i \in C \;\; \forall j \in J \;\; \forall k \in V$
(5.12)
$\theta p_{jk} - \theta m_{jk} = \theta d_{jk}$ $\forall j \in J \;\; \forall k \in V$
(5.13)
$\theta d_{jk} \leq \epsilon$ $\forall j \in J \;\; \forall k \in V$ (5.14)
$\sum_i y_{ijk} = Cam_{jk}$ $\forall i \in C \;\; \forall j \in J \;\; \forall k \in V$ (5.15)
$Cam_{jk} \leq c$ $\forall j \in J \;\; \forall k \in V$ (5.16)
$x_{ij}, y_{ijk} \in \{0,1\}$ $\forall i \in C \; \forall j \in J \; \forall k \in V$
(5.17)
$cap_j, \theta m_{jk}, \theta p_{jk}, Cam_{jk}, \theta d_{jk} \geq 0$ $\forall j \in J \; \forall k \in V$
(5.18)
$F_i, K_i, C_k, \theta_i, M, capmax, \epsilon, c \geq 0$ $\forall i \in C \; \forall k \in V$
(5.19)

La función objetivo (5.1) del modelo busca minimizar las cargas diarias de los camiones. La restricción (5.2) programa a todos los clientes según su frecuencia dependiendo de la cantidad de veces que debe ser asignado el cliente durante el mes, a su vez asegura que los clientes mensuales y diarios sean asignados una vez al mes y todos los días respectivamente.

Las siguientes restricciones ayudan a la replicabilidad de las frecuencias, es decir que se programe al mismo cliente al mismo día según su frecuencia durante el mes. La restricción (5.3) asegura que los clientes quincenales sean programados cada diez días, por ende, dos veces al mes siempre el mismo día. La restricción (5.4) programa a los clientes semanales cada cinco días por ende cuatro veces a la semana, siempre el mismo día durante el mes. La restricción (5.5) programa a los clientes bisemanales, ocho veces al mes, en las combinaciones lunes y miércoles o martes y jueves, siempre los mismos días durante el mes.

Las restricciones (5.6) y (5.7) no permiten que los clientes bisemanales sean programados los días viernes, ya que este día se dejará para que otros clientes con otras frecuencias sean asignados y que los clientes trisemanales no sean asignados los días martes y jueves del mes, respectivamente.

La restricción (5.8) almacena la demanda del cliente i del día j y la restricción (5.9) guarda todas las demandas diarias para ser minimizadas posteriormente.

Las restricciones (5.10), (5.11), (5.12) (5.13) y (5.14) forman los clústeres geográficos de los clientes ya programados, en donde cada clúster corresponde a un camión recolector, por ende los clientes i asignados al día j y al camión k representarán un clúster, desde ahora denominado clúster de clientes. La restricción (5.10) permite que cada cliente i sea asignado solamente a un único camión k durante el día j. La restricción (5.11) asegura que el cliente i asignado al día j y al camión k respete la capacidad de cada camión diariamente.

La restricción (5.12) almacena el ángulo formado entre cada cliente i asignado al día j y al camión k y el depósito, lo almacena en las variables θm_{jk} y θp_{jk} según corresponda para posteriormente en la restricción (5.13) y (5.14) restar ambos ángulos y formar los clústeres geográficos según la variable ϵ dada.

Las restricciones (5.15) y (5.16) balancean la cantidad de clientes i asignados al día j de cada camión k.

Las restricciones (5.17) y (5.18) son de no negatividad.

3 Técnica de solución

El sistema de información presenta tres etapas como se describe en la Figura 1 [29]. Ingreso de datos, segmentado por zonas geográficas, incluyendo así también todas las restricciones presentes en el domino del negocio. Una etapa para procesar los datos con un modelo matemático de programación lineal [22]. El sistema se integra, a la capa de optimización, mediante un Pipe and Filters de Unix [30]. Un archivo de texto interpreta AMPL (A Mathematical Programming Language) [27], y para resolver las instancias se utilizó el software solver SCPI [28]. La solución óptima encontrada, exportada a un archivo, es incorporada mediante un proceso interno. Finalmente, se presenta tanto un calendario, programación de visita de clientes, como las rutas asignadas a los operarios por día, visualizadas en un mapa.

Figura 1 Proceso general del sistema.

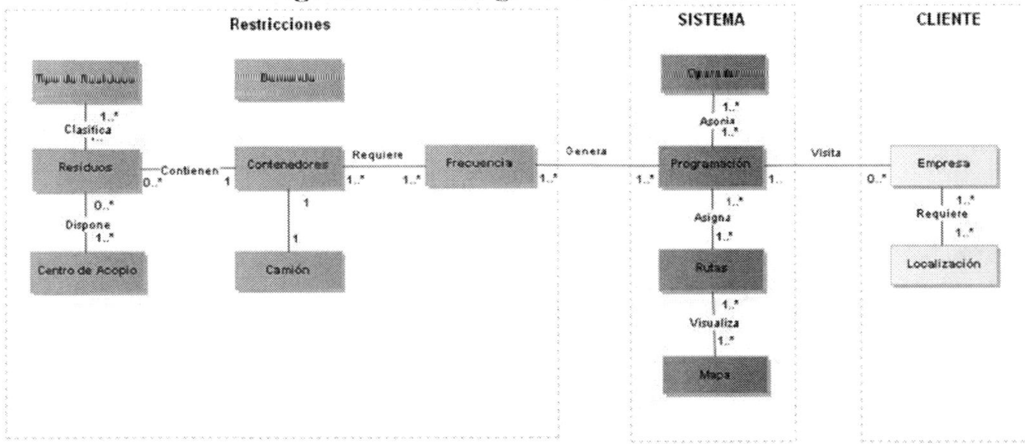

3.1 Arquitectura de la solución

La arquitectura definida para el desarrollo de la aplicación es híbrida [24], dado los requerimientos no funcionales [31], como así también la necesidad del cumplimiento de atributos de calidad. El marco de trabajo seleccionado es SYMFONY [32], versión 3.2. La arquitectura proporciona atributos de calidad como productividad, mantenibilidad y adaptabilidad [25].

La aplicación se desarrolló utilizando la metodología Rapid Application Development (RAD) [33]. El proceso de captura de requerimientos fue mediante reuniones con expertos.

3.2 Diseño

El objetivo es conseguir un modelo orientado a objetos que refleje el conocimiento de un dominio dado e independiente de cualquier concepto de comunicación, ya sea con elementos de infraestructura como de interfaz gráfica, etc.

Otro atributo de calidad aplicado es el lenguaje ubicuo, ya que está demostrado que el principal motivo de fracaso de los proyectos de software es la dificultad de comunicación entre los expertos de negocio y los desarrolladores [34] [35]. Por lo tanto, es necesario establecer un lenguaje de uso común que contenga los principales conceptos del dominio y facilite la comunicación entre partes [36].

El diseño arquitectónico establece la separación de los elementos que conforman el dominio [37]. La primera separación se hace a alto nivel y consiste en tres grandes grupos: presentación, backend y datos [24]. A partir de esta separación los dos primeros grupos se subdividen a su vez en capas, éstas pueden ser físicas o lógicas y deben ser cohesivas y tener idéntico nivel de abstracción para cada capa de primer nivel, con un mínimo acoplamiento posible con el resto de capas [38]. La Figura. 2, presenta las cuatro mayores capas que componen el sistema, presentación, aplicación, transversal y optimización.

Figura. 2 Arquitectura general del proyecto

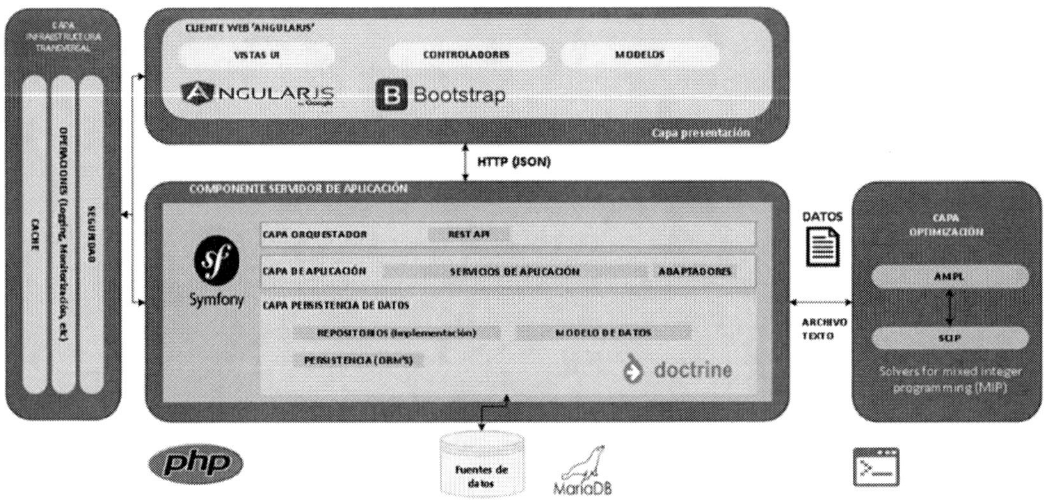

3.3 Interfaz de usuario

La interfaz de usuario se diseñó con el objeto de plasmar el contenido y funcionalidad de una manera intuitiva, para ello se utilizaron las normativas de usabilidad propuestas por Nielsen [39], además se cumple con el estándar de calidad, establecido en la ISO 9126 [25].

Figura. 3 Programación de visitas

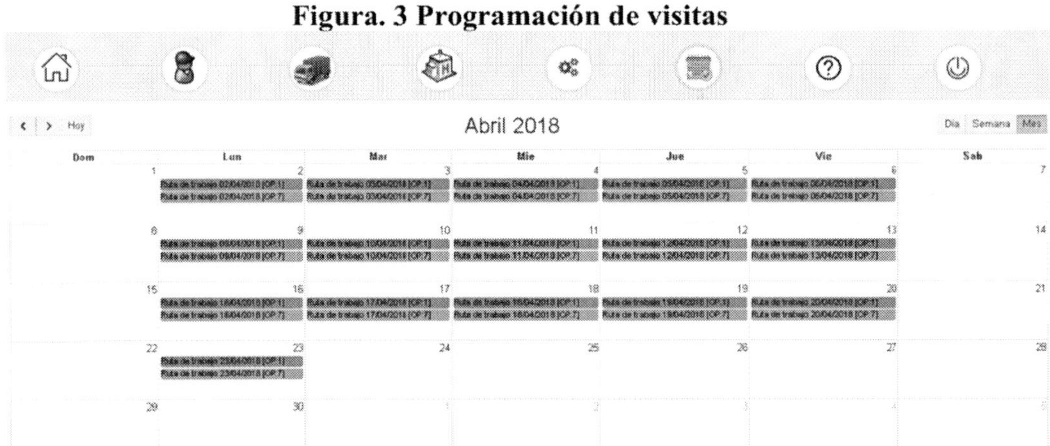

Un ejemplo de la interfaz se puede visualizar en la Figura 3, desde ahí se puede revisar la programación de los clientes para todo el mes.

Figura 4 Ruteo de vehículos, día 10

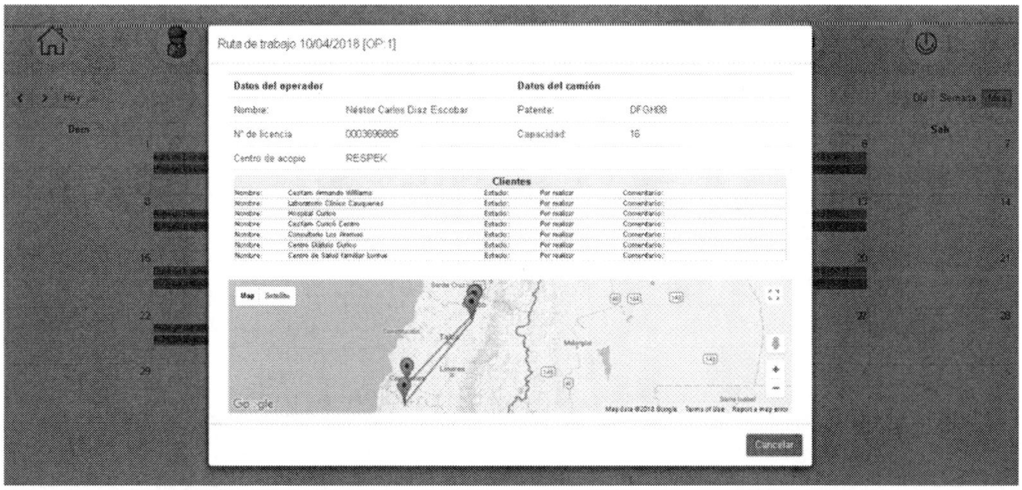

También al pulsar el detalle de cada evento en el calendario, se despliega un mapa con las rutas a ser visitadas Figura 4. El sistema cuenta con mantenedores específicos, con el objeto de realizar acciones correctivas a los datos en el sistema.

3.4 Atributos de calidad

La aplicación desarrollada no tiene inconvenientes de operatividad, dado que permite al usuario ejecutar la aplicación con cualquiera de los navegadores web que utilicen el estándar HTML5. La aplicación dispone de una estructura de capas desacopladas [40]. También es tolerante a fallas, dado que permite realizar los ruteos utilizando la información de la base de datos. El posterior desarrollo de nuevos aplicativos, está validado por el uso de los servicios expuesto mediante el REST API [41].

4 Resultados preliminares

El modelo matemático de programación lineal, se programó utilizando el lenguaje AMPL y resuelto con el solver SCIP 4.0. El hardware del servidor del proyecto en estado piloto tiene las características, descritas en la Tabla 1, como también se exponen las versiones de la arquitectura tecnológica empleada.

Todas las instancias se presentarán con un time CPU máximo de 35.000 segundos (9,7 horas), el cual se consideró razonable para obtener una buena solución o hasta que encuentre el óptimo.

Tabla 1 Configuración del hardware utilizado

Hardware	Procesador doble núcleo (vCPU) Dos GB RAM Cincuenta GB DD, SSD
LAMP (Linux, Apache, MariaDB, PHP) [26]	CentOS 7 Kernel: Linux 3.10.0-514.16.1.el7.x86_64 Architecture: x86-64, Apache 2.4,PHP MariaDB 5.5, Php 5,6,
Symfony [32] Angular JS [42]	3.2 1.6
Ampl [27]	20170207 (Linux x86_64)
SCIP [28]	4.0.0 [precisión: 8 byte]

4.1 Programación y asignación clientes Región del Maule

A continuación, en la Figura 5, se presenta la distribución de los clientes presentes en la región del Maule.

Figura 5 Clientes Región del Maule

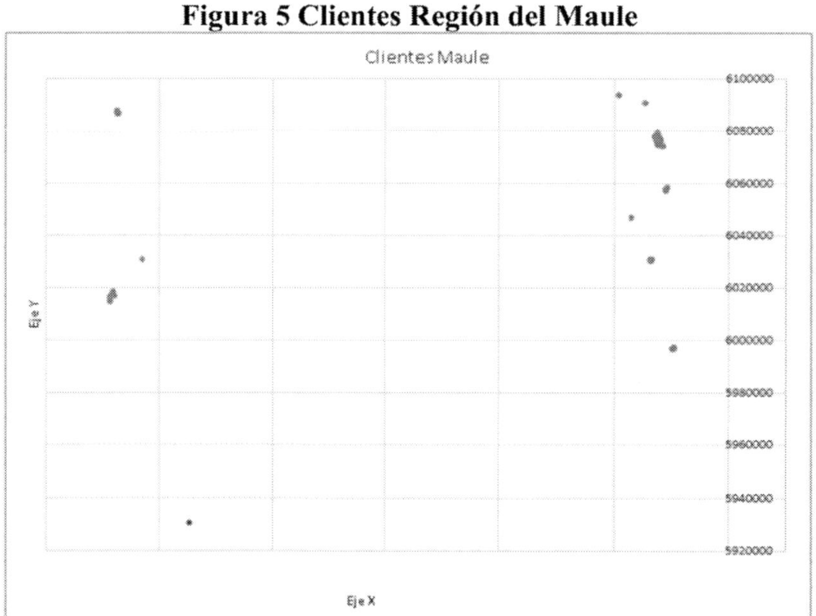

Utilizando el software diseñado, se procesan los datos de 77 clientes correspondientes a la región del Maule, restringiendo a dos camiones con una capacidad de 16 contenedores cada uno, un ángulo de dispersión de la región que se desea tomar para cada clúster diariamente de 20°, debido al comportamiento de los datos y una máxima de 7 clientes diarios por camión [22].

En la Tabla 2, se presentan los resultados de la programación realizada por el software para 20 días. Está balanceada la cantidad de clientes asignados a los camiones y los contenedores utilizados diariamente.

Tabla 2 Clientes programados y asignados región del Maule solver SCIP.

Día	Clientes Camión 1	Clientes Camión 2	Capacidad
1	41, 45, 55, 60, 69	2, 4, 9, 10, 12, 14, 30	3.22
2	1, 11, 21, 25, 29, 34	54, 70, 71, 74, 75, 76	5.02
3	36, 53, 55	44, 47	8.59
4	15, 22, 26, 54, 58, 59, 63	16, 27, 31, 33, 51, 57, 66	5.63
5	8, 17, 18, 20, 35, 56, 65	19, 28, 50, 62, 64, 67, 68	5.68
6	3, 9, 13, 14, 32, 48	41, 43, 55, 60,	6.19
7	1, 5, 21, 23, 25, 34	11, 54, 70, 71, 74, 75, 76	4.64
8	24, 53	36, 44, 55	9.83
9	33, 37, 39, 57, 58, 59, 63	15, 16, 26, 27, 51, 54, 66	5.64
10	8, 19, 28, 35, 52, 64, 67	17, 18, 50, 56, 65, 68, 73	5.71
11	2, 4, 9, 10, 12, 14, 30	41, 45, 55, 60, 69	4.96
12	25, 54, 70, 71, 74, 75, 76	1, 6, 7, 11, 21, 34	3.04
13	44, 47, 53	36, 55	10.83
14	15, 26, 27, 51, 58, 59, 63	16, 22, 31, 33, 54, 57, 66	5.65
15	8, 50, 62, 64, 65, 67, 68	17, 18, 19, 20, 28, 35, 56	5.53
16	3, 9, 13, 14, 32, 49	41, 42, 43, 46, 55, 60, 61	4.78
17	1, 5, 11, 21, 23, 34	25, 54, 70, 71, 74, 75, 76	4.64
18	40	36, 44, 53, 55	11.49
19	15, 51, 54, 57, 58, 59, 63	16, 26, 27, 33, 37, 38, 66	5.65
20	8, 19, 28, 35, 64, 67, 72	17, 18, 50, 52, 56, 65, 68	5.71

Fuente: Elaboración propia.

5 Conclusiones y trabajos futuros

El modelo propuesto cumple todas las visitas correspondientes durante el mes, los clientes diarios son asignados veinte veces al mes, los bisemanales ocho veces, trisemanales doce veces, semanales cuatro veces, quincenales dos veces al mes y los clientes mensuales una vez al mes, en cuanto a la asignación a los distintos camiones estos fueron asignados solo uno por día, minimizando la distancia entre éstos como se aprecia en la Figura 4 y respetando la capacidad de los camiones.

La arquitectura de software definida y utilizada es portable, administrable, con componentes reutilizables, evolutiva, y permite modificaciones y extensibilidad, además de ser escalable. Esto se debido a un conjunto de divisiones, módulos y capas, interactuando entre sí, expuestos en servicios REST.

Uno de los aspectos en los cuales se está trabajando, es el procesamiento de las direcciones de los clientes, para obtener la longitud y latitud mediante el API de Google Maps ®, y así el modelo proveerá una solución inicial para ser procesada, por la API antes indicada.

6 Agradecimientos

This work has been partially supported by CONICYT FONDECYT by grant 11150370, FONDEF IT17M10012 and the "Grupo de Logística y Transporte" at the Universidad del Bío-Bío. This support is gratefully acknowledged.

7 Referencias

[1] Ministerio de Salud, *Reglamento sobre el manejo de residuos de estableciemintos de atención de salud (REAS),* Santiago: Gobierno de Chile, 2009.

[2] P. P. Ballesteros Silva y C. J. Duque Vanegas , «Apliación del fraccionamiento de operaciones en una heurística constructiva en programación secuencial para la asignación de varios trabajos a varias máquinas en paralelo,» *Scientia et Technica,* vol. 18, nº 4, pp. 664-671, 2013.

[3] S.-S. Oksana, «The development of green logistics for implementation sustainable development strategy in companies,» *Czestochowa University of Technology, Faculty of Management, ul. Armii Krajowej, Częstochowa, Poland,* vol. 36b, pp. 42-201 , 2014.

[4] S. Nripendra, C. David y L. Seoki, «Green strategies for hotels: Estimation of recycling benefits,» *International Journal of Hospitality Management ,* nº 43, p. 13–22, 2014.

[5] S. I. Pirani y H. A. Arafat, «Reduction of food waste generation in the hospitality industry,» *Journal of Cleaner Production,* nº 132, p. 129e145, 2016.

[6] H. Teng-Yuan, C. Chung-Ming, N.-W. Kuoc y S. M.-F. Yud, «Establishing attributes of an environmental management system for green hotel evaluation,» *International Journal of Hospitality Management,* nº 36, p. 197–208, 2014.

[7] A. Pérez y I. Rodríguez del Bosque, «Sustainable development and stakeholder relations management: Exploring sustainability reporting in the hospitality industry from a SD-SRM approach,» *University of Cantabria, Spain, International Journal of Hospitality Management,* nº 42, p. 174–187, 2014.

[8] J. A. Aragon-Correa, «Sustainability issues and hospitality and tourism firms' strategies,» *International Journal of Contemporary Hospitality Management,* vol. 27, nº 3, pp. 498-522, 2015.

[9] A. Bruns-Smith, V. Choy, H. Chong y R. Verma, «Environmental sustainability in the hospitality industry: Best practices, guest participation, and customer satisfaction [Electronic article],» *Cornell Hospitality Report,* nº 15, pp. 6-16, 2015.

[10] E. Fraj, J. Matute y I. Melero, «Environmental strategies and organizational competitiveness in the hotel industry: The role of learning and innovation as determinants of environmental success,» *Tourism Management,* nº 46, p. 30e42, 2105.

[11] P. Jones, D. Hillier y D. Comfort, «Sustainability in the hospitality industry: Some personal reflections on corporate challenges and research agendas,» *International Journal of Contemporary Hospitality Management,* vol. 28, pp. 36-67, 2016.

[12] B. Prud'homme y L. Raymond, «Implementation of sustainable development practices in the hospitality industry: a case study of five Canadian hotels,» *International Journal of Contemporary Hospitality Management,* vol. 28, p. 3, 2016.

[13] S. Debnath, «Integrated waste management framework: a business case from hospitality industry,» *Int. J. Business Excellence,* vol. 8, nº 5, 2015.

[14] X. Xun y G. Dogan, «A Conceptual Framework of Sustainable Hospitality Supply Chain Management,» *Journal of Hospitality Marketing & Management, 24:3, 229-259,* nº 24, pp. 229-259, 2015.

[15] X. Xun y G. Dogan, «Influence of sustainable hospitality supply chain management on customers' attitudes and behaviors,» *International Journal of Hospitality Management,* nº 49, p. 105–116, 2015.

[16] J. F. Molina-Azorín, J. ,.-M. TaríJuan, M. D. Lopez-Gamero y E. M. Pertusa-Ortega, «The effects of quality and environmental management on competitive advantage: A mixed methods study in the hotel industry,» *Tourism Management,* nº 50, p. 41e54, 2015.

[17] E. Papargyropoulou, N. Wright, R. Lozano, J. Steinberger, R. Padfield y Z. Ujang, «Conceptual framework for the study of food waste generation and prevention in the hospitality sector,» *Waste Management,* nº 49, p. 326–336, 2106.

[18] M. L. Weng, «Creativity and sustainability in hospitality and tourism,» *Tourism Management Perspectives,* nº 18, p. 161–167, 2016.

[19] E. S. C. C. H. Hsu, «Environmental management research in hospitality,» *International Journal of Contemporary Hospitality Management,* vol. 28, pp. 886 - 923, 2016.

[20] P. P. Ballesteros Silva , D. P. Ballesteros Riveros y J. E. Bravo Bolívar, «Aplicación de una heurística constructiva en programación secuencial para la asignación de trabajos a varias máquinas en paralelo,» *Scientia et Technica,* vol.

18, nº 1, pp. 120-125, 2013.
[21] R. d. l. Á. Junco Díaz y D. S. & Rodríguez Sordía, Desechos hospitalarios: aspectos metodológicos de su manejo, Vols. %1 de %2122-126, Habana, Cuba: Revista Cubana de Higiene y Epidemiología, 38(2), 122-126., 2000, pp. 38(2),.
[22] M. K. R. Ruiz, Tesis pre grado, propuesta de un modelo de programación lineal entera para la programación y asignación de clientes para las rutas transporte de los camiones recolectores de la empresa procesos sanitarios SPA, Concepción: Universidad Bio Bio, 2017.
[23] M. G. Baldoquin de la Peña , R. Linfati y A. Escalera Fariñas , «Modelos y algoritmos en la solución de una problema real de agrupamiento y planificación de visitas a clientes,» de *Congreso Latino-Iberoamericano de Investigación de Operaciones* , Río de Janeiro , 2012.
[24] P. Clements, D. Garlan, L. Bass, J. Stafford, R. Nord, J. vers y R. Little, Documenting software architectures: views and beyond, Pearson Education, 2002.
[25] I. S. Organization, ISO/IEC Standard 9126-1: Software Engineering – Product Quality – Part 1: Quality Model; Part 2: External Metrics; Part 3: Internal Metrics; Part 4: Quality in Use Metrics, ISO/IEC 2003, 2001-2004.
[26] J. Gerner, E. Naramore, M. Owens y M. Warden, Professional LAMP: Linux, Apache, MySQL and PHP5 Web Development, Indianapolis, USA: Wiley Publishing, Inc., 2005.
[27] R. Fourer, D. M. Gay y B. W. Kernighan, AMPL, Boston, USA: Cen-gage Learning., 2002.
[28] T. Berthold, G. Gamrath, A. M. Gleixner, S. Heinz, T. Koch y Y. Shinano, Solving mixed integer linear and nonlinear problems using the SCIP Optimization Suite, Berlin, Germany: Zuse Institute Berlin, 2012.
[29] R. Cruz Herrera y N. Díaz Escobar, Tesis pre grado, Sistema de Información Web, para la Consignación y Ruteo de Vehículos con Datos Determinísticos, Santiago: Universidad Andrés Bello, 2018.
[30] J. Peek, G. Todino y J. Strang, Learning the UNIX Operating System, California, USA: O'Reilly Media, 2001.
[31] I. Sommerville, Ingeniería de Software, México: PEARSON EDUCACIÓN, 2011.
[32] J. Lockhart, Modern PHP, California, USA: O'Reilly Media, Inc., 2015.
[33] J. Martin, Rapid application development, Macmillan Publishing Co., Inc., 1991.
[34] C. De La Torre, U. Zorrilla, J. Calvarro y M. Á. Ramos, Arquitectura N-Capas DDD .NET 4.0, Madrid, España: Krasis Consulting, 2010.
[35] M. J. Gallivan y M. Keil, «The user–developer communication process: a critical case study.,» *Information Systems Journal, 13: 37-68. doi:10.1046/j.1365-2575.2003.00138.x,* 2003.
[36] M. P. &. P. Team, Microsoft® Application Architecture Guide, Washington, USA: Microsoft Press, 2009.
[37] E. Evans, Domain-Driven Design: tackling complexity in the heart of software, Boston, USA: Addison Wesley, 2003.
[38] M. Richards, Software Architecture Patterns: Understanding Common Architecture Patterns and When to Use Them, California, USA: O'Reilly Media, 2015.

[39] J. Nielsen, Designing web usability: The practice of simplicity., New Riders Publishing, 1999.
[40] B. F. a. J. Yoder, Big Ball of Mud, Addison-Wesley, 1999.
[41] L. Richardson, S. Ruby y A. Mike, RESTful Web APIs: Services for a Changing World, California, USA: O'Reilly Media, 2013.
[42] B. Green y S. Seshadri, AngularJS, California, USA: O'Reilly Media, 2013.

Díaz et al., 2018

Modeling of the Teniente Converter through Artificial Neural Networks

Alejandro Pulgar Sandoval[1], Karina Carvajal Cuello[1]

[1] Departamento de Ingeniería Informática y Ciencias de la Computación, Universidad de Atacama. Copayapu 485, Copiapó, Chile
alejandro.pulgar@alumnos.uda.cl, karina.carvajal@uda.cl

Abstract. The Teniente Converter is the main fusion plant of the Hernán Videla Lira Smelter. It produces matte, slag and gases. The slag contains magnetite in varying amounts. High percentages of magnetite imply higher copper losses due to mechanical entrapment in the slag stage. The objective of this work is to create a model with artificial neural networks to predict the percentage of magnetite that is generated in the slag that occurs in the operation of the Converter. For the creation of the neural network, the multilayer perceptron has been chosen. The results obtained are promising. They present an average square error of 0.23, a standard residual error of 0.1 and an adequacy index of 0.8 for a test data set of 60 subjects.

Keywords: Teniente Converter, Artificial Neural Networks, Predictive Model, Magnetite.

1 Introducción

A través de un proceso pirometalúrgico, la Fundición Hernán Videla Lira, o Fundición Paipote, procesa una gran variedad de concentrados de súlfuros de cobre. La Fundición cuenta con una capacidad nominal de procesamiento de 340.000 toneladas anuales de Carga Nueva Util, de material que proviene de plantas propias y de compras realizadas a terceros [1]. El equipo principal encargado de este proceso es el Convertidor Teniente (CT), un reactor que genera escoria, metal blanco y gases [2]. La escoria, proveniente del CT, posteriormente, es procesada en un Horno Eléctrico para la obtención de cobre en forma de metal blanco. La escoria contiene cantidades variables de magnetita; que se genera en función de las variables de entrada y de operación del equipo. La magnetita que se genera en el proceso de fusión, cumple la función de proteger el ladrillo refractario que reviste el interior del CT, por lo que porcentajes de magnetita inferiores a 18% pueden significar que el equipo resulte dañado en la operación. Porcentajes de magnetita superiores al 21% implican dificultades operacionales en el Horno Eléctrico para la obtención del cobre en la escoria. La magnetita que se genera en el CT arrastra el cobre en la escoria por atrapamiento mecánico durante la etapa de escoriado del equipo. Por lo que, mayores porcentajes de magnetita, implican un mayor porcentaje de cobre en la escoria que se dirige al Horno Eléctrico y la disminución de la producción de cobre en forma de metal blanco que se obtiene en el CT. Por lo tanto, según los encargados de la operación de este equipo, el rango óptimo del porcentaje de magnetita en la escoria, que se espera, es entre 18% y 21%.

Por otra parte, porcentajes altos de magnetita en el Horno Eléctrico genera un aumento del tiempo de residencia de la escoria en el equipo, generando un cuello de botella operacional en el proceso de fundición. Esto trae como consecuencia: i) interrupción del proceso de reducción llevado a cabo en el Horno Eléctrico, enviando la escoria a los escoriales con porcentajes elevados de cobre; ii) disminución de la producción en la fundición debido a la reducción de la inyección de los concentrados de cobre en el CT y iii) el aumento de los costos operacionales, debido al mayor consumo energético del Horno Eléctrico, entre otros.

Dentro de las investigaciones realizadas en el CT se encuentran, por ejemplo, la creación de un sensor virtual con redes neuronales para la predicción de la temperatura del CT [3], la creación de un modelo de simulación del comportamiento de los gases de fundición con un error relativo aceptable [4] y la creación de un modelo geometalurgico predictivo de la viscosidad de escorias de fusión en función de la cantidad de minerales de arcilla en concentrados de cobre [5], entre otras. Respecto a trabajos realizados con redes neuronales se encontraron trabajos de modelamientos de procesos ligados a la metalurgia y la química [6]-[12]. Los resultados muestran la capacidad de las redes neuronales para el modelamiento de los procesos, dada su capacidad de modelar sistemas multivariables complejos y de generalizar en base al conjunto de datos de entrenamiento.

En base a la revisión bibliográfica, no se encontró un modelo predictivo del porcentaje de magnetita en la escoria que se genera en la operación del CT. Por otra parte, la Fundición ha tenido dificultades para controlar la magnetita de la escoria, siendo este porcentaje, mayoritariamente superior al 21% y por ende trayendo los problemas antes mencionados. Es por esto que se propone crear un modelo predictivo que permita estimar el porcentaje de magnetita que se genera en el CT. La predicción de esta variable permitiría un mejor control del proceso y reducirían las consecuencias expuestas anteriormente.

El documento, a continuación, se organiza de la siguiente forma. En la sección 2 se describen los fundamentos y el contexto de este trabajo. La sección 3 muestra la metodología utilizada, incluyendo los indicadores que permiten indicar la efectividad de esta predicción. Finalmente, las secciones 4 y 5 muestran los principales resultados y conclusiones de este trabajo, respectivamente.

2 Marco Teórico

En esta sección se realizará una descripción del proceso de fusión, de las variables que intervienen en el proceso y del funcionamiento de las redes neuronales.

2.1 Descripción del Convertidor Teniente (CT) y del proceso de fusión

El Convertidor Teniente es el equipo en donde se lleva a cabo la fusión de los con centrados de súlfuros de cobre, lo que permite que estos pasen de estado sólido a líquido. El CT es un horno basculante metálico de forma cilíndrica, instalado de manera horizontal y revestido por ladrillos refractarios en su interior. Posee 4 metros de diámetro y un largo de 16 metros [13].

El CT es una innovación creada en Chile en la década de 1970, es un reactor pirometalúrgico capaz de fundir y convertir concentrado de cobre a metal blanco, en un único equipo y sin aporte de energía externa [14]. Cuenta con 28 toberas de inyección de concentrado seco. A través del Garr-Gun[1] ingresa el fundente, el material circulante y el concentrado húmedo. Las toberas de soplado suministran el aire enriquecido en oxígeno. Además, posee una campana que captura los gases sulfurados que se producen en el proceso de fusión, como se muestra en la figura 1.

El objetivo del CT es fundir el concentrado de cobre para la obtención de metal blanco, escoria y los gases sulfurados. El reactor logra el proceso de fusión gracias a la oxidación del azufre y el fierro contenido en los concentrados de cobre. Esta es una reacción exotérmica, por lo que el concentrado se funde de manera autónoma y sin requerir energía externa para el proceso. Además, el proceso es semi-continuo, ya que se obtiene el metal blanco y la escoria sin que el proceso de fusión se detenga [15].

El concentrado seco es inyectado de manera neumática a través de las toberas de inyección, directamente al baño de cobre del CT. También se inyecta aire enriquecido en oxígeno de baja presión a través de las toberas de soplado. El rango de temperatura óptimo de operación del equipo varía entre 1100°C y 1200°C. Estas temperaturas permiten el proceso de fusión, para así lograr la conversión y separación de fases entre la escoria y el metal blanco como consecuencia de su diferencia de densidades. La escoria y el metal blanco al interior del CT es separada por material de escoria fayalítica que compone la interfase [16].

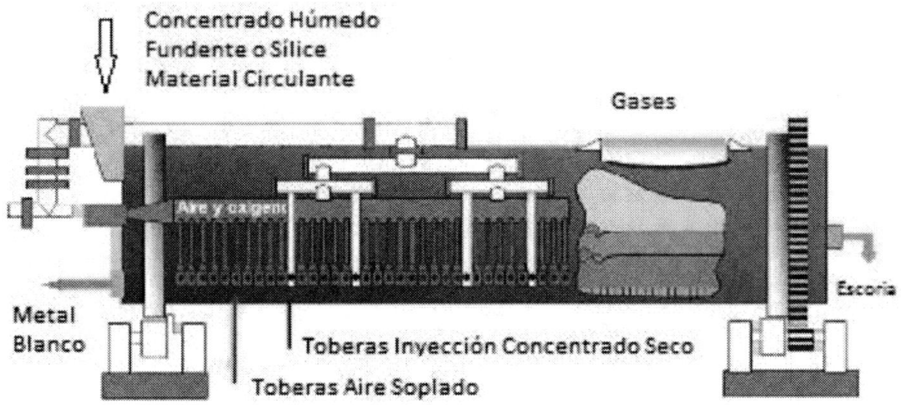

[1] Boquilla metálica por la cual ingresa el material sólido al CT

Fig. 1. Representación del Convertidor Teniente (Fuente: Obtención del cobre, Fernando Quezada Pérez. Modificado)

Las variables operacionales del Convertidor Teniente se pueden clasificar en sólidas y gaseosas. En las sólidas encontramos el concentrado seco, el fundente o sílice, el concentrado húmedo y el material circulante. Las entradas en estado gaseoso son el aire de inyección y el aire de soplado [17], [18]. Los productos que se obtienen del proceso llevado a cabo en el CT son metal blanco, escoria y gases sulfurados [2].

2.2 Generación de Magnetita en el Convertidor Teniente

La magnetita se genera en la escoria durante el proceso de fusión en el CT. Los concentrados de cobre que ingresan al reactor son ricos en azufre y hierro. El proceso de fusión consiste en la oxidación del azufre de los concentrados por efecto del oxígeno que se suministra al equipo. Esta oxidación no solo afecta al azufre, sino también al hierro contenido en el material de inyección. Es decir, la magnetita se genera por la sobre oxidación de los minerales ferrosos que componen el concentrado de cobre [17].

Según los datos obtenidos entre los años 2016 (octubre) al 2017 (marzo) la magnetita en la escoria varía entre 16% y 33%. La magnetita que se genera en el proceso de fusión cumple la función de proteger el ladrillo refractario que reviste el interior del CT, por lo que porcentajes de magnetita inferiores a 18% pueden significar que el equipo resulte dañado en la operación. Porcentajes de magnetita superiores al 21% implican dificultades operacionales en el Horno Eléctrico para la obtención del cobre en la escoria. Además, la magnetita que se genera en el CT arrastra el cobre en la escoria por atrapamiento mecánico durante la etapa de escoriado del equipo. Por lo que, mayores porcentajes de magnetita implican un mayor porcentaje de cobre en la escoria que se dirige al Horno Eléctrico y por lo tanto, la disminución de la producción de cobre en forma de metal blanco que se obtiene en el CT. De esta forma, el rango óptimo del porcentaje de magnetita en la escoria debería estar entre 18% y 21%, según los operadores del CT.

Para evitar la generación de magnetita, es posible disminuir el oxígeno que ingresa al reactor. Sin embargo, esto repercute en la disminución de la temperatura del equipo, lo cual entorpece la operación y la ley de cobre del metal blanco resultante del proceso [17]. Otra estrategia utilizada para reducir la generación de magnetita consiste en añadir sílice o fundente, pero esto implica un mayor costo energético, además del costo en sí de adicionar este flujo. Por otro lado, la viscosidad de la escoria aumenta con el contenido de sílice [19].

En el Horno Eléctrico se lleva a cabo el proceso de reducción de la magnetita de la escoria, con el objetivo de extraer el remanente de cobre como metal blanco. Cuando la escoria que se procesa en el Horno Eléctrico posee una composición de magnetita superior a 21%, se dificulta el proceso de reducción de la magnetita. Esto genera un aumento del tiempo de residencia de la escoria en el equipo, generando un cuello de botella operacional en el proceso de fundición. Como consecuencia se debe interrumpir el proceso de reducción llevado a cabo en el Horno Eléctrico y se envía la escoria a los escoriales con porcentajes elevados de cobre. Debido al cuello de botella operacional generado, también es necesario reducir la inyección de los concentrados de cobre en el CT, lo cual trae como consecuencia la disminución de la producción en la fundición.

Por otra parte, el elevado porcentaje de magnetita en la escoria incide negativamente en el consumo de electricidad del Horno Eléctrico para el proceso de reducción, aumentando significativamente los costos operacionales.

Por lo tanto, si existiera un modelo capaz de predecir o estimar el porcentaje de magnetita en la escoria permitiría controlare la operación de tal forma de trabajar con los porcentajes adecuados de magnetita y así reducir las desventajas del desconocimiento de la misma, en el proceso.

2.3 Redes Neuronales Artificiales

Las redes neuronales artificiales se pueden definir como modelos matemáticos computacionales inspirados en el funcionamiento de los sistemas neuronales biológicos. Están compuestas por unidades de procesamiento adaptativas de información llamadas neuronas que están interconectadas entre sí. La red neuronal más utilizada es el perceptrón multicapa [20].

En la figura 2 se puede observar un esquema de la red neuronal perceptrón multicapa. El perceptrón multicapa se compone de un conjunto de neuronas que se distribuyen en las distintas capas de la red neuronal. En la primera capa se encuentran las neuronas de entrada y la última capa corresponde a las neuronas de salida. Las neuronas ubicadas entre la capa de entrada y las neuronas de salida se encuentran ubicadas en la capa oculta. Cada capa posee un número determinado de neuronas con sus respectivas funciones de transferencia. Las neuronas de una capa están conectadas con las neuronas de la capa siguiente, de modo tal que las señales enviadas por las neuronas de la capa n-1 son las señales de entrada de la capa n.

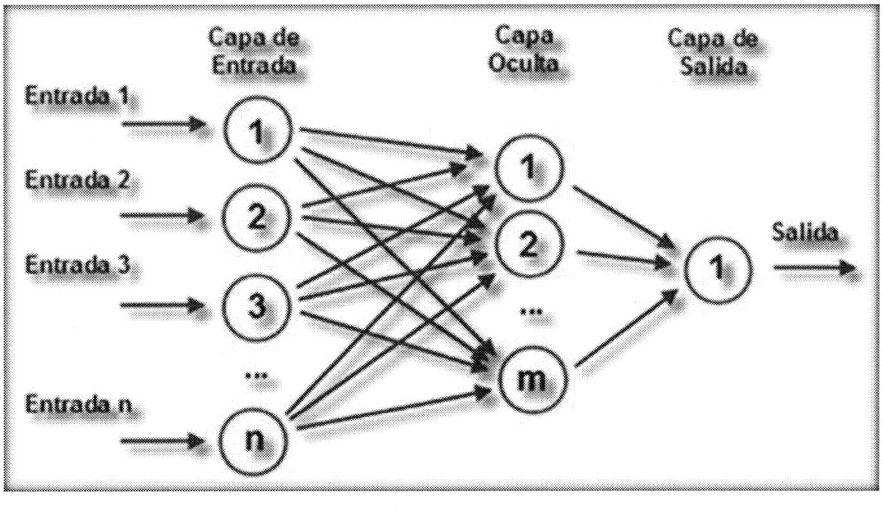

Fig. 2. Esquema del perceptrón multicapa. (Fuente: Redes Neuronales, Carlos Nuñez y Freddy Zapata)

Los parámetros de la red neuronal se expresan matemáticamente como vectores y matrices. La red neuronal se debe entrenar para ajustar sus pesos sinápticos, reduciendo el error de la salida. Este proceso consiste en proporcionar un conjunto de datos de entrenamiento a la red, de modo que se minimice el error de la señal de salida [21].

3 Metodología

Dada la problemática planteada y considerando los posibles beneficios de modelar el proceso se presenta un modelo en base a redes neuronales artificiales, utilizando el perceptrón multicapa, que sea capaz de simular el proceso de fusión y de predecir el porcentaje de magnetita que se genera en la escoria del Convertidor Teniente. Este modelo permitirá, en un trabajo posterior, plantear un modelo de control que, basado en la estimación a futuro de la magnetita se puedan monitorizar y ajustar las variables de entrada para regular el porcentaje de magnetita.

La metodología general de trabajo, para la solución propuesta, se puede dividir en 3 etapas: preprocesamiento de datos, modelamiento y prueba.

3.1 Preprocesamiento de datos

Los datos utilizados en el modelo se extrajeron del reporte operacional diario y de la base de datos del sistema de control distribuido (DCS) PlantPax de la fundición. Los datos del reporte operacional diario son extraídos manualmente por la imposibilidad de ser exportados. La figura 3 muestra una imagen de una parte del reporte operacional diario.

Los datos recabados del DCS se obtienen mediante su exportación a una planilla Excel. La figura 4 muestra una parte de esta exportación. Del DCS se extrajo la información de las siguientes variables: inyección, sílice, circulante, húmedo, aire de soplado, oxígeno de soplado y del aire de inyección y porcentaje de magnetita que se genera en la extracción de la escoria.

	Turno C							
METAL BLANCO HE	0	1	2	3	4	5	6	7
Hora								
OLLAS			1		1			
Ley Cu			73,9		73,4			
						Total Turno C		2
ESCORIA CT	0	1	2	3	4	5	6	7
Hora								
OLLAS	4			6		4		4
Ley Cu	3,8			4,6		4,2		3,0
Ley Fe3O4	26,4			26,8		26,0		25,1
Ley SiO2	23,6			25,9		22,8		24,2
Ley Fe	37,9			37,4		37,2		37,6
Fe/SiO2	1,61			1,44		1,63		1,55
						Total Turno C		18
METAL BLANCO	0	1	2	3	4	5	6	7
Hora								
OLLAS		3			3		3	
Ley Cu		74,4			73,5		72,7	
Ley Fe		1,8			1,6		1,4	
Ley S		20,1			19,8		18,8	
Destino		CPS3			CPS2		CPS3	
						Total Turno C		9
HORA	0	1	2	3	4	5	6	7
Tiempo Soplado								
Tiempo Inyección								
Tiempo Carga								

Fig. 3. Imagen de una parte del reporte operacional diario, en donde se entregan datos de la operación del CT. De este reporte se puede extraer la información referente a duración de los escoriados, porcentaje de magnetita en la escoria y tiempo de interescoriado.

	DATOS DCS							
	Variables entrada							
Fecha y hora	Circulante	Humedo	Silice	Aire inyec	Air Garr-Gun	Aire sopla	Ox soplado	Tasa prom iny
08/10/16 11:40:00	2,035233839	1,275471809	4,15076043	27,0391003	79,126986	279,854752	88,7431154	42
08/10/16 11:50:00	2,019304846	1,213145234	4,24534798	27,2227444	78,2574705	289,709215	92,8553179	39,5
08/10/16 12:00:00	2,054711143	1,259109544	4,23274541	27,0781482	79,4121444	289,909799	93,1490754	43
08/10/16 12:10:00	2,008214444	1,199229704	4,30897171	27,3200684	77,2480328	291,978064	92,6330892	38
08/10/16 12:20:00	2,030746877	1,668670384	4,62314265	27,2716061	78,3654801	288,03215	85,9717763	44
08/10/16 12:30:00	2,007297103	1,859484285	4,56058466	27,2651784	77,8112636	282,268893	84,336152	42,5
08/10/16 12:40:00	1,950294513	1,915346403	4,20723	27,2345462	78,7217087	272,49218	80,8966688	47
08/10/16 12:50:00	1,164343248	1,900030725	2,61297697	27,1930123	77,5909283	283,471284	83,0108374	41,5
08/10/16 13:00:00	1,93517627	1,537314435	2,89471561	27,1645051	76,974917	270,896447	80,5666197	44,5
08/10/16 13:10:00	1,952780706	1,550863585	3,25768735	27,1266227	77,5071807	274,515283	81,2404496	42
08/10/16 13:20:00	2,116975883	1,49403926	2,80144036	27,1821908	76,629587	256,085562	74,4208918	38
08/10/16 13:30:00	2,032761503	1,828491055	4,39568051	27,1806617	78,824056	279,617051	83,3117801	41
08/10/16 13:40:00	2,048123119	1,969205894	4,20452571	27,3507266	77,0371982	276,083273	81,4258557	41
08/10/16 13:50:00	2,04022972	1,975894357	4,28000164	27,2780647	77,1673071	289,217742	85,7689716	47

Fig. 4. Imagen de una parte de los datos exportados del DCS.

Luego de la extracción de datos, se realizó una depuración de los mismos, eliminando períodos de operación en donde los datos de producción se alteran debido a restricciones ambientales. También se eliminan los datos de los períodos en que hay problemas de soplado, inyección, o en las correas que alimentan al Garr-Gun. Se descarta la información de los periodos en que hubo problemas operacionales por fallas en el equipo y su instrumentación. Finalmente se suprime la información de los períodos de operación en que no estaba completa la información acerca de las variables seleccionadas.

La Tabla 1. muestra algunos ejemplos de los datos, sin normalizar, obtenidos luego del preprocesamiento de los datos. En el caso de las variables de entrada de material sólido, se realiza la transformación de unidades a kg / (10 min). Para el caso de las variables de entrada en estado gaseoso, se realiza la transformación de unidades a m^3 / (10 min). De este modo se trabaja con las tasas de entrada en el mismo marco temporal. Las variables de entrada de los ciclos de operación del Convertidor Teniente son insertadas en las columnas de la planilla de manera descendente. Las filas de la planilla representan los ciclos de operación.

Tabla 1. Ejemplo de datos sin normalizar, preprocesados, para trabajar con el Modelo Neuronal.

Inyección kg/10min	Sílice kg/10min	Circulante kg/10min	Húmedo kg/10min	Oxígeno de inyección m^3/10min	Oxígeno de soplado m^3/10min	Tiempo de ciclo. 10 min	Fe_3O_4 t-1 %	Fe_3O_4 %
7000	635	322	256	362	1860	11	22	21
7119	682	330	314	362	1891	7	21	18
7375	655	533	243	360	1914	12	18	22
7276	639	661	83	361	1831	13	22	21
7152	654	630	181	357	1911	11	21	26
7028	648	615	175	358	1870	12	26	24
6750	664	193	190	358	1738	16	24	21
7359	626	469	118	379	1888	13	20	20
7032	648	598	155	376	1798	13	20	23
7403	639	551	0	373	1931	12	23	23
7399	665	336	52	372	1697	14	23	21
7347	662	306	0	370	1711	12	21	23
7871	687	273	0	372	1838	11	23	24
7878	632	190	0	377	1893	13	24	26

Luego del proceso anterior se normalizan los datos de entrada de la red neuronal, utilizando la ecuación 1. La normalización de los datos de entrada permite que los pesos sinápticos de la red sean consistentes, para evitar desproporciones en los pesos iniciales de la red. En este caso las variables fueron normalizadas entre 0 y 1 [11]. Finalmente se tiene 433 registros con los cuales se trabajará para crear el modelo neuronal.

$$p_n = \frac{(p_i - p_{min})}{(p_{max} - p_{min})}. \quad (1)$$

Donde,

p_n= Valor normalizado del enésimo elemento del vector de entrada.

p_i= Valor del i-ésimo elemento que se desea normalizar del vector de entrada.

p_{min}= Valor mínimo de cada elemento del vector de entrada del conjunto de datos.

p_{max}= Valor máximo de cada elemento del vector de entrada del conjunto de datos.

3.2 Diseño del Modelo Neuronal

El modelo neuronal creado tiene una capa de entrada, una capa oculta y una capa de salida. En la capa de entrada se consideran 8 variables, correspondiente a las primeras 8 variables de la tabla 1. En la capa oculta se consideran 8 neuronas y la capa de salida contiene 1 neurona que corresponde al porcentaje de magnetita. La función de activación de cada neurona es la función logaritmo-sigmoide. Este modelo se obtuvo después de realizar varias pruebas, modificando los parámetros de la red neuronal como número de neuronas en la capa oculta, función de activación, etc.

De los 433 registros se utilizaron 377 para entrenamiento y 60 para prueba. El conjunto de datos de entrenamiento debe ser representativo en términos de dispersión para que la red sea capaz de incorporar los distintos escenarios del conjunto de datos de prueba [12].

3.3 Prueba del Modelo

Para probar la efectividad de este modelo y su capacidad de generalización se utilizaron los índices de error cuadrático medio (RMSE), error residual estándar (RSD) e índice de adecuación (IA), que se muestran en las ecuaciones (2), (3) y (4). El rango de estos estadígrafos varía entre 0 y 1. Valores cercanos a 0 indican un buen desempeño predictivo para el error cuadrático medio y el error residual estándar, mientras que valores cercanos a 1 indican una buena estimación para el índice de adecuación.

$$RMSE = \sqrt{\frac{\sum_{i=1}^{n}(o_i - p_i)^2}{\sum_{i=1}^{n} o_i^2}} \quad (2)$$

$$RSD = \sqrt{\frac{\sum_{i=1}^{n}(o_i - p_i)^2}{N}} \quad (3)$$

$$IA = 1 - \frac{\sum_{i=1}^{n}(o_i - p_i)^2}{\sum_{i=1}^{n}(|o_i - o_m| + |p_i - o_m|)^2} \quad (4)$$

Siendo:

o_i= El valor deseado de predicción para i.

p_i= El valor predicho para i.

N= El número total de datos.

o_m= El valor medio de las predicciones deseadas.

4 Resultados

Después de las pruebas realizadas, el mejor modelo de red neuronal obtenido fue el que presentó los siguientes indicadores, considerando que se realizó el entrenamiento con un total de 377 escoriados del conjunto de datos:

- Índice de adecuación (IA) = 0,87
- Error cuadrático medio (RMSE) = 0,19
- Error residual estándar (RSD) = 0,09

La prueba para verificar el nivel de predicción del modelo se realizó con los datos de 60 escoriados. La figura 5 muestra los datos de porcentaje de magnetita real y el porcentaje de magnetita estimado por el modelo neuronal. En el eje Y de la figura 3, se puede apreciar el porcentaje de magnetita normalizado entre 0 y 1. Los resultados se presentan en esta escala por los motivos de confidencialidad establecidos con la empresa que ha proveído los datos. El eje X corresponde a la medición del porcentaje de magnetita de 60 escoriados de la operación del Convertidor Teniente.

Los indicadores para la medición del error, presentan los siguientes resultados para un total de 60 escoriados del conjunto de datos de prueba:

- Índice de adecuación (IA) = 0,8
- Error cuadrático medio (RMSE) = 0,23
- Error residual estándar (RSD) = 0,1

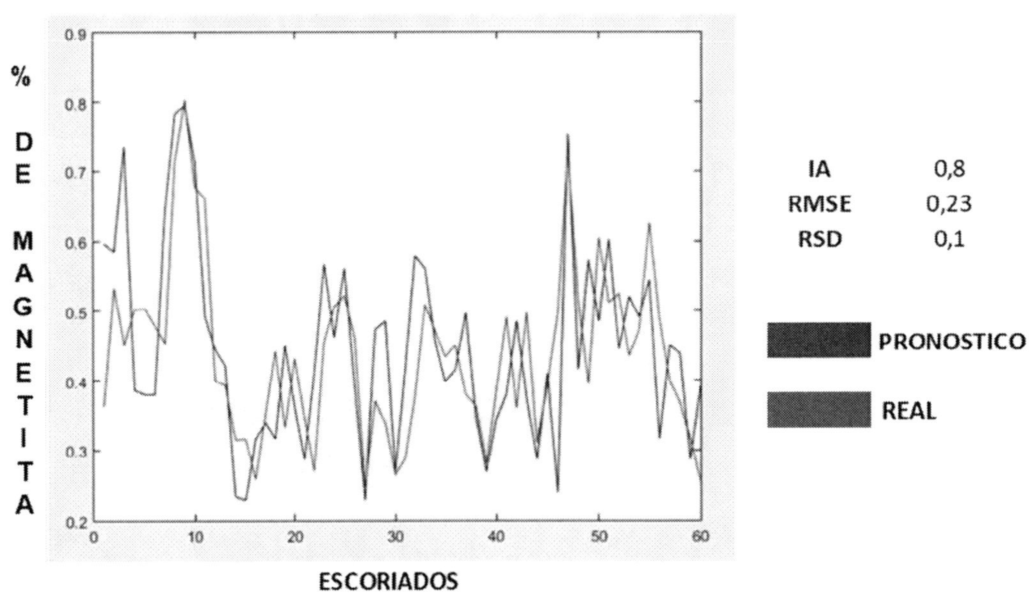

Fig. 5. Pronóstico de la red neuronal v/s Porcentaje real de magnetita. El eje Y muestra el porcentaje de magnetita real y predicho y en el eje X se consideran los 60 ejemplos de prueba.

5 Conclusiones

El modelo neuronal creado para la predicción del porcentaje generado de magnetita en la operación del Convertidor Teniente, permite predecir con un error cuadrático medio (RMSE) menor a 0,3. Por lo tanto, se puede crear un modelo para predecir el porcentaje de magnetita generado en la operación del Convertidor Teniente mediante redes neuronales artificiales. El bajo error residual estándar y los índices de adecuación obtenidos reafirman la capacidad de las redes neuronales para la estimación de la magnetita que se genera en la operación del Convertidor Teniente.

Los datos que fueron extraídos del sistema de control distribuido (DCS) PlantPax, permitieron obtener adecuadamente los datos para el entrenamiento y prueba de la red neuronal. Fueron generados en total 433 datos, de los cuales, en forma excluyente, se utilizaron 377 datos para entrenamiento y 60 para prueba.

A pesar de que se excluye la variable operacional de temperatura por motivo de no contar con el registro instrumental de dicha variable, las 8 variables escogidas para el modelo lograron predecir de manera satisfactoria el porcentaje de magnetita generado en la escoria.

Los resultados obtenidos son prometedores. Sin embargo, se debe contrastar el modelo neuronal creado con pruebas en terreno controladas, para poder validarlo completamente.

Agradecimientos

Se agradece a la Empresa Nacional de Minería (ENAMI) por aportar los datos e infraestructura necesarios para realizar esta investigación y al profesor Jonathan Castillo, profesor del Departamento de Ingeniería en Metalurgia de la Universidad de Atacama por su apoyo en la descripción del proceso y selección de variables.

Referencias

1. www.enami.cl
2. Collao, C.: Diseño e Implementación de Lazo de Control de Adisión de Fundente en Convertidor Teniente. (2008)
3. Suárez, A., Gómez, Z.: Sensor virtual neuronal con variables instrumentals y su aplicación en un Convertidor Teniente. (2011).
4. Pérez, S., Aguilera, Y., Hurtado, J., Vargas, J.: Modelación y simulación fluido-dinámica computacional de sistema de enfriamiento de gases para fundición de cobre mediante Convertidor Teniente con enfriador. Science Direct, Vol. 33 (2017) 179-187
5. Jeldres, G.: Modelo geometalurgico predictivo de la viscosidad de escorias de fusion en funcion de la cantidad de minerales de arcilla en concentrados de cobre. Tesis de Magister (2016)
6. Fardis, N., Mehdi, I.: Application and comparison of RNN, RBFNN and MNLR approaches on prediction of flotation column performance. International Journal of Mining Science and Technology, Vol. 25 (2015) 983-990

7. Đurić, I., Mihajlovi, I., Živkovi, Ž., Kešelj, D.: Artificial neural network prediction of aluminum extraction from bauxite in the Bayer process. Journal of the Serbian Chemical Society, Vol. 77 (2012) 1259-1271
8. Alhajreeb, I., Zahedia, G., Manan, Z. A., Zadeh, S. M.: Modeling and optimization of an industrial hydrocracker plant.. Journal of Petroleum Science and Engineering, Vol. 78 (2011) 627-636
9. Azizi, A., Ghaedrahmati, R., Ghahramani, N., Rooki, R.: Modelling and simulation of the cyanidation process of Aghdareh gold ore using artificial neural network and and multiple linear regression. International Journal of Mining and Mineral Engineering, Vol. 7 (2011)
10. Nakhaei, F., Mosavi, M. R., Sam, A., Vaghei, Y.: Recovery and grade accurate prediction of pilot plant flotation column concentrate: Neural network and statistical techniques. International Journal of Mineral Processing, Vol 110-112 (2012) 140-154
11. Hagan, M., Demuth, H., Beale, M., De Jesús, O.: Neural Network Design. Segunda Edición (2014)
12. Jaque, M.: Modelos de redes neuronales aplicado en la predicción del signo de los fondos de AFP Cuprum. Tesis de Magister. Universidad de Chile (2014)
13. P. Cuadra y B. Martinich, «www.codelcoeduca.cl,» 2000. [En línea].
14. Santelices, B., Lund, F., Cooper, T., Asemjo, J.: Innovación basada en conocimiento científico. Estudio en homenaje a los 50 años del Instituto de Chile y de la Academia Chilena de Ciencias Academia Chilena de Ciencias
15. Codelco: Manual Anual de Apoyo Operacional. (2005)
16. Suárez, A., Gómez, Z.: Sensor virtual neuronal con variables instrumentales y su aplicación en un Convertidor Teniente. Revista Iberoamericana de Automática e Informática Industrial, Vol. 8 (2011) 54-63
17. Cardona, N.: Contribución al Análisis Fisicoquímico de las Pérdidas de Cobre en Escorias. Tesis de Magister. Universidad de Concepción (2011)
18. Berríos, R.: Desarrollo de un Programa Código Abierto para la Fusión de Concentrado en el Convertidor Teniente. Trabajo de Título. Universidad de Santiago de Chile (2010)
19. Yucra, H. G.: Evaluación de los factores que afectan las propiedades mecánicas de los refractarios en convertidor pierce-smith. Tesis (2017).
20. Serrano, A., Soria, E., Martín, J.: Redes Neuronales Artificiales. (2009)
21. López, J.: Sistema de inversión en bolsa de corto plazo. (2008)

SMMicro: A Methodological Proposal for Migrating from Monolithic Architecture to Microservices

Carlos Arboleda[1], Pamela Flores[1], Jenny Torres[1]

[1] Escuela Politécnica Nacional, Faculty of Systems Engineering, Ladrón de Guevara E11-253, P.O. Box 17-012759,
Quito, Ecuador

{carlos.arboleda, pamela.flores, jenny.torres}@epn.edu.ec

Abstract. Microservices architecture is an approach based on the construction of systems as independent suites of services, focused on stability, reliability, resilience and easy scaling. Therefore, this architecture is among the most used in the software industry due to its versatility. However, some issues are identified with it, one of them is a migration from legacy architectures that at the beginning fulfilled their functionality, but over the time, they became obsolete. Up to now, there are no guidelines that lead to a migration between monolithic architectures to microservices, being this the main motivation for this research, which aims to investigate the difficulties in migrating monolithic to microservices and establishing a methodological proposal called SMMicro. SMMicro is a conceptual model that allows establishing guidelines to provide a migration focused on decomposition and the subsequent association of components in the layers of an ecosystem of microservices. In addition, SMMicro was implemented on a case study selected from a set of academic software systems, resulting in the design of the system migrated with new components and with the expected benefits of a microservices architecture.

Keywords: Software Engineering, Microservices, Migration, Monolithic Architecture.

1 Introduction

The study of different software architectures has become crucial for the continuous improvement of Software Engineering. This is how the definition of a Microservices-based Architecture has appeared, based on the difficulties of the traditional monolithic approach. Nowadays we can find different architectural styles that have advantages and disadvantages depending on the context of use. There are a number of limitations regarding monolithic systems that have exceeded their initial scope and need to scale their functions to meet the requirements of the consumer. In addition, if we make a

comparison of the main characteristics that influence in a system, we find some observations that [1] and [2] analyze in different studies.
Scalability. Each microservice can be scaled independently of other services. In contrast to monolithic architectures, it avoids the need to scale the whole system when there are only a few functionalities that are used intensively.
Resilience. Unlike monolithic architectures, microservices can be easily replaced. Therefore, recovering from a failure is relatively simple. A new microservice does not need to use part of the code base or the technologies of the old microservice. Small microservices facilitate their updating and when the decision of a technology or approach is limited to a microservice, it can be completely rewritten if necessary.
Continuous Delivery. Microservices allow a better time to place them on the market. If the different teams that work in a large system are responsible for one or more microservices and if it is required changes to these microservices, each team can develop and bring features into production without the time-consuming coordination with other teams. The deployment of a single microservice is associated with less risk than the deployment of a large monolithic.
Flexibility. When developing microservices there are no restrictions on the use of technologies. This, unlike monolithic architectures, reduces the potential risk, allows independent technological decisions for different microservices, increases the productivity of developers and prevents the technological platform from becoming obsolete.
All these potential features of a Microservices architecture are based on the expected benefits of an efficient software development. Nevertheless, until today the migration from monolithic architectures towards microservices has been partially studied and in the literature, there are no guidelines that allow to lead towards a migration between those architectures. For this reason, this study presents a methodological proposal for the migration from monolithic systems to systems based on microservices based in a case study.
The rest of the article is structured as follows. Section 2 shows several related works by other authors and the contribution that our work has regarding them. Section 3 presents the methodological proposal called "Scheme for Migration towards Microservices" (SMMicro) that facilitates its understanding and serves as a reference in the architecture transition. Section 4 presents the results obtained from a first implementation of SMMicro. It should be noted that this model and therefore its validation, is characterized by being mostly theoretical, so there are empirical implications that are not within the scope of the project. Finally, Section 5 details conclusions.

2 Related Work

Based on the difficulties that the traditional monolithic approach has, Villamizar [3] analyze the evolution to microservices through Service Oriented Architecture (SOA), and Balalaie [4] focus on the use of microservices and the different components of a distributed architecture. In a more detailed way Salah [5] shows an analysis of how was the evolution of this approach and the types of tools that have been used, such as Remote Procedure Call (RPC), Simple Object Access Protocol (SOAP), Representa-

tional State Transfer (REST), among others. In this context, the decomposition of monolithic systems is not detailed, unlike researchers such as Escobar [6], Levcovitz [7] or Ahmadvand [8] that clearly define decomposition as one of the most relevant aspects in a migration. They deal with several decomposition methodologies and some problems and limitations that can be found in case studies. Fowler [9] and Dragoni [10] analyze the future impact that can have a migration to microservices and therefore the elements that must be discussed for a successful objectives fulfillment. In the same context, it is vital to associate these principles with the different components that structure microservices, so Bakshi [11] and Sanchez [12] expose some key elements that facilitate the construction and deployment of distributed architectures.
Finally, as we have seen, the microservices architecture, is constantly evolving and growing, so, within the goals proposed in this work, we have the construction of a scheme that facilitates the transition to microservices, focus on the decomposition of monolithic web systems and the different elements involved in a migration. This work is elaborated trying to integrate and organize ideas, techniques and methodologies already proposed in the literature, as well as validate it on a case study that allows us to refine certain empirical aspects and discover new experiences that complement our study. Thus, the contribution of the work is significant in three well-defined aspects: facilitate design decisions for transition to microservices, reduce the number of software risks when migrating to microservices, and to improve the comprehensibility of the main changes in a decomposition to microservices.

3 Methodological proposal

This section develops the methodological proposal that will and also presents the construction of the SMMicro scheme, since, although there is no mechanical process to follow, there are several strategies defined by authors that facilitate the extraction of transition guidelines.

3.1 Migration from Monolithic Architecture to Microservices

It is important to emphasize that, from the point of view of the microservice system, the organizational design includes the structure, authority direction, granularity and composition of the equipment. A good design of microservice systems covers the implications of changing these organizational properties, considering that a good service design is a byproduct of a good organizational design. It is also important to analyze how the application is structured prior to a migration.
Organizational Impact. In the article titled "How Committees In-vent" from 1967, it was argued that the design of a software system will imitate the communication structure of the organization that produced it [2]. Conway's law, as known, has had a recent renaissance in microservice circles. Most of the pioneers of microservice architectures propose faster software delivery by optimizing organizational design instead of addressing software architecture, agreeing Conway's decades-old assertion [2]. Therefore, it is crucial to examine the organizational structure and the current state of

the system to be migrated. In order to apply a transformation strategy, it is important to: analyze the status and documentation of the system to be migrated in relation to the organization. Identify problematic areas in the organizational design. Identify safe transformations (changes that do not change existing behavior).

Decomposition of monolithic systems. The difficulties of division into microservices depend entirely on the complexity of the monolithic application. An application with many features will require great architectural effort and careful deliberation to decompose successfully. There are several steps to fragment a monolithic, among them, to identify the components that can be used as independent services. Authors like [1] and [13] recommend selecting the main general functionalities of the monolithic and then to divide those functionalities into small independent components. However, there are other proposals such as decomposition by context, maturity or access to data, each one of them employed in a way that the microservices should be as simple as possible, or the company will replace a monolithic software with several smaller monoliths [14].

Microservices ecosystem. It is considered as microservices ecosystem the environment where they will be built and deployed; this because the microservices are extracted from an entire infrastructure that includes hardware, networks, generation stack, distribution, detection of services and load balancers [15]. All of this is part of the infrastructure of the microservice ecosystem, its construction, standardization and maintenance must therefore be stable, scalable, fault tolerant and reliable. A proposal that covers these aspects for microservices can be divided into four layers, the three lower layers are the infrastructure layers. At the bottom of the model we find the hardware layer and the communication layer, followed by the application platform and finally the fourth layer where there are all the microservices [15].

Components for architectures with microservices. Once the different aspects of the microservice ecosystem have been analyzed, we can carry out a detailed study by specifying each component separately and then fitting them into each layer in order to obtain a clearer scheme of an architecture based on microservices. It should be emphasized that the use of the components detailed below will depend on the analyzed system and the requirements that it needs.

- *Discovery Server:* The so-called registration server or discovery server is used to delimit and provide the end-points of the services to be consumed. It obtains available instances of each microservice and allows to each microservice to know what another one executes in case of having some type of communication [15]. It should be considered that it can also be include a *Configuration Server* component that centralizes and remotely provides the configuration of each microservice. It is responsible for making changes to our APIs without re-implementing code. This also refers to the minimum dependence that must exist between each service.
- *Load Balancing:* It allows a balance between the different instances in a transparent way when consuming a service. It can be implemented as part of the service orchestration and in addition, it can obtain available instances of the registration server [1].
- *Circuit Breaker:* When having a distributed architecture, the risk of failure in the communication is evident. For this reason, this component is responsible for preventing the propagation of a failure to the rest of the application and ensure at least the performance of some services. It is based mainly on three status [1]: Closed (occurs

when the microservice works normally); Open (occurs when there is some type of failure); SemiOpen (occurs every certain time to know if the service is already available to enable it or it is down to keep it isolated).

- *Edge Server:* This edge or perimeter service in most cases is an API Gateway where the services to be consumed are exposed. Its main function is to become a single entry point to handle customer requests, regardless the means of access (mobile or web), or even, although it is more complex several APIs can be created depending on the requirements of each consumer group [13]. In this way, it isolates the customers of the application divided into microservices and all the outside traffic is routed to the corresponding internal services.
- *Message Broker:* When talking about this component we can find two different contexts. In one hand, we have a messaging pattern between microservices, and, on the other hand, an architecture based on events to manage data [13]. Thus, the communication between microservices can be synchronous if they communicate directly with each other, or asynchronous if there is a message broker that manages their communication. However, this component is more relevant in terms of data management, since each microservice manages its own relational or non-relational database, there will always be a dependency between them and therefore a message broker responsible for managing its transactions and for keeping an event log that guarantee the transactions in case of a failure. Given its close relationship between the communication and application layer, it can be applied in any of them.
- *Logging:* It refers to monitoring, and a log of all the relevant information, which allows developers to understand the status of the microservice with a log of information to prevent future problems [15]. Once the record of logs is matured, an additional component, such as *Alerts,* can be proposed to notify when a microservice is having an unusual behavior. In general, this type of alerts are programmed based on a record of the behavior that a service has had, whether in a normal, dangerous or critical state. Later, this will allow us to establish behavior rules to identify minimum damages that may evolve in catastrophes.
- *Dashboards:* They focus on monitoring that all the functionalities of the system are active and their respective connections with the database [15]. They accurately reflect the state of the microservices, are easily coupled with the components such as Service Discovery or Message Broker and are built in such a way that anyone could understand the software's status.
- *Hardware:* While hardware is not a component, when dealing with microservices we must choose an adequate physical environment to execute them. Nowadays there are a large number of technologies that offer services in the cloud, for not spend on physical servers to host software components. So, it is well known that the most relevant aspects to analyze in a migration are the use of IaaS and PaaS, since they encapsulate our microservices in such a way that they are isolated in containers or virtual machines to achieve better stability and resistance. However, this will depend on the amount of resources used by the system to be migrated, and also on the resources available in the company, since you can contract services in the cloud or use your own servers.

3.2 Delimitation of a Conceptual Model

In the methodological proposal there is a crucial point that is the delimitation of a conceptual model that allows to encapsulate the guidelines that will later be used for migration to microservices. A conceptual model, if correctly applied, must achieve the following fundamental objectives [16], [17]: Improve the understanding of the individuals regarding representative system. Provide a reference point to extract future specifications. Be sufficiently transparent so that those interested in the project feel comfortable using it to discuss the mechanisms that are relevant in the system.
Thus, we have composed our conceptual model through the following stages.
1. Comprehension. Once analyzed the different studies and theories about microservices, the first step is to understand the activities to be carried out by the managers of the company that owns the system. The institution should be informed and motivated on what is the schedule, objectives, scope and the benefits that will be obtained by including a transformation not only of the application, but also of possible changes in the organizational culture when developing software. Thus, as assistance tools to facilitate the change in the company, we proposed: migration planning and migration scope documentation.
When we talk about *understanding* we also refer to the understanding of the system to be migrated. This is important because we must understand how the application was built, including its background, development methodology, domain model, database structure, architecture, among others. It should be noted that in case the information is not updated it is recommended to carry out an analysis divided into two parts. First, a background section that helps us to understand the requirements for which the application was created, and second, an analysis of the current state that allows us to understand how the system evolved and the implications of making a transformation to microservices on that application. To do this, it can be done an analysis of: Development methodologies; Functional Requirements; Non-Functional Requirements; Global Package Diagram; Classes belonging to system packages; Logical Scheme; Physical Scheme; Initial Domain Model; Design pattern; Physical Architecture.
2. Decomposition. Once the comprehension stage is completed, the decomposition of the monolith continues. For this purpose, the different existing decomposition patterns are analyzed and the ones that best adapt to our application are selected, both in software modules and in the database. For an optimal decomposition, as already mentioned in [13], the operations of the system must be defined, therefore, we can use the following tools to facilitate the study: Class model; Domain Model; Table with functionalities.
At this point it should be emphasized that this proposal is limited to minimally constructed systems with software layered model, since once the functions of the system are identified, we proceed to group these functionalities in future microservices on the business and data layers, through: List of possible microservices; Divided Domain Model Diagram; Diagram of Decomposed Database; Entities Database Model; Table with sensitive entities by number of relations; Querys on the Database; Comparative table of reading and writing entities. Once the diagrams of possible decompositions are structured, a comparison is done to determine the level of dependence between

the business and data layer, to finally define an optimal decomposition. It is proposed the use and realization of: Testing in the system production environment; Matrix with calls from the persistence layer to the Database; Final decomposition diagram.

3. Association. Once the final decomposition is done, each element must be coupled within the layers of the microservice ecosystem. This is proposed as the third stage of our model, where the components and tools that best adapt to our case study should be used. It must be considered that, although all the layers of the ecosystem are necessary, the components that each one uses will depend on the analyzed application, that is, based on the resources of the company and the different scenarios where it is proposed to put into production the system. They can be chosen several, all, or even more components of those that have been stated throughout this proposal. Thus, we start from layer four where our ecosystem core is built with the microservices previously decomposed, both in the business and data layers. We continue with layer three where we analyze the application platform, so, in conjunction with the necessary components that can be adapted to layer four we can have everything referred to communication and finally the deployment of the different functionalities that were proposed for every microservice. For this, we use consecutively: List of feasible components to integrate in the analyzed system; Components diagram for each layer of microservice ecosystem; System diagram based on the entire microservices ecosystem.

4. Validation. Once the distributed architecture has been established within the microservice ecosystem, we can establish two stages for its validation. The first stage is responsible for the overall operation of the system, simulating that the internal structure of each microservice is unknown, and focusing on ensuring that the integration has not affected the interoperability between them. It must be considered that the system must comply with the same functionalities that it had prior to the migration. This verification can be done with black box testing, in different environments with compatibility testing. The second stage is responsible for evaluating intrinsic factors in a microservice ecosystem such as stability, reliability, scalability and performance, through questions that can be selected from the study of Susan Fowler [15].

3.3 Scheme for Migration towards Microservices

The SMMicro Guideline is defined with the previously defined conceptual model in section 3.2. Figure 1 presents these guidelines with its respective justifications and activities, in an easy way to understand and use. For its implementation on a system, first we must verify the observations proposed for each stage. Once considered it, we can follow the guidelines shown in Figure #, starting from stage 1 to stage 4. This model only proposes a general framework to mitigate errors during the migration to microservices. It doesn't define step by step what the development team, testing team or other members of the migration team must do. Depending on the monolith, different strategies will be implemented such as Strangler Application Pattern developed, presented in depth by Kyle G. Brown [18].

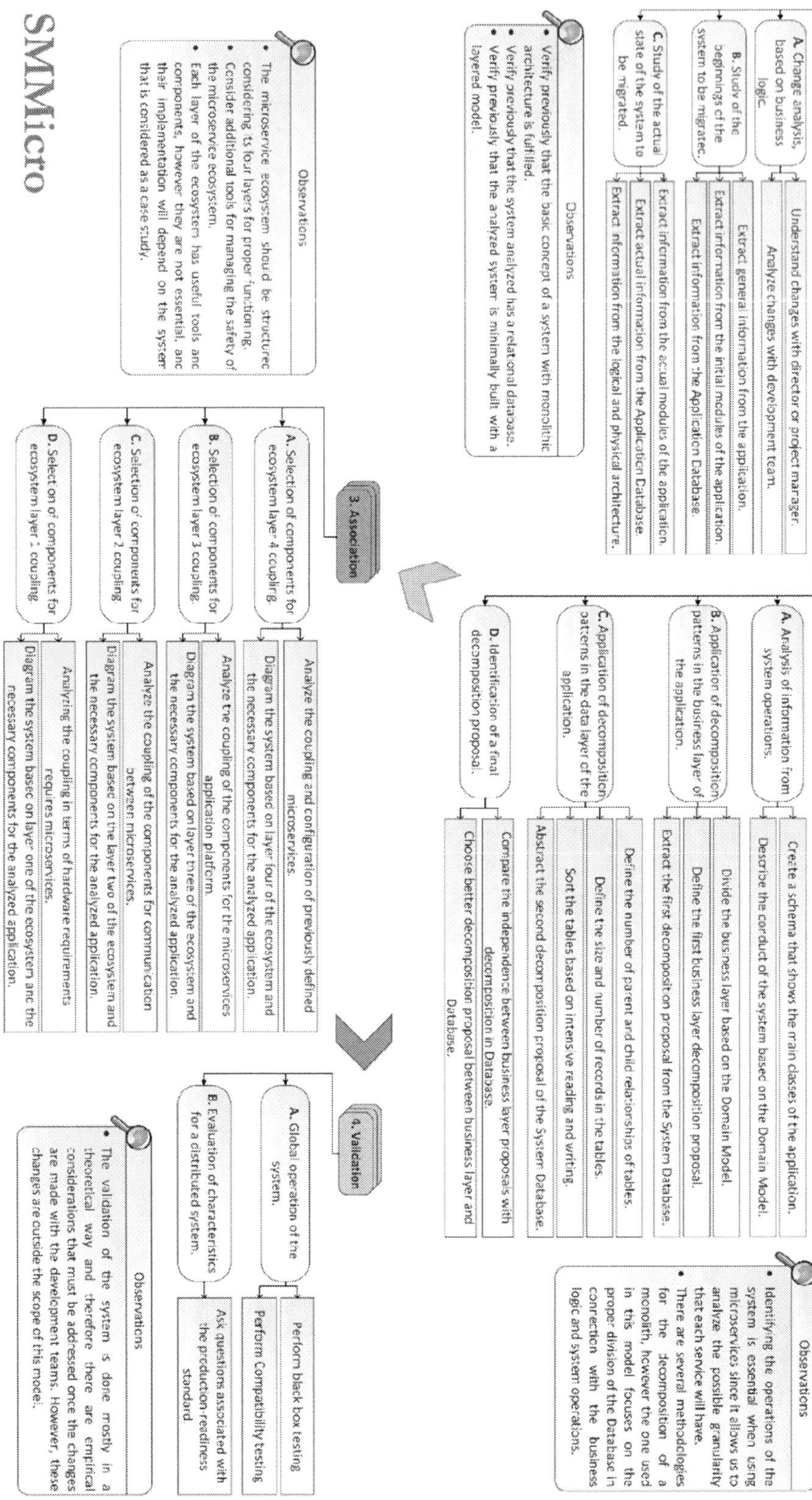

Fig. 1. SMMIcro

4 Implementation of the Methodological Proposal

This Section focuses on the results obtained from a first implementation of the methodological proposal in conjunction with the SMMicro scheme. To carry out this implementation, a case study has been established as a research methodology, which is defined as the intensive study of an object of study. As case study, we took a Management and Administration System for Laboratories (SISLAB) in a University where the software is in a process of optimization and improvement of architectures. We could identify a convenient case study defining a minimum set of requirements based on the difficulties of the previously analyzed monolithic architectures. The system chosen was developed as a web application that allows users to take control of inventories, as well as billing and administration of the services offered to the student community and the public in general. However, there are some changes in the business logic since adaptations were implemented due to the large scale of laboratories that the institution currently has. It was coded in JAVA language and developed based on the J2EE business standard, using a layer architecture: The Data Layer, implemented using PostgreSQL, the Intermediate Layer, implemented using the JBoss Server and JSF Framework. And finally, the communication of the client is through the Presentation Layer.

4.1 Analysis of Results

Among the most relevant results we have the final decomposition of the database of the SISLAB, according to the previously founded decomposition methodologies. With this, each schema of the database responds to its corresponding microservice of the business logic, therefore, we have a reduction of dependence compared with the structure of the system's initial database. As a point of consideration, the existing dependence can only be reduced, but not mitigated, since, with the migration there are factors of business logic that will remain constant over the time, and the only way to change them is redesigning the system from scratch, which is not considered nor making changes that affect the consumer customer's functionality experience.

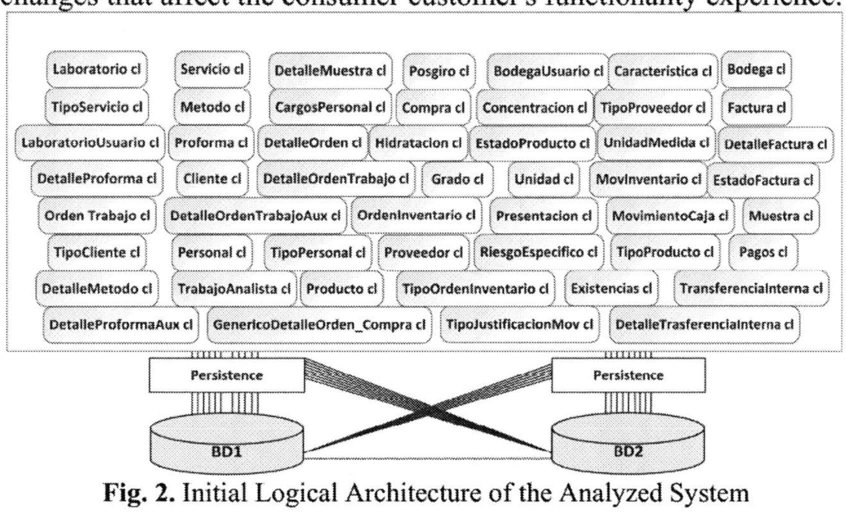

Fig. 2. Initial Logical Architecture of the Analyzed System

Figure 3 shows the scheme obtained from the relationship between the business and the data layers. It shows the decomposition that best groups the existing classes in the system, considering that now it is intended to use three databases for the three proposed microservices, a fourth database for the billing module that is currently managed separately, and finally a fifth database that manages the isolated tables from the functions of the application, as well as future implementations that need to expand the number of entities or tables in the system.
As a transcendental result, we also show the structure of the system in the different layers of the microservice ecosystem. It should also be noted that prior to the hardware layer there is already an important structure where its implementation will depend only on the entity that owns the application. In this case, the institution must decide if it proposes an implementation based on cloud, or if it makes use of the physical servers available and uses an implementation like the one shown in Figure 4 with hybrid cloud. The results also show that there is a considerable increase in the number of components so that the system can be managed properly. However, as mentioned at the beginning, SMMicro is not a recipe that can be followed to obtain the best result with microservices.

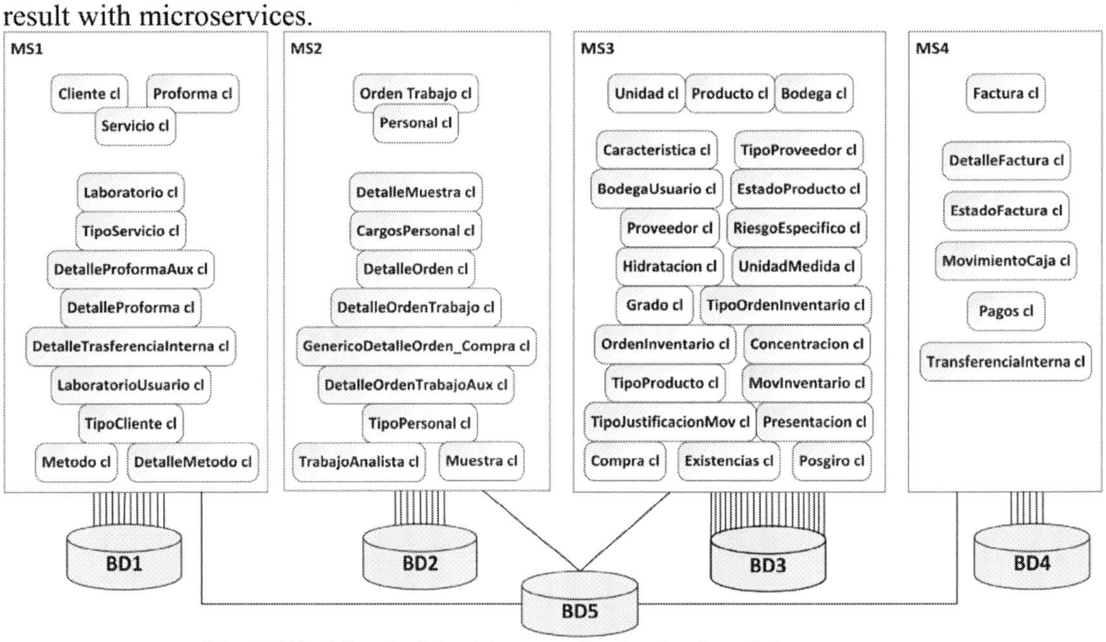

Fig. 3. Final Logical Architecture for the Analyzed System

The methodological proposal is only a point of reference that helps those in charge of migration to have a more adequate vision about the changes, so many components will be necessary or not, according to the analyzed application.

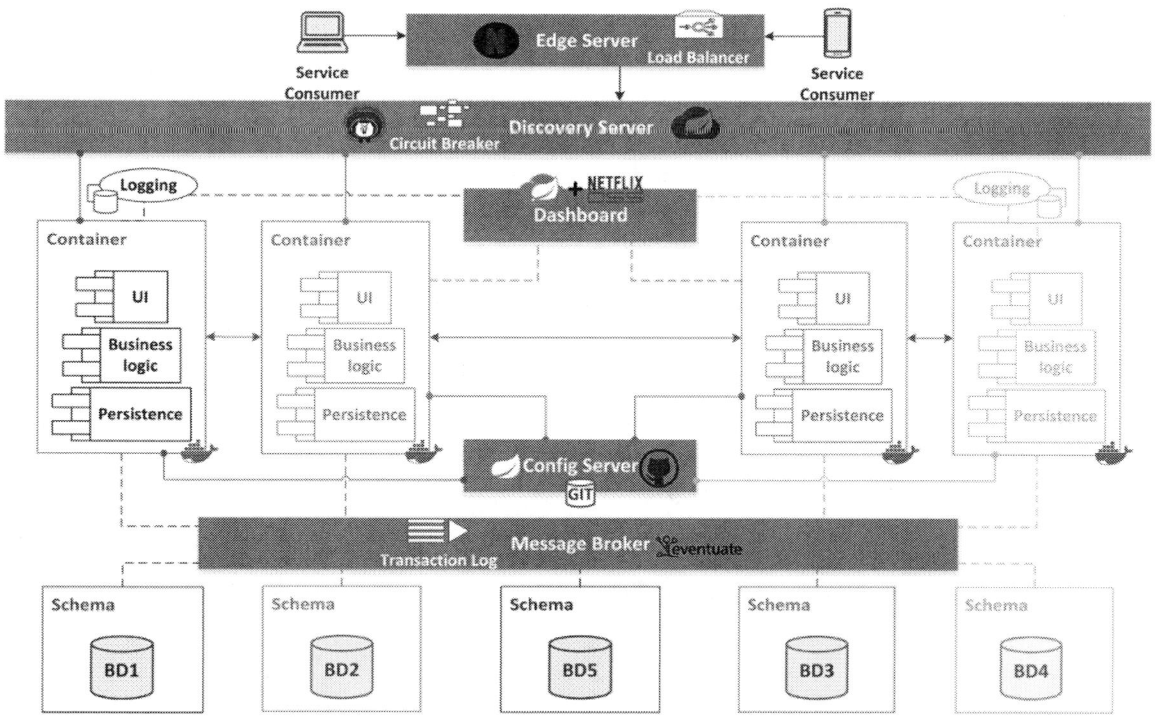

Fig.4. Final Physical Architecture for the Analyzed System

5 Conclusions

The general objective of this project, which was to elaborate a methodological proposal for the migration towards an architecture based on microservices, was carried out and shaped through four stages. Each stage proposed guidelines with their respective justifications, activities to perform, possible tools that can be used, and the pertinent considerations and recommendations. It is also proposed to encapsulate the methodological proposal, easy to abstract, through a graphic scheme called Scheme for Migration towards Microservices (SMMicro).

In order to determine the necessary components for a decomposition of microservices starting from a monolithic architecture, an analysis of the state of the art was carried out with different articles and books where several main components coincided. However, the implementation of each one of these depend on the case study system since they cannot be treated in a standard way. It was also found that not only certain components are necessary for the architecture, but also a complete ecosystem of microservices where they can coexist. Finally, in the validation on a case study, it was not possible to identify the total use of the proposed components for microservices, since the system was only adapted to the scope of this project, and there is still the stage of implementation of the design for future work, where evidently new observations, corrections and additions will be found to this first version of SMMicro.

In the analysis of the methodological proposal, some types of decomposition were examined, although not all of them since there may be *n* strategies that will depend on the context in which they are going to be applied. An important recommendation is to be clear that we do not only handle microservices, but also a range of components and tools that must be implemented in different layers within an ecosystem. In addition, it is recommended to previously establish how the application evolved over time, since there are functionalities that can be discarded due to lack of use or, on the contrary, functionalities that need greater scalability for certain scenarios. A key axis is the Domain Model since it allows us to define the functions of the application and define a starting point for a decomposition strategy. Regarding the association stage, an analysis based on the different layers of the microservices ecosystem was seen, where the selection of the necessary components for the proper functioning of the proposed microservices is emphasized. It is also highlighted that the hardware layer evidences the work in conjunction with the infrastructure area of the institution, showing once again the need for a collaborative work of the entire institution for the production of an efficient distributed architecture. As a final conclusion, an architecture based on microservices provides multiple benefits, taking into account several complications in its implementation. Therefore, our methodological proposal through SMMicro can become a point of reference to facilitate a migration starting from a monolith, however, it must be validated in more case studies according to similar contexts that were taken in the selection of the analyzed system.

References

1. E. Wolff, Microservices Flexible Software Architecture. United States: Addison-Wesley, 2017.
2. I. Nadareishvili, R. Mitra, M. McLarty, and M. Amundsen, Microservice Architecture Aligning Principles, Practices and Culture. United States: O'Reilly, 2016.
3. M. Villamizar et al., "Evaluating the monolithic and the microservice architecture pattern to deploy web applications in the cloud," in Computing Colombian Conference (10CCC), 2015 10th, 2015, pp. 583-590: IEEE.
4. A. Balalaie, A. Heydarnoori, and P. Jamshidi, "Migrating to cloud-native architectures using microservices: an experience report," in European Conference on Service-Oriented and Cloud Computing, 2015, pp. 201-215: Springer.
5. T. Salah, M. J. Zemerly, C. Y. Yeun, M. Al-Qutayri, and Y. Al-Hammadi, "The evolution of distributed systems towards microservices architecture," in Internet Technology and Secured Transactions (ICITST), 2016 11th International Conference, 2016, pp. 318-325: IEEE.
6. D. Escobar et al., "Towards the understanding and evolution of monolithic applications as microservices," in Computing Conference (CLEI), 2016 XLII Latin American, 2016, pp. 1-11: IEEE.
7. A. Levcovitz, R. Terra, and M. T. Valente, "Towards a Technique for Extracting Microservices from Monolithic Enterprise Systems," arXiv preprint arXiv:1605.03175, 2016.
8. M. Ahmadvand and A. Ibrahim, "Requirements Reconciliation for Scalable and Secure Microservice (De) composition," in Requirements Engineering Conference Workshops (REW), IEEE International, 2016, pp. 68-73: IEEE.
9. M. Fowler, "Microservices a definition of this new architectural term," Accessed on: 2017-03Available: https://martinfowler.com/articles/microservices.html

10. N. Dragoni, S. Dustdar, S. T. Larsen, and M. Mazzara, "Microservices: Migration of a mission critical system," arXiv preprint arXiv:1704.04173, 2017.
11. K. Bakshi, "Microservices-based software architecture and approaches," in Aerospace Conference, 2017 IEEE, 2017, pp. 1-8: IEEE.
12. D. Sánchez, "Arquitectura de microservicios," Accessed on: 2017-07Available: http://enmilocalfunciona.io/arquitectura-microservicios-1/
13. C. Richardson, Microservice Patterns MEAP. United States of America: Manning Publications Co, 2017.
14. C. Carneiro and T. Schmelmer, Microservices from day One. Florida: Apress, 2016.
15. S. J. Fowler, Production-Ready Microservices. United States of America: O'Reilly, 2016.
16. C. Kung and A. Soelvberg, "Activity modeling and behavior modeling," in Proc. of the IFIP WG 8.1 working conference on Information systems design methodologies: improving the practice, 1986, pp. 145-171: North-Holland Publishing Co.
17. S. Robinson, G. Arbez, L. G. Birta, A. Tolk, and G. Wagner, "Conceptual modeling: definition, purpose and benefits," in Proceedings of the 2015 Winter Simulation Conference, 2015, pp. 2812-2826: IEEE Press.
18. K. Brown "Apply the Strangler Application pattern to microservices applications," *IBM Developer Works,* p. 6, 2017.

MoProPEI-MP an Adaptation in the Selection of Process Mining Tools for Software Processes

Silvia Jaqueline Urrea-Contreras[1], Brenda Leticia Flores-Rios[1], María Angélica Astorga-Vargas[2], Jorge Eduardo Ibarra Esquer[2], Félix Fernando González-Navarro[1]

[1] Universidad Autónoma de Baja California, Instituto de Ingeniería, Mexicali, B. C. México
{jaqueline.urrea, brenda.flores, fernando.gonzalez}@uabc.edu.mx
[2] Universidad Autónoma de Baja California, Facultad de Ingeniería, Mexicali, B. C. México
{angelicaastorga,jorge.ibarra}@uabc.edu.mx

Abstract. Software organizations produce evidence of the execution of their activities, which can be processed with algorithms, supported by process mining tools, and used to discover, monitor and improve processes. Different kinds of process mining tools have been developed, which has resulted in challenges for their selection or adoption according to the algorithms or techniques that each one of them handles. MoProPEI-MP is presented as an adaptation of a process model for information exploitation projects, oriented to guide in the identification and selection of algorithms and tools of process mining. The evaluation of the adaptation of the model was endorsed by 17 primary studies obtained from a literature review, identifying the most reported process mining tools used in software processes case studies. Also, it presents the traceability with all the tasks of the activities of MoProPEI-MP.

Keywords: Process mining, software processes, process mining tools, MoPro-PEI-MP.

1 Introduction

Process Mining (PM) can be considered a proficient means for helping organizations understand their actual way of carrying out the activities (event log) of each process and serves as a foundation for process improvement [1]. Also, PM provides the techniques, algorithms or tools needed to explore and exploit the event log [2]. According to [3], PM applied to Software Engineering contributes to solve critical problems in monitoring, control and improvement of the software development process. However, this transdisciplinarity is not trivial. There are organizations dedicated to software development and maintenance that face challenges in management and implementation of software projects or Software Process Improvement (SPI), highlighting among them the need to exploit existing information in their repositories or use tools to collect, record, classify and evaluate evidence of the execution of activities when the volume and complexity of the information are significant [4]. A practitioner in the software area or responsible of SPI project knows that the data stored in their different repositories (process model repositories) are not the most relevant for monitoring or determining the capacity level of the processes. The implicit knowledge (tacit knowledge) exists between relationships and dependencies of the event logs that are stored in database tables, message logs, mail archives, transaction logs and other data sources [1]. In Latin America, the experience that these types of organizations have acquired in SPI projects, since about ten years ago, has challenged them to search for algorithms, techniques and tools for PM and Business Intelligence that allow them to comply more rigorously with software process models or standards, establish the validity and reliability of the analysis of evidence and/or seek solutions to problems in the scalability of information [4]. Recently, various PM tools have been developed and when using PM, a resource to be considered is the time invested on locating, selecting, converting and filtering the events logs in an admissible format required as input by the PM tools, such as: csv, xls, mxml, xes. This becomes a critical scenario for the responsible for knowledge base that requires knowing some aspects related to the characteristics and volume of information that you wish to manipulate, while others indicate how they should present the information for its exploitation [5]. For example, answer questions such as which PM tools exist in the market, which PM algorithms or techniques should be selected to assist software project management team, or what is the expected outcome.

Under this context, the importance of having an evaluation framework or process model for the selection of PM algorithms and tools that impact on SPI projects of software development organizations. The process model for information exploitation projects (MoProPEI - Modelo de Procesos para Proyectos de Explotación de Información) proposed by [6] was selected because it offers the creation of tacit knowledge from a data mining process, focused on management [6]. Also, MoProPEI allows the adaptation of activities and artifacts (work-products) oriented to the identification and selection of PM algorithms and tools that can be used in software projects or software processes. We present an adaptation of MoProPEI with a focus on PM applied to software processes called MoProPEI-MP.

This document is structured as follows: section 2 shows the state of the art related to data mining, PM and PM tools. Section 3 describes the characteristics of MoProPEI and functional features of MoProPEI-MP. Section 4 evaluates its impact by means of the identification of 17 primary studies oriented to PM tools used by software process improvement case studies. Using four tasks of the Modeling process of MoProPEI-MP, we can compare 17 primary studies that provide the difference in terms of the way of to identify, select and implement PM tools. Finally, the conclusions and future work are presented in section 5.

2 State of the art

The exploitation of information focuses on the generation of pieces of knowledge from the implementation of algorithms belonging to the field of data mining, or other types of mining [6]. This document is focused on Process Mining (PM), so the following section presents its definition, its relationship with data mining, and PM tools.

2.1 Data Mining and Process Mining

Data mining is one of the stages in the knowledge extraction process from databases [7]. In general, data mining refers to the application of specific algorithms to extract patterns (models) from the data by using automatic tools that use sophisticated algorithms to discover patterns, associations, anomalies and/or structures of the large amount of data existing and to filter the necessary information from large databases [8,9]. Besides, PM is a discipline that is located between the computational intelligence and data mining, and it is composed of a series of tools and techniques based on data mining [10] and related algorithms [1]. The main purpose of PM is to discover, monitor and improve the processes identified by organizations based on their event logs [11]. In the last decade, a variety of PM algorithms and PM tools have been proposed [12] that at the same time represent a point of reference due to the difficulty of comparing them because they show differences in functionality and performance [11]. Some of them are: the rules of association, petri nets, alpha algorithm, clustering, genetic miner, heuristic miner, and decision trees.

In the research of [13] a comparative study between heuristic, fuzzy and genetic PM algorithms has been carried out, providing a guide, explaining and specifying the output that will be obtained, when using them, the behavior and challenging problems that can be present with its their implementation. Likewise, [12] presents a framework for the selection of PM algorithms and the measurement of their efficiency based on data mining techniques. Also, it highlights the existence of metrics for the measurement of the quality of the results of mining processes; such as adjustment, simplicity, precision and generalization [11].

2.2 Process Mining Tools

There are two types of PM tools. Some of the commercial PM tools are: Disco developed by Fluxicon, ARIS Process Performance Manager (PPM) by Software AG, Futura Reflect by Futura Process Intelligence, ProcessAnalyzer by QPR, Comprehend, and BPM One. Besides, in the open-source tools, currently, version 6.7 of ProM is available, which can be downloaded for free and implemented in java with a variety of algorithms and process mining techniques (heuristic, genetic, fuzzy, alpha, region-based, among others), which are handled as complements. Nevertheless, based on the vendor every PM tool can either support partial or extended PM techniques [1].

A problem that arises with these technological proposals is the lack of standardization and the fact that the tools use their own guidelines and formats (csv, xls, mxml, xes). This can be confusing for a PM user to decide which (is) the most suitable tool (s) for his project [14]. Sometimes, the selection or acquisition of an inadequate tool derives from the existence of diverse suppliers and commercial and open-source tools that allow performing the task without having an objective method of selection.

3 An Adaptation of the MoProPEI Model to Process Mining (MoProPEI-MP)

MoProPEI is focused on the development of information exploitation engineering projects, establishing phases, activities, tasks, techniques and procedures [6]. The right side of Fig. 1 shows the Development sub-process, composed of six phases: Understanding the domain, Understanding the data, Modeling, Data preparation, Implementation, Evaluation and presentation.

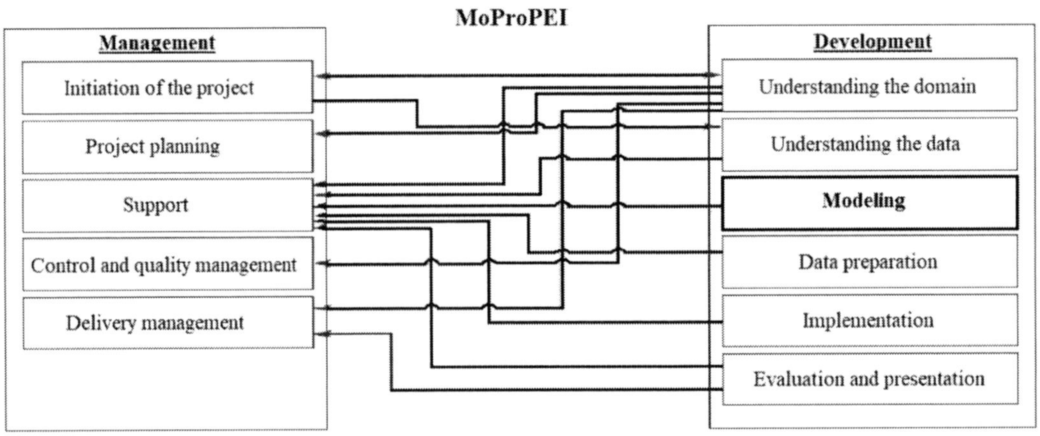

Fig. 1. General Structure of MoProPEI (Translated from [6])

From these phases, we found that the Modeling phase contains two activities related to identifying and selecting data mining algorithms and tools. The objective of the first activity, A1.Modeling the problem, is to define the problem by means of a technical vocabulary and to determine techniques for exploiting information to be implemented in order to solve the identified problems. This activity comprises the following tasks: T1.1 Define the problem of exploiting information and T1.2 Model the problem of exploitation of information. Otherwise, the second activity, A2.Setting the model, has the objective of establishing the tools and algorithms to be applied based on the problem and the previously identified techniques. It includes the tasks: T2.1 Identify alternative tools, T2.2 Select tools, T2.3 Identify data mining algorithms, and T2.4 Select data mining algorithms [6].

The most important characteristic of MoProPEI is the adaptability to the needs of the project that is under development [6]. So, it was contextualized for its use under a PM approach. This adaptation was called MoProPEI-MP. This way, the sub-processes Management and Development are considered as category of processes, the phases are analyzed as processes, and the activities, tasks and work-products are specified towards the identification and selection of algorithms and tools for PM.

In this document, we present only the activities (A1 and A2), tasks (T1.1, T1.2, T2.1, T2.2, T2.3 and T2.4) and work-products of the Modeling process of Development category. In the Modeling process, the tasks of A1.Modeling of the problem are: T1.1. Define the problem to be solved based on the business problems identified under a PM approach, and T1.2. Model the problem to solve for the identification of the solution. The tasks of A2. Setting the model are: T2.1. Identify the PM algorithms from the problems to solve and the identification of the solution, T2.2. Select the PM algorithms based on the identified PM algorithms, T2.3. Identify the PM tools from the problems to solve with the identification of the solution and the selected processes PM algorithms, and T2.4. Select the PM tool taking into account the PM tools identified. Table 1 lists the seven work-products created and used by activities A1 and A2. Both activities were defined by a process pattern (Table 2) consisting of the tasks, objectives, and input and output work-products.

Table 1. Work-products identified in MoProPEI-MP Modeling process

Work products
WP1. Business problems identified.
WP2. Problems to be solve.
WP3. Identification of the solution.
WP4. Process mining algorithms identified.
WP5. Selected process mining algorithms.
WP6. Process mining tools identified.
WP7. Selected process mining tools.

In the original model MoProPEI, the activities were not subject to a consecutive flow. However, in MoProPEI-MP a sequential workflow was established (Fig. 2) to guide in the most appropriate selection of the PM tool according to the problem identified. Fig. 2 shows how the output work-product of T2.2 (WP5) is an input work-product of T2.3 and the output work-product of T2.3 (WP6) is an input work-product of T2.4.

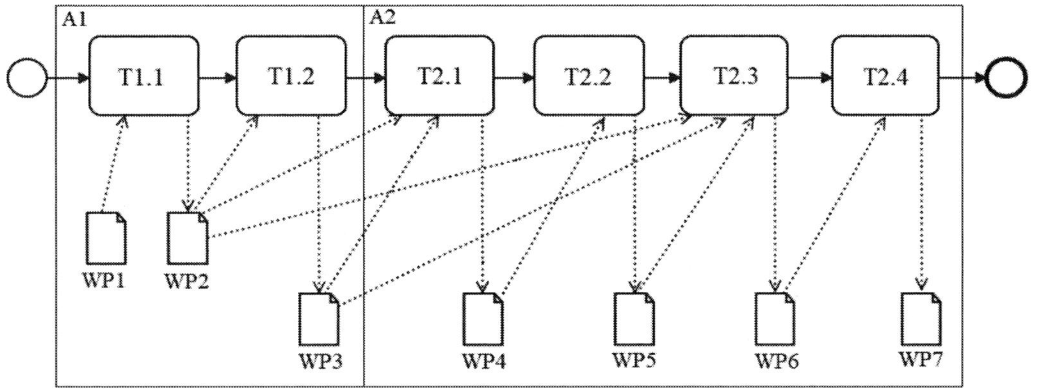

Fig. 2. Workflow of tasks related to activities A1 and A2 for the MoProPEI-MP Modeling process

Mature software organizations have been effective in collecting, organizing and storing a large amount of data from their daily activities (event log). However, they do not have PM algorithms or tools as to turn them into knowledge to be employed in SPI activities. In this section, we present the MoProPEI-MP as a feasible and useful PM model for these organizations (Table 2), which assures the reliability in the identification and selection of PM algorithms and tools through six tasks.

Table 2. Description of the MoProPEI-MP Modeling process as a process pattern

Modeling Process	
Activities	
A1. Modeling the problem	A2. Setting the model
Objectives	
O1.1 Determine by technical vocabulary the problems to be solved according to the identified business problems. O1.2 Represent the problem through an event log or a process model so that it is possible to identify the process mining algorithms to be used.	O2.1 Determine the process mining algorithms to be used based on the characteristics of the identification of the solution. O2.2 Determine the set of process mining tools in the market that satisfy the identification demands of the solution, analyzing its advantages and disadvantages and the algorithms that support it. O2.3 Formalize the selection of the chosen tool(s) to solve the problem.
Tasks	
T1.1 Define the *Problems to be solved* based on the *Business problems identified* under a process mining approach. T1.2 Model the *Problem to be solve* for the *Identification of the solution* under the process mining approach.	T2.1 Identify the *Process mining algorithms* from the *Problems to be solved* and the *Identification of the solution.* T2.2 Select the *Process mining algorithms* based on the *Process mining algorithms identified.* T2.3 Identify the *Process mining tools* from the *Problems to be solve* with the *Identification of the solution* and the *Selected process mining algorithms.* T2.4 Select the *Process mining tool* taking into account the *Process mining tools identified.*
Input work-products	
T1.1: WP1 T1.2: WP2	T2.1: WP2, WP3 T2.2: WP4 T2.3: WP2, WP3, WP5 T2.4: WP6
Output work-products	
T1.1: WP2 T1.2: WP3	T2.1: WP4 T2.2: WP5 T2.3: WP6 T2.4: WP7

4 Evaluation of MoProPEI-MP

Some papers have already proposed the application of PM in the software process context [1]. To evaluate a traceability of the tasks of MoProPEI-MP with the related work in the discipline of PM since 2007, a literature review was carried out under the methodology presented in [15]. The main goal was to identify updated information on the PM algorithms and tools that are reported in SPI projects. The following sections present the results of each of the phases used in the review.

4.1 Identify the Primary Studies

The Primary Studies (PS) identification process consisted of the following seven steps:

- Step 1: List the selected information sources to monitor and compare the results obtained from them. The sources were: 1) IEEE Xplore, 2) Elsevier ScienceDirect, 3) Springer Link, and 4) ACM Digital Library.
- Step 2: Adapt the search string depending on the source of information in order to achieve a successful search. The search string was: ((Process Mining) AND (Software process improvement) AND (Process Mining Software OR Analysis and Adoption of Process Mining tools) AND (Organizations OR Enterprises OR Entities OR SMEs)).
- Step 3: Apply the first 3 inclusion criteria based on studies in the Spanish or English languages carried out during the period from 2007 to 2017 and which contain at least two words of the search string in the title and abstract.
- Step 4: Apply the remaining inclusion criteria to filter a document with important relevance in the research topic.
- Step 5: Apply exclusion criteria in order to eliminate those documents that are not relevant in information, repeated in two or more sources of information or that cannot be accessed.
- Step 6: Obtain filtered PS in accordance with the inclusion and exclusion criteria.
- Step 7: Save each PS with an identification number (PS1, PS2,..., PSn) for a later handling in the data extraction.

At the beginning of the process, we identified 23,127 studies in the information sources. Some of them mentioned PM algorithms and tools, but they were limited to presenting their titles as a work reference and clearly there is a gap in terms of how to apply PM algorithms and tools. So, after executing the search chain, complying with the inclusion and exclusion criteria, we analyzed the studies that present PM algorithms and tools giving a brief application of them and the scenario of use within SPI project. In this way, 17 PS were selected, assigned an identifier and classified by year of publication, author(s), title, type of document, validation of the use scenario, algorithms and tools that were used (Table 3).

Table 3. Summary of proposals that present process mining algorithms and tools in software process projects

ID	Year	Author(s)	Title
PS1	2011	Wouter Poncin, Alexander Serebrenik, Mark van den Brand	Process mining software repositories.
PS2	2011	Irina-Maria Ailenei	Process Mining Tools: A Comparative Analysis.
PS3	2011	Artini M. Lemos, et al.	Using Process Mining in Software Development.
PS4	2012	Wil van der Aalst, el al.	Process Mining Manifesto.
PS5	2012	Wil van der Aalst	Process Mining: Overview and Opportunities.
PS6	2012	Damián Pérez Alfonso, Raykenler Yzquierdo Herrera, Rogelio Silverio Castro, Manuel Lazo Cortés	Utilización de técnicas de minería de proceso en el entorno empresarial cubano.
PS7	2013	Damián Pérez Alfonso, Raykenler Yzquierdo Herrera, Manuel Lazo Cortés	Recommendation of Process Discovery Algorithms: a Classification Problem.
PS8	2014	Vladimir Rubin, Irina Lomazova, Wil van der Aalst	Agile Development with Software Process Mining.
PS9	2014	Esmita .P. Gupta	Process Mining A Comparative Study.
PS10	2014	Santiago Aguirre Mayorga, Carlos Parra	Metodología para la aplicación de minería de procesos.
PS11	2015	Wil van der Aalst	Extracting Event Data from Databases to Unleash Process Mining.
PS12	2015	Hugo Santiago Aguirre Mayorga, Nicolás Rincón García	Minería de procesos: desarrollo, aplicaciones y factores críticos.
PS13	2015	Swapnali B. Sonawane, Ravi P. Patki	Process Mining by using Event Logs.
PS14	2015	Anna A. Kalenkova, Wil van der Aalst, Irina A. Lomazova, Vladimir A. Rubin	Process mining using BPMN: relating event logs and process models.
PS15	2016	Paola E. Velazquez-Solis, et al.	Empiric Evidence of Process Mining in CMMI-DEV Implementation.
PS16	2016	Arturo Orellana García, Damián Pérez Alfonso, Vivian Estrada Sentí	Revisión de los principales modelos para aplicar técnicas de Minería de procesos.
PS17	2017	Arthur M. Valle, Eduardo A.P. Santos, Eduardo R. Loures	Applying process mining techniques in software process appraisals.

4.2 Implement and evaluate MoProPEI-MP

In this and the next steps, the 17 PS were analyzed in order to identify how they selected or proposed algorithms and PM tools. So, the tasks T1.1, T1.2, T2.1, T2.2, T2.3 and T2.4 of activities A1 and A2 of the MoProPEI-MP Modeling process were associated with the 17 PS, where ID={PS1, PS2, PS3, ..., PS17}. The tasks were grouped for the identification of both the PM algorithms and tools, in the tasks T2.1 with T2.3 and T2.2 with T2.4. The result is shown in Table 4, highlighting with gray the rows of the PS that meet the requirements of the A1 and A2 activities. PS1, PS2, PS3, PS6, PS8, PS11, PS12, PS17 fulfilled the tasks where at least one case study was described and used PM tools. It should be noted that 100% fulfilled the tasks T2.1 and T2.3 focused on the identification of algorithms and tools, 76.47% on the selection of algorithms and tools with tasks T2.2 and T2.4. For the A1 activity, we observed that only 58.82% of the PS defined the problem (T1.1) and 64.7% modeled the problem (T1.2).

Table 4. Mapping PS with the tasks of the MoProPEI-MP Modeling process

	A1 Modeling of the problem		A2 Setting the model	
ID	T1.1	T1.2	T2.1, T2.3	T2.2, T2.4
PS1	x	x	x	x
PS2	x	x	x	x
PS3	x	x	x	x
PS4			x	
PS5			x	x
PS6	x	x	x	x
PS7	x		x	x
PS8	x	x	x	x
PS9			x	x
PS10			x	x
PS11	x	x	x	x
PS12	x	x	x	x
PS13	x	x	x	
PS14		x	x	x
PS15			x	
PS16		x	x	
PS17	x	x	x	x

Besides, Table 5 presents the PM tools that were identified by the 17 PS. Some examples are: ProM, Futura Reflect, Aris PPM, Flow, Process Analyzer, Disco, Perceptive Process Mining and Celonis. We detected that some tools were proposed on more than one occasion and some PS did not implement the identified or selected PM tools. For these reason, in the same table we highlighted in gray only the PM tools that were used or implemented by the case studies in the PS.

The use of PM Tools has already been proposed by [16] to demonstrate that SCAMPI assessments are more objective by reducing human intervention. In PS1, PS3, PS6, and PS17, the implementation of PM tools is shown to support SPI projects. The case studies expose benefits in improved processes such as discovering the actual process compared to the documented process, and identification of practitioners executing activities in process. PS8 considered that software process mining approach improves communication with the customer and initiates continuous improvement into the agile development lifecycle.

Table 5. Identification and Implementation of process mining tools for each PS

PM Tools	PS1	PS2	PS3	PS6	PS8	PS11	PS12	PS17
ProM	x	x	x	x	x	x		x
Futura Reflect	x	x						
CPN Tools		x						
Aris PPM		x			x	x		
Flow		x						
ProcessAnalyzer		x			x			
Process Discovery Focus		x						
Comprehend		x						
Interstage Process Discovery		x				x		
Discovery Analyst		x				x		
Disco					x	x	x	
Perceptive Process Mining					x	x		
Celonis					x	x		
XMAnalyzer						x		

4.3 Identify the Process Mining algorithms and tools

Table 6 presents the percentage of PS in which each PM algorithms and tools were mentioned. Heuristic, genetic and fuzzy algorithms were mentioned only by 5.8%. The most mentioned tool was ProM, appearing in 76.4% of the PS. ProM is a free and open source PM toolset, developed by the Eindhoven University of Technology, and it has the capacity of storing unlimited records; it also generates BPMN models, workflows, Petri networks, among others and offers information filtering, process discovery, verification of the conformity and visualization of groupings. ProM imports event logs compliant with MXML or XES formats and can load process model definitions in different standards.

5 Conclusions

Since PM is a young discipline, the proposals in practical as well as theoretical cases, both in their algorithms and in tools, are constant, so this line of research must be persistent in order to be able to contrast the factors that can be offered. We show how PM can be embedded into software process because once we have a real workflow of processes; it will be possible to solve problems related to the efficiency in monitoring and control, conformance checking and enhancement of them.

Table 6. List of process mining tools and algorithms identified in 17 PS

PM tool and algorithms	Percentage
ProM	76.4%
Disco	41.1%
Aris PPM	35.3%
Futura Reflect, CPN Tools, Process Analyzer, Interstage Process Discovery, XESame, Perceptive Process Mining y Celonis	17.6%
FRASR, Flow, Comprehend, XMAnalyzer, In Concert, Enterprise Visualization Suite, Eventifier, Reflect one	5.8%
Heuristic, genetic and fuzzy algorithms	5.8%

The main objective of this document is the identification and selection of PM algorithms and tools that impact on SPI projects. We presented an adaptation of MoProPEI with a focus on PM applied to software processes called MoProPEI-MP. The process pattern of MoProPEI-MP is presented with the description of activities, tasks and work-products focused on the analysis of the characteristics to establish a clear approach in the processes of identification and selection of PM algorithms and tools. MoProPEI-MP was evaluated through the analysis of 17 PS from which it was possible to identify that the process mining algorithms and tools offer less interest in the tasks of problem identification and modeling (T1.1 and T1.2), giving greater emphasis to the identification and selection of PM algorithms and tools (T2.1, T2.2, T2.3 and T2.4). These latter tasks are handled jointly, which does not allow a deeper analysis of the advantages and disadvantages that they may offer. The ProM tool was identified and selected as the one that had the greatest application in the case studies of process improvement in the PS.

In addition, specifying new requirements related to PM algorithms in the development or use of software tools allows extracting or exploiting existing tacit and explicit knowledge in the repositories, intranets or information systems.

Acknowledgement

Scholarship from the Consejo Nacional de Ciencia y Tecnología (CONACYT) under number 634421 to the first author to carry out this project; and, financial support from Maestría y Doctorado en Ciencia e Ingeniería (MyDCI) program under number 001867.

References

1. Valle, Arthur M., Santos, Eduardo A.P., Loures, Eduardo R. Applying process mining techniques in software process appraisals. Elsevier. (2017) 19-30
2. Yzquierdo Herrera, R. Minería de proceso como herramienta para la auditoria. Ciencias de la Información. 44(2), (2013) 25-32

3. Samalikova, J., Kusters, R., Trienekens, J., Weijters, T., Siemons, P. Toward objetctive software process information: experiences from a case study. Software Qual J. (2011) 101-118
4. Astorga-Vargas, A., Morales-Bustamante, J., Flores-Rios, B., Ibarra-Esquer, J. Determining software process capability in conformity to the process assessment model NMX-I -15504 applied to the reference model NMX-I-059 supported by the AURAP tool. Iberian Conference on Information Systems and Technologies (CISTI 2014). España. (2014) 283-288
5. Pollo Cattaneo, M. F., García Martínez, R., Britos, P., Pesado, P. M., & Bertone, R. Elementos para una Ingeniería de Explotación de Información. Proyecciones, 10. (2012)
6. Martins, S., Pesado, P., García-Martínez, R. Propuesta de Modelo de Procesos para una Ingeniería de Explotación de Información: MoProPEI. Revista Latinoamericana de Ingeniería de Software. (2014) 313-332
7. Piatetsky-Shapiro, G. Data mining and knowledge discovery 1996 to 2005: overcoming the hype and moving from "university" to "business" and "analytics". Data Mining and Knowledge Discovery, 15(1), (2007) 99-105
8. S. Mitra and T. Acharya. Data mining: multimedia, soft computing and bioinformatics. John Wiley & Sons, 2003
9. Riquelme Santos, J. C., Ruiz, R., & Gilbert, K. Mineria de datos: Conceptos y tendencias. Inteligencia artificial: Revista Iberoamericana de Inteligencia Artificial, 10(29), (2006) 11-18
10. Aguirre Mayorga, H., Rincón García, N. Minería de procesos: desarrollo, aplicaciones y factores críticos. Revistas Javeriana. (2015) 137-155
11. Van der Aalst, W. M. P., Adriansyah, A., de Medeiros, A.K.A., Arcieri, F., Baier, T., Blickle, T., Bose, J.C., van den Brand, P., Brandtjen, R., Buijs, J., et al. Process mining manifesto. In: Daniel, F., Barkaoui, K., Dustdar, S. (eds.) BPM 2011 Workshops, Part I. LNBIP, Springer, Heidelberg. (2012) 169–194
12. Wang, J., Wong, R. K., Ding, J., Guo, Q., & Wen, L. Efficient selection of process mining algorithms. IEEE Transactions on Services Computing, 6(4), (2013) 484-496
13. Gupta, E. P. Process mining a comparative study. International Journal of Advanced Research in Computer and Communications Engineering, 3(11), 5. (2014)
14. Ailenei, Irina-Maria. Process Mining Tools: A Comparative Analysis. Thesis. (2011)
15. Kitchenham, B. Guidelines for performing Systematic Literature Reviews in Software Engineering. Technical Report, Software Engineering Group, Department of Computer Science, University of Durham. UK. (2007) 3-5
16. Astromskis, S., Janes, A., Sillitti, A., & Succi, G. Continuous CMMI assessment using non-invasive measurement and process mining. International Journal of Software Engineering and Knowledge Engineering, 24(09), (2014) 1255-1272

Cyberbullying in developing countries: Uncovering the profiles of the aggressors, victims, manifestations and dynamics

Javiera Aliaga[1], Diego Fuentealba[2,3][0000-0001-5284-0448],
Cherie Flores-Fernández [4][0000-0001-5294-7157], Katherina Kuschel [5][0000-0002-1465-3411],
Raúl Carrasco[1,6][0000-0002-5023-9349]], Marcelo Pizarro[7][0000-0002-2707-8604]

[1] Facultad de Administración y Economía, Universidad de Santiago de Chile, Santiago 9170022, Chile. Corresponding author: raul.carrasco.a@usach.cl
[2] Informatics Research Centre, University of Reading, Reading, UK
[3] School of Informatics and Telecommunications, Universidad Tecnológica de Chile-INACAP
[4] Escuela de Bibliotecología, Universidad Tecnológica Metropolitana, Santiago, Chile
[5] Researcher at Dirección de Investigación y Desarrollo Académico, Universidad Tecnológica Metropolitana, Santiago, Chile
[6] Facultad de Ingeniería, Ciencia y Tecnología, Universidad Bernardo O'Higgins, Santiago 8370993, Chile
[7] Facultad de Ingeniería, Universidad Nacional Andrés Bello, Santiago, Chile

Abstract. This research reviews the literature about a new form of harassment, the cyberbullying. This harassment uses technologies such as Internet, smartphones, social networks, e-mail, to annoy, assault and harass other individuals. This work analyses why does this happen, who is the cyber-bully and who the cybervictim, in what contexts, how does the cyberbullying look like, and what can be done to prevent or diminish the threat. Results reveal that men are more prone to act both as an aggressor and as a victim, mainly between the ages of 9 and 17 years old. The cyberbully is generally older than the victim. Although not very frequent, cyberbullying is also present among adults. Additionally, the amount of time spent on the use of the Internet is highly related to the frequency and magnitude of the cyberbullying. The chances of being attacked are higher when students have access to Internet in the classroom. The role of parents is critical to prevent and diminish the threat.

Keywords: Cyberbullying, Internet, underage, developing countries.

1 Introduction

Cyberbullying (or cyber-bullying) is a phenomenon that has been constantly growing as a complex psychosocial abnormality among all the schools in the world. Cyberbullying is defined as the intentional and constant violence of the students aimed at their psychologically or physically weaker peers[1].

The term cyberbullying is derived from traditional face-to-face bullying behaviors, which are observed mainly among elementary-school students, such as verbal abuse, teasing, insults and threats, as well as physical aggression, such as hitting, kicking, punching and damaging the belongings of others. Such behaviors must occur repeatedly and systematically against an individual who fails or is unable to defend himself or herself, in order to be classified as bullying [2].

1.1 Cyberbullying: The "unstoppable" trend

Cyberbullying -as a particular type of bullying- involves the use of information and technological communication such as smartphones, web pages, personal blogs, e-mail and immediate text message, in a defamatory manner, with the purpose of harming another and repetitively [3]. On the other hand, there are several theories about those responsible for displaying and transmitting harmful or illicit content, such as intimate or damaging images of those who do not want to show them. The legal argument suggests that the Internet -as a social communication network- should be regulated and eventually, prohibit those types of exhibitions. On the other hand, the providers of such pages cannot be blamed if they warn about the type of information provided or the nature of the publications [4].

According to these studies, it can be said that internet providers are not chasing to the responsible of this kind of content, because how pleasant or unpleasant is the content depends on the point of view of each person. Internet providers are delegating the responsibility to the users, because they decide what they want to see or do in the web pages. Therefore, most cybervictims are children, who don't have proper supervision of this kind of resources.

Children from an early age have started a life surrounded by technology, but they are not aware of possible threats when new opportunities for interaction and communication are born, such as Facebook, Twitter, WhatsApp, and Instagram. The irresponsible access to new forms of communication has brought new ways to hurt, extort and intimidate, generating fear of personal integrity [5]. This fact could justify the increase in cyberbullying compared to data from old research, as well as a greater concentration of cyberbullying in countries such as the United States and Canada compared to European countries.

1.2 All types of bullying are part of "human nature". Can it be eradicate?

The most common element that incite this threat is the imbalance from differences in power, strength, defence capacity, along with the fact that the perpetrator, when using this method, does not have to face his/her victim and, he/she can remain anonymous. All these are advantages that the aggressor has to set to achieve its objective. Bullying is a form of abuse that is based on an imbalance of power; it can be defined as a systematic imbalance of power [6, 7].

In adolescence is a peak period for involvement in cyberbullying associated with that both computer proficiency and time spent online[8]. Where girls are usually more involved compared to traditional bullying. According to Hinduja and Patchin [9] there are inconsistencies in the among the studies in gender due to methodological, sample and cultural differences.

2 Literature review

Although there are already some reviews of cyberbullying [8, 11–14], the field is developing very rapidly, in part as new technologies develop and new fashions (such as particular social network sites) appear.

2.1 Risk factors associated with cyberbullying

The most relevant factors associated with cyberbullying are: 1) three hours or more of daily internet use, 2) use of instant messaging, 3) relationship problems, 4) hyper-activity-inattention problems, 5) behavior problems, 6) school-related problems, and 7) risky behavior on the internet (e.g., posting personal information, using a web camera and harassment of others online) [15].

2.2 Relevance: Consequences of being a victim of cyberbullying

Cyberbullying can cause wide health problems on the victims, such as emotional and psychosomatic problems, discomfort, moderate to severe depression, and anxiety, and it has even been said that cyberbullying is a threat with higher risks of substance use and suicide. It can also involve other individuals, who support or observe the victims. They even can adopt both functions and greatly influence the decisions that could be taken by the affected party [16].

Finally, it is easy to intimidate others in cyberspace, being more necessary to control the access to an electronic device (e.g., mobile phone or computer) and control the access to the individual information (e.g., name, phone number, mail address, username) of the victim to whom the intimidation will be performed [17]. Most of the time, cyberbullying begins with harmless intent and grows from there, which is unable to be measured in terms of the results and the damages that can be caused to the individuals who are affected and even those around them [18].

2.3 Prevalence rates vary among cultures

A report from the Cyberbullying Research Center in the United States revealed that from June 2004 to February 2010, the number of cyberbullying victimizations varied between 18.8% and 40.6% [19]. Adolescent girls are more likely to be victimized by cyberbullying (25% versus 16%); they are more likely to tell an adult (21% versus 18%) [19]. The nature of bullying among girls varies from boys in that the former tend to spread rumors in cyberspace while the latter are more likely to post photos. Cyberbullying can start as early as age 10, and may continue into adulthood [20]. Just about half (51%) of young people report giving consideration to the fact that their online postings might have personal repercussions. Furthermore, there is a strong personal component to cyberbullying in that 73% of students report being confident that they knew the identity of their perpetrator [19]. Finally, according to a recent survey of 1,247 participants that were 14-to-24 year old, 50% report having experienced some form of digital abuse [21], including spreading lies, violation of trust, and digital disrespec.

On the other hand, developing countries have less Internet access than the U.S. population. Therefore, the prevalence rates of cyberbullying are lower. Contrary to the U.S. -where adolescent girls were more likely to be victimized by cyberbullying than boys- in Latin American countries young boys seem to be most victimized by cyberbullying. There are broad differences in digital literacy and citizenship education among schools, cities, cultures and countries. Although research has demonstrated the relationship between traditional bullying and cyberbullying with homophobic, sexist, racist, and discriminatory situations, most of the studies have ignored the systemic relationships of the phenomenon with attitudes reinforced and modeled by the adult society [22].

The magnitude of the consequences of cyberbullying on the victim may also vary among different locations. The Centers for Disease Control lists suicide as one of the leading causes of death among kids aged 15-19 years in the U.S. In the UK, half of youth suicides are sourced to bullying. And in Latin American countries the youth suicide rates are lower.

In some countries the cyberbullying might be considered illegal. For example, in the US, cyberbullying can result in a charge of juvenile delinquency or a misdemeanor cyber-harassment charge. Identity theft, password theft, or hacking can violate state and federal laws. In some states, "sexting" or even forwarding on a "sext" (text messages of a sexual nature) is punishable as possessing or distributing child pornography. If convicted, a sexter may be required to register as a sex offender, even if they are minors. If an adult perpetrates or allows cyberbullying, they can be arrested for cyber-harassment or cyberstalking, which can result in felony or misdemeanor punishment. In the UK, online harassment and cyberbullying can violate various laws like the Defamation Act 2013, Communications Act 2003, Protection From Harassment Act 1997, and others.

3 Scope of the review

3.1 Search strategy

The search strategy was restricted to peer-reviewed journal articles published in EBSCO, WoS, ScienceDirect, and Google Scholar between January 1, 2013 to December 31, 2017. This search included only empirical studies (all data types).

The initial search string of "Cyberbullying AND Latin America" yielded 350 results (Fig. 1).

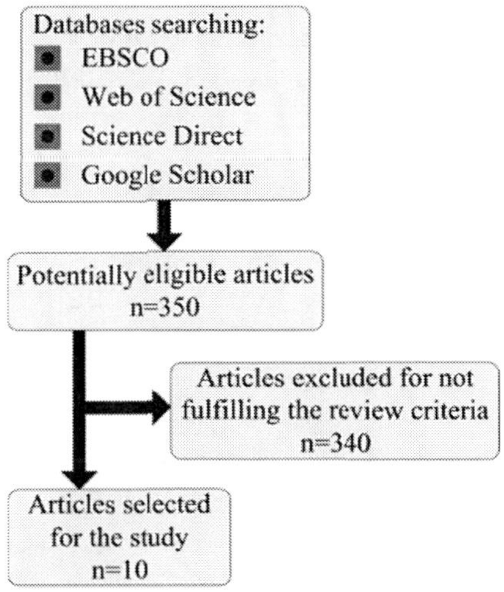

Fig. 1. Flowchart of articles evaluated for the literature review.

3.2 Study selection and procedure

The inclusion criteria applied to select the documents, were;

- papers that studied cyberbullying among children and adults (causes and effects, victims, anonymity, cyberstalking, social media, sexting, aggressors, perpetrators, bystanders, cybervictims, cyberbullies).
- special focus on developing countries such as Mexico, Argentina and Colombia, because the main inquiries on this subject are concentrated in these countries, scarcer in Latin America[23].

The hand search was assisted by Mendeley, a web-based reference manager that can suggest literature related to what is contained in a folder. Finally, the step of full review excluded publications:

- that were literature reviews and theoretical essays,
- with low methodological quality,
- that did not satisfy the regionality criteria,
- that addressed traditional face-to-face bullying, not related to digital technologies,
- on specific adolescent populations, such as, adolescents at risk of psychosis, those with intellectual disabilities, developmental issues or obesity, homosexuals or adolescents who were in jail,
- that explicitly addressed those who reported experiences both as a cybervictim and as a cyberbully at the same time, and
- that addressed suicidal behaviors/attempts and suicide.

Titles and abstracts were assessed independently by two evaluators. Whenever there was disagreement between the evaluators, another reviewer was called to give his opinion.

According to these criteria, the analysis is based on the full review of 10 studies conducted in 6 different countries around the world that studied cyberbullying among children and adults between 7 to 65 years old.

3.3 Research questions

This article aims to answer why does cyberbullying happen, what are the characteristics (demographics and psychological patterns) of the cyberbully and the cybervictim, in what contexts does cyberbullying take place (classroom) or trigger (the potential irregularities related to their social and family environment), how does the cyberbullying look like, and what can be done to prevent or diminish the threat.

4 Overview of the results

Tables 1, 2 and 3 show the scientific research identifying the authors, country, characteristics of the sample (location, gender and age of the participants), research questions and main findings.

5 The risk of becoming a cybervictim

Several reasons can be given of why a person can be vulnerable to cyberbullying. One of the most common reasons is that the victim has a family with recognizably lower self-esteem. Normally, families with high self-esteem and confidence, provide greater security and reinforce the emotional bond of young people with adults[34]. Another factor of the same nature is that there are low levels of parental participation in children's access to the Internet, in which there is a greater risk of becoming a cyber stalker or victim. It should be noted that children with more difficulties to socialize are more likely to become addicted to the Internet because it offers more likelihood of communication and at the same time a refuge, evasion or escape from the reality in their life. These children could be victims of the Internet to the point of becoming harassed.

Therefore, it can be concluded that the influence of the family is related to the problem of cyberbullying [34]. A study showed that around 80% of the parents and guardians try to regulate the access to Internet of their children, meaning that they have a notion on cyberbullying and are aware of the exposition of children in elementary school, because around of the 80 percent informed that they [35]. It is important to emphasize that parents play a fundamental role to prevent and eradicate this type of behavior, since they are the main source to acquire moral values and then shape the behavior towards society [36].

Table 1. Results of cyberbullying studies in developing countries

Authors	Country	Sample and method	Research question (RQ)	Main findings (MF)
[24]	Argentina	Male and female participants. (non specific) 7 to 11 years old. Quantitative	How old are you most exposed to bullying? Why?	Those who were more exposed to cyberbullying and other incidents, were children between 8 and 9 years old, confirming that they have been victims of bullies older than them. It was found that men were the more likely to be harassed than women. Some of the explanations are that at that age those involved begin to develop defensive mechanisms and those young children do not have the perception of danger as deep-rooted as adults.
[25]	Turkey	136 students. 18 to 29 years old. Quantitative	Does the experience as a delinquent or victim of cyberbullying is associated with personality factors?	Being a criminal, cybernetic or being a victim was related to being psychotic (this is a magnitude about the vulnerability to impulsive, violent or low ability to put oneself in the place of another person). Regarding the sex of the members, it could be seen that university students were representative more likely to present cybercriminal behavior than women. On the other hand, men perceived that intimidation behaviors were harmless in women. The main implication that emerges from the present findings is that young Internet users are not aware of the level of humiliation of their online actions and their effects on other people's lives.
[26]	Colombia	2000 male and female students of public and private schools. 11 to 19 years Quantitative.	Distinctive characteristics to be harassed?	The analysis was based on sentences which made references to "have hit or bothered someone", someone has said bad things about you "and other phrases of the same nature. On the other hand, the research was divided into different categories, such as sex, age, social stratum, public or private school, among others. The results were moderate to high discrimination. Regarding the gender, more men were reported as victims than women, but there are no significant differences.
[27]	Mexico	191 teenagers. 14 to 15 years old. Quantitative	How cybervictims seek for help?	The way the victim seeks for help with, first; parents and teachers (with 78% and 85% respectively), second; brothers, third; classmates, and fourth; friends of the same age. On the other hand, there are factors that influence being a victim of cyberbullying. One factor without major differences was having a computer, Internet access or Smartphone. However, students who reported to use the cellphone in the classroom were twice bullied as many victims as those who did not.

Table 2. Results of cyberbullying studies in developing countries (continuation).

Authors	Country	Sample and method	Research question (RQ)	Main findings (MF)
[28]	Colombia	223 students in Bogotá. 15 years old. Qualitative	What is the use that the students give to Internet, computers and mobile phones in the classroom?	The main use is to gather information that would help them to develop school assignments. The second use is entertaining (games, videos, listening to music or chatting with friends and family). In the field of cyberbullying, many had a notion of what it means and the damage that it causes to people. However certain students gave reasons why they practiced this threat, arguing that "they did it because they liked their partner" or "they thought differently from him".
[29]	Mexico	717 victims of cyberbullying, distributed in 504 women and 204 men. 16 to 65 years old. Qualitative	How do you use the cell phone if you want to harass someone?	In the first place the answer that had the highest average was, to look for interaction, that is to say, sending messages by social networks, electronic mails and calls, in reiterative form. The second place was the sexual harassment, given in the same way previously said, but obscenely, for example very revealing images of his body, messages such as 'let's get together', 'give me another chance' and aggressive emails, insulting the person . Third, the social discredit, this is sabotaging the reputation of someone in your private life or work, also get private information without your permission and then expose it to others. Fourth, gradual approach that is, knowing the person online and then interfering in their life, hurting, harassing or following it. And finally in fifth place, surveillance, as for example, monitoring through GPS, cameras, computer or microphone.
[30]	Spain	300 male and female students from 3 different schools. 12 to 18 years old. Quantitative	Does having few friends online influence cyberbullying?	A series of questionnaires was carried out, which were rated with scores, those who obtained high scores wanted to say that they were more prone to harass, and on the contrary, those who obtained low scores were less prone to harass. Those that obtained high score, obtained them in all the questions except in those that made reference to have friends online.Girls are the hardest hit, taking children as stalkers.

Table 3. Results of cyberbullying studies in developing countries (continuation).

Authors	Country	Sample and method	Research question (RQ)	Main findings (MF)
[31]	Mexico	300 students from different campuses of the ENP and the CCH. 15 to 18 years old. Qualitative.	Are friends necessary to prevent acts that involve being harassed?	Friends in the adolescence phase are fundamental because the given support in this phase is related to self-esteem and emotional well-being. It influences the feeling of being accepted, rejected or ignored by their peers. The ideal for young people is to belong to a group and grow with them, which leads to more intimate relationships, more confidence to talk about everyday problems or secrets, among other things. Potential offenders have different qualities that can make them more likely to practice harassment, such as excessive use of computers or cellphones, having many accounts on social networks and webpages, turn off the screen used when someone approaches, anger after using this tool, among others.
[32]	Greece	146 students. 12 to 16 years Quantitative.	What are the potential individual characteristics associated with cyberbullying and victimization?	Cyber-attacks 10.3%, cyberbullies 8.9%, cybervictims 15.1%, and not involved 65.8.
[33]	Mexico	300 young males and females (12-20 years) Mixed-methods.	Do you know what cyber bullying is? How many have been affected?	No significant differences by gender. One-fifth of the total sample were participants in cyberbullying. One third practice it without knowing what it is.

5.1 How can parents help prevent cyberbullying?

Parents can have a significant influence on the degree that affects the victim of cyberbullying, so they should first inform the children about the appropriate use the internet. Then, they should monitor the environment in which they are inserted and thus be able to be more attached to the reality their children live.Finally, they should encourage their self-esteem as much as possible and increase their security so that when faced with this problem it will not be so difficult to face it [37].
However, in the first place, they should detect opportunely: changes in behavior, school performance, and school attendance. Children tend to decrease the desire to go out on the streets, their communication and everything that entails victim of bullying, in short, parents must be able to realize that something is happening to their children and try to help them cope with their problems [38].

6 Internet uses according to students

According to the students, the most important use regarding technology is the Internet since it helps them to complete their homework, and it entertains them (e.g., listen to music, play games, communicate, and a smaller amount says to watch pornography). As time goes by, students get older and they decrease their number of contacts in their social networks and become more meticulous with their privacy [18]. The frequent use of the Internet and technological devices such as learning, entertainment, and communication, generates isolation and dependency, causing a constant communication between the aggressors and victims, a dynamic that makes harder and harder to stop the aggressions [39].

6.1 Unpleasant content everywhere

Due to the expansion of technology, and the easy access to the Internet, people are more prone to receive or see unpleasant photos, aggressive and intimidating emails, texts or despicable videos, which in any case or form has a negative impact on people [24, 28].

6.2 Fun or cyberbullying?

The study conducted in Mexico found that one third practice cyberbullying without knowing what it is [33, 37]. It needs to be taught the difference of being fun or being annoying, and a proper use of technology.

7 Conclusion

7.1 Contribution

As shown in this review, the population that is most affected are joung children, and mostly men. At an early age they are normally not aware of the consequences of their actions on their environment. Our findings also show that those who use the Smartphone with Internet in the classroom are more prone to cyberbullying.

However, cyberbullying is also present in adults, mostly men, that are normally the aggressors.

Researchers agree that cyberbullying can be considered a new type of aggression, and it is growing, due to the increase in the spread of Internet among young people and the development of new social networking platforms. The assessment of the preponderance and nature of cyberbullying could be complex, since that there is still a lack of consensus on how cyberbullying should be defined and measured [40].

In order to prevent and tackle cyberbullying, parents and teachers have a great influence in teaching children (potential victims) the correct use of the internet, and limit their time spent on-line.

7.2 How can parents help to tackle cyberbullying?

Parents can have a significant influence on the degree that affects the victim of cyberbullying, so they should first inform the children about the appropriate use the internet. Then, they should monitor the environment in which they are inserted and thus be able to be more attached to the reality their children live.Finally, they should encourage their self-esteem as much as possible and increase their security so that when faced with this problem it will not be so difficult to face it [37].
However, in the first place, they should detect opportunely: changes in behavior, school performance, and school attendance. Children tend to decrease the desire to go out on the streets, their communication and everything that entails victim of bullying, in short, parents must be able to realize that something is happening to their children and try to help them cope with their problems [38].

7.3 How can schools help to tackle cyberbullying?

In an educational environment, the use of internet, computers and mobile phones, generates a very good opportunity, offering students easier learning as it allows to corroborate information or correct errors immediately, strengthening the knowledge. However, despite these advantages, this tool has generated a new way of attacking, humiliating and threatening [32].

As those who use the Smartphone with Internet in the classroom are more prone to cyberbullying [31, 32], teachers and instructors may avoid the use of those devices during classes.

7.4 How can software, apps and devices be designed to avoid cyberbullying?

There are a number of applications about school bullying that can be downloaded or purchased through the markets on cell phones, Google Play and Apps Store. Some of these applications are: Stoppit, Bullysemaforo, bully block, bullying bully, bully button, brave up, bully tag, among others. All made for the purpose of preventing and combating harassment, as follows, for example: detect inappropriate insults, messages and photos and then are sent to the respective attorneys to be informed and can control the situation, also allow you to send recordings, photos, audios at any time to parents or teachers to stop the situation, also others work as a daily life where they ask questions like someone has hit you today? or has anyone ignored you today? to detect harassment. [41].

Currently, there are social networks that allow people to denounce the bad acts for society, such as robberies, mistreatment, scams, among others, and crimes committed by some people, which can be shared and reach many parts of the world, including the television press. Also on the internet, most of the pages that correspond to being seen by people of legal age due to their morbid, violent or sexual content, include notices in which they ask the age to be able to show what they contain and If you do not meet the minimum age the subject can not be accessed. So it helps to give notice to children who enter that the content is not appropiate for them. Therefore these tools are very useful to face and prevent harassment.

Aliaga et al., 2018

Finally to avoid, fight and solve the problems of harassment, everyone must provide either parents, teachers, relatives, authorities and the community in general.

References

1. Zych, I., Ortega-Ruiz, R., Del Rey, R.: Scientific research on bullying and cyberbullying: Where have we been and where are we going. Aggression and Violent Behavior. 24, 188–198 (2015).
2. Monks, C.P., Smith, P.K.: Definitions of bullying: Age differences in understanding of the term, and the role of experience. British Journal of Developmental Psychology. 24, 801–821 (2006).
3. Parés Soliva, M.: Ciber acoso. Un tema de reflexión. Confederación de Adolescencia y Juventud de Iberoamérica y el Caribe. 1–5 (2007).
4. Verdejo, M.: Ciberacoso y violencia de género en redes sociales. Universidad Internacional de Andalucía, Sevilla (2015).
5. García-Maldonado, G., Joffre-Velázquez, V.M., Martínez-Salazar, G.J., Llanes-Castillo, A.: Ciberbullying: forma virtual de intimidación escolar. Revista Colombiana de Psiquiatría. 40, 115–130 (2011).
6. Rigby, K.: New perspectives on bullying. Jessica Kingsley Publishers, London, England (2002).
7. Smith, P.K., Sharp, S. eds: School bullying: Insights and perspectives. Routledge, London (1994).
8. Tokunaga, R.S.: Following you home from school: A critical review and synthesis of research on cyberbullying victimization. Computers in Human Behavior. 26, 277–287 (2010).
9. Hinduja, S., Patchin, J.W.: Cyberbullying: An Exploratory Analysis of Factors Related to Offending and Victimization. Deviant Behavior. 29, 129–156 (2008).
10. Alonso, C., Avilés, C., Notó, C., Ruiz, G., Teijeira, E., Uruñuela, P., Díez, P., Grado, A.: Acoso entre iguales . ciberacoso, (2013).
11. Mora-Merchán, J., Jäger, T. eds: Cyberbullying: A cross-national comparison. Presented at the (2010).
12. Smith, P.K.: Cyberbullying and cyber aggression. In: Jimerson, S., Nickerson, A., Mayer, M.J., and Furlong, M.J. (eds.) Handbook of school violence and school safety. pp. 111–121. Routledge, New York, NY (2012).
13. Smith, P.K., Slonje, R.: Cyberbullying: the nature and extent of a new kind of bullying, in and out of school. In: Jimerson, S.R., Swearer, S.M., and Espelage, D.L. (eds.) Handbook of Bullying in Schools: An International Perspective. pp. 249–262. Routledge (2010).
14. Kowalski, R.M., Giumetti, G.W., Schroeder, A.N., Lattanner, M.R.: Bullying in the digital age: A critical review and meta-analysis of cyberbullying research among youth. Psychological bulletin. 140, 1073–1137 (2014).
15. Borges Bottino, S.M., Bottino, C.M.C., Gomez Regina, C., Lobo Correia, A.V., Silva Ribeiro, W.: Cyberbullying and adolescent mental health: systematic review. Cadernos de saude publica. 31, 463–475 (2015).
16. Salmerón, M.A., Blanco, A., Casas, J.: Ciberacoso y adolescentes. Anales de Pediatria Continuada. 12, 269–273 (2014).
17. El Asam, A., Samara, M.: Cyberbullying and the law: A review of psychological and legal challenges. Computers in Human Behavior. 65, 127–141 (2016).
18. Gutiérrez, A.N., Navarro, A., Dueñas, A.M., Carreño, A., Muños, B., Torres, D.: Sistematización de experiencias de acompañamiento in situ. Instituto para la Investigación Educativa y el Desarrollo Pedagógico, IDEP, Bogotá, Colombia (2016).

19. Li, Q.: Cyberbullying in schools: A research of gender differences. School Psychology International. 27, 157–170 (2006).
20. Williams, S.G., Godfrey, A.J.: What is Cyberbullying & How Can Psychiatric-Mental Health Nurses Recognize It? Journal of Psychosocial Nursing and Mental Health Services. 49, 36–41 (2011).
21. PureSight Online Child Safety: The dangers of cyberbullying, http://www.puresight.com/Cyberbullying/the-dangers-of-cyber-bullying.html.
22. Cabra Torres, F., Marciales Vivas, G.: Cyberbullying and Education: A Review of Emergent Issues in Latin America Research. In: Navarro, R., Yubero, S., and Larrañaga, E. (eds.) Cyberbullying Across the Globe. pp. 131–147. Springer International Publishing, Cham (2016).
23. Romera Félix, E.M., Del Rey Alamillo, R., Ortega Ruiz, R.: Prevalencia y aspectos diferenciales relativos al génerodel fenómeno bullying en países pobres. Psicothema. 23, 624–629 (2011).
24. Lugani, C., Rizzo, A.: Ciber-acoso en niñas y niños. In: STS 2015, 2° Simposio Argentino sobre Tecnología y Sociedad. pp. 215–227. , Rosario, Argentina (2015).
25. Seray Ozden, M., Icellioglu, S.: The perception of cyberbullying and cybervictimization by university students in terms of their personality factors. In: Garcia Laborda, J., Ozdamli, F., and Maasoglu, Y. (eds.) Procedia - Social and Behavioral Sciences. pp. 4379–4383. Elsevier Ltd., Istanbul, Turkey (2014).
26. Herrera-López, M., Romera, E., Ortega-Ruiz, R.: Bullying and cyberbullying in Colombia; co-occurrence in adolescent schoolchildren. Revista Latinoamericana de Psicologia. 49, 163–172 (2017).
27. Vega López, M.G., González Pérez, G.J., Quintero Vega, P.P.: Ciberacoso: victimización de alumnos en escuelas secundarias públicas de Tlaquepaque, Jalisco, México. Revista de Educación y Desarrollo. 25, 13–20 (2013).
28. Pinilla Mondragón, R.: Prácticas de ciberbullying entre estudiantes del grado 10 de educación media. Revista de investigación educativa de la escuela de graduados en educación. 3, 16–23 (2013).
29. Retana Franco, B.E., Sánchez Aragón, R.: Acoso Cibernético: Validación en México del ORI-82. Acta de Investigación Psicológica. 5, 2097–2111 (2015).
30. Louise, H., Guillén, S., Ivorra, D., Fernández, Y.: Factores que aumentan la probabilidad de que una persona sea un ciberacosador. Revista de fundamentos de psicología. 6, 13–20 (2014).
31. Avendaño, S., Figueroa, M.: Un estudio del acoso cibernético "cyberbullying" en estudiantes de la ENP y CCH de la UNAM: Incidencia y tipos, perfiles de agresores y víctimas y acciones de afrontamiento. XII Congreso Nacional de Investigación Educativa. 3, 1–11 (2013).
32. Antoniadou, N., Kokkinos, C.M., Markos, A.: Possible common correlates between bullying and cyber-bullying among adolescents. In: Ortega, R. and Zych, I. (eds.) Psicologia Educativa. pp. 27–38. Colegio Oficial de Psicólogos de Madrid (2016).
33. Zapata, L., Guerrero, Y.: El ciberbulling, otra enfermedad de la escuela. Revista Electrónica de la red Durango de Investigadores Educativos. 7, 69–84 (2015).
34. Ortega Barón, J., Buelga, S., Cava, M.J.: The Influence of School Climate and Family Climate among Adolescents Victims of Cyberbullying. Comunicar. 24, 57–65 (2016).
35. Monks, C.P., Mahdavi, J., Rix, K.: The emergence of cyberbullying in childhood: Parent and teacher perspectives. Psicologia Educativa. 22, 39–48 (2016).
36. Garaigordobil, M.: Ciberbullying en adolescentes y jóvenes del País Vasco: Cambios con la edad. Anales de Psicología. 31, 1069–1076 (2015).
37. Rojas Pardo, G.M.: El ciberbullying como medio de victimación en línea a los menores de 18 años de edad dentro de las instituciones educativas y hogares del cantón Santo Domingo. Tesis de grado previo a la obtención del título de Abogada de

los Tribunales de la República, Facultad de Jurisprudencia, Universidad Regional Autónoma de Los Andes. 90 (2015).

38. Gutiérrez Marco, A.: Ciberacoso : propuesta de intervención. Trabajo final de máster oficial universitario en mediación e intervención familiar, Universidad Jaime I. 31 (2015).
39. Sabater Fernández, C., López-Hernáez, L.: Factores de Riesgo en el Ciberbullying. Frecuencia y Exposición de los Datos Personales en Internet. RISE – International Journal of Sociology of Education. 4, 1–25 (2015).
40. Baldry, A.C., Farrington, D.P., Sorrentino, A.: Cyberbullying in youth: A pattern of disruptive behaviour. Psicologia Educativa. 22, 19–26 (2016).
41. Peinado Miguel, Fernando; Mateos Abarca, Juan Pablo. 2015. "Aplicaciones Móviles Contra El Acoso Escolar." : 72–91.

Digital Catalogue of Software Acquisition Patterns

Ítalo Donoso-Barraza[1], Vianca Vega-Zepeda[1], Diego Bravo-Rojas[1]

[1]Departamento de Ingeniería de Sistemas y Computación, Universidad Católica del Norte, Angamos 0610, 1270709, Antofagasta, Chile
{italo.donoso, vvega}@ucn.cl, dbr005@alumnos.ucn.cl

Abstract. Today there are several methods to acquire a software product among which it is possible to refer: the purchase of a Commercial Off-The-Shelf (COTS) product, custom software development, components acquisition, among others. Despite of the chosen method, it is important to take into account activities and tasks that support the acquisition process and that guide the purchaser to acquire a product that meets the required quality criteria. In this scenario, this paper describes the development of a web tool that allows users to gather, share and complement the present knowledge about software acquisition. Furthermore, this web tool helps users to synthesize this knowledge on a digital catalogue that supports the purchaser in the acquisition process, from early stages to implantation and acquired product start-up.

Keywords: Software Acquisition, Software Acquisition Patterns, Quality Management, Knowledge Management

1 Introducción

La adquisición de productos de software es un aspecto estratégico para las organizaciones, porque mejora la eficiencia operacional de las soluciones tecnológicas que se requieren, disminuyendo los costos que supone el desarrollo de manera interna [1]. Al iniciar un proyecto de adquisición, el adquiriente debe evaluar las distintas alternativas que puedan dar solución a las necesidades inmediatas de la organización, considerando el tiempo a invertir para su desarrollo interno o externo, los recursos monetarios y humanos asociados, entre otros, que pueden afectar los márgenes aceptables para considerarlo como un proyecto de adquisición exitoso. En la actualidad se han identificado nueve posibles alternativas de adquisición de productos de software que han sido denominadas *patrones de proyectos de adquisición* [2], todos ellos con características y enfoques diferentes que se basan en los siguientes criterios: tipo de producto a adquirir, metodologías utilizadas para el desarrollo del producto, adaptabilidad del producto adquirido, y la relación entre el cliente y el equipo de desarrollo [3].

Dentro del contexto del presente trabajo, un *patrón* se puede definir, de manera general, como una propuesta de solución a problemas específicos que ha sido probada con anterioridad demostrando su eficiencia, por lo que se espera que al aplicarlos en contextos similares se obtengan resultados equivalentes [4]. La diferencia entre

adquirir un producto software y contar con un patrón homónimo, radica en las etapas del ciclo de adquisición. Por una parte, la adquisición de software describe un proceso transversal aplicable a la obtención de cualquier producto, y en este punto un patrón de adquisición está elaborado y adaptado a un producto software específico. De esta manera, y con base en la información que hasta hoy se tiene en esta materia, se cuenta con la definición completa de dos de los nueve patrones identificados, a saber: productos desarrollados a medida utilizando métodos tradicionales, y la adquisición de un producto comercial completo.
Es en este punto donde nace el desarrollo de una herramienta web que está enfocada en reunir y compartir el conocimiento en materia de adquisición de software que hasta hoy han desarrollado académicos y estudiantes en el Departamento de Ingeniería de Sistemas y Computación de la Universidad Católica del Norte, mediante una herramienta que entregará al adquiriente las diferentes opciones frente a su problemática mediante un *catálogo digital* que busca apoyar a los interesados (empresas desarrolladoras de software, estudiantes y/o organizaciones que adquieren productos de software), en la elección correcta de la metodología que debe guiar el proceso de adquisición, para asegurarse de esta manera que el producto software adquirido es de calidad.
El artículo se organiza de la siguiente manera: en la segunda sección se presentan brevemente los patrones de adquisición de software que son la base de conocimiento que la herramienta busca compartir, la sección tres explica detalladamente la herramienta desarrollada y la última sección muestra las conclusiones y trabajo futuro.

2 Patrones de Proyectos de Adquisición

La ventaja de contar con patrones en una determinada área radica en que permiten abstraer la esencia de las soluciones a ciertos problemas típicos, y la documentación asociada a éstos permite que sea fácil de entender y aplicar por quienes no son expertos en el área [4]. Ahora bien, dentro de la Ingeniería de Software, Vega et al. [2] indican que contar con patrones de proyectos de adquisición de software permiten que cada estrategia aplicada pueda organizarse de mejor manera incrementando así el éxito en el proyecto de adquisición.
Como se mencionó anteriormente, dentro de la Ingeniería de Software y en concreto, dentro del desarrollo y/o adquisición de software, actualmente se cuenta con la identificación de nueve patrones de proyectos de adquisición (aquellos destacados en color gris en la Fig. 1) a través de la utilización de un método para la construcción de taxonomías denominado MECT [2]. Adicionalmente, se cuenta con la definición completa de dos de estos nueve patrones, es decir, el desarrollo de productos a la medida utilizando métodos tradicionales, y la adquisición de un producto comercial completo denominados COTS (Commercial Off-The-Shelf, de sus siglas en inglés), estos dos patrones han sido adaptados al formato propuesto en [4] el cual define quince campos que cada nuevo patrón de proyecto de adquisición debiera describir (ver Tabla 1). Los campos que se mencionan en la Tabla 1 se enfocan principalmente en describir las gestiones que debe realizar el adquiriente para obtener un producto

software de calidad. Estos campos abarcan información que va desde el enfoque y la problemática que aborda el patrón, hasta la descripción en detalle de cada una de las actividades a realizar durante el ciclo de adquisición

Tabla 1. Descripción de los campos del formato propuesto para la formalización de patrones de proyectos de adquisición de software [4].

Campo	**Descripción**
Nombre	Describe al patrón de manera concisa
Contexto	Describe el ambiente en donde reside el problema, incluido el dominio de la aplicación
Objetivo	Describe qué hace el patrón y cuál es su intención
Problema	Visión general del problema, describiendo las condiciones que motivan aplicar el patrón.
Bases para la solución	Se identifican los modelos, estándares y buenas prácticas que se consideran para el planteamiento de la solución.
Solución	Se identifican los modelos, estándares y buenas prácticas que se consideran para el planteamiento de la solución.
Roles participantes	Se identifican y describen los roles involucrados en el proyecto de adquisición de software.
Actividades de la metodología	Especifica mediante un diagrama las actividades de la metodología y su relación con las etapas del ciclo de vida de la adquisición del software.
Diagrama general de la metodología	Diagrama de flujo que muestra el orden de ejecución de cada una de las actividades que comprende la metodología.
Detalle de actividades	Detalle de cada actividad de la metodología a través de una tabla descriptiva que muestra los roles participantes, las entradas y salidas de la actividad, su descripción, tareas que la componen y los activos de los procesos relacionados.
Diagrama de actividades	Por cada actividad se presenta un diagrama que muestra la secuencia de tareas necesarias para ejecutarla. También se muestra la interacción de las distintas tareas con los activos que apoyan su realización.
Responsables y participantes	Se presenta en una tabla la relación roles-actividades.
Consecuencias	Describe las potenciales negociaciones a considerar cuando se implementa el patrón y los resultados de su aplicación.
Descripción de activos	Se presenta la descripción de cada activo, organizado según el elemento o actividad a la cual están asociados.
Patrones relacionados	Listado de patrones que se asemejan a éste.

Adicionalmente, los patrones de proyectos de adquisición de software influyen o determinan las estrategias o técnicas de control que deben aplicarse para garantizar el éxito de su aplicación en un determinado proyecto de adquisición [2]. Estas estrategias o técnicas difieren unas de otras según el patrón, ya sea por las características propias del producto a adquirir o por la relación que existe entre quien lo provee y quien lo adquiere, siendo este último quien debe contar con la debida información para ajustar el proyecto de adquisición al patrón adecuado, y por ende la aplicación de dichas estrategias de la manera correcta.

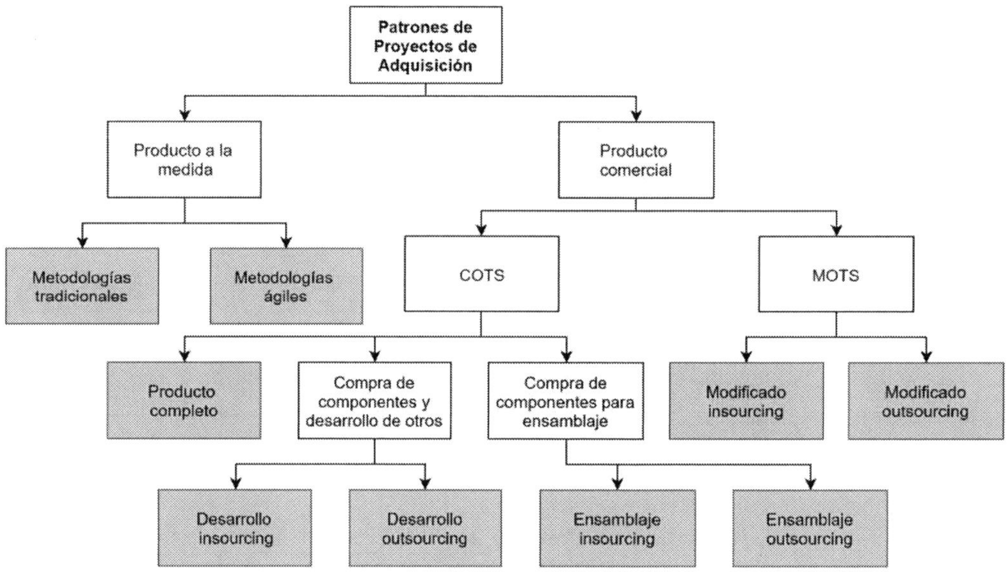

Fig. 1. Patrones de Proyectos de Adquisición de Software [2]

3 Herramienta web

Con la identificación de los nueve patrones mencionados anteriormente y la definición de los campos que cada patrón relacionado a un proyecto de adquisición debiera tener, nace el objetivo de crear una herramienta que sintetice todo este conocimiento y deje a disposición del adquiriente las distintas metodologías y recursos a considerar al momento de iniciar un proyecto de adquisición.
El desarrollo del sistema web comenzó con la determinación de los elementos o recursos que permitieran la administración de la información contenida en cada uno de los campos del formato y que facilitaran su difusión a otras personas. Para ello, se consideró el análisis de algunas plataformas gratuitas como: Moodle [5] y Claroline [6] y otra comercial: BlackBoard [7], con el fin de abstraer sus características más relevantes. Estas plataformas de e-learning fueron analizadas y revisadas antes de comenzar con el desarrollo del catálogo y de la plataforma para, de esta manera, comprender qué funcionalidades permiten la difusión de contenido desde un punto de vista pragmático, es decir, permitiendo que el conocimiento que se tiene en materia de adquisición de software y aquel que surja como resultado de futuras investigaciones, pueda ser compartido en una plataforma web que permita que tanto estudiantes, académicos, y profesionales del mundo laboral, puedan complementar dicho conocimiento con el propósito de mejorar los patrones ya existentes, o la identificación de nuevos patrones que estén enfocados en apoyar las distintas tareas

de adquisición que surgen al momento de comprar y/o desarrollar productos de software.
Del resultado de este análisis se determinaron elementos comunes de las plataformas descritas anteriormente. Estas características más relevantes pueden resumirse en:

- Descripciones globales y ayuda en línea
- Gestión de archivos y documentos incluyendo múltiples formatos
- Creación y administración de foros y encuestas
- Utilización de glosarios sobre conceptos clave relacionados a los patrones disponibles en el catálogo
- Colaboración constante entre estudiantes, académicos, investigadores y aquellos vinculados al mundo laboral

Dichas características conforman una parte de la plataforma, ya que ésta se sustenta en tres ejes: uso de patrones, herramientas e interacción con el adquiriente. Sin embargo, es importante mencionar que estas características fueron desarrolladas en completitud para la herramienta web presentada en este artículo, es decir, las plataformas de e-learning nombradas anteriormente no fueron incorporadas a la herramienta web, ya que sus funcionalidades más relevantes fueron desarrolladas totalmente para el catálogo y la plataforma.
Actualmente no existen plataformas o herramientas que guíen completamente el ciclo de adquisición de un producto software desde etapas tempranas hasta la implantación y puesta en marcha de este, procurando en todo momento la calidad del sistema adquirido o desarrollado.

3.1 Desarrollo de la plataforma y del Catálogo Digital

El desarrollo de esta herramienta, que corresponde a un sistema web, se divide en dos pilares fundamentales: la plataforma y el catálogo
La Plataforma. La plataforma ha sido nombrada Plataforma CDPAS, siendo CDPAS las iniciales del Catálogo Digital de Patrones de Adquisición de Software. A grandes rasgos la plataforma es el núcleo que sustenta el catálogo digital, ya que a través de ella se gestiona la información de los patrones, encuestas, foros, glosarios, entre otros, que se comparten al público mediante el catálogo. Sin la plataforma no es posible visualizar información en este último. Lo anterior es la razón del porqué la plataforma es precisamente el núcleo del CDPAS y en ella el usuario puede definir nueva información para los patrones disponibles, o bien, crear su propia versión de un nuevo patrón propuesto o de los nueve ya identificados. En concreto, toda la información que se puede crear, editar, gestionar y compartir dentro de la plataforma se describe en la Fig. 2.

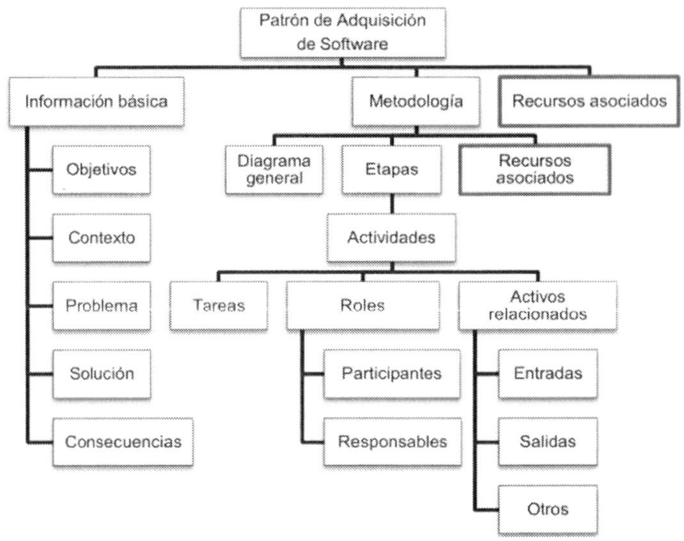

Fig. 2. Generalidades de un Patrón de Adquisición de Software [elaboración propia]

El Catálogo. El catálogo digital es la cara visible de la Plataforma, todo el contenido que se gestionará entre estudiantes, investigadores, académicos y el público en general tendrá su equivalente en la publicación de los patrones de adquisición. Conforme se avanza en la definición de los patrones restantes el catálogo irá progresivamente abarcando los diferentes proyectos de adquisición a los que se pueda enfrentar al adquiriente, guiándolo y transformándose en una herramienta que apoyará la gestión de este sobre el control de las actividades propias derivadas del proceso de adquisición.

Es importante mencionar que todo nuevo patrón identificado o propuesto debe someterse a un proceso de revisión antes de ser publicado en el catálogo (ver Fig. 3), de este modo se valida que toda la información que en él se encuentra publicada es idónea, correcta, e incorpora los procedimientos necesarios para la adquisición de un producto de calidad. Una vez que al patrón ha sido publicado, este queda visible para todos los usuarios sintetizando toda la información relevante con base en el formato descrito anteriormente e incorporando todos los elementos definidos por su creador (ver Fig. 4).

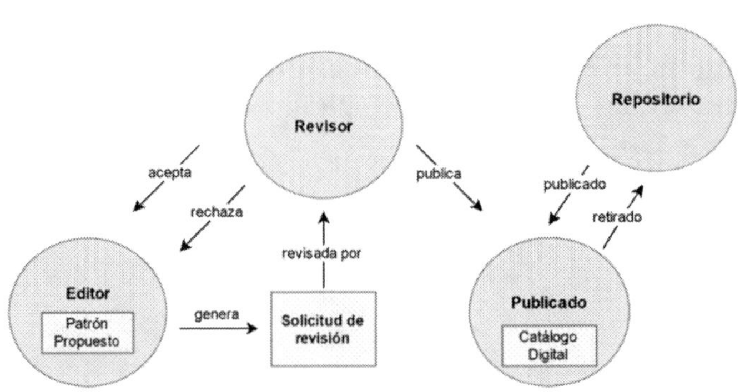

Fig. 3. Proceso de Revisión de un Patrón Propuesto [elaboración propia]

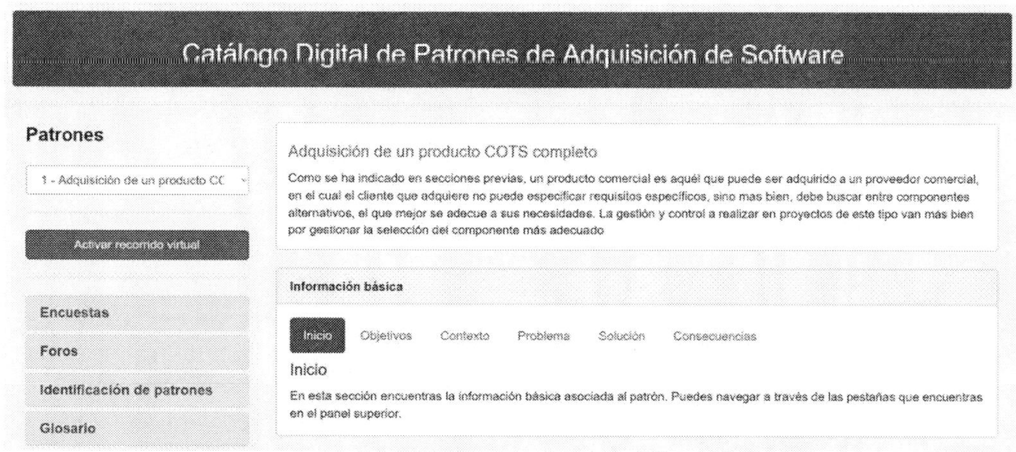

Fig. 4. Página del Catálogo - Información básica

3.2 Usuarios y público objetivo

En la Tabla 2 se definen los usuarios en los cuales está enfocado el catálogo digital.

Tabla 2. Tipos de usuarios y roles dentro de la herramienta

Campo	Descripción
Administrador	Es el encargado de definir nuevos usuarios en el sistema, además otorga privilegios a éstos junto con modificaciones y eliminaciones. Es el administrador transversal a cualquier sistema web.
Estudiante	Puede ingresar, editar y eliminación información asociada a la definición de los nueve patrones identificados. Además, puede enviar revisiones de sus patrones para ser publicados en el catálogo una vez que éstos hayan sido aprobados por los investigadores y/o académicos.
Académicos e Investigadores	Puede ingresar, editar, eliminar y publicar información asociada a la definición de los nueve patrones identificados. Además, es quien aprueba o rechaza las distintas variantes de patrones antes de ser publicados en el catálogo digital.
Adquiriente	Es uno de los usuarios principales tanto de la Plataforma como del Catálogo ya que es el principal actor que utilizará como base la metodología definida por el patrón escogido para guiar su proceso de adquisición.
Público en general	Cualquier persona que desee acceder al catálogo, previo registro en el sistema.

4 Conclusiones y trabajo futuro

La herramienta web presentada, abarca tanto la plataforma como el catálogo digital. Su uso está enfocado a dos aspectos: en primer lugar, facilitar el trabajo colaborativo y difusión de la investigación realizada en torno al conocimiento de adquisición de software entre investigadores y estudiantes; y en segundo lugar busca ser una herramienta que permita difundir al público en general (empresas desarrolladoras o adquirientes de productos de software) el trabajo desarrollado por el Departamento de Ingeniería de Sistemas y Computación de la Universidad Católica del Norte.
En cuanto a la validación de la herramienta, el componente enfocado en los investigadores fue validado por académicos ligados a la Ingeniería de Software y a la gestión del conocimiento. La validación del público general está aún pendiente y se espera como parte de esta publicación, recoger los comentarios y sugerencias de los asistentes al Congreso. Asimismo, se espera obtener la retroalimentación como resultado del uso del Catálogo en entornos reales y con usuarios reales. Por otra parte, como desafío futuro, se espera contar con la definición de los nueve patrones que hasta ahora se han identificado, y de los cuales dos ya han sido incorporados completamente al Catálogo. Respecto al uso de esta herramienta, se pretende realizar una segunda versión en donde se incorporen funcionalidades que permitan al adquiriente utilizar la plataforma y el catálogo en un sentido mucho más pragmático por sobre el informativo, respecto a las actividades que describen los patrones y el soporte de dichas actividades dentro de esta.
Finalmente, es importante señalar que tanto la Plataforma como el Catálogo están en funcionamiento y se encuentran a disposición del público en general para su uso.

5 Referencias

[1] Software Engineering Institute, "CMMI for Development, Version 1.3," no. November, 2010.

[2] V. Vega, G. Gasga, and J. Calvo-Manzano, "Identificación de Patrones de Proyectos de Adquisición del Software mediante la aplicación del método MECT," Madrid, España, 2010.

[3] V. Vega, "Metodología de Aseguramiento de la Calidad en el proceso de Adquisición de Software, incluyendo las dimensiones de Proceso y de Producto (MACAD-PP)," Universidad Politécnica de Madrid, 2012.

[4] A. Flores and H. Soto, "Especificación de Patrones de Proyectos de Adquisición de Software," Universidad Católica del Norte, 2014.

[5] "Moodle." [Online]. Available: https://moodle.org/?lang=es. [Accessed: 29-Mar-2018].

[6] "Claroline Connect: tu plataforma de aprendizaje en linea." [Online]. Available: https://www.claroline.net/ES/index.html. [Accessed: 29-Mar-2018].

[7] "Online Learning Platforms | Blackboard Products." [Online]. Available: http://www.blackboard.com/products.html. [Accessed: 29-Mar-2018].

Evaluating the impact of training software engineers using the R&G methodology

Mauricio Diéguez[1], Ricardo Gacitúa[1] and Elizabeth Vidal[2]

[1] Universidad de La Frontera, Temuco, Chile
{mauricio.dieguez,ricardo.gacitua}@ufrontera.cl

[2] Universidad La Salle, Arequipa, Perú
evidal@ulasalle.edu.pe

Abstract. The increase in the complexity of the computer systems and the relevance acquired by the attributes of quality (for example, security) make it necessary to include in the early stages of software development the techniques of prevention and correction of failures. A first published study evaluated the impact of using a systematic methodology, called Rapid & Global (R&G). This was introduced in a first programming course with the objectives of facilitating the teaching of programming and introducing disciplined and systematic practices in the solution of problems. This article presents a second phase of this study and aims to present the results of the academic follow-up of students in a second programming course, after the introduction of the methodology, in an environment that does not encourage its use. The aim is to determine if there is evidence in this adverse environment that the students persist in its use or is completely discarded. A training evaluation model is used to determine the extent to which the practices learned in the first course are conserved and how they contribute to the final result obtained. This study reveals four important results: (i) The students faced, in a second course, adverse conditions and completely different to the conditions provided in the first course, which did not favor a better adoption of the methodology, (ii) There is evidence of the use of the methodology, despite the environment in which it does not favor its use, (iii) Although the results of the final evaluations show no significant differences in relation to the number of approved, this results suggest an improvement in the final qualification obtained, (iv) Achieving greater adoption of disciplined and systematic practices requires the existence of coordinated activities in subsequent courses, in order to favor the adoption and reinforcement of the acquired practices. The results of this study suggest that the introduction of a systematic methodology used in the teaching of programming, focused on the design of solutions, should be reinforced in subsequent courses in order to improve the level of adoption.

Keywords: Software Architecture, programming, modeling, design.

1 Introducción

Considerando que el tamaño y la complejidad de los sistemas informáticos es creciente, y que los atributos de calidad - tales como seguridad y eficiencia - adquieren mayor relevancia, los algoritmos y las estructuras de datos ya no constituyen los principales desafíos del desarrollo de software. Cuando los sistemas constan de muchos componentes, su organización - la arquitectura de software - adquiere mayor relevancia que el código, puesto que los principales desafíos son de diseño, entre los que se cuentan el modelado de la interacción entre componentes, su secuenciación y la semántica de los modelos [1]. Sin embargo, en los primeros cursos de programación el principal foco está centrado principalmente en aspectos de lenguaje y sintáxis de un lenguaje de programación más que en el modelado de la solución [2]. Esto es, existe interés sólo en el *Qué* (Problema) y en el *Con qué* (Herramientas), pero escasamente en el *Cómo* (proceso) [3]. Según Garlan y Shaw [4] *"más allá de los algoritmos y estructuras de datos de la computación; el diseño y especificación de la estructura global del sistema es un nuevo tipo de problema"*. Parnas [5], advierte acerca de los peligros del desarrollo de software indisciplinado- definido básicamente como la construcción de productos de software sin guías metodológicas y basadas en estrategias de prueba y error. Lamentablemente al día de hoy aún persisten posturas y enfoques que enfatizan que el software depende exclusivamente de las habilidades de codificación de los desarrolladores y no en aspectos metodológicos innecesarios [6]. Esta postura predomina en la formación inicial de desarrolladores de software. Sin embargo la propuesta de Gacitúa et al. [3] muestra que la introducción de una metodología para enseñar a programar, basada en guías sistemáticas y disciplinadas, es posible y presenta beneficios.

Este estudio presenta los resultados de una segunda fase del estudio realizado en [3] y tiene por objeto determinar si en un ambiente adverso existe evidencia de que los alumnos persisten en utilizar la metodología aprendida o ésta se descarta completamente. La pregunta de investigación que motiva este trabajo es: ¿Existe evidencia de que la práctica adquirida en un primer curso de programación, relativa al uso de una metodología para diseñar el proceso de una solución computacional, es conservada en un curso posterior el cual no considera el uso de metodologías y además agrega restricciones para centrarse principalmente en el código? Para responder la pregunta anterior, se realizan dos evaluaciones las cuales busca determinar: (a) si existe evidencia que los alumnos continúan usando la metodología y (b) si la formación basada en la metodología R&G muestra impacto en el rendimiento académico de los alumnos, en comparación con alumnos que no fueron formados con ella.

La estructura del artículo es como sigue: La sección 2 presenta una breve descripción de la metodología y de las condiciones que se requiere para su uso. La sección 3 describe la metodología que se utiliza para responder a la pregunta de investigación. Luego, la sección 4 ilustra los resultados obtenidos. La sección 5 presenta una breve discusión respecto de los resultados y finalmente, la sección 6 resume las principales conclusiones y trabajos futuros.

2 Antecedentes básicos

Esta sección describe la metodología Rápida & Global (R&G), y las condiciones que favorecen su uso. La metodología R&G es una metodología propuesta para el análisis y estructuración de problemas, y se ha utilizado en la enseñanza de programación de computadores [3]. En particular, hemos utilizamos la metodología con el objeto de desarrollar el pensamiento lógico-computacional en etapas tempranas, pues permite promover la inclusión temprana de conceptos de arquitectura y paradigmas de programación. La metodología, tal como ilustra la Figura1, define cuatro etapas principales, (i) Definición del Problema, (ii) Definición de Entradas y Salidas, (iii) Diseño - Refinamiento Conceptual, (iv) Pseudo-código. Cada etapa utiliza templates que guían a los estudiantes tanto en la identificación, descripción y especificación de elementos que componen un algoritmo [3].

La metodología fue utilizada para enseñar a programar a un grupo de estudiantes de primer año de la carrera de ingeniería informática, en su primer curso de programación el año 2017. La experiencia anterior, demostró que la utilización de la metodología R&G, en la enseñanza de programación, favorece la formación de estudiantes sistemáticos y disciplinados [3]. Estos resultados preliminares han motivado la realización de un seguimiento de estos estudiantes en su segunda asignatura de programación, dictada durante el segundo semestre del año 2017 (asignatura que no utiliza R&G), de manera de evaluar el impacto de la utilización de R&G en las prácticas de programación de los estudiantes.

Este estudio propone realizar un seguimiento de los alumnos en otras asignaturas para determinar el impacto que ha tenido el uso de este enfoque metodológico en su desempeño futuro. Posteriormente, se espera determinar el grado de adopción de esta metodología, por parte de los estudiantes, en las condiciones más desfavorables dado que se someten a una asignatura en la que no se propicia ni se fortalece el uso de alguna metodología. Ciertas condiciones de la asignatura posterior, evidentemente constituyen barreras para que los alumnos puedan destinar tiempo a seguir una metodología que se concentra en las etapas de diseño, por sobre la codificación. El escenario anterior, por tanto, se puede caracterizar de la siguiente manera:

- No se fomenta la continuación de uso de la metodología;
- Se tiene como foco de atención principal el código final y el modelo de datos, no de procesos;
- Los resultados producidos por la metodología no son exigidos; y
- Los tiempos definidos para las actividades no favorecen el tiempo requerido para el diseño conceptual de procesos.

Estableciendo este escenario adverso, se persigue evidenciar el uso de una práctica adquirida (i.e. uso de metodología para el diseño de código) introducida en una asignatura previa. Se pretende determinar si es que, a pesar del escenario más adverso, existe alguna evidencia que los alumnos aún mantienen la práctica adquirida de diseñar la lógica del algoritmo.

3 Metodología

Esta sección presenta la metodología que guía el proceso para determinar: (1) si existe evidencia acerca de que los alumnos aún mantienen la práctica adquirida de diseñar la lógica de un algoritmo, y (2) si la formación basada en la metodología R&G muestra algún impacto en el rendimiento académico de éstos. Se incluye al final de esta sección una discusión de la validez de los resultados.

Este estudio utilizó una metodología basada en el estudio de caso, como es descrito en [7]. En la Figura 1, se muestran las etapas del estudio.

Fig. 1. Metodología utilizada en el estudio.

La metodología se basa en una investigación del comportamiento de los actores involucrados en una situación determinada, sobre la que no se tiene control de los acontecimientos y en la que se estudian acontecimientos contemporáneos [8].

3.1 Semblanza del estudio

En esta etapa se presenta la descripción de la situación y los elementos relevantes del estudio.

El objetivo de la experiencia consiste en determinar la evidencia de uso de una práctica adquirida y evaluar el impacto de la metodología R&G en las prácticas de programación de los estudiantes, basado en la comparación del rendimiento académico de grupos de estudiantes. De este modo, se busca determinar si los estudiantes han adoptado la metodología como parte habitual de sus prácticas de programación y si esta metodología significa un aporte en el aprendizaje del estudiante. Para lograr lo anterior, se realiza un seguimiento académico de los estudiantes que fueron formados en una primera asignatura con la metodología R&G, analizando su comportamiento y desempeño académico en una segunda asignatura de programación de la carrera de Ingeniería Informática de la Universidad de La Frontera, Chile. Esta segunda asignatura utiliza el enfoque tradicional centrado en el lenguaje de programación para fortalecer la enseñanza de programación. Se requiere determinar si los estudiantes han continuado, de manera autónoma, utilizando los procesos y las herramientas proporcionadas en la metodología R&G.

Este estudio posee tanto una componente cuantitativa como una cualitativa para el logro de los objetivos planteados, como se describe a continuación:

- **Objetivo 1: Demostrar evidencia de uso de la Metodología R&G**. Para responder a este objetivo, se requiere el uso de un instrumento cualitativo que recoja la apreciación de los estudiantes respecto del uso de la metodología en un ambiente que no favorece su uso. Los estudiantes son consultados respecto de si la metodología R&G favorece su desempeño académico.

- **Objetivo 2: Determinar impacto de la práctica de uso de la Metodología R&G**. Para responder este punto, se utiliza un instrumento cualitativo y uno cuantitativo. Primeramente, se consulta al profesor de la asignatura su apreciación respecto de diferencias significativas entre los grupos de estudio. Se analiza además, el rendimiento académico de ambos grupos de modo de determinar la existencia de diferencias en rendimiento favorecidos por el uso de una metodología.

Caracterización de los grupos a analizar. La totalidad de los estudiantes a analizar, rindieron la asignatura inicial de programación durante el primer semestre del año 2017. Algunos de ellos utilizaron la metodología R&G y otros utilizaron los métodos tradicionales centrados en código. Para efectos de responder a los objetivos antes mencionados, se clasifican los estudiantes en dos grupos de acuerdo a su experiencia con la metodología.

- Grupo 1: El primer grupo está compuesto por 9 estudiantes que no tienen experiencia con R&G, sino que fueron enseñados con los métodos tradicionales enfocados al código. Estos estudiantes no han sido analizados anteriormente, por lo que cual no se cuenta con antecedentes cualitativos respecto de sus prácticas de programación.
- Grupo 2: Este grupo está compuesto por 11 estudiantes, quienes ya han trabajado con R&G, durante la primera asignatura de programación. Este grupo, durante la intervención que se realizó en el primer semestre, demostró la adopción de prácticas de programación tendientes al diseño y demostró un desarrollo metódico y disciplinado.

3.2 Preguntas del estudio de caso

Considerando que se requiere obtener evidencias respecto del impacto de la metodología R&G en las prácticas de programación de un grupo de estudiantes de la carrera de Ingeniería Informática, se ha propuesto la siguiente pregunta general de investigación: ¿Existe evidencia de que la práctica adquirida en un primer curso de programación - relativa al uso de una metodología para diseñar el proceso de una solución computacional – se conserva en un curso posterior, el cual no considera el uso de la metodología y además agrega restricciones para centrarse principalmente en el código?
Dicha pregunta general puede desglosarse en las siguientes preguntas, y se relaciona a los objetivos definidos en la sección anterior:

1. ¿Existe evidencia de que los estudiantes continúan utilizando la metodología R&G?
2. ¿Existe alguna relación entre el rendimiento de los estudiantes y la utilización de la metodología R&G?

3.3 Procedimientos a realizar

Para cumplir con el estudio y la metodología propuesta, se realizarán las siguientes actividades, asociadas a los objetivos:

Estudio Cuantitativo: El estudio cuantitativo, consiste en la comparación de las calificaciones de los estudiantes de ambos grupos. Para esto, se revisarán los promedios de los estudiantes, la cantidad de estudiantes que aprobaron la asignatura y los niveles de las calificaciones obtenidos. Se requiere determinar si los estudiantes que trabajaron anteriormente con R&G presentan diferencias en los promedios con aquellos estudiantes que no conocen la metodología.

Estudio Cualitativo: Este estudio tiene por objetivo determinar el aporte de la metodología R&G en los estudiantes y su grado de adopción, mediante la realización de dos consultas de percepción, ambas medidas en base a una escala Likert de 5 niveles [9]. La primera consulta busca recoger la opinión del profesor de la asignatura respecto del desempeño de ambos grupos de estudiantes, tal como se ilustra en la Figura 4.

La segunda consulta, está dirigida hacia los estudiantes que trabajaron con R&G en la asignatura anterior, y busca recoger la percepción de éstos respecto de la influencia de R&G en sus prácticas de programación durante esta segunda asignatura. Las afirmaciones que forman parte de esta consulta se ilustran en la Figura 2.

3.4 Reporte del estudio de caso

Para finalizar, se presentarán las principales conclusiones del estudio, derivadas tanto del estudio cuantitativo como del estudio cualitativo, presentando las respuestas a las preguntas de investigación planteadas.

4 Resultados

Esta sección presenta los resultados del estudio propuesto.

4. 1. Demostrar evidencia de uso de la Metodología R&G.

Consulta Estudiantes: La Figura 3 presenta los resultados de la consulta a los estudiantes. Cabe señalar que 6 estudiantes respondieron la consulta. En términos generales, la apreciación de los estudiantes es que el enfoque tradicional utilizada en este asignatura ha sido más adecuado que R&G para responder a las exigencias impuestas. La mayoría expresa que no la utilizado para resolver los ejercicios propuestos en la asignatura.

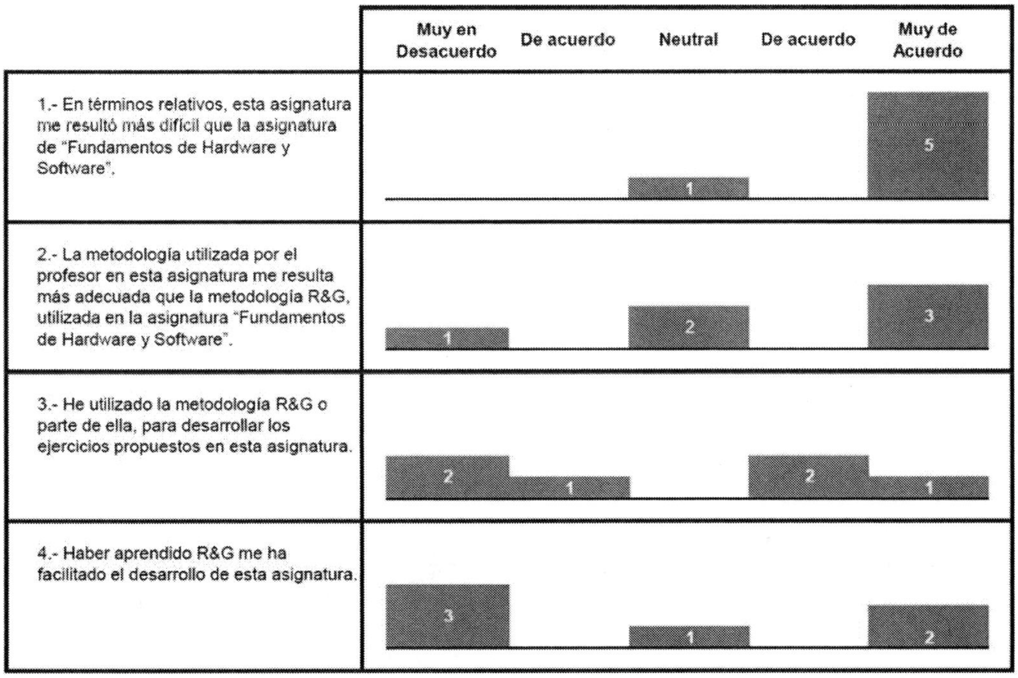

Fig. 2. Respuesta Estudiantes.

De las observaciones de los estudiantes, presentadas en la Figura 3, se desprende que el enfoque de esta segunda asignatura, si bien a la mayoría le resulta más fácil de seguir, presenta condiciones adversas para la continuidad en la utilización de R&G.

> 5,- En esta sección incluya cualquier comentario que estime conveniente respecto de la Metodología R&G y su impacto en su aprendizaje.
>
> La Metodologia R&G me ayudó a poder entender la lógica de los problemas que se planteaban en las evaluaciones de una manera más eficiente. Entiéndase que la pude incorporar solo por la práctica que llevaba después de la primera evaluación, ya que noté que el tiempo que se otorga en las evaluaciones son muy acotados. Este no alcanza para diseñar el software junto con su diagrama de clases y el código, considerando que la programación orientada a objetos requiere mayor detenimiento en temas de lógica, sintaxis, orden, entre otros elementos, que en programación estructurada.
>
> Hay pasos muy engorrosos que pueden ser resumidos o simplemente quitados, todo esto dudo que afecte al desarrollo correcto de los problemas
>
> es útil para mentalizar funciones de un programa pero no para cuando el programa tiene muchas divisiones como por ejemplo la parte grafica u que otras extensiones requiere pero sin embargo es útil cuando quiere se quiere hacer la parte de lógica del programa

Fig. 3. Opiniones de los estudiantes.

Los estudiantes declaran que los tiempos asignados a la resolución de los ejercicio, no permite el desarrollo de un análisis y diseño utilizando R&G y, por sobre todo, los resultados exigidos para cada actividad - esto son modelos de clases y código, no son los mismos resultados generados por la metodología R&G. A pesar de que la asignatura no provee de las condiciones para utilizar R&G, existe evidencia que un grupo de los estudiantes utiliza y destaca la importancia de utilizar R&G en las etapas primarias del desarrollo de software.

4.2. Determinar impacto de la práctica de uso de la Metodología R&G.

Consulta Profesor: La Figura 4, presenta los resultados de la encuesta realizada al profesor.

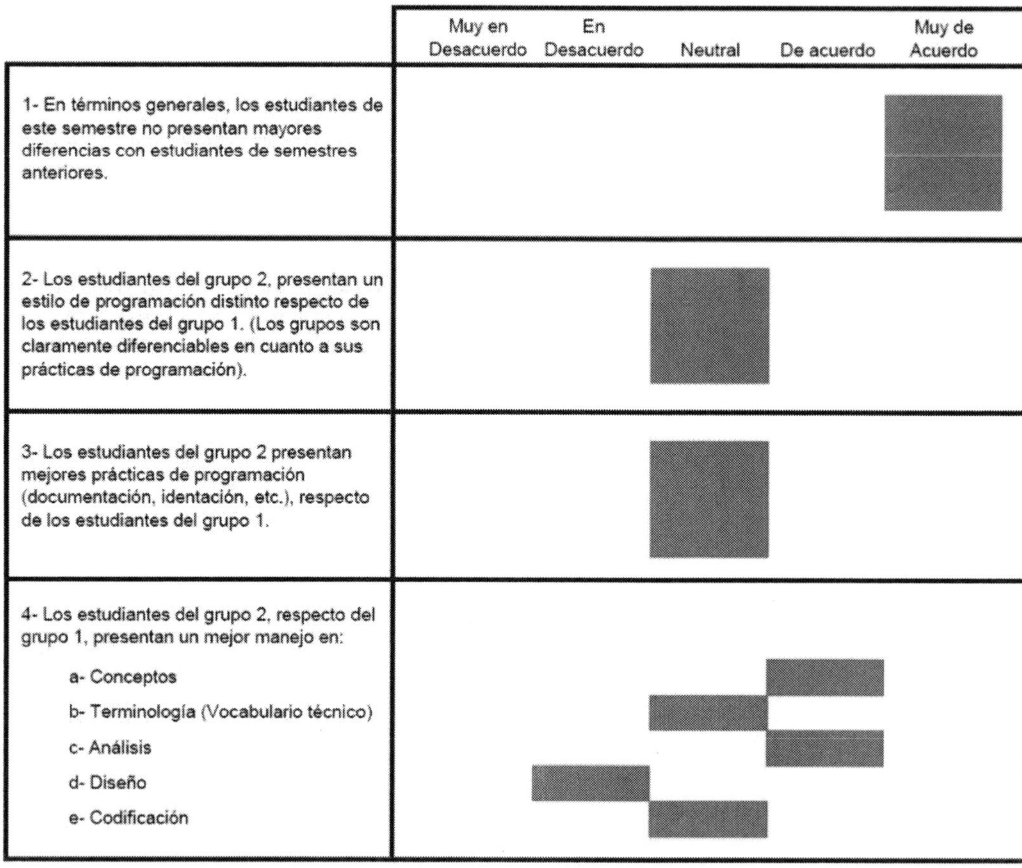

Fig. 4. Respuestas Profesor de la asignatura.

Se aprecia que el docente, en términos generales, no observa una mayor diferencia entre ambos grupos. Sin embargo, si da testimonio que los estudiantes del grupo 2 destacan del grupo 1 en lo referente a la conceptualización y el análisis, pero no en el diseño (etapas en las que enfatiza la metodología R&G). Se puede, por tanto, determinar que los estudiantes del grupo 2 han adquirido mejores prácticas de Análisis, sin perder habilidades de codificación (etapa en la que centran las metodologías actuales de enseñanza de programación). En relación a la etapa de diseño, se puede explicar teniendo en cuenta que esta segunda asignatura de programación, se centra en un diseño de modelado de datos (diagramas de clases) y no en un diseño de arquitectura, como lo hace R&G.

Estudio cuantitativo: El estudio cuantitativo consistió en el análisis de las calificaciones de los estudiantes. La Tabla 1, presenta el resumen de las estadísticas de ambos grupos. Se aprecia que los porcentajes de aprobación son muy similares en ambos grupos, por lo que no es posible determinar si el uso de la metodología marca una diferencia en las estadísticas globales de aprobación.

Tabla 1. Estadísticas del curso "Fundamentos de Programación"

Grupo	Estudiantes	Aprobados	Reprobados	% Aprob.	% Resprob.
Grupo 1	9	3	6	33.33%	66.67%
Grupo 2	11	4	7	36.36%	63.64%

Sin embargo, la Figura 5 muestra que los promedios de los estudiantes del grupo 2 son ligeramente superiores a los promedios de los estudiantes del grupo 1, es decir que, en general, el rendimiento de los alumnos que han trabajado con R&G es superior al alcanzado por el otro grupo. Esto, podría ser un indicador de que la metodología generó un impacto positivo en los estudiantes.

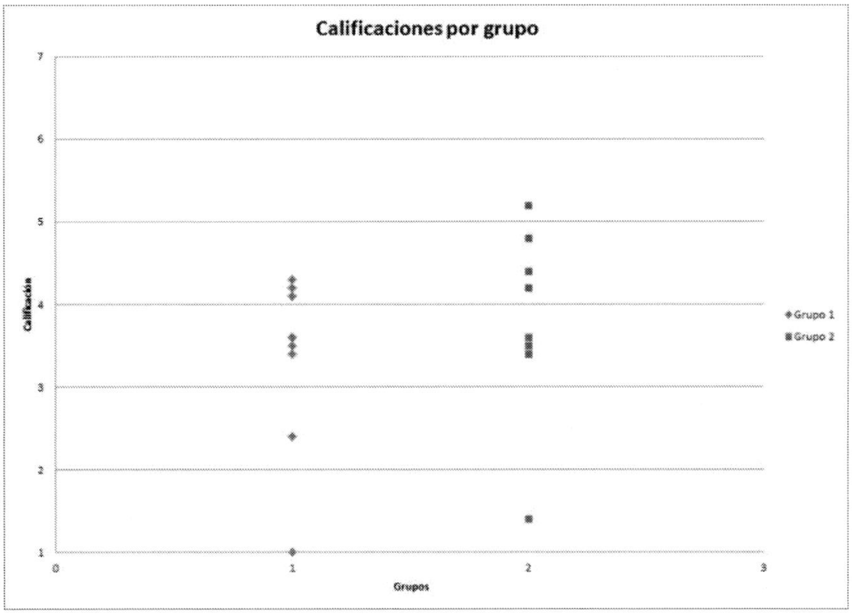

Fig. 5. Gráfico de calificaciones por grupo.

En la Tabla 2, se muestra el detalle de los promedios de los estudiantes, tanto para la primera como para la segunda asignatura, además del grupo al cual pertenece cada estudiante.

Se aprecia que para el grupo 1, la tendencia en los promedios se mantiene de una asignatura a otra, es decir, que en términos generales, los estudiantes que tuvieron los promedios más altos en la primera asignatura son los que mantienen los promedios más altos en ésta segunda asignatura. Para el segundo grupo, se aprecia la situación contraria. Esto es, los estudiantes que presentaron los mejores promedios en la asignatura anterior, en ésta presentan los promedios más bajos. Esto se puede explicar por el cambio a una metodología a la que no están habituados.

Tabla 2. Calificaciones de los estudiantes

Grupo 1			Grupo 2		
1° Asig.	2° Asig.		1° Asig.	2° Asig.	
Promedio	Promedio	Estado	Promedio	Promedio	Estado
5,3	4,1	Aprobado	4,5	3,6	Reprobado
5,3	4,2	Aprobado	5,0	3,6	Reprobado
5,1	4,3	Aprobado	4,6	1,4	Reprobado
4,4	3,6	Reprobado	4,0	3,5	Reprobado
4,5	3,4	Reprobado	4,2	3,5	Reprobado
4,2	1,0	Reprobado	6,1	4,8	Aprobado
4,2	3,6	Reprobado	4,0	4,2	Aprobado
4,1	3,5	Reprobado	4,0	4,4	Aprobado
5,9	2,4	Reprobado	4,9	3,4	Reprobado
			5,0	3,4	Reprobado
			4,0	5,2	Aprobado

5 Discusión

5.1 Discusión acerca de los resultados

Esta sección presenta la discusión de los resultados del estudio. Se discuten las principales observaciones recogidas de los distintos estudios.

La evidencia recabada de las respuestas de los estudiantes da cuenta de lo siguiente:

- Existe evidencia de que un 50% de los estudiantes ha utilizado R&G para resolver los ejercicios propuestos, a pesar de que las condiciones impuesta por la asignatura no lo facilitaba.
- La utilización de R&G ha facilitado el aprendizaje de un 33% de los estudiantes en esta segunda asignatura, a pesar de no ser la metodología utilizada en la asignatura.
- Un 50% de estudiantes manifiesta que la metodologia utilizada en este curso le ha resultado más adecuada que R&G.

De las respuestas obtenidas del profesor responsable se desprende lo siguiente:

- No existe una diferencia apreciable en las prácticas de programación de los estudiantes de ambos grupos de estudio.
- Se aprecia que los estudiantes formados con R&G presentan un mejor desempeño en la conceptualización y en el análisis de los problemas.
- Se aprecia que los estudiantes que no fueron formados con R&G presentan levemente un mejor desempeño en el diseño de las soluciones .
- No se aprecian diferencias en la codificación de las soluciones de ambos grupos de estudiantes.

De este estudio, se deriva que sí existe evidencia de la utilización de la metodología en una segunda asignatura. Algunos estudiantes declaran explícitamente que utilizaron R&G en la resolución de los ejercicios de la asignatura, aun cuando manifiestan las dificultades y barreras que tuvieron para su uso, tales como restricciones de tiempo, resultados exigidos sólo a nivel de código, entre otras. El uso de la metodología en el primer curso, por tanto, logró un impacto en el estudiante. El cambio metodológico, en la segunda asignatura, afectó negativamente en los estudiantes que han aprendido con R&G, no así con el resto de los estudiantes. Esto puede indicar que cambios en el proceso de enseñanza-aprendizaje no son recomendables ni agregan valor al desarrollo de las competencias que un estudiante del área de desarrollo de software requiere. Se requiere por tanto, articular las asignaturas de programación con un enfoque metodológico común inicial. En cursos avanzados, los estudiantes deben ser capaces de concebir soluciones lógicas y procedimentales, por tanto no basta que solo posean dominio de un lenguaje de programación. Se sostiene, por tanto, que en los cursos superiores debería hacerse evidente la diferencia entre quienes se forman utilizando una metodología y quienes sólo se focalizan en el código final. Del estudio, también, se desprende que el foco en el diseño no ha generado un desmedro en el uso y dominio de un lenguaje de programación - de acuerdo a observación realizada por el profesor. Lo anterior, indica que R&G no afecta negativamente el desarrollo de habilidad en la codificación de los estudiantes. Por el contrario, se agrega una mejor preparación para el análisis de problemas y el diseña de soluciones y su posterior implementación como código fuente, siendo este mejor estructurado y documentado.

5.2 Limitaciones a la validez del estudio

Una de las limitaciones a la validez de los resultados, se relaciona con el tamaño de la muestra sobre el cual se extraen las conclusiones de nuestro trabajo. En efecto, el número de alumnos que cursa un primer y un segundo curso de programación no son numerosos y varía en un rango por semestre de entre 10 a 20 alumnos. Reconocemos que esto no permite extraer conclusiones más generalizadas, puesto que no se provee una muestra estadística mayor. Sin embargo, como una manera de enfrentar esta limitación, se definió el estudio del comportamiento de los estudiantes desde varios puntos de vista. Por ejemplo, se diseñó un estudio cuantitativo con el análisis de los promedios de los estudiantes. Además, se analizó la opinión de los estudiantes y del profesor de la asignatura, de manera tal de aumentar la objetividad del análisis.

6 Conclusión

Este artículo presenta los resultados de un estudio de seguimiento realizado sobre un grupo de alumnos a quienes se les enseñó a programar utilizando la metodología R&G, la cual pone el centro de interés en el diseño de una solución por sobre el código. Se evidenció que a pesar de ser sometidos a un ambiente adverso, en el cual no se favorece el uso de esta metodología, existe evidencia de que los alumnos persisten en utilizar la metodología aprendida. De este estudio se derivan cuatro conclusiones principales: (i) Los estudiantes se enfrentaron, en un segundo curso, a condiciones adversas y completamente diferentes a las condiciones provistas en el primer curso, lo cual no favoreció una mejor adopción de la metodologías. (ii) Existe evidencia del uso de la metodología, a pesar del ambiente en que no favorece su uso. (iii) Aun cuando los resultados de las evaluaciones finales no muestran diferencias significativas en relación al número de aprobados, dicho resultados sugieren una mejora en la calificación final obtenida. (iv) Lograr una mayor adopción de prácticas disciplinadas y sistemáticas requiere la existencia de actividades coordinadas, en los cursos posteriores, de manera de favorecer la adopción y refuerzo de las prácticas adquiridas.

El trabajo futuro comprende el diseño y desarrollo de una plataforma web que apoye el diseño de los algoritmos en un ambiente gráfico, incluyendo la generación automática de código. Se propone, además, ampliar el estudio de manera tal, de validar las conclusiones obtenidas en este estudio preliminar. Se ampliará la muestra de estudio, incluyendo a una Universidad del Perú, la cual dispone de un mayor número de estudiantes, 50 alumnos en el grupo de control y 50 alumnos en el grupo test, bajo igualdad de lenguajes de programación.

References

1. Garlan, D.: Software architecture: A roadmap, in Proceedings of the Conference on The Future of Software Engineering, ser. ICSE '00. New York, NY, USA: ACM, (2000), pp. 91–101. [Online]. Available: http://doi.acm.org/10.1145/336512.336537
2. Fincher, S.: What are we doing when we teach programming? in Frontiers in Education Conference. FIE '99. 29th Annual, vol. 1, Nov (1999), pp. 12A4/1–12A4/5 vol.1.
3. Gacitúa, R., Diéguez, M., Vidal, E.: Forming software architects in early stages: From craft to engineering. In: Proceedings of the XVIII Congreso Chileno de Educación en Computación (2017).
4. Garlan D. and Shaw, M.: An introduction to software architecture, Pittsburgh, PA, USA, Tech. Rep., (1994).
5. Parnas, D.L.: Risks of undisciplined development. Commun. ACM 53(10), 25–27 (Oct 2010), http://doi.acm.org/10.1145/1831407.1831419
6. McBreen, P. Software Craftsmanship: The New Imperative. Addison-Wesley, (2002). [Online]. Available: https://books.google.cl/books?id=JqJQAAAAMAAJ.
7. Martínez Carazo, P.C.: El método de estudio de caso: estrategia metodológica de la investigación científica. Pensamiento & gestión (20) (2006)
8. Yin, R.K.: Case study research: Design and methods. Sage Publications (1994).
9. Allen, I.E., Seaman, C.A.: Likert scales and data analyses. Quality progress 40(7), 64 (2007).

Traceability of requirements in Agile Methodologies: A systematic mapping

Héctor Cornide[1] and Rodolfo Villarroel[2]

[1] Departamento Ingeniería Informática y Ciencias de la Computación, Universidad de Atacama, Avenida Copayapu 485, Copiapó, Chile
hector.cornide@uda.cl
[2] Escuela Ingeniería Informática, Pontificia Universidad Católica de Valparaíso, Avenida Brasil 2241, Valparaíso, Chile

Abstract.
Background: Today, agile methodologies (MA) enjoy great popularity, however, there are not many papers that show in recent years the incorporation of requirements traceability in MA.
Goal: This study aims to analyze the way in which MA face scenarios of changes in requirements and if there is evidence of incorporation of traceability requirements in the MA.
Method: A Systematic Mapping of the Literature was carried out to obtain a visualization regarding the scientific contributions existing in this subject.
Result: We recovered a total of 20 primary studies, which we classified according to four criteria: process, tools, models and revisions. The increase in the number of publications in recent years shows the attractiveness of the subject.
Conclusions: The results obtained allow us to draw important conclusions that will help to conduct future research on this topic. The formalization of AgileRE could help the incorporation of requirements traceability.

Keywords: Agile Methodology, traceability, requirements, Systematic Mapping.

1 Introducción

En la actualidad, las metodologías ágiles gozan de una mayor y mejor presencia en la industria de desarrollo de software. La comunidad científica se ha mostrado muy activa en este tema, contribuyendo con publicaciones basadas en propuestas de mejora para: sus procesos de desarrollo, metodologías de enseñanza, experiencias de adopción en la industria, aspectos claves para formación de equipos ágiles, entre otras.

Cada vez, aumenta la utilización de MA debido a la simplicidad de sus reglas y prácticas, además de su orientación a equipos de desarrollos pequeños, la flexibilidad ante los cambios y su ideología de colaboración [1]. Estos proyectos se caracterizan por un énfasis sobre las interacciones humanas y colaboraciones, aligerando el desarrollo de procesos, entregas frecuentes y documentación mínima.

Dentro de las MA, los métodos empleados para gestionar los requerimientos son siempre discutidos y cuestionados, a diferencia de lo que sucede en los métodos tradicionales donde la trazabilidad de requisitos es adoptada sin mayores problemas. Son muchas las definiciones que se dan acerca de la trazabilidad de requerimientos, pero casi todos tienen opiniones muy parecidas a las que se presentan a continuación:

- "*Una especificación de un requerimiento de software es trazable si (i) el origen de cada requerimiento está claro y (ii) si se facilita la referencia de cada requerimiento en el desarrollo futuro o en la documentación*" [2]
- "*Es la capacidad de describir y de seguir la vida de un requisito, tanto en dirección hacia adelante y hacia atrás, es decir, desde sus orígenes, a través de su desarrollo y especificación, a su despliegue y uso subsecuentes, y a través de períodos de refinamiento y de la iteración en curso en cualesquiera de estas fases*" [3].
- Doorn [4], describe la trazabilidad desde el origen del requisito hasta la implementación de este requisito en el sistema y viceversa, es decir, hacia adelante y hacia atrás. Esto implica que un requerimiento debe de ser rastreable desde que se define y durante todo el desarrollo del software, lo cual garantiza una adecuada administración del cambio con el fin de evaluar el impacto en el resto del sistema.

En el caso de estar en la etapa de desarrollo de los requerimientos, se podrá evaluar cómo afectaría un cambio de un requisito en otro. Por otro lado, estando en etapa de implementación y en caso de que haya un cambio en los requerimientos, la trazabilidad permitirá hacer una evaluación en el diseño y en la implementación. Si el cambio se da cuando el sistema está implementado, la trazabilidad permitirá hacer una evaluación de cómo serán afectados los involucrados.

Aplicar trazabilidad es un proceso delicado, ya que, durante todo el desarrollo de un sistema, independientemente del modelo que se utilice, se deben de tomar en cuenta aquellos elementos que permitan rastrear el requerimiento desde su nacimiento hasta su puesta en marcha y viceversa.

Actualmente, los modelos de trazabilidad parecieran ser incompatibles con las prácticas de desarrollo ágil, porque la Ingeniería de Requisitos (IR) hace un marcado énfasis en la documentación para compartir e intercambiar conocimiento. Las metodologías ágiles buscan un punto medio entre ningún proceso y demasiados procesos, proporcionando sólo lo suficiente para que el esfuerzo sea redituable.

La motivación principal de esta investigación es analizar las evidencias científicas más recientes (últimos cinco años) respecto a las técnicas de trazabilidad de requisitos utilizadas en las MA. Como motivación secundaria, se espera identificar algunos nuevos métodos, técnicas y herramientas que permitan mejorar la gestión de cambios de requisitos en las MA.

Este artículo se encuentra organizado como sigue: en la sección 2, se describe el método de investigación utilizado. En la sección 3, se muestran los resultados obtenidos en la ejecución del Mapeo Sistemático con las evidencias encontradas para responder las preguntas de investigación y finalmente, en la sección 4 las conclusiones.

2 Metodología del mapeo

El mapeo sistemático de la literatura es un método definido para construir clasificaciones y conducir análisis temáticos a los efectos de obtener un mapa visual del conocimiento existente dentro de un tema amplio [5]. El análisis de los resultados se realiza categorizando los hallazgos y contando la frecuencia de publicaciones dentro de cada categoría para determinar la cobertura de las distintas áreas de un tema de investigación específico. La información generada se puede combinar para responder a preguntas de investigación más específicas y ahorrar tiempo y esfuerzo de investigación. Por lo anterior, los mapeos sistemáticos deben ser de calidad en términos de completitud y rigurosidad. El uso de esta herramienta permite identificar tópicos donde existen suficientes estudios primarios para conducir revisiones sistema áticas y tópicos donde se necesiten generar más estudios primarios [6]. Otro tipo de estudio secundario son las revisiones sistemáticas de la literatura. Las mismas, a diferencia del mapeo sistemático, son utilizadas para encontrar, evaluar y realizar la agregación de toda la evidencia presente en los artículos de investigación relevantes respecto a una pregunta específica de investigación. El objetivo es asegurar que la revisión de la literatura es objetiva, rigurosa y auditable [6]. Sin embargo, tiene como principal inconveniente el esfuerzo considerable requerido para su realización [5]. Se decide realizar un mapeo sistemático de la literatura debido a la necesidad de obtener una visión general respecto a los procesos de trazabilidad de requisitos en MA. En [5] sugieren un procedimiento que consta de 5 etapas (ver figura 1):

A. Definir preguntas de investigación.
B. Realizar la búsqueda literaria.
C. Seleccionar estudios.
D. Clasificar artículos.
E. Extraer y realizar la agregación de datos.

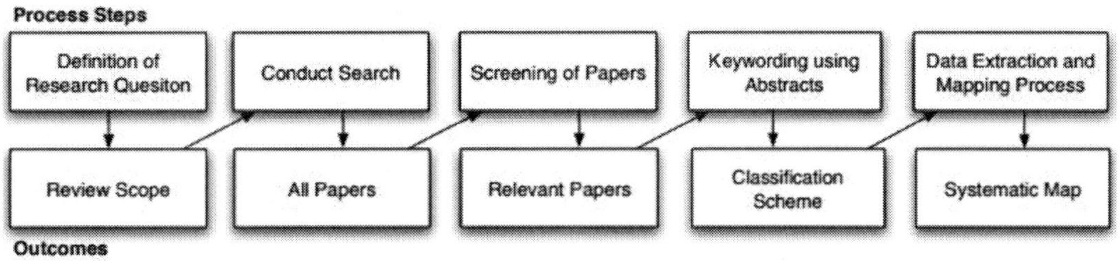

Fig. 1. Proceso para el Mapeo Sistemático [5]

2.1 Preguntas de investigación

El objetivo de esta investigación es analizar el escenario actual del proceso de trazabilidad de requisitos en MA y sus proyecciones de uso en este ámbito.

Este objetivo se divide en tres preguntas de investigación concretas para obtener un conocimiento más detallado y una visión integral del tema. Las preguntas de investigación a responder en este estudio son las siguientes:

- •RQ.1. ¿Qué propuestas formales existen para realizar la trazabilidad de requisitos en MA?
- •RQ.2. ¿Existen evidencias que permitan señalar que MA tiene una mejor adaptación a la trazabilidad de requerimientos?
- •RQ.3. En el contexto de los equipos de trabajo ágiles, ¿Cuáles son los desafíos que se deben considerar para realizar una adecuada trazabilidad ágil?

2.2 Fuente de datos y cadena de búsqueda.

La cadena de búsqueda se determinó sistemáticamente realizando distintas búsquedas relacionadas con el tema de investigación. De esta forma se pudo refinar el vocabulario y conocer el uso de sinónimos para poder generar cadenas más potentes. Las bases de datos de citaciones utilizadas fueron: Web of Science (WOS) y SCOPUS, mientras que la base de dato de publicaciones científicas fue: ScienceDirect.

La selección anterior, se debe a la gran reputación que poseen estas bases de datos y porque se contaba con acceso total al material publicado. Como fuente de datos externa, se consideraron dos artículos adicionales que provienen de la investigación exploratoria realizada de forma previa.

La cadena de búsqueda adaptada a cada motor considerando lo siguiente: ((agile OR agil OR agility) AND (traceability OR requierement OR requierements OR çhange management"))

- •**SCOPUS**: TITLE-ABS-KEY ((agile OR agil OR agility) AND (traceability OR requirement OR requirements OR (change AND management))) AND PUBYEAR >2011 AND (LIMIT-TO (SUBJAREA, ÇOMP "))
- •**WOS**: TITLE: (((agile OR agil) OR agility) AND (((traceability OR requirement) OR requirements) OR change management")) Timespan: 2012-2017.
- •**ScienceDirect**: pub-date >2011 and TITLE-ABSTR-KEY (agile OR agil OR agility) and TITLE-ABSTR-KEY ((traceability OR requirement OR requirements OR change management")) [All Sources (Computer Science)]

2.3 Criterios de inclusión y exclusión.

Serán elegibles todas aquellas publicaciones científicas que tengan relación con la Ingeniería de Software. Si el motor lo permitía, se filtró por la disciplina *Computer Science* y por la subdisciplina *Software Engineering*. Cómo el interés es analizar la forma en que se han ido incorporando los procesos de trazabilidad de requisitos en MA, sólo se consideran los artículos publicados a partir del 2012. Se excluyen los artículos que no mencionan algo relacionado con trazabilidad de requisitos en metodologías ágiles.

2.4 Extracción de datos y síntesis.

El formulario de extracción de datos se desarrolló con los siguientes campos: Título del artículo, Año, Autor, Tipo (Journal, Conferencia), N° de citaciones, Foco (Herramientas, Proceso, Modelo, Revisiones); Método utilizado; Principales contribuciones; Evidencias RQ1; Evidencias RQ3; Evidencias RQ3.

La conducta de búsqueda se definió de la siguiente manera:

- Como primer filtro (1F), se procedió a revisar todos los títulos y palabras claves de los artículos arrojados por cada base de datos. Luego se procedió a eliminar los artículos repetidos.
- Como segundo filtro (2F), se procedió a la lectura de abstract para todos aquellos artículos que pasaron el primer filtro.
- Finalmente, los artículos seleccionados fueron descargados desde la web, se leyeron completamente y se agregaron al formulario de registro de información creado en Microsoft Excel según el protocolo definido.

3 Ejecución del Mapeo sistemático

Una vez definido el protocolo de investigación, se ejecutó la revisión. Como resultado de la aplicación de la cadena de búsqueda, se obtuvo un total de 1003 artículos. En la figura 2, es posible observar el proceso de ejecución del Mapeo, seleccionando finalmente 20 estudios primarios.

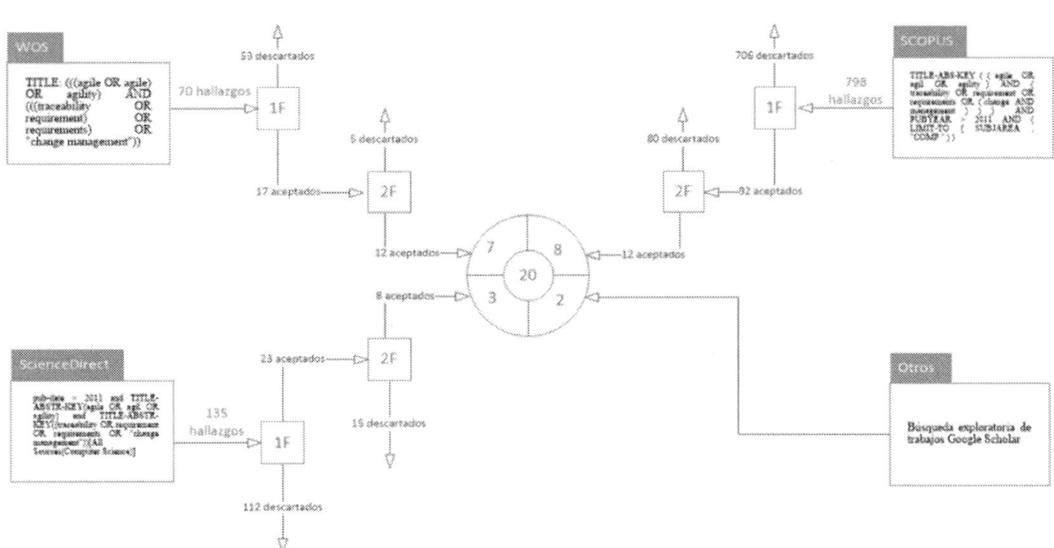

Fig. 2. Resultados del proceso de Mapeo sistemático

3.1 Vista general de los artículos

En la figura 3, se muestra la distribución de estudios primarios seleccionados por año y por base de datos científica utilizada.

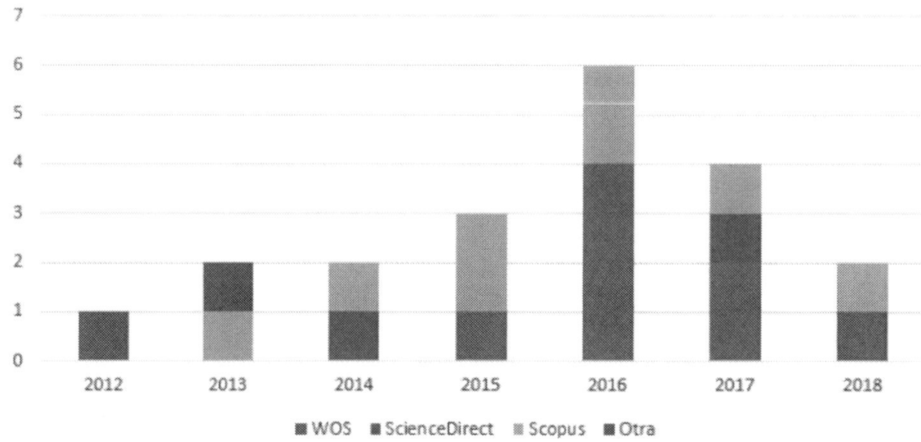

Fig. 3. Distribución de estudios primarios por año y por base de datos.

En la figura 4 se observa la distribución según el foco de los estudios primarios donde el mayor porcentaje responde a propuestas teóricas (propuestas de mejora de procesos, nuevos modelos y revisiones de literatura) lo que provoca un escaso número de artículos que posean validaciones empíricas.

De las figuras anteriores, sólo es posible constatar el gran interés que existe respecto a la trazabilidad de requisitos en metodologías ágiles.

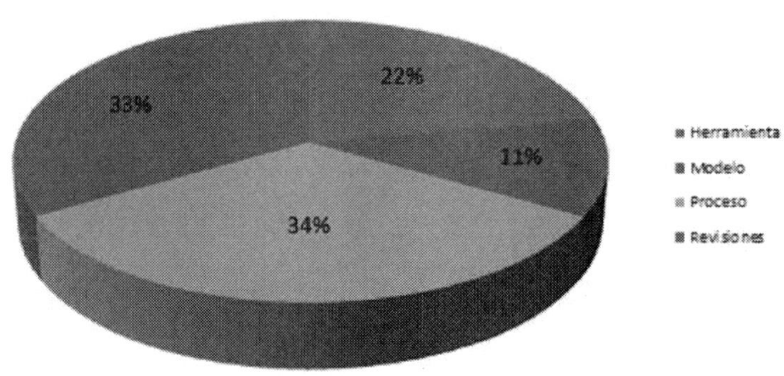

Fig. 4. Distribución según foco de los estudios primarios seleccionados.

Tabla 1. Estudios primarios seleccionados en el proceso de Mapeo.

N°	Estudio Primario	Autor	Año
P1	A supporting tool for requirements change management in distributed agile development	Domia Lloyd, Ramadan Moawad, Mona Kadry	2017
P2	A systematic review of requirements change management	Shalinka Jayatilleke, Richard Lai	2018
P3	The Essential Nature of Product Traceability and its Relation to Agile Approaches	Kent D. Palmer	2014
P4	A multi-faceted roadmap of requirements traceability types adoption in SCRUM: An empirical study	Alaa G., Samir Z.	2015
P5	A survey on product backlog change management and requirement traceability in agile (Scrum)	Alsalemi A.M., Yeoh E.-T.	2016
P6	Achieving lightweight trustworthy traceability	Cleland-Huang J., Rahimi M., Mäder P	2014
P7	AgileRE: Agile Requirements Management Tool	Gaikwad V., Joeg P., Joshi S.,	2018
P8	Requirements engineering in agile projects: A systematic mapping based in evidences of industry	Medeiros J.D.R.V., Alves D.C.P., Vasconcelos A., Silva C., Wanderley E.,	2015
P9	Trace++: A Traceability Approach to Support Transitioning to Agile Software Engineering	Furtado F., Zisman A.	2016
P10	Traceability in agile projects	Cleland-Huang J.	2013
P11	Tracepp requeriments traceability tool: Extending the scalability of the trace++ technique	Naves F.	2017
P12	A systematic literature review on agile requirements engineering practices and challenges	Inayat, Irum; Salim, Siti Salwah; Marczak, Sabrina; Daneva, Maya; Shamshirband,	2015
P13	Agile Development as a Change Management Approach in Software Projects: Applied Case Study	Alawairdhi, Mohammed	2016
P14	Agile Requirements Engineering: A systematic literature review	Schon, Eva-Maria; Thomaschewski, Joerg; Jose Escalona, Maria	2017
P15	Impact and Challenges of Requirement Engineering in Agile Methodologies: A Systematic Review	Alam, Sehrish; Shah, S. Asim Ali; Bhatti, Shahid Nazir; Jadi, Amr Mohsen	2017
P16	Lightweight Traceability for the Agile Architect	Gayer, Sebastian; Herrmann, Andrea; Keuler, Thorsten; Riebisch, Matthias; Antonino, Pablo Oliveira	2016
P17	Reviewon Agile Requirements Engineering Challenges	Elghariani, Kaiss; Kama, Nazri	2016
P18	Trace plus plus : A Traceability Approach to Support Transitioning to Agile Software Engineering	Furtado, Felipe; Zisman, Andrea	2016
P19	Trazabilidad de Requisitos Adaptada a las Necesidades del proyecto: Un Caso de Estudio Usando Alternativamente RUP y XP	Víctor Anaya, Patricio Letelier	2012
P20	Sistema de control de trazabilidad de requerimientos en ambientes ágiles de desarrollo de software	José Manuel Hernández Reyes ; Carlos Enríquez Ramírez	2013

4 Discusión de resultados

El análisis de la información para discutir los resultados se realizó analizando y clasificando los estudios primarios seleccionados, según las preguntas de investigación que dieron origen al presente estudio.

4.1 RQ.1. ¿Qué propuestas formales existen para realizar la trazabilidad de requisitos en MA?

Al revisar los estudios primarios seleccionados, fue posible analizar las distintas propuestas para conducir un proceso de trazabilidad en las metodologías ágiles.

De los estudios primarios, es rescatable el valor que la comunidad científica le otorga al proceso de trazabilidad de requisitos, a pesar, de que parte de la industria del desarrollo del software, tiende a no otorgar el mismo valor a esta actividad por considerar que la inclusión de este tipo de tareas haría más pesada la metodología que por principios tienen que ser livianas.

En la tabla 2, se describen las propuestas plasmadas en los estudios primarios seleccionados luego del proceso de mapeo sistemático realizado.

Tabla 2. Tipos de propuestas para trazabilidad

N°	Propuesta de Trazabilidad	Estudio primario relacionado
1	Herramienta de apoyo	P1; P9; P18; P19
2	Mejora de procesos	P3; P4; P5; P6; P13; P16
3	Modelo	P10; P20
4	Revisiones/Mapeo Sistemáticas	P2; P8; P12; P14; P15; P17

Un aspecto que llamó la atención, fue la cantidad de revisiones/mapeos sistemáticas existentes en la literatura. Esta situación se evalúa positivamente y es producto al gran interés en la búsqueda de soluciones que ayuden a clarificar los temas relativos a trazabilidad de requisitos en MA.

El estudio que posee la mayor cantidad de citaciones (102), es precisamente una reciente revisión sistemática de la literatura [7] que busca evidencias para conocer si existe o no, la Ingeniería de Requerimientos Ágil. Como resultado, pudieron identificar 17 prácticas para realizar este proceso, siendo la más frecuente la priorización de requerimientos.

En [8], se analiza la problemática que tiene el desarrollo distribuido de software ágil y el aumento de probabilidad de fracaso de los proyectos sino se mejora la gestión de los requerimientos. Para abordar este problema se desarrolla una herramienta web que muestra resultados muy prometedores.

En [9] se presenta la herramienta Trace++ y en [10] aparece la herramienta SharpTrace. En ambos casos son herramientas que muestran buenos resultados, pero, carecen de evidencia empírica que permita indicar que los resultados pueden ser replicables en otros entornos.

Las propuestas relacionadas a mejoras en los procesos de las MA [11] [12] [13] [14] [15] [16], tienen por objetivo "limpiar" y "optimizar" algunos elementos de forma que permitan realizar procesos de trazabilidad de requisitos sin sobrecargar de actividades la metodología que, por principios, siempre se espera que sea liviana. Sin embargo, se reconoce la necesidad y casi obligatoriedad de incorporar elementos debido a que las MA se han comenzado a utilizar en desarrollos de software con características complejas.

En la investigación realizada por [17], se analizaron algunos modelos de trazabilidad para el desarrollo de software. Los modelos analizados fueron:

1. Modelo de Lindvall & Sandahl [18].
2. Modelo de Gotel, Mader, Philippow [19].
3. Modelo de Ramesh-Jarke [20].

4. Modelo de Letelier, Anaya [21] [22].
5. Modelo de Egyed [23].
6. Enterprise Architect [24].

Estos modelos han sido ampliamente utilizados y aplicados bajo metodologías tradicionales, pero no han sido aún considerados para las MA, principalmente debido a la confianza de los equipos de trabajo en la propia MA.

4.2 RQ.2. ¿Existen evidencias que permitan señalar que MA tiene una mejor adaptación a la trazabilidad de requerimientos?

Compleja fue la tarea de encontrar evidencias para identificar cuál MA se ajusta mejor a procesos de trazabilidad de requisitos. Al iniciar la investigación, se consideraba que se encontrarían evidencias con claras tendencias hacia Scrum, debido a que es la metodología ágil mayormente utilizada. Sin embargo, sólo los estudios [12] [13], abordan el tema de trazabilidad de requisitos en Scrum, mientras que en [10] lo hace en XP.

Lo anterior, se debe a que las propuestas son aún teóricas resultando difícil y costoso lograr una validación empírica en alguna MA. Por lo general, la retroalimentación respecto a este tipo de temas se obtiene mediante encuestas de opinión que recogen las percepciones de los involucrados en el proceso.

4.3 RQ.3. En el contexto de los equipos de trabajo ágiles, ¿Cuáles son los desafíos que se deben considerar para realizar una adecuada trazabilidad ágil?

Al revisar los estudios primarios, se evidencia que los equipos de trabajo ágiles no están muy convencidos de añadir elementos de trazabilidad a la metodología de trabajo, es más, en [7] los autores indican que muchos equipos de trabajo ágiles visualizan la Ingeniería de Requerimientos como un proceso que sólo le pertenece a las metodologías tradicionales y que sus principios, conceptos y métodos no son replicables en MA. Sin embargo, en los equipos de trabajo ágiles que han enfrentado proyectos un poco más largos y complejos, la postura es distinta. Se reconoce el concepto de AgileRE, en [25] se visualizan avances formales en su utilización y en [7] plantean los siguientes desafíos:

- Los equipos de desarrollo ágiles plantean la necesidad de mantener una mínima documentación.
- Mejorar el involucramiento con el cliente.
- Estimación de presupuestos y planes de trabajo.
- Descuido por los requerimientos no-funcionales.
- Limitaciones contractuales
- Evaluación de los cambios en los requerimientos.

En [12] y [13] abordan la problemática de trazabilidad basados en Scrum. [12] propone una taxonomía de trazabilidad de los requisitos en el contexto del desarrollo ágil.

También se realizó un estudio empírico, focus group, donde los hallazgos indican que una visión multifacética resulta importante para el diseño de herramientas de trazabilidad de requisitos. En [13], a través de una encuesta, logran observar que los cambios de requerimientos en el product backlog no se registran porque son considerados como un nuevo requisito. Lo anterior, hace que el concepto de trazabilidad no aplique en Scrum. Sin embargo, a través de la misma encuesta, se observa que las prácticas AgileRE son bien percibidas por los equipos Scrum. Lamentablemente, falta un método específico para la trazabilidad de requisitos para los proyectos de Scrum

5 Conclusiones

En este artículo, se realizó un Mapeo Sistemático para poder analizar la problemática actual de la trazabilidad de requisitos en las metodologías ágiles y para identificar desafíos que enfrentan los equipos de trabajo ágiles.

Las prácticas AgileRE, tiene muchas oportunidades de adopción en los equipos ágiles, debido a que las MA están siendo utilizadas para enfrentar proyectos cada vez más grandes y complejos, lo que obliga a tomar acciones concretas sobre los requerimientos para garantizar el éxito del proyecto.

Se pudo identificar a través de evidencias de la industria, que existen dos grandes problemas para desarrollar adecuadamente el proceso de AgileRE. Estos son: la baja calidad en la participación de los usuarios en los proyectos y la gestión inadecuada de los cambios. En la medida que se formalicen métodos formales en estos aspectos, AgileRE cobrará cada vez más y mejor importancia para los equipos de trabajo ágiles.

A través de las revisiones sistemáticas de la literatura existentes, se pudo constatar que se han propuesto un gran número de métodos, prácticas y herramientas para dar soporte a la trazabilidad, sin embargo, al carecer de evidencias empíricas que validen las contribuciones, dichos trabajos van quedando registrados en la literatura, pero no adoptados por la industria del desarrollo de software.

Si bien muchos desarrolladores ágiles descartan la idea de incorporar técnicas de trazabilidad de requisitos en proyectos MA, el tamaño y la creciente complejidad de los proyectos ágiles obliga a encontrar formas de lograr los beneficios de la trazabilidad sin el costo y el esfuerzo de los enfoques tradicionales.

Como trabajo futuro, se realizará un análisis comparativo entre las técnicas de trazabilidad detectadas en esta investigación para determinar cuál es la que reúne mejores condiciones para ser considerada por los equipos ágiles.

Agradecimientos

Héctor Cornide Reyes es beneficiario de la Beca INF-PUCV 2016 en la realización de sus estudios de Doctorado en Ingeniería Informática en la Pontificia Universidad Católica de Valparaíso.

Referencias

1. Reyes, J. M. H., & Ramírez, C. E. Sistema de control de trazabilidad de requerimientos en ambientes ágiles de desarrollo de software.
2. Antonelli, R. L., & Oliveros, A. (2000). Traceability en la Etapa de Elicitación de Requerimientos. In II Workshop de Investigadores en Ciencias de la Computación.
3. Gotel, O. C., & Finkelstein, C. W. (1994, April). An analysis of the requirements traceability problem. In Requirements Engineering, 1994., Proceedings of the First International Conference on (pp. 94-101). IEEE.
4. Jorge H. Doorn, Carmen Leonardi, Marcela Ridao, Universidad Central de Buenos Aires. DOI=http: www.exa.unicen.edu.ar/catedras/ingrequi/index_archivos/2007_lunes8_inicio.ppt
5. Kai Petersen, Robert Feldt, Shahid Mujtaba, and Michael Mattsson. Systematic mapping studies in software engineering. In EASE, volume 8, pages 68-77, 2008.
6. Barbara A Kitchenham, David Budgen, and O Pearl Brereton. Using mapping studies as the basis for further research a participant-observer case study. Information and Software Technology, 53(6):638-651, 2011.
7. Inayat, I., Salim, S. S., Marczak, S., Daneva, M., & Shamshirband, S. (2015). A systematic literature review on agile requirements engineering practices and challenges. Computers in human behavior, 51, 915-929.
8. Lloyd, D., Moawad, R., & Kadry, M. (2017). A supporting tool for requirements change management in distributed agile development. Future Computing and Informatics Journal.
9. Furtado, F., & Zisman, A. (2016, September). Trace++: A Traceability Approach to Support Transitioning to Agile Software Engineering. In Requirements Engineering Conference (RE), 2016 IEEE 24th International (pp. 66-75). IEEE.
10. Anaya, V., & Letelier, P. (2002). Trazabilidad de Requisitos Adaptada a Las Necesidades Del Proyecto: Un Caso de Estudio Usando Alterativamente RUP Y XP.
11. Palmer, K. D. (2014). The Essential Nature of Product Traceability and its Relation to Agile Approaches. Procedia Computer Science, 28, 44-53.
12. Alaa, G., & Samir, Z. (2014, December). A multi-faceted roadmap of requirements traceability types adoption in SCRUM: An empirical study. In Informatics and Systems (INFOS), 2014 9th International Conference on (pp. SW-1). IEEE.
13. Alsalemi, A. M., & Yeoh, E. T. (2015, December). A survey on product backlog change management and requirement traceability in agile (Scrum). In Software Engineering Conference (MySEC), 2015 9th Malaysian (pp. 189-194). IEEE.
14. Cleland-Huang, J., Rahimi, M., & Mäder, P. (2014, November). Achieving lightweight trustworthy traceability. In Proceedings of the 22nd ACM SIGSOFT International Symposium on Foundations of Software Engineering (pp. 849-852). ACM.
15. Alawairdhi, M. (2016, May). Agile development as a change management approach in software projects: Applied case study. In Information Management (ICIM), 2016 2nd International Conference on (pp. 100-104). IEEE.
16. Gayer, S., Herrmann, A., Keuler, T., Riebisch, M., & Antonino, P. O. (2016). Lightweight traceability for the Agile architect. Computer, 49(5), 64-71.
17. Lina María Montoya Suarez and Gabriel Jaime Correa Henao. Modelos de trazabilidad de requisitos para el desarrollo de software. QUID: Investigación, Ciencia y Tecnología, (20):29-38, 2013.
18. Mikael Lindvall and Kristian Sandahl. Traceability aspects of impact analysis in object-oriented systems. Journal of Software: Evolution and Process, 10(1):37-57, 1998.

19. Orlena CZ Gotel and CW Finkelstein. An analysis of the requirements traceability problem. In Requirements Engineering, 1994., Proceedings of the First International Conference on, pages 94-101. IEEE, 1994.
20. Balasubramaniam Ramesh and Matthias Jarke. Toward reference models for requirements traceability. IEEE transactions on software engineering, 27(1):58-93, 2001.
21. Víctor Anaya and Patricio Letelier. Smarttrace: Una herramienta para trazabilidad de requisitos en proyectos basados en uml. In WER, pages 210-224, 2002.
22. Patricio Letelier and Víctor Anaya. Entregrando especificaciones textuales y elementos de modelado uml en un marco de trabajo para trazabilidad de requisitos. In JISBD, pages 151-162, 2002.
23. Alexander Egyed. A scenario-driven approach to trace dependency analysis. IEEE Transactions on Software Engineering, 29(2):116-132, 2003.
24. Enterprise architect - sparx system, visited 11/2017.
25. Cao, L., & Ramesh, B. (2008). Agile requirements engineering practices: An empirical study. IEEE software, 25(1).

Guide for the selection of software development methodologies for small projects and small equipment

Nahur M. Meléndez Araya[1], Claudio Salazar Cortes[1]

[1] Universidad de Atacama, Avd Copayapu #485, Copiapó, Chile
{nahur.melendez, claudio.salazar}@uda.cl

Abstract. There is no single and universal software development methodology that applies to all cases, but there is one that is best suited for each type of project. There are a large number of them that could be used in a software development project, however, the particularity of each project requires a thorough disposition of the activities, whether they are associated with traditional, agile or hybrid methodologies. Considering that the small projects and small teams are those that mostly lack a methodological framework to guide them, the article presents a guide that supports the project manager in make decision the most appropriate methodology, considering the characteristics and scope of the project. For this, the dimensions of the triangle of projects (cost, scope and time) are considered, as well as the methodology of Function Points.

Keywords: Selection of Methodologies, Development Methodologies, Traditional Methodologies, Agile Methodologies, Software Engineering.

1 Introducción.

El éxito o fracaso de cada proyecto está condicionado por una gran cantidad de variables, como el equipo de desarrollo, los solicitantes y la manera en que se organizará el proyecto (gestión de proyectos) [1]. Considerando lo anterior, el trabajo presentado por Pérez [2], expone que una mala gestión de los requisitos en un proyecto de software representa alrededor del 65% de los problemas en gestión de proyectos.

Estudios como el presentado por Carrizo y colegas [3], así como el de Eia [4] y el de Hernández [5], han demostrado un crecimiento vertiginoso en la industria del software latinoamericana, sin embargo esta aun es incipiente e inmadura, lo cual conlleva a una falta de competitividad, que a su vez dificulta su crecimiento [6].

Sin embargo, para lograr un resultado positivo para el cliente, no sólo hay que gestionar correctamente el proyecto, sino que también hay que aplicar técnicas y métodos adecuados para el desarrollo de software. Un problema común es aplicar una metodología de desarrollo de software determinada sin mayor análisis, trayendo como consecuencia que los involucrados no harán lo que se supone deben hacer, impactando negativamente en el proyecto. Pérez en [2], plantea que muchas veces esto se debe por una falta de entrenamiento adecuado o por una resistencia al cambio de las personas, así como una mayor valorización al aspecto técnico por sobre el metodológico. Una forma de dar solución a esta compleja problemática es aplicando un modelo de gestión del software adecuado que sea entendido por todos y lo suficientemente flexible para adaptarse a proyectos de distinta envergadura [7].

Los fracasos de los proyectos se pueden atribuir a distintas causas, Morreale en [1] indica que estas pueden darse en las etapas de desarrollo, en la implementación o un tiempo después de ser implementado el proyecto, siendo una de sus principales causas la poca experiencia y preparación de los profesionales participantes en el proyecto. De igual modo, otros trabajos [8] [9] [10], informan que el costo que implica reparar errores (o defectos) cometidos durante el desarrollo del software, una vez realizada la entrega del producto, representa entre 60% y 100% de sobrecosto en comparación con lo que hubiera implicado detectarlos en fases más tempranas.

Según plantea Morreale [1], los desarrolladores individuales y los pequeños equipos de trabajo presentan serios problemas de madurez en sus procesos de desarrollo (en muchos casos no existe un proceso real), debido al desconocimiento del cómo aplicar una u otra metodología, esto conduce a software desarrollado de forma fortuita, cuyo resultado en calidad es deficiente y posiblemente destinado a fallar.

Entendiendo que los proyectos de software que cumplen con las necesidades y satisfacen al usuario son exitosos, en contraste con aquellos que no fueron debidamente definidos y documentados [11] [12] y considerando que los proyectos pequeños son los que mayoritariamente carecen de un marco metodológico que los guíe, el presente trabajo propone una guía metodológica que ayude a los pequeños grupos de desarrolladores, a visualizar cuál es la metodología a aplicar para enfrentar de mejor manera el proyecto software y disminuir los riesgos en él.

2 Metodologías de desarrollo de software.

Aunque teóricamente las metodologías clásicas de desarrollo podrían servir para cualquier tipo y tamaño de proyecto, en la realidad se consideran apropiadas para proyectos y equipos grandes de 10 o más miembros [13], ya que para un proyecto pequeño sólo la exhaustiva documentación que exige, podría demandar más recursos de los disponibles y aumentar considerablemente los tiempos.

Asimismo, se suele pensar que las metodologías ágiles tendrían que resolver los problemas y críticas anteriores, por ser uno de sus puntos fuertes la entrega rápida de versiones para obtener retroalimentación que ayude a desarrollos más apropiados a las necesidades del cliente, así como ser apropiadas para equipos de 3 a 20 personas [13].

Sin embargo la particularidad de cada proyecto de desarrollo de software, obliga a disponer minuciosamente las actividades, ya sea que éstas se encuentren asociadas a metodologías tradicionales, ágiles o híbridas. Akther y Miniruzzaman [14] a partir de su estudio de los modelos de Ciclo de Vida para el desarrollo de software, presentan las definiciones y características de las principales metodologías (Tabla 1).

Tabla 1. Comparación de perspectivas en el Desarrollo de Software [14].

Aspecto Evaluado	Enfoque Tradicional	Enfoque Ágil
Ciclo de vida del desarrollo	Modelo del ciclo de vida lineal (Cascada, espiral o variación)	Iterativa, Modelo de entregas evolutivas.
Estilo de desarrollo	Anticipatorio	Adaptativo
Requisitos	Conocidos tempranamente, ampliamente y estables. Claramente definido y documentado	Emergente, de cambio rápido, desconocido. Descubierto durante el proyecto.
Arquitectura	Arquitectura pesada para los actuales y futuros requisitos posibles	Se basa en el dicho "Sólo haz lo necesario"
Administración	Centrada en el proceso, comando y control	Centrada en las personas, liderazgo y colaboración.
Documentación	Pesada/Detallada. Conocimiento explícito	Liviana. Comunicación cara a cara. Conocimiento tácito.
Metas	Previsibilidad y optimización	Exploración o adaptación
Cambio	Tendencia a ser adverso a los cambios.	Se adhiere a los cambios
Miembros del equipo	Equipos de especialistas distribuidos. Las habilidades se adaptan a un plan.	Ágiles, conocidos, colaborativos.
Organización del equipo	Equipos preestructurados	Equipos autorganizados
Involucramiento del cliente	Bajo involucramiento, pasivo.	Cliente en el sitio y considerado como miembro del equipo. Activo/proactivo
Cultura organizacional	Cultura de jerarquía y control	Cultura de liderazgo y colaboración
Proceso de desarrollo de software	Enfoque universal y hacia una solución predecible y segura.	Enfoque flexible, adaptable al conocimiento colectivo entendiendo las necesidades contextuales para proveer un desarrollo rápido.
Medición del éxito	Conforme al plan	Valor entregado al negocio

3 Equipos Pequeños y Proyectos Pequeños

Douglas Smith [15] define equipo de trabajo como, dos o más personas con habilidades complementarias, que están comprometidas con un propósito, un conjunto de metas de desempeño y un enfoque común, por los cuales se hacen mutuamente responsables. Los resultados de Putnam [16] evidenciaron algo que muchos desarrolladores sospechaban: cuando el tamaño del equipo crecía más allá de un número de personas establecido, el esfuerzo aumentaba pero el tiempo del proyecto no se reducía.

Por un lado, nuestra propuesta metodológica considera "Equipo Pequeño de Desarrollo de Software" el compuesto por 2 a 5 integrantes, los cuales cubren todas las capacidades requeridas. Así mismo, la clara identificación de los roles ayuda a estructurar y organizar el equipo, y sus respectivas responsabilidades; en este aspecto, nuestra propuesta, toma como base los cinco roles principales definidos en Metrica v3 [17]: i) Directivo, ii) Jefe de Proyecto (JP), iii) Consultor, iv) Analista y v) Programador. Además, se considera relevante la definición de un nuevo rol, el "Cliente", debido a que en las diversas metodologías analizadas cumple un rol importante, pero no está incluido entre roles especificados originalmente en Métrica v3.

Por otro lado, definimos un "Proyecto Pequeño de Desarrollo de Software" en base a tres criterios. El primero asume que los requisitos son relativamente estables y que el proyecto será administrado por el cliente y el desarrollador. El segundo criterio es el entregado por Putnam [16], que se basa en la cantidad de líneas de código que pueden llegar a tener los proyectos. Y tercero, la forma de estimar sería en base a criterios y juicios de expertos.

Por último, los tipos de proyectos pequeños de desarrollo de software, para los cuales es aplicable esta guía son: i) de mantenimiento, ii) mejora funcional, iii) mejora técnica, iv) nuevo desarrollo, v) desarrollo breve, vi) capacitación, vii) revisión de calidad, viii) reingeniería, ix) web, x) empresariales y xi) móviles.

4 Criterios de selección.

No existe una metodología de desarrollo de software única y universal que se aplique a todos los proyectos, pero si existe una metodología que se adapta mejor para cada tipo de proyecto [18]. En el momento de elegir y adoptar un estándar o construir una metodología, hay que considerar algunos requisitos importantes, así las variables más relevantes presentadas por Asensio en [19] consideran que la metodología debe:

- Ajustarse a los objetivos, cada aproximación al desarrollo de software está basada en unos objetivos.
- Cubrir totalmente el ciclo de vida del desarrollo de software.
- Integrar las distintas fases del ciclo de vida de desarrollo de software.
- Incluir la realización de validaciones.
- Soportar la determinación de la exactitud del sistema en del ciclo de desarrollo.
- Ser la base de una comunicación efectiva.
- Funcionar en un entorno dinámico orientado al usuario.
- Especificar claramente los responsables de resultados.
- Poder emplearse en un entorno amplio de proyectos software.
- Poder ser enseñada.
- Estar soportada por herramientas CASE.
- Soportar la eventual evolución del sistema.
- Contener actividades conducentes a mejorar el proceso de desarrollo de software.

La cuantificación de los criterios se llevó a cabo a partir del estudio de las características, ventajas y desventajas de las metodologías según la bibliografía revisada, no obstante la cuantificación principal se obtiene del trabajo de Ahmed [20] y del realizado por Qumer [21]. En base a lo anterior, se cuantificaron un total de quince metodologías repartidas entre tradicionales y ágiles, evaluando aspectos desde la teoría (y en algunos casos de forma empírica) que se consideran relevantes en su uso (Tabla 2). La participación del cliente es un criterio que se debe agregar a las tradicionales, "Flexibilidad", "Velocidad" y "Bajo Costo" que se revisan sistemáticamente cuando se intenta encontrar criterios unificadores, es así que para el desarrollo de esta propuesta se define lo siguiente:

- *Presupuesto asignado*: Nivel de presupuesto que demanda trabajar con la metodología. 5 presupuesto más alto, 1 menor presupuesto.
- *Tiempo asignado:* El tiempo asignado al proyecto es relevante para esta metodología. 5 es importante, 1 es poco importante.
- *Documentación:* La metodología requiere documentación exhaustiva. 5 Mayor documentación, 1 Menor documentación
- *Equipo de trabajo:* La metodología requiere de varios roles para poder ser implementada. 5 Mas roles, 1 menos roles.
- *Respuestas al cambio:* La metodología no permite cambios en etapas avanzadas del proyecto. 5 Permite cambios, 1 no permite cambios.
- *Cliente:* La metodología integra a cliente como parte del equipo en todo el proceso de desarrollo. 5 (siempre presente) - 1 (presente esporádicamente).

Para esta evaluación la escala se considera: el cumplimiento total asignando un valor de 5 (100%), cumplimiento parcial 4 (80%), cumplimiento equilibrado valor 3 (60%), 2 cumplimiento bajo (40%) o mínimo asignando el número 1 con un 20%.

Tabla 2. Cuantificación Criterios v/s Metodologías (Elaboraba en base a [14]).

Criterio Evaluado	**Cascada**	**Modelo V**	**Iterativo**	**Incremental**	**Espiral**	**Prototipo**	**Evolutivo**	**RAD**	**RUP**	**XP**	**DAS**	**Scrum**	**DSDM**	**Crystal**	**Mobile-D**
Presupuesto asignado	1	1	1	1	1	1	1	1	1	2	1	1	1	1	1
Tiempo asignado	2	1	3	3	5	2	1	4	5	4	5	5	4	5	1
Documentación	4	2	1	1	2	4	2	4	4	5	5	5	4	4	3
Equipo de trabajo	4	4	2	3	5	4	4	4	3	4	5	5	5	5	4
Respuestas al cambio	2	2	2	1	2	3	3	1	3	4	4	5	5	5	1
Cliente	2	1	1	1	2	3	3	5	2	4	5	5	5	5	3

5 Guía metodológica propuesta

Los equipos pequeños presentan ventajas respecto a la comunicación y la distribución de los roles necesarios para enfrentar el proyecto, sin embargo, la mayoría de las veces estos grupos desconocen o no aplican metodologías de desarrollo de software que les permitan poder planificar y desarrollar de mejor manera un proyecto. La propuesta pretende orientar al JP respecto a la selección de la metodología que mejor se adapta a un proyecto dado sus características. Los desarrollos que en su ejecución o alguna de sus etapas, como el levantamiento de requisitos o implementación, requieran de un equipo grande quedan fuera del alcance de esta guía.

La guía para la selección de metodologías, hace uso de variables como tiempo, costo y alcance, las cuales derivan de una secuencia de etapas, que comienzan en la definición que realiza el JP respecto al nivel de presupuesto disponible, que pudiera estar sujeto a un presupuesto general para proyectos de desarrollo o bien derivado de su apreciación personal en calidad de experto. También debe indicar si el proyecto es de tamaño pequeño, considerando que en general, se puede definir en función de una experiencia de desarrollo anterior, la cantidad de líneas de código o la duración del proyecto. En cuanto a la documentación que se exige, podrían ser simples manuales de usuario o una documentación técnica exhaustiva debido a las características propias y que son conocidas por el JP. La disponibilidad de desarrolladores y miembros del equipo en general también es una entrada conocida que se analizará de acuerdo a la cantidad de miembros y los roles que asuman a la hora de comenzar el proyecto.

5.1 Variables costo, tiempo y alcance

La guía propuesta considera las dimensiones del triángulo de proyectos por cuanto se basa en una combinación de costo, alcance y tiempo. Si una de estas dimensiones es grande, el proyecto se vuelve más pesado. El triángulo de proyectos permite visualizar de manera gráfica el comportamiento de las variables, mientras mayor sea el nivel de equivalencia entre los lados del triángulo, más equilibrado será su desarrollo. Un cambio en el alcance, por ejemplo, provocará que tanto el tiempo como el costo se vean afectados para mantener su equilibrio.

Se debe considerar que en el desarrollo de software utilizando metodologías tradicionales del tipo en cascada, el tiempo y los recursos estimados son los que se imponen en la base del triángulo e intentan ajustar los recursos a requisitos que se consideran fijos, ya que resultan de un análisis detallado de las reglas del negocio. Por su parte, las metodologías ágiles intentan invertir este triángulo considerando fijos el tiempo y los recursos; en cambio las características del producto son las que se estiman, siendo los requisitos posibles de modificar a medida que el proyecto avanza.

5.2 Determinación del tamaño

Para seleccionar el tamaño del esfuerzo, tiempo y la cantidad de personal necesario, se utiliza la metodología de Puntos de Función (PF). Este método trata de determinar el número total de PF de un sistema basándose únicamente en los documentos técnicos que recogen la especificación de requisitos funcionales, cabe señalar que una las características principales de este método, es que su aplicación es factible desde las primeras etapas del ciclo de vida de la aplicación de software, es decir, desde el momento en que se elaboran dichos documentos técnicos. Los PF tratan de determinar, lo más pronto posible, la funcionalidad que proporciona a los usuarios una determinada aplicación software. Los puntos de función siguen una serie de pasos concretos basados en reglas y criterios específicos definidos por la International Function Point Uses Group (IFPUG) [22]:

- Contar del número total de Puntos de Función sin ajustar (PFsA), para cada componente del sistema (Entradas Externas, Salidas Externas, Consultas Externas, Ficheros Lógicos Internos y Ficheros Externos de Interfaz).
- Ajustar mediante un Factor de Ajuste (VAF) ó Factor de Complejidad Técnica y contar el número de Puntos de Función ajustados.
- Validar resultados.

Estimación de PFsA. Medición del tamaño funcional del software desde el punto de vista del cliente, no considera ningún aspecto de implementación de la solución. Cuantifica los requisitos funcionales del usuario, visualiza las funcionalidades del software y le asigna un puntaje de acuerdo a una métrica de complejidad (Tabla 3). Todo sistema tiene un Buscar (EQ), Actualizar (EI), Insertar (EI), Listar (EO), Eliminar (EI), Informes o reportes (EO) y tablas en la base de datos (ILF). El procedimiento considera clasificar los componentes identificados y obtener el valor en PF mediante la aplicación de (1). Posterior para mejorar la estimación se deben ajustar los PFsA.

$$\text{PFsA} = \sum_{i=1}^{5}(n^{\underline{o}}\ componentes\ de\ tipo\ i * peso\ del\ componente\ i\ ) \quad (1)$$

Tabla 3. Valores estándar IFPUG [22].

Componente/ Complejidad	Baja	Media	Alta
Entradas Externa (EI)	3PF	4PF	6PF
Salida Externa (EO)	4PF	5PF	7PF
Consulta Externa (EQ)	3PF	4PF	6PF
Archivo Lógico Interno (ILF)	7PF	10PF	15PF
Archivo de Interfaz Externo (EIF)	5PF	7PF	10PF

$$\text{VAF} = 0.65 + 0.01 \sum_{i=1}^{14} F_i \quad (2)$$

Cálculo de VAF. Basado en 14 características generales del sistema (General System Characteristics ó GSC's) que evalúan la funcionalidad general de la aplicación que se está midiendo mediante la aplicación de la formula (2), siendo Fi el valor ajustado de las GSC. Cada GSC tiene asociada una serie de cuestiones o preguntas acerca de la misma, cuya respuesta ayuda a determinar su grado de importancia dentro del sistema (Tabla 4) en función de una escala de 0-5: Sin Influencia (0), Incidental (1), Moderado (2), Medio (3), Significativo (4) y Esencial (5).

Roles según metodología. Las metodologías contemplan distintos roles en su estructura, estos también se pueden adaptar a los distintos equipos de trabajo, que enfrentan un proyecto de software. Para el uso de la guía metodológica, estos roles según su funcionalidad, deben ser identificados y posteriormente homologados a los seis perfiles definidos en la propuesta.

Tabla 4. Las 14 características generales del sistema, para el cálculo de PF [14].

	Enfoque Tradicional	Enfoque Ágil
1	Comunicación de datos	¿Qué necesidades de comunicación requiere el sistema para transferencia o intercambio de información?
2	Procesamiento de datos distribuido	¿Existen funciones de procesamiento distribuido? ¿Cómo son manejados los datos distribuidos?
3	Rendimiento	¿Es importante el tiempo de respuesta? ¿Es crítico el rendimiento?
4	Uso del hardware existente	¿En qué medida se está utilizando la plataforma hardware en donde se ejecutará la aplicación?
5	Transacciones	¿Con qué frecuencia se ejecutan las transacciones? (diariamente, semanalmente, mensualmente, etc..)
6	Entrada de datos interactiva	¿Requiere el sistema entrada de datos interactiva? ¿Cuánta información se captura on-line? (en%)
7	Eficiencia	¿Se diseñó la aplicación pensando en que fuera eficiente y fácilmente utilizable por el usuario?
8	Actualizaciones on-line	¿Cuántos ficheros lógicos internos se actualizan interactivamente?
9	Complejidad de procesamiento	¿Existe mucha carga en cuanto a procesamiento. Lógico y/o matemático? ¿Es complejo el procesamiento interno?
10	Reusabilidad	¿Se desarrolló la aplicación para cumplir las necesidades de más de un usuario. ¿Se ha diseñado el código para ser reutilizable?
11	Facilidad de conversión e instalación	¿Cómo son de difíciles la conversión y la instalación? ¿Se ha incluido en el diseño la conversión y la instalación?
12	Facilidad de Operación	¿Requiere el sistema copias de seguridad y de recuperación fiables?
13	Múltiples instalaciones.	¿Se diseñó y desarrollo el sistema, para soportar múltiples instalaciones en diferentes organizaciones?
14	Facilidad de mantenimiento	¿Se diseñó y desarrollo el sistema pensando en facilitar el posterior proceso de mantenimiento?

5.3 Evaluación inicial de condiciones para selección de metodología.

El primer paso que debe ejecutar el JP para utilizar correctamente la guía de selección, es completar la Tabla 5 con las condiciones iniciales del proyecto de acuerdo a sus apreciaciones y respuestas que pueda consensuar entre los involucrados respecto a las características particulares del proyecto.

En segundo lugar el JP interpreta las necesidades del Cliente, en esta interacción define los PF ajustados, logrando una estimación del esfuerzo de desarrollo. En tercer lugar se realizará una ponderación de los seis criterios definidos asignando un peso relativo expresado como porcentaje que indique la mayor incidencia de un factor respecto a otro. Cuarto, la aplicación de la formula (3) permite obtener el Valor Total Ponderado (VTP), donde:

- *Valor Total Ponderado*: Valor sobre el cual se toma la decisión de adoptar la mejor metodología (la mejor metodología obtiene el valor ponderado más alto)

Tabla 5. Evaluación Inicial de Condiciones.

Evaluación de las Condiciones	Si(1) No(0)
¿El proyecto está sujeto a un presupuesto acotado?	
¿El proyecto tiene un tiempo corto para el desarrollo?	
¿Es necesaria una documentación exhaustiva para cada etapa del proyecto?	
¿Se necesita un equipo de trabajo pequeño?	
¿El proyecto podría considerar cambios durante su ejecución?	
¿El cliente es parte del desarrollo del proyecto durante toda su creación?	

- REC_i: Vector de Respuestas a la Evaluación de Condiciones Iniciales del proyecto para cada una de los 6 factores evaluados: Presupuesto, tiempo, documentación, equipo de trabajo, respuestas al cambio y el cliente.
- $Peso_i$: Es el peso representado como porcentaje para definir la importancia relativa de un factor respecto de otro.
- VM_i: Representa la Matriz de Valorización de los factores para cada una de las metodologías.

$$\text{Valor Total Ponderado} = \sum_{i=1}^{6} \text{REC}_i \text{ x } \text{Peso}_i \text{ x } \text{VM}_i \quad (3)$$

Con ello se logra un puntaje comparable entre las 15 metodologías consideradas, siendo la que mejor se adapta a las condiciones del proyecto aquella cuyo VTP es mayor. En caso que dos o más metodologías obtengan VTP altos, el JP podrá decidir utilizar cualquiera de ellas, considerando la facilidad de homologación de roles de cada una de ellas con las características de su equipo. Finalmente el JP adapta la metodología al equipo a través de la homologación de los roles.

6 Ilustración de la Propuesta

Se propone ilustrar la aplicación de la guía con el proyecto de desarrollo de software "Sistema de control para entrega de juguetes en DIDECO Vallenar" (SC-DIDECO) abordado por el Departamento de Informática (DI) de la Ilustre Municipalidad de Vallenar (IMV), quienes contaban con un equipo pequeño de desarrollo (2 personas) para llevarlo a cabo. El JP será el Jefe del DI - IMV.

- *Problemática:* Por años la IMV aplicaba un sistema manual de entrega de juguetes a niños de la comuna, esto ocasionaba un desorden administrativo y de gestión. El ingreso de los registros de los beneficiarios era manual y muchas veces se duplicaba u omitía alguna información. Esto provocaba que la municipalidad quedara en tela de juicio por parte de la comunidad que cuestionaba la equidad del proceso.
- *Objetivo:* Crear una herramienta informática que disminuyera los errores del ingreso, selección y entrega de juguetes para los niños menores de 8 años de la comuna de Vallenar. Ademas de entrega de reportes e información estadística.
- *Desarrollo:* Los encargados de crear este software trabajaron directamente con la asistente social y un administrativo de la Dirección de Desarrollo Comunitario (DIDECO) de IMV, quienes entregaron los requerimientos al equipo desarrollador.

El primer paso es definir el tamaño del proyecto de acuerdo a puntos de función, los cuales el JP determina a partir de aplicación de la Tabla 3, esta instanciación se aprecia en Tabla 6. Así mismo, mediante la aplicación de Tabla 4, establece un factor de ajuste de 28, el cual al ser aplicado a la formula (2) nos entrega un VAF de 49PF .

Tabla 6. Estimación de PFsA de SC-DIDECO.

Componente/ Complejidad	Baja	Total
Entradas Externa (EI)	3*3PF	9PF
Salida Externa (EO)	4*4PF	16PF
Consulta Externa (EQ)	3*3PF	9PF
Archivo Lógico Interno (ILF)	2*7PF	14PF
Archivo de Interfaz Externo (EIF)	1*5PF	5PF
Total PFsA		53PF

En segundo lugar, con la información anteriormente recabada el JP estima las horas promedio (8) y las líneas de código por PF (20) para un desarrollo con tecnologías de cuarta generación (PHP y PostgreSQL). Esto le permite determinar un esfuerzo de 392 horas hombre (HH), 1.96 meses de desarrollo, que significa un costo total estimado de $2.552.000. Tercero, el JP llena con sus apreciaciones la encuesta de Evaluación Inicial de Condiciones (Tabla 5), cuya información es cruzada con la Cuantificación Criterios v/s Metodologías presentada en la Tabla 2. Para facilitación de los cálculos se ha creado una aplicación semiautomatizada mediante tablas Excel, donde la Figura 1 muestra los resultados finales obtenidos para el caso de SC-DIDECO.

Respuesta Evaluación de Condiciones	Guía de Selección de Metodología	Peso	RUP	Resultado Ponderado	Valor	XP	Resultado Ponderado	Valor	DAS	Resultado Ponderado	Valor	SCRUM	Resultado Ponderado	Valor	DSDM	Resultado Ponderado	Valor	CRYTAL CLEAR	Resultado Ponderado	Valor
1	Presupuesto asignado al proyecto	20%	1	0,2	0,2	2	0,4	0,4	1	0,2	0,2	1	0,2	0,2	1	0,2	0,2	1	0,2	0,2
0	El tiempo asignado	20%	5	1	0	4	0,8	0	5	1,0	0,0	5	1,0	0,0	4	0,8	0,0	5	1,0	0,0
1	Documentación del proyecto	10%	4	0,4	0,4	5	0,5	0,5	5	0,5	0,5	5	0,5	0,5	4	0,4	0,4	4	0,4	0,4
1	Equipo de trabajo	20%	3	0,6	0,6	4	0,8	0,8	5	1,0	1,0	5	1,0	1,0	5	1,0	1,0	5	1,0	1,0
1	Respuestas al cambio	20%	3	0,6	0,6	4	0,8	0,8	4	0,8	0,8	5	1,0	1,0	4	0,8	0,8	5	1,0	1,0
1	El cliente	10%	2	0,2	0,2	4	0,4	0,4	5	0,5	0,5	5	0,5	0,5	4	0,4	0,4	5	0,5	0,5
		100%			2,0			2,9			3,0			3,2			2,8			3,1

Fig. 1. Valores respuestas a evaluación de condiciones para caso estudio SC-DIDECO.

Cuarto, tal como se aprecia en Figura 1, la Matriz de Valorización de Factores entrega la mayor VTP a la metodología Scrum (3,2) y en segunda opción la metodología Cristal Clear (3,1). Finalmente, tal como fue planteado en sección 5.3, el JP adapta la metodología al equipo homologando los roles a su equipo (Tabla 7).

Tabla 7. Homologación de Roles Scrum - Metrica v3.

Scrum	Metrica v3
Propietario del proyecto, determina las prioridades	Directivo
Scrum Manager, gestiona y facilita la ejecución del proceso	Jefe de Proyecto
Interesados asesoran y observan	Consultor
Equipo, construye el producto (programadores)	Analista
	Programador

7 Conclusiones

Como se ha dicho no existe una metodología única que garantice el 100% de éxito en un proyecto de software. El desconocimiento y la baja calidad de la información, hace que muchas veces se tome una decisión errónea, respecto a que metodología debiera utilizarse al considerar las características y alcances de un proyecto. Siendo mayoritariamente los proyectos pequeños y los equipos pequeños quienes evidencian esta falta de guía, con resultados de calidad deficiente y posiblemente destinados a fallar.

A pesar de que las metodologías ágiles se ajustan muy bien a pequeños equipos de trabajo y proyectos cortos en virtud de su facilidad de aprendizaje y sus costos reducidos de implementación, existen ventajas de las metodologías tradicionales que ayudan a asegurar una mejor calidad del producto, las cuales deben ser consideradas.

Los resultados preliminares, demuestran la efectividad de la propuesta, siendo bien evaluada en los proyectos involucrados en los casos de prueba. Sin embargo, se detecta la necesidad de automatizar la metodología, especialmente en lo que respecta a la homologación de roles.

Finalmente, se puede afirmar que se logró la creación de una guía para la selección de metodologías de desarrollo de software para proyectos y equipos pequeños, que oriente al jefe de proyecto en la toma de decisión de la metodología más adecuada para ser utilizada, considerando las características y alcances del proyecto en cuestión.

Las etapas siguientes a seguir respecto a la propuesta metodológica, se enmarcan en la incorporación de un mayor número de casos de estudios que permitan el ajuste y refinamiento de la metodología. Así como expandir su alcance para dar soporte a desarrolladores individuales y a equipos y proyectos medianos.

Agradecimientos

Se agradece la participación del Jefe del Departamento de Informática de la Ilustre Municipalidad de Vallenar, Sr. Pedro Zamarca Paz, quien junto a su equipo, han colaborado en el ajuste de esta propuesta al aplicarla en sus proyectos de desarrollo, siendo uno de ellos el presentado en este artículo.

References

1. Morreale, R.: The Top Reasons Projects are Unsuccessful, PM World Journal, (2012).
2. Pérez, H. F.: Conoces el informe chaos, (2013), recuperado el 29/03/2018 desde http://fuenteperez.es/blog/conoces-el-informe-chaos
3. Carrizo, D., Rojas, J.: How Do Software Development Enterprises in Latin America Do Requirements Engineering? An Empirical Study. 29th IBIMA Conference, Vienna, Austria (2017).
4. Eia, R.: The growth of the Colombian software industry: O Crescimento da industria do software na Colombia vol 57, (2016) 95-106.
5. Hernández, V.S: La industria del Software. Estudio a nivel global y America Latina (2006).
6. Mayer & Bunge Informática LTDA. "Panorama de la Industria Latinoamericana de Software". Brasil (2004). Pág 97.
7. Ruiz, J. J., ¿Por Qué Fracasan los Proyectos de Software? Mexico DF, (2004).
8. Boehm, B., Some Experience with Automated Aids to the Design of Large-Scale Reliable Software, IEEE Transactions on Software Engineering, (1975), 125-133.
9. Daly, E., "Management of Software Development". IEEE Transactions on Software Engineering, (1977), 199-242.
10. Selby, R. y Boehm, B., Software engineering: Barry W. Boehm's lifetime contributions to software development, management, and research, Wiley-IEEE, (2007), 75-78, 978-0470148730.
11. Pressman, R. S., Ingeniería de Software, Mexico, McGrill, (2010)
12. Pressman, R. S., Ingenieria de Software 7ª Edición, Mexico, McGrill, (2014).
13. Beck, k.: Extreme programming Explainer: Embrece Change. Addison-Wesley, (2002).
14. Moniruzzaman, A.B.M., Hossain, A.B.: Comparative Study on Agile software development methodologies, (2013), recuperado el 29/03/2018 desde https://arxiv.org/ftp/arxiv/papers/1307/1307.3356.pdf
15. Smith, J. K.-D., Sabiduría de los Equipos. Mckinsey & Company, (1993).
16. Ganzas, J.: Por qué los equipos con mucha gente (más de 7) son menos productivos, (2013), recuperado el 29/03/2018 desde http://www.javiergarzas.com/2013/11/equipos-con-mucha-gente.html
17. Metrica v3., recuperado el 29/03/2018 desde http://administracionelectronica.gob.es/
18. Canós, J.H., Letelier, P., Penadés, M.C.: Métodologías Ágiles en el Desarrollo de Software, JISBD 2003: VIII Jornadas de Ingeniería del Software y Bases de Datos, (2003).
19. Asensio, R.M.: Informática Aplicada a la Gestión Pública, Universidad de Murcia, (2011).
20. Ahmed, D.: Is your project's best estimation method Agile or conventional?, (2015), recuperado el 29/03/2018 desde http://www.ibm.com/developerworks/library/d-estimation-agile-or-conventional-trs/index.html
21. Qumer, A. &.-S.: Measuring agility and adoptability of agile methods: A 4-dimensional analytical tool, IADIS International Conference Applied Computing, (2007).
22. Rodriguez, F. S.: Planificación y Gestión de Sistemas de Información: Medida del Tamaño Funcional (1999).

Gaps Regarding Requirements Engineering Protocol: A Preliminary Empirical Study

Richard Esparza[1], Paola Peláez[1], John W. Castro[2] and Efraín R. Fonseca C. [1]

[1] Universidad de las Fuerzas Armadas ESPE, Departamento de Ciencias de la Computación, Sangolquí, Ecuador
{rsesparza, pspelaez, erfonseca}@espe.edu.ec
[2] Universidad de Atacama, Departamento de Ingeniería Informática y Ciencias de la Computación, Copiapó, Chile
john.castro@uda.cl

Abstract. —**Background:** Research in Requirements Engineering (RE) has increased significantly in the last few years, due to requirements are the first primary input into the software development process. However, there remain severe problems regarding requirements that even have caused the failure of several software development projects. **Aim:** To structure an artifact that provides a panoramic view of problems regarding the RE, its causes and the characteristics of solutions proposed. **Method:** We conduct the preliminary stages of a systematic mapping study (SMS). **Results:** From the information available on 8 primary studies we find that implicit activities of requirements engineering have been subject to an arduous research work, which has been intensified over the last years. **Conclusions:** Despite the importance of RE in the software development process and a significant amount of research carried out in this field; there is no a robust model to guide the practice of RE based on a vast base of empirical knowledge.

Keywords: software engineering, requirements engineering, systematic mapping study.

1 Introduction

El ímpetu tecnológico de los últimos tiempos ha demandado el incremento exponencial en el desarrollo de software [1]. Hoy en día el software se encuentra omnipresente en la cotidianidad de las personas, lo que ha incidido en la transformación del aparato productivo a nivel mundial [2]. Anecdóticamente, un alto porcentaje de proyectos de software fracasan por distintos factores [3]. De acuerdo con el Chaos Report [4] publicado por Standish Group, en el año 2015 solamente el 29% de proyectos de desarrollo de software fueron exitosos, mientras que la finalización del 52% se tornó en un desafío y el 19% fracasaron. En términos generales, un proyecto de desarrollo de software es de calidad cuando es entregado a tiempo, dentro del presupuesto establecido y cumpliendo con todos los requisitos especificados por el cliente [5]. La calidad es considerada una característica vital del software, ya que representa una herramienta esencial para que las empresas tengan una ventaja competitiva respecto a la competencia [6]. Bajo esta perspectiva, la calidad del software ha sido objeto de numerosos estudios empíricos (por ejemplo, [7][8][9][10][11]), los cuales resaltan la existencia de distintos factores que inciden en esta característica y por ende en el éxito de un proyecto, siendo uno de ellos los requisitos de software [12].

De acuerdo a la IEEE, la ingeniería de requisitos (IR) es *"la primera etapa y una de las más fundamentales en el proceso de desarrollo de software cuyo objetivo es obtener una comprensión clara del dominio del problema y las necesidades de los clientes con el fin de aumentar la calidad del software y la efectividad del proceso de desarrollo"* [13][14] ; es decir, que si no se comprende y define claramente los requisitos del producto software, su calidad estará comprometida desde un inicio [15][16]. Pese a los esfuerzos realizados en miras de determinar el protocolo idóneo para la IR y obtener requisitos de calidad, un gran número de proyectos de software han fracasado debido a problemas de requisitos [12]; posiblemente debido a su naturaleza altamente cambiante, a problemas sociales, humanos, complejidad, y también quizá debido al costo de corregir los problemas subyacentes [13][17].

Por este motivo, llevamos a cabo las fases iniciales de un mapeo sistemático de literatura (SMS de las siglas del inglés *Systematic Mapping Study*) con el propósito de estructurar un modelo base para la construcción de un repositorio de conocimiento empírico que almacene de forma estructurada la información referente a la problemática identificada en la IR, sus causas y los detalles de las soluciones propuestas; de modo que guíe adecuadamente la práctica de la IR de acuerdo con las circunstancias particulares del desarrollo de software en curso. En miras de estudiar la factibilidad de la construcción de dicho repositorio, como estudio inicial nos propusimos construir una estructura que provea una vista panorámica de los problemas en torno a la IR, sus causas y las características de las soluciones propuestas para dichos problemas. Los resultados preliminares del SMS han mostrado que detrás de los requisitos de software existe un arduo trabajo de investigación que se ha ido intensificando con el paso de los años, dada su importancia en el proceso de desarrollo y por que no decirlo en la calidad resultante del producto software; sin embargo, no existe aún un repositorio robusto de conocimiento empírico que guíe adecuadamente la práctica de la IR en las circunstancias particulares de cada proyecto de desarrollo de software.

Lo que resta del artículo está estructurado como sigue. En la Sección 2, se analizan los trabajos relacionados. La Sección 3 describe el SMS. En la Sección 4 se responden a las preguntas de investigación. En la Sección 5, se discuten los hallazgos obtenidos. En la Sección 6, se presentan las amenazas a la validez. Finalmente, en la Sección 7 se presentan las conclusiones

2 Trabajos Relacionados

La IR representan una fase fundamental del proceso desarrollo de software, dado que tiene como finalidad comprender de forma clara, concisa y precisa las necesidades de los clientes y por ende el sistema a ser desarrollado [3]. La IR nació con el propósito de aumentar la calidad del software y la efectividad del proceso de desarrollo [12]. Los costos relacionados con la detección y corrección de errores guardan una estrecha relación con las fases del proceso en la que son detectados; es decir que, si se detectan errores al inicio, el impacto será menor para el desarrollo del proyecto. Como resultado se minimizan costos, tiempo y se incrementa la satisfacción del cliente [12]. No obstante, a pesar de los numerosos intentos de mejorar la IR en las pequeñas y medianas empresas de software, los principales problemas relacionados a esta temática aún persisten. Dichos inconvenientes están relacionados con requisitos incompatibles e incompletos y con el manejo inadecuado de herramientas de gestión de requisitos [18]. Daniel Méndez, investigador de NaPiRE [19], señala que la obtención, especificación y validación de requisitos precisos y apropiados para las partes interesadas, son un factor crítico de la calidad del software; no obstante, también menciona que los requisitos son altamente volatiles e inherentemente complejos por naturaleza [20].

Badariah Solemon y colegas en su estudio [15] realizado a 63 pequeñas y medianas empresas de software en Malasia en el que identificó los desafíos críticos de IR, indica que en la actualidad cada vez más compañías consideran a la IR como uno de los principales retos en el desarrollo de software.

De la misma manera, Kalinowski y colegas, en su trabajo sobre los problemas críticos y causas comunes en la IR [12], afirman que muchos proyectos de software fallan debido a problemas en el proceso de IR. Este estudio se realizó en Brasil y corresponde a una replicación de la familia de encuestas NaPiRE [19]. Como resultado, los autores obtuvieron un diagrama probabilístico de causa-efecto de los problemas comunes de la IR. En este estudio se encuestó a 74 empresas, incluyendo pequeñas, medianas y grandes, la cuales utilizaban metodologías de desarrollo ágiles, así como tradicionales. En el trabajo realizado por la Facultad de Ingeniería y Ciencias Exactas de la UADE en diferentes empresas argentinas, llamado *"Prácticas de Ingeniería de Requisitos en el desarrollo de aplicaciones Web"* [21], se constató debilidad en investigaciones previas sobre el proceso de la IR.

En términos generales los estudios revisados presentan resultados que muestran diversos problemas de la IR, desde la perspectiva de las prácticas de ingeniería adoptadas por un país o región específica. Sin embargo, se carece de un enfoque global de los problemas y causas comunes de la industria del software. Por lo tanto, se precisa estudiar de forma más exhaustiva y sistemática la literatura para identificar en un amplio espectro las carencias en torno a la IR.

3 Mapeo Sistemático de Literatura

El método de investigación seleccionado fue un SMS, el cual permite realizar un análisis estructurado de un tema de interés, detectando condiciones comunes y puntos no tratados acerca del tema; así mismo da las pautas para hacer reproducible el estudio en revisiones sistemáticas futuras que permita expandir el área de investigación con el descubrimiento de nuevos estudios [22]. Es preciso aclarar que la selección de un mapeo sistemático (SMS) de literatura en lugar de una revisión revisión sistemática de literatura (SLR de las siglas del inglés *Systematic Literature Review*), obedece a que nuestra intención era buscar información específica en los artículos primarios para dar respuesta a las preguntas de investigación, más no una síntesis de datos, que es lo que usualmente se realiza en una SLR.

Este estudio se basó en los lineamientos propuestos por Kitchenham y Charters [22] con algunas variantes. El protocolo restructurado propone el planteamiento de: (1) el SMS, (2) los criterios de inclusión y exclusión, (3) la estrategia de búsqueda y, (4) el proceso de selección de estudios y extracción de datos.

3.1 Planteamiento del SMS

Con base en la problemática en torno a la IR identificada en la sección 1, como objetivo de búsqueda nos planteamos: *Estructurar un modelo base para la construcción de un repositorio de conocimiento empírico que almacene de forma estructurada la información referente a la problemática identificada en la de la IR, sus causas y los detalles de las soluciones propuestas; de modo que guíe adecuadamente la práctica de la IR de acuerdo con las circunstancias particulares del desarrollo de software en curso.*

Como estudio preliminar nos interesó conocer la factibilidad de la creación de este modelo, por lo que nos propusimos en primera instancia: *Construir una estructura que provea una vista panorámica de los problemas en torno a la IR, sus causas y las características de las soluciones propuestas para dichos problemas.*

Con el propósito de definir el sub-objetivo de búsqueda como alcanzable definimos las siguientes preguntas de investigación:

RQ1: ¿Con qué frecuencia se han presentado estudios en torno a la IR?

RQ2: ¿Cuáles son los problemas y causas más comunes relacionados a la IR?

RQ3: ¿Qué métodos de investigación han sido utilizados en los estudios realizadas en torno a la IR?

RQ4: ¿Cuál es la tendencia en torno a las propuestas realizadas con miras a tratar los problemas vinculados a la IR?

3.2 Criterios de Inclusión y Exclusión

Los criterios de inclusión y exclusión definen de forma explícita las características que deben cumplir los estudios para ser o no considerados en el proceso de SMS. Para esta investigación se definieron los siguientes criterios:

Criterios de inclusion. El artículo:

- Describe estudios empíricos relacionados con la problemática de la calidad de los requisitos de software
- Describe detalladamente los problemas que afectan a la calidad de los requisitos de software
- Describe las diferentes técnicas o usos para evaluar la calidad de los requisitos de software
- Describe propuestas para abordar los problemas que inciden en la calidad de los requisitos de software
- Debe haber sido publicado a partir del año 2016 en adelante.

Criterios de exclusion. Serán excluidos:

- Artículos cortos, tutoriales y resúmenes de presentaciones o conferencias en torno a la temática de los requisitos
- Artículos que solo reporten detalles meramente técnicos de soluciones a la problemática de la IR
- Artículos escritos en un idioma diferente al inglés
- Artículos no accesibles en texto completo

3.3 Definición de la Estrategia de Búsqueda

La estrategia de búsqueda constituye el procedimiento a través del cual se determina el conjunto de estudios que constituyen la fuente fiable de la cual se obtiene la información que da respuesta a las preguntas de investigación. Para el caso de esta investigación, la estrategia planteada consta de tres actividades: (1) Conformación del grupo de control de literatura, (2) construcción de la cadena de búsqueda y, (3) búsqueda de estudios candidatos.

3.3.1. Conformación del grupo de control. El grupo de control (GC) de literatura es un conjunto de estudios que cumplen con los criterios definidos en la sección 3.2. El GC se conforma con el propósito de ser la fuente de la cual se seleccionan los términos que servirán como base para la conformación de la cadena de búsqueda. Los estudios del GC son seleccionados en consenso por los participantes de la investigación. Para conformar el GC se tuvo la participación de tres investigadores, los cuales propusieron estudios conocidos y de buena fuente como candidatos para conformar el GC [23]. Por medio de una validación cruzada se seleccionaron 6 artículos de los propuestos por los investigadores para el GC. La Tabla 1 muestra los estudios que integran el grupo de control.

3.3.2. Construcción de la cadena de búsqueda. La construcción de la cadena de búsqueda inicia con el análisis detallado de los artículos que conforman el GC, con el objetivo de identificar términos significativos relativos a la investigación. Cada investigador identificó términos comunes entre artículos y términos particulares de cada artículo, todos consecuentes con el objetivo del SMS. A paso seguido se realizó una validación cruzada entre los investigadores para clasificar los términos por afinidad, de lo que se identificaron 5 contextos relacionados con el objetivo del SMS: Entorno, Problema, Propuesta, Propósito y Herramienta. A continuación, se estableció una matriz de datos que conjugó la actividad manual de los investigadores con el uso de herramientas informáticas, en este caso el software CATMA, que permite el análisis cualitativo de datos. La matriz incluye: (1) el conteo total de cada término, es decir, cuántas veces un término aparece en cada artículo del GC y la suma total de las repeticiones, (2) el número de artículos en los que cada término se repite y, (3) el número de investigadores que consideraron el término como relevante.

Tabla 1. Tabla de control

No.	Título	Palabras clave
EC1	A Review of Practice and Problems in Requirements Engineering in Small and Medium Software Enterprises in Thailand	Software Engineering, Requirements Engineering, SMEs, Process Improvement
EC2	A study on the software requirements elicitation issues - Its causes and effects	Software requirements engineering, software requirements elicitation, elicitation issues, systematic literature review, cause-and-effect
EC3	A Survey on Current Requirement Process Practices in Software Companies and Requirement Process Problems	SRS, Requirement Process, Software Requirement Engineering, Requirement Elicitation, Requirement Specifications
EC4	State-of-art practices to detect Inconsistencies and Ambiguities from Software Requirements	Inconsistency, Ambiguity, Requirement Engineering
EC5	Towards Building Knowledge on Causes of Critical Requirements Engineering Problems	NaPiRE; Knowledge Building; Requirements Engineering; Problems; Causes; Causal Analysis
EC6	Towards Guidelines for Preventing Critical Requirements Engineering Problems	Guidelines; problem prevention; defect prevention; requirements engineering

Con ayuda de la matriz se determinaron los términos más relevantes que formarían la cadena de búsqueda los cuales fueron combinados a través de operadores lógicos: OR para agregar sinónimos del mismo contexto y AND para combinar los contextos. La cadena de búsqueda fue probada iterativamente en la base SCOPUS tras cada ajuste hasta que se encontró la cadena de búsqueda ideal, entendiéndose como cadena ideal aquella que cumple con las tres condiciones siguientes: (i) obtiene un número de estudios razonable (cientos no miles), (ii) los títulos de los estudios que obtiene están muy relacionados con el objetivo de la búsqueda y, (iii) la mayoría de los estudios del GC son parte del conjunto de estudios que obtiene la cadena. Desde esta perspectiva la cadena de búsqueda que fue considerada la ideal obtiene 211 estudios dentro de los cuales aparecen los 6 estudios de control; dicha cadena es la siguiente:

ALL({requirements engineering}) AND ALL({problems} OR {issues}) AND ALL({quality}) AND ALL({practices} OR {guidelines}) AND ALL({survey} OR {review}).

3.4 Proceso de Selección de Estudios Primarios y Extracción de Datos

Como se indicó anteriormente, a partir de la cadena de búsqueda se obtuvieron 211 estudios en la base digital SCOPUS. De acuerdo con el protocolo adoptado, el siguiente paso por dar es adaptar la cadena de búsqueda a cuantas bases digitales sea posible, tomando en cuenta que mientras más sean la validez de la investigación aumentará. Sin embargo, antes de continuar con la SMS nos propusimos estudiar la factibilidad del objetivo principal de la búsqueda, para lo que fueron aplicados filtros en los estudios obtenidos en SCOPUS. Los filtros aplicados corresponden a restringir la búsqueda a los años 2014 a 2018; así como también restringir sólo a revistas y congresos. Como resultado de esta actividad se obtuvieron 36 estudios (denominados estudios seleccionados). A paso seguido se accedió al texto completo de los estudios, los cuales fueron revisados por al menos dos investigadores y a través de una validación cruzada seleccionaron finalmente 8 estudios [20][24][25][27][28][29][30][31], que fueron denominados estudios primarios. Con el propósito de dar respuesta a las preguntas de investigación planteadas, la información más relevante para la investigación contenida en los estudios primarios fue extraída (ver sección 4).

4 Resultados

Esta sección presenta los resultados obtenidos del SMS preliminar. Se muestra entonces la síntesis del análisis de los estudios primarios, a partir del cual se respon-dieron las preguntas de investigación.

RQ1 ¿Con qué frecuencia se han presentado estudios en torno a la IR?

Identificamos que el trabajo empírico en la IR empezó en los años 90 [24][25]. Sin embargo, esta no fue considerada relevante hasta el año 2000 fecha a partir de la cual se ha visto un incremento significativo en cuanto al número de estudios publicados en torno a la IR [24][26][27]. A partir del año 2012 se han publicado diversos artículos enmarcados dentro de la iniciativa NaPiRE [26][28][29] enfocada en determinar el estatus de las prácticas y problemas a los que se enfrentan los profesionales del área de la IR. La Figura 1 muestra la tendencia de publicación de estudios en torno a la IR, la cual evidencia el aumento de interés de los investigadores en torno a la temática en los últimos años.

Fig. 1. Publicación de estudios por años

RQ2 ¿Cuáles son los problemas y causas más comunes relacionados a la IR?

Identificamos diversos problemas específicos de la IR presentados en la Tabla 2, donde se puede observar que los 4 problemas más citados en la literatura son: Falta de comunicación y retroalimentación, falta de conocimiento del contexto, requisitos no especificados que son muy abstractos, falta de colaboración del cliente y requisitos ocultos o incompletos.

Por otro lado, identificamos que las principales causas más citadas en la literatura, para los diversos problemas que se presenta en la IR son la falta de experiencia y las barreras en el lenguaje, como se puede ver en la Tabla 3.

Se puede observar cierta discrepancia entre los autores ya que como se puede evidenciar en las tablas anteriores, una causa como por ejemplo *"tiempo insuficiente"* [31] es considerado también como un problema [28][29].

RQ3 ¿Qué métodos de investigación han sido utilizados en los estudios realizadas en torno a la IR?

El 50% de los estudios primarios han utilizado como método de investigación los casos de estudio [26][29][30][31]. El 25% de estudios utilizaron encuestas [25][28] y el 25% restante emplearon revisiones de literatura [24][27].

Tabla 2. Principales problemas de IR

Problemas	Estudios Primarios
Falta de conocimiento del producto	[30]
Falta de conocimiento del contexto	[25][27][29][30]
Falta de comunicación y retroalimentación	[26][28][29][30][31]
Responsabilidades poco claras	[29][30]
Recursos insuficientes para el entendimiento y mantenimiento de los requisitos	[25][30]
Requisitos ocultos o incompletos	[26][28][29][30][31]
Objetivos cambiantes	[26][28][29]
Requisitos no especificados que son muy abstractos	[26][28][29][30][31]
Tiempo Insuficiente	[26][28][29]
Stakeholders con dificultad para separar requisitos de diseños de soluciones existentes	[26][28][29]
Falta de colaboración del cliente	[25][26][27][28][29][31]
Requisitos inconsistentes	[26][28][29]
Dificultad en el acceso a las necesidades del cliente y a la información del negocio	[26][28][29]
Falta de habilidades	[25][30]
Personal de trabajo inestable	[25]
Falta de Involucramiento del usuario final	[25]
Requisitos no funcionales poco claros	[29]
Requisitos implícitos no especificados	[29]
Falta de colaboración del líder de proyecto	[29]
Implementación de características que no corresponden a los requisitos especificados	[27][29]
Barreras en el lenguaje	[29]

Tabla 3. Causas identificadas

Causas	Estudios Primarios
Poco tiempo para contratación de personal	[28][30]
Stakeholders con diferentes requisitos	[26][30]
Stakeholders con dificultad para separar requisitos de diseños de soluciones existentes	[30]
Barreras en el lenguaje	[26][27][28]
Falta de colaboración del cliente	[28]
Tiempo Insuficiente	[31]
Falta de conocimiento del contexto	[31]
Requisitos ocultos o incompletos	[29]
Falta de experiencia	[25][26][27][29][30][31]
Técnicas de elicitación pobres	[26]
Requisitos no especificados que son muy abstractos	[26]

RQ4 ¿Cuál es la tendencia en torno a las propuestas realizadas con miras a tratar los problemas vinculados a la IR?

Con base en los estudios primarios identificados en el SMS, se han logrado identificar tres diferentes tipos de contribución que proponen los investigadores. En primer lugar, se encuentran los lineamientos [25][29][30] presentes en el 43% de los estudios primarios. En segundo lugar, están los modelos [27][28][31], también presentes en el 43% de los estudios primarios. Finalmente, solo un estudio primario [26] propone como tipo de contribución una herramienta.

Por un lado, los lineamientos proponen una tendencia a cambiar hacia procesos ágiles, que incluyan la participación del cliente que ayudará a obtener un mejor entendimiento de los requisitos [25][30]. Por otro lado, la tendencia hacia procesos más estrictos basados en revisiones formales, modelos y un mayor seguimiento también es un lineamiento propuesto [30]. Para proporcionar una visión más completa de los problemas críticos que enfrenta la IR, Méndez y colegas [26] construyen diagramas probabilísticos de casusa-efecto. Mientras que Méndez y colegas [28] y Kalinowski y colegas [31] proponen un nuevo enfoque de análisis causal de efectos basado en la evidencia de datos entre empresas. Para ello, los autores utilizan la infe-rencia diagnostica de las redes bayesianas que permite determiner las causas principales de los problemas asociados con la IR.

5 Discusión

Los problemas más reportados en la literatura son la falta de comunicación y retroalimentación, falta de conocimiento del contexto, requisitos no especificados que son muy abstractos, falta de colaboración del cliente y requisitos ocultos o incompletos. Sin embargo, que sean citados con mayor frecuencia no implica que éstos sean los problemas más críticos que se presentan en la IR, ni mucho menos que éstos sean los que más impacto tienen en la calidad del software resultante. Con respecto a las causas identificadas encontramos la falta de experiencia y las barreras en el lenguaje como las principales, pero hay que considerar que una causa puede dar origen a más de un problema específico.

Identificamos que dentro de la literatura se da el caso de que lo que para unos autores es considerado como causa, para otros es un problema. Esto evidencia la falta de consenso en este apartado, pudiendo afectar a la correcta identificación de los problemas que afectan a la IR junto con sus causas. Los enfoques de investigación empleados en los estudios primarios son los casos de estudio, encuestas y revisiones de literatura. En cuanto al tipo de contribución que proponen los estudios primarios identificados, encontramos que muchos de éstos aportan lineamientos, modelos y herramientas. Sin embargo, aún no existe una guía que especifique los problemas que se pueden presentar en la IR, con sus correspondientes causas y posibles soluciones.

6 Amenazas a la Validez

Identificamos como posibles amenazas a la validez en este estudio: (i) cobertura de las RQ, (ii) sesgo hacia ciertas publicaciones, (iii) calidad de la evaluación, y (iv) desconocimiento del área. Es probable que las RQ planteadas podrían cubrir parcialmente la temática de estudio, lo que intentamos mitigar definiendo un objetivo de trabajo y planteando varias RQ en consenso, con el propósito de hacer alcanzable el objetivo. Es posible que en un SMS se tienda a encaminar el proceso hacia un grupo específico de estudios, lo cual evitamos conformando un GC de literatura y planteando en consenso una cadena de búsqueda con términos de control explícitos. Es probable que la calidad de la evaluación de los estudios no sea la adecuada por desconocimiento del área de investigación, lo cual mitigamos incluyendo en el equipo de SMS a dos investigadores con experiencia en temas de IR y realización de SMS.

7 Conclusiones

Este trabajo preliminar describe a breves rasgos el estado actual de las carencias en torno a la IR. Se identificaron un total de 211 estudios candidatos, de los cuales 8 fueron seleccionados como estudios primarios para el SMS. Los principales hallazgos de nuestra investigación son tres. En primer lugar, a pesar de que el número de estudios seleccionados es relativamente pequeño, es posible notar que el interés de la comunidad por la temática de investigación se ha incrementado en los últimos años. En segundo lugar, existen muchos problemas que afectan a la IR así como causas, pero existe discrepancia entre los autores sobre si un factor identificado es un problema o una causa, ya que la valoración de estos factores es muy subjetiva y está sujeta a consideración de cada autor. En tercer lugar, muchos esfuerzos se han realizado para tratar los problemas en torno a la IR. Sin embargo, aún no se ha llegado a una solución definitive, ni mucho menos a un modelo o guía que permita identificar claramente los problemas en torno a la IR, sus causas y alternativas de solución.

Las dos principales limitaciones de nuestra investigación son el corto periodo de la búsqueda, el número de bases de datos consultadas y el número de estudios primarios seleccionados. Como trabajos futuros proponemos: (i) ampliar el periodo de la búsqueda, así como también las bases de datos y la cantidad de estudios seleccionados para obtener una vision más amplia y complete sobre la temática bajo estudio, (ii) crear un conjunto de guías y lineamientos para tratar los problemas vinculados a la IR. Los resultados de este estudio presentan a los investigadores futuras direcciones de investigación.

Referencias

1. Sun, Y., Shinde, K.: Template-Based Code Generation Framework for Data-Driven Software Development. 4th Int. Conf. on Applied Computing and Information Technology/3rd Int. Conf. on Computational Science/Intelligence and Applied Informatics/1st Int. Conf. on Big Data, Cloud Computing, Data Science & Engineering (ACIT-CSII-BCD), Las Vegas (2016) 55-60
2. Nadir, S., Streitferdt, D., Burggraf, C.: Industrial Software Developments Effort Estimation. Int. Conf. on Computational Science and Computational Intelligence, Las Vegas (2016) 1248-1252
3. Fernández, L., Bernad, P.: Risk Management in Software Development Projects in Spain: A State of Art. Rev. Facultad de Ingeniería Universidad de Antioquia, no. 70 (2014) 233-243
4. The Standing Group: Chaos Report. Online [http://www.standishgroup.com/] (2015)
5. Frese, R., Sauter, V.: Improving Your Odds for Software Project Success. IEEE Engineering Management Review, Vol. 46(4): 125-131, (2014)
6. Olaperi, Y.S., Sanjay, M.: An Empirical Evaluation of Software Quality Assurance Practices and Challenges in a Developing Country. IEEE Int. Conf. on Computer and Information Technology; Ubiquitous Computing and Comunications; Dependable, Autonomic and Secure Computing; Pervasive Intelligence and Computing, Liverpool (2015) 867-871
7. Fitzgerald, C., Letier, E., Finkelstein, A.: Early Failure Prediction in Feature Request Managment Systems. IEEE 19th Int. Requirements Eng. Conf., Trento (2011) 229-238
8. Nagappan, N., Murphy, B., Basili, V.: The Influence of Organizational Structure on Software Quality: An Empirical Case Study. 30th Int. Conf. on Software Engineering, Leipzig (2008) 521-530
9. Nagappan, N., Ball, T., Zeller, A.: Mining Metrics to Predict Component Failures. 28th Int. Conf. on Software Engineering, Shanghai (2006) 452-461
10. Kpodjedo, S., Ricca, F., Galinier, P., Guéhéneuc, Y.G., Antoniol, G.: Desing Evaluation Metrics for Defect Prediction in Objet Oriented Systems. Journal Empirical Software Engineering, Vol. 16(1): 141-175, (2011)
11. Rempel, P., Mäder, P.: Preventing Defects: The Impact of Requirements Traceability Completeness on Software Quality. IEEE Transactions on Software Engineering (2016) 777-797
12. Kalinowski, M., Oliveira, R., Conte, T., Prikladnicki, R., Méndez, D., Wagner, S.: Towards Building Knowledge on Causes of Critical Requirements Engineering Problems. 27th Int. Conf. on Software Engineering and Knowledge Engineering (SEKE), Pittsburgh (2015)
13. Ouhbi, S., Idri, A., Fernandez-Aleman, J.L., Toval, A.: Software Quality Requirements: A Systematic Mapping Study. 20th Asia-Pacific Software Engineering Conf. (APSEC), Bangkok (2013) 231-238
14. Neill, C. J., Laplante, P. A.: Requirements engineering: the state of the practice. IEEE Software, Vol. 20(6): 40-45, (2003)

15. Solemon, B., Sahibuddin, S., Abd, A.A.: Requirements Engineering Problems in 63 Software Companies in Malaysia. Int. Symposium on Information Technology, Kuala Lumpur (2008) 1-6
16. Suranto, B.: Software Prototypes: Enhancing The Quality of Requirements Engineering Process. Int. Symposium on Technology Managment and Emerging Technologies (ISTMET), Langkawi (2015) 148-156
17. Mafra, P., Kalinowski, M., Méndez, D., Felderer, M., Wagner, S.: Towards Guidelines for Preventing Critical Requirements Engineering Problems. 42th Euromicro Conference on Software Engineering and Advanced Applications (SEAA), Limasol (2016) 25-29
18. Khankaew, S., Riddle, S.: A Review of Practice and Problems in Requirements Engineering in Small and Medium Software Enterprises in Thailand. IEEE 4th Int. Workshop on Empirical Requirements Engineering (EmpiRE), Karlskrona (2014) 1-8
19. NaPiRE: Naming the Pain in Requirement Engineering. Online [http://www.mendezfe.org/projects/napire/] 2012
20. Fernández, D., Wagner, S.: Naming the Pain in Requirements Engineering: A Design for a Global Family of Surveys and First Results from Germany. Information and Software Technology, Vol. 57, (2014) 616-643
21. Oliveros, A., Napolillo, F., López, F.: Requirements in Web Applications Development. IEEE Congreso Argentino de Ciencias de la Informática y Desarrollos de Investigación (CACIDI) - IEEE Conference on Computer Sciences, Buenos Aires Argentina (2016)
22. Kitchenham, B., Charters, S.; Guidelines for Performing Systematic Literature Reviews in Software Engineering. EBSE. Keele University and Durham University Joint Report (2007)
23. Zhang, H., Ali Babar, M., Teli, P.: Identifying Relevant Studies in Software Engineering. Information and Software Technology, Vol. 53: 625-637, (2011)
24. Ambreen, T., Ikram, N., Usman, M., Niazi, M.: Empirical Research in Requirements Engineering: Trends and Opportunities. Requirements Engineering, Vol. 23(1): 63-95 (2016)
25. Ilyas, F., Zahra, K.: A Survey on Current Requirement Process Practices in Software Companies and Requirement Process Problems. Int. Conf. on Computational Science and Computational Intelligence, LasVegas (2016) 1280-1285
26. Méndez, D., Wagner, S., Kalinowski, M., Felderer, M., Mafra, P., Vetrò, A., Conde, T., Christiansson, M., Greer, D., Männistö, T., Nayabi, M., Oivo, M., Penzenstadler, B., Pfahl, D., Prikladnicki, R., Ruhe, G., Schekelmann, A., Sen, S., Spinola, R., Tuzcu, A., de la Vara, J.L., Wieringa, R.: Naming the Pain in Requirements Engineering Contemporary Problems, Causes, and Effects in Practice. Empirical Soft. Engineering, Vol. 22(5): 2298-2338, (2017)
27. Reddivari, S., Asaithambi, A., Niu, N., Wang, W., Da Xu, L., Cheng, J.-R.: Ethnographic Field Work in Requirements Engineering. Journal Enterprise Information Systems, Vol. 11(1): 137-159 (2015)
28. Méndez, D., Tießler, M., Kalinowski, M., Felderer, M., Kuhrmann, M.: On Evidence-Based Risk Management in Requirements Engineering. Software Quality: Methods and Tools for Better Software and Systems (SWQD), Vienna (2017), 39-59
29. Wagner, S., Méndez, D., Felderer, M., Kalinowski, M.: Requirements Engineering Practice and Problems in Agile Projects: Results from an International Survey. XX Ibero-American Conference on Software Engineering CIbSE, Buenos Aires (2017)
30. Liebel, G., Tichy, M., Knauss, E., Ljungkrantz, O., Stieglbauer, G.: Organisation and Communication Problems in Automotive Requirements Engineering. Requirements Engineering, Vol. 23(1): 145-167, (2018)
31. Kalinowski, M., Curty, P., Paes, A., Ferreira, A., Spinola, R., Méndez, D., Felderer, M., Wagner, S.: Supporting Defect Causal Analysis in Practice with Cross-Company Data on Causes of Requirements Engineering Problems. IEEE/ACM 39th Int. Conf. on Software Engineering: Software Engineering in Practice Track (ICSE-SEIP), Buenos Aires (2017) 223-232

Adding sensitivity analysis to component selection reduced effort yet increased difficulty, hurting acceptance

Fabián Villarroel, Hernán Astudillo and Bernhard Hitpass

Departamento de Informática
Universidad Técnica Federico Santa María
Santiago, Chile

fabian.villarroel@alumnos.usm.cl,]
{hernan, bernhard.hitpass} @inf.utfsm.cl

Abstract. Commercial off-The Shelf (COTS) products are increasingly used by organizations to automate (partial o totally) their business processes. Choosing the proper combination of components is not a trivial task, usually requiring thorough assessment; existing techniques address selection of ERP's, TPS and other kinds of business software, but do not extend to general COTS-based systems. This article describes the extension of the existing PBEC-OTSS (Process-Based Evaluation and Comparison Off-the-Shelf software), originally published in 2013, to enable measuring stability of recommended solutions under changes in information. An experimental study was conducted to compare the updated technique with the original one; study participants were IT professionals and an expert; the case study is a real scenario from a Chilean public sector institution; and effort, satisfaction and assessment quality were measured. The study showed that both techniques yield similar results to the expert, but PBEC-OTSS presented better results for non-expert professionals. It remains to be explored why acceptance was correlated with difficulty rather than effort.

Keywords: Business/IT Alignment, Off-The-Shelf software, Multi-criteria Decision-making, Business Process Management, Analytic Hierarchic Process, Sensitivity Analysis

1 Introduction

The software selection process reveals a challenging task that has to consider increasingly diverse factors to guide organizations in selecting the best approach. Besides this complexity, there are many similar commercial applications in the market with diverse capabilities and qualities. Any wrong decision in the COTS selection will be reflected adversely in the entire project, increasing the cost, time, effort, performance, and/or quality of the final system.

Although it is a significant process for organizations, software selection remains a subjective and uncertain decision process [1], which is complex and takes time to satisfy the specific needs of the organization [2].

Many proposed methods for assessment and selection of commercial software are still fairly limited, which inhibits them to be applied and accepted as a formal method in the industry [27]. In practice:

- Many organizations lack a rigorous software selection process [3], risking investing in wrong technological alternatives or spending too much time in the selection process [4].
- Software selection is often made hastily by evaluators with neither time nor experience to plan it [5] or who choose only according to their intuition or experience [6].

Determining the proper IT applications is not a trivial task for organizations, and it demands a rigorous assessment process. Therefore, the key question is: How to identify the most adequate application to satisfy organizational needs? The goal is to choose the right level and type of IT, to allow alignment between organizational strategy and structure to reach higher levels of organizational performance [8]. However, the (dis)advantages of any software application in an organization are generally known only after some time of using it [9].

The reminder of this article is structured as follows: Section 2 presents related work; Section 3 describes the PBEC-OTSS technique; Section 4 details an experimental comparison of PBEC-2016 against PBEC-2013 and ESA; Sections 5 and 6 expound the comparison results for PBEC-2013 and ESA, respectively; and Section 7 summarizes and concludes.

2 Related Work

Many techniques have been proposed for OTSS selection decision-making. Especially relevant are those for assessment and selection of specific software types like ERP's [11], Data Warehouse Systems [12], BPM suites, and Transaction Processing Systems [13].

However, generally these solutions cannot be applied to select smaller COTS components, and also software assessment criteria are recurrent or very similar, leaving out the assessment of component alignment with the specific organization's processes. Most assessment proposals rank components according to some criteria; at best, the organization can select a component with general criteria and adapt it to its specific processes [7].

Expert System for Software Assessment [1] uses Expert System Prototypes to assess software, incorporating MCDA (Multiple Criteria Decision Aid) aspects. It allows assessment automation, and depending on the problem and information available, it suggests an assessment model and assists in the valuation of the criteria. It consists of Intelligent Front End, Inference Engine, and Knowledge Base.

Enterprise Software Selection Method [7] uses a Decision Support System that combines qualitative and quantitative assessments to select business software.

Decision Making Framework for Software Selection [2] consists of a methodology for software selection, common criteria for assessment, and a Hybrid Knowledge Based System (HKBS).

Comella-Dorda et al. [15] propose a sensitivity analysis of the obtained OTSS systems that considers how assessment results react to changes in assumptions, like weight of criteria or ratings by evaluators. By assessing sensitivity to changes in assumptions, it is possible to determine the effect of minor changes in judgements on the product recommendations. However, it proposes neither a specific technique nor establishes criteria and metrics, only describing a method to follow, leaving the specific problem unsolved.

Summarizing, despite the countless assessment proposals, to the best of our knowledge there are currently no process model-based techniques to assess and compare OTSS on the basis of their possible contribution to a specific organization, much less techniques to identify trade-offs among OTSS.

3 PBEC-OTSS

PBEC-OTSS (Process-Based Evaluation and Comparison Off-the-Shelf software) [14] (also known as PBEC-2013) was proposed in 2013 to assess and compare Off-the-Shelf Software (OTSS) components based on their possible contribution to the organization. It evaluated alternative software configurations for the target business process models, and fuzzy inference to synthesize global scores from individual criteria evaluations. Its main benefits are: (i) favoring Business/IT alignment; (ii) contributing to Business Process Management (BPM) and OTSS selection area; (iii) improving decision making, i.e., decision making is well informed and with less uncertainty; and (iv) gathering additional information that may help to decrease time, cost, and effort.

Actual experience with PBEC-2013 in the intervening time has shown a few deficiencies:

- Some criteria were always assessed with 0 by evaluators, raising the question of whether these criteria were actually useful and if evaluators truly understand how to measure them.
- The visual elements in the assessment were not clearly understandable by everyone.
- It did not allow trade-off analysis among alternative selections.

This article describes a modified version of PBEC-OTSS (from now on called PBEC-2016). It differs from PBEC-2013 in the set of evaluation criteria, the use of visual aids and tool, and the possibility of trade-off and decision stability analysis.

PBEC-OTSS has three main elements:

- Input: The OTSS documentation to be assessed, Problems and Systems implemented in the organization, Models and Business Documentation.
- Components: 7 steps and 5 criteria of assessment, defined from the Processes perspective.

- Output: Sensitivity Analysis, Alternative Process Models Configurations, Ranking, and OTSS scoring.

If the organization does not have all the input documentation, it will be obtained by going through the initial steps.

PBEC-OTSS uses three measurement models:

- Assessment Criteria: specific criteria to measure process models, OTSS, implemented systems, and organizational problems.
- Process Models Alternative Configurations: variations in assignment and execution of the process activities to actors (persons and areas) and systems (implemented and OTSS).
- Refined Process Models: the impact of each alternative OTSS configuration on the specific business processes (efficacy) and use of existing systems (efficiency).

PBEC-2013 utilized a fuzzy calculator to synthesize alternative OTSS configurations global score and ranking from individual inputs. PBEC-2016 is supported by an interactive Assessment Tool that supports alternatives assessment and pairwise comparison; computes scores and rankings; and allows sensitivity analysis to identify decision trade-offs and improve the stability of recommendation. All the figures in this article have been generated by this tool.

PBEC-OTSS has seven steps:

1. Define Scope: to establish the assessment dimension and purpose, identify:

- Motivation: Identify the problems and/or situations to be solved or improved, and the objectives and/or organizational needs to be achieved or met with the acquisition of the OTSS.
- Business processes: Identify the Motivation-related business processes.
- Implemented Systems: Systems already in place in the organizations that participate in the identified Business Processes and/or are involved with the Motivation.
- Use objectives: From the Motivation and as a complementary measure, determine whether the OTSS acquisition is to reduce, maintain, or increase the amount of activities carried on with every Implemented System within the organization.

2. Refine Process Models: Review the identified business process models and confirm their completeness regarding events, activities, roles, and implemented systems. If the organization business processes are not completely modeled, or if they are documented as a black box (see Fig. 1.), the original model is refined, improving its representation: for each role, specify events, users' activities that cover the implemented systems (individualizing each system), automated activities executed by the system, and manual activities not performed by any system (see Fig. 2.).

Fig. 1. Example of not refined Process

3. Generate Alternative Process Models Configurations: Review and revise all the documentation of each OTSS to be assessed (identified in the first step). Subsequently, a new process model including the OTSS is generated for each process model of the previous stage. Each process activity able to cover the OTSS (user's or automated activities) will depend on the functionalities identified in the reviewed documentation. The name and/or amount of process activities shall not be changed, just the type (e.g. manual activity transformed in user activity).

In general, all the involved systems (whether purpose-built or OTSS) appear in each generated process model alternative configuration, and no system may appear as a black box.

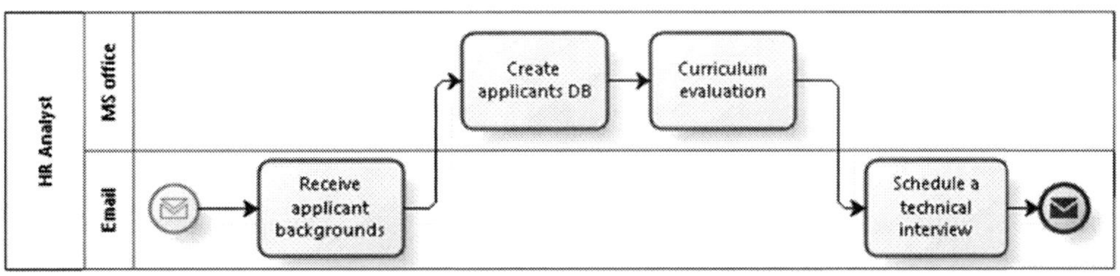

Fig. 2. Example of Refined Process

4. Measure Criteria: There are five assessment criteria, defined with a process perspective. The measurement of each criterion is specific to each project, since PBEC does not consider general criteria (Cost, Supplier, Ease of Use) unlike most assessment techniques. The criteria are:

- Degree of Coverage: Amount of activities possible to be performed by users in the assessed OTSS.
- Degree of Automation: Variation of the automated activities.
- Degree of Integration: OTSS collaboration with the already-implemented systems.
- Degree of Interoperability: The effort required to connect one system to another.
- Fraction of Users with automated tasks: Percentage of users whose tasks would appear automated respect to the total of users.

In many practical situations, the model of human preference decisions is uncertain and those responsible for deciding might be reluctant or unable to assign exact numerical values to their judgments. PBEC makes use of the Analytic Hierarchy Process (AHP) [1], a well-known multi-criteria decision making (MCDM) technique based in pairwise comparison [10]; using a discrete Saaty scale of 1-9 and pairwise comparison has the advantage of simplicity [18] (see Fig. 2.).

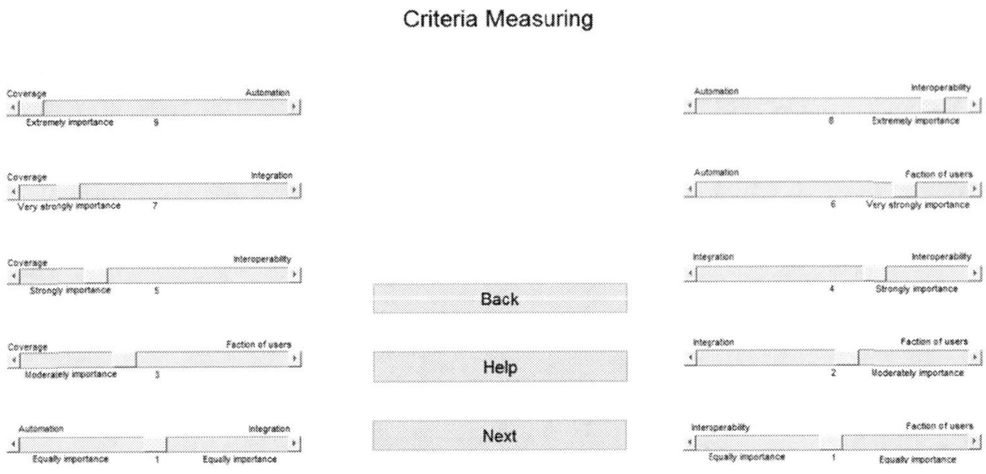

Fig. 3. Criteria Measuring

Initial weights are assigned to each criterion, and can be changed by each evaluator (see Fig. 4.).

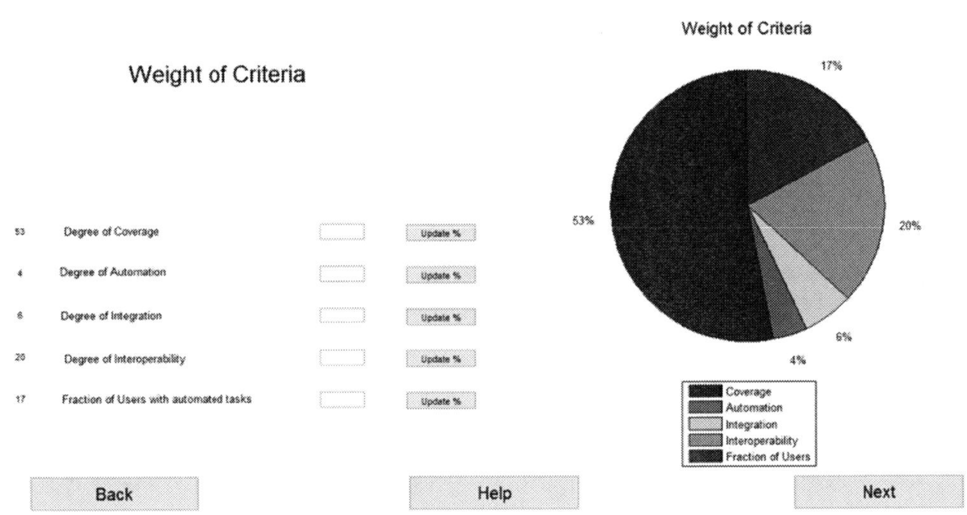

Fig. 4. Weight of Criteria

5. Alternative Measurements: Once criteria weights are obtained, they are used to evaluate each alternative COTS component, using pairwise comparisons and the same 1-9 scale (see Fig. 5.).

This yields quantitative assessments for each alternative regarding all criteria (see spider chart in Fig. 6).

6. General Assessment: The general score and criteria score of each alternative are calculated from the weight of each criterion and its evaluation for each alternative (see Fig. 7. ; the highest scoring alternative is highlighted).

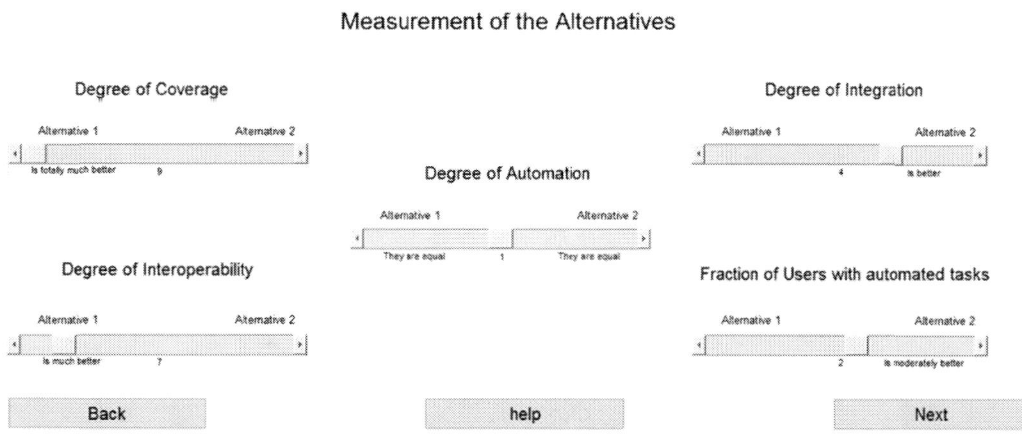

Fig. 5. Measurement of the Alternatives

7. Sensitivity Analysis: A sensitivity analysis can be done to have a more stable recommendation is available; this is especially useful when there are alternatives with similar scores and small assessment changes might change the recommendation. This variation is defined as ±10% and can be applied in both the weight of each criterion and the performance of an alternative in a criterion (see Fig. 8.).

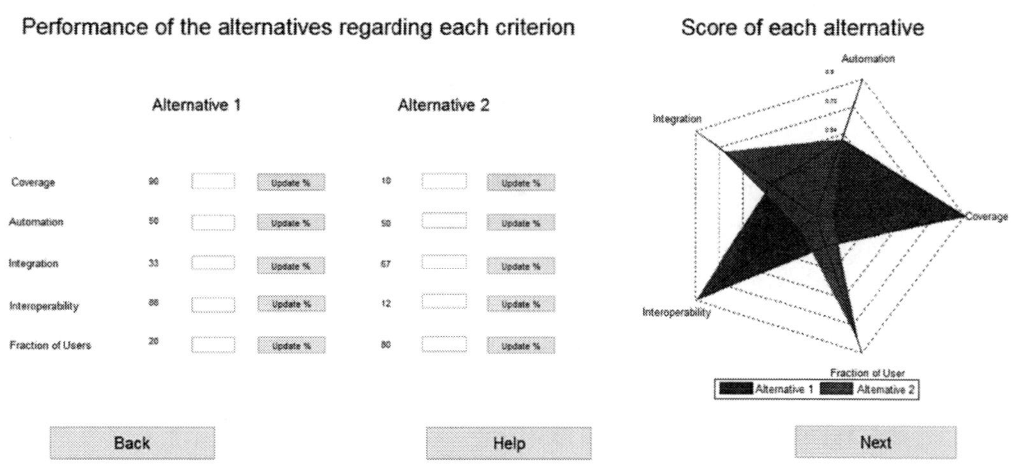

Fig. 6. Performance of the alternatives regarding each criterion

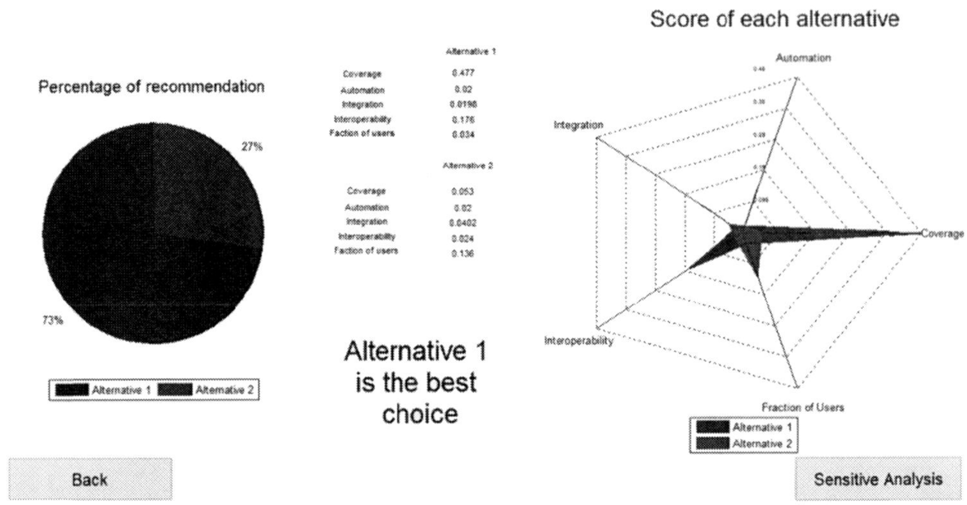

Fig. 7. General Assessment

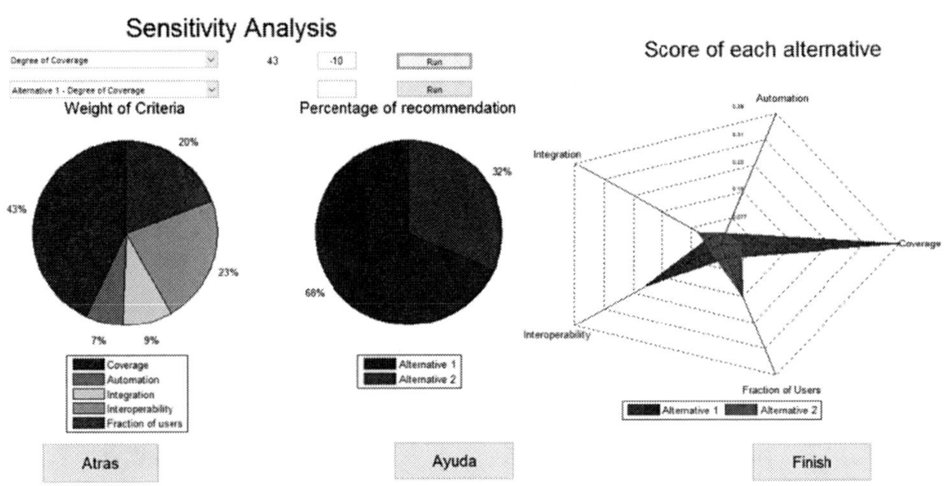

Fig. 8. Example of Sensitivity Analysis

4 Experimental Comparison

An experimental study was carried out to evaluate and compare both versions of PBEC-OTSS. Assessment effort, evaluator satisfaction and assessment quality were measured for an actual project at FOSIS, a Chilean public sector institution. The case has been described in detail in [14].

FOSIS requested evaluation of software options to support the staff recruitment process. The existing situation used Microsoft Office (Word, Excel, and Access) and e-mail. The project goals were:

- Reduce the staff recruitment process cycle times.
- Standardize the staff recruitment process.
- Automation of the main tasks of the process.

Two COTS alternatives were compared: PeopleNet Recruitment (Alternative 1) and Email2DB (Alternative 2).

Two assessment techniques were used: PBEC-OTSS (described in Section III), and Enterprise Software Analyzer (ESA) (described below).

The study participants were 15 professionals with experience in process modeling, from which 9 used PBEC and 6 used ESA to evaluate the FOSIS system.

Participants' results were compared with those of a BPM expert, who used both techniques and the same example. This allowed measuring the "quality" of a participant's assessment as similarity to the expert's assessment.

Enterprise Software Analyzer (ESA) is a formalized description of the technique used for COTS software assessment on a published study (by other authors) performed to 126 Management Information Systems (MIS) [6]. ESA has four steps:

1: Review the COTS software documentation.

2: Assess each of the following criteria in 1 to 10 scale (1=lowest and 10=highest):

- Functionality: level of compliance of the characteristics and functions required by the organization.
- Reliability: COTS software general quality.
- Cost: total cost of the acquisition and implementation of the COTS software (1=expensive, 10=economic)
- Ease of Customization: ease of the COTS software to be modified, satisfying the specific needs of the organization. Ease of use: user interface friendliness

3: Compute the weighted score for each criterion; the weights were fixed at: Functionality*3.5; Reliability*3.3; Cost*1.6; Ease of Customization*0.9; Ease of Use*0.7.

4: Calculate the final core by adding all the values of the previous step. Table 1 shows the mapping of each numeric score to a fuzzy concept.

Table 1. Value of OTSS for ESA

Score	10-28	29-46	47-64	65-82	83-100
Value of OTSS	Low	Mid-Low	Mid	Mid-High	High

ESA was selected to compare the results obtained with the technique proposed in this work. The main reason is that the first version of PBEC-OTSS [14] was used in its experimental study, since it shows greater significance as it is based on a study with many participants with outstanding job titles (126 MIS managers). Therefore, to have a good point of comparison, ESA will be used again.

5 Results: PBEC-2016 v/s ESA

The key results of comparing PBEC-2016 and ESA (see Table 2).were (see some statistical values for both techniques in Table 3):

- The PeopleNet Recruitment alternative got better scores that Email2DB using both techniques, but the spread is much lower in ESA than in PBEC-

2016; we attribute this to ESA assessing alternatives separately but PBEC assessing them together.

- ESA assigns fixed weights to criteria, but since PBEC depends on the importance the evaluator assigns to each criterion and the environment where the assessment will be performed, it is not possible to determine such values in PBEC.
- In general, the criteria Degree of Coverage and Degree of Automation were the most important to participants, with an average weight of 26.2 and 23.2, respectively.
- With ESA, the average gap between the expert and the participant's opinion is about a 7% lower, but with PBEC it is approximately a 9% higher.

Table 2. General results

	ESA		PBEC-2016	
Measure	A1	A2	A1	A2
Expert	61,2	38,2	67	33
Mean	54,7	45,3	76	24
Median	54,6	45,4	78	22
Min-Max	51,1-57,5	42,5-48,9	59-84	16-41

Table 3. Subjects evaluation of PBEC-2016 and ESA

	Effort		Ease of Use		Satisfaction	
Measure	ESA	PBEC	ESA	PBEC	ESA	PBEC
Expert	20	40	3	4	5	5
Mean	30	43,3	3,7	3,9	4	3,8
Median	30	40	3,5	4	4	4
Min-Max	30-40	30-60	2-5	2-5	2-4	2-5
Recomm.?	ESA	5/7	PBEC		8/10	

6 Results: PBEC- 2013 v/s PBEC-2016

Since outcomes from both versions of PBEC-OTSS (PBEC-2013) and PBEC-2016 are not directly comparable), some changes had to be made to allow the comparison.

- PBEC-2013 did not define weights for criteria, but it allows direct assessment of each alternative regarding a criterion; hence, to allow comparison it will be considered that each criterion has the same weight (16.6%).
- Evaluation assigned to each study participant who used the original technique must be standardized, so all alternatives assessments sum up 100%, giving another point of comparison regarding the criteria participation.

- The values obtained when applying the Sensitivity Analysis will not be considered for comparison purposes. The item Effort in the Survey of Applied Technique was renamed as Ease, for a better understanding of the evaluators.

Table 4. Results with PBEC-2013

Alternatives	P1	P2	P3	P4	P5	P6	Exp
A1	50	51	54	51	52	50	53
A2	50	49	46	49	48	50	47

Table 5. Results with PBEC-2016

Alts	P1	P2	P3	P4	P5	P6	P7	P8	P9	Exp
A1	75	76	84	59	81	78	69	81	84	67
A2	25	24	16	41	19	22	31	19	16	33

PBEC-2013 and PBEC-2016 can be compared using the previous assumptions; see Table 4 and Table 5 for details.

- The results obtained with PBEC-2013 show that PeopleNet Recruitment (Alternative 1) is just a couple of points best evaluated than Email2DB (Alternative 2), contrary to using PBEC-2016 where the gap is evident. The main reason is the way in which the assessment is performed; PBEC-2013 assessed each alternative separately, resulting in a score, but PBEC-2016 used graphical pairwise comparison and score ranking.
- In PBEC-2013 evaluators' preferences, the Implementation and Participation criteria were assessed with 0 (except for one case); therefore, these two criteria seem not to add value to the model and, as they are interrelated, it does affect the general assessment.
- In PBEC-2016 the criteria are no longer interrelated, being in a more delimited range, where it is possible to distinguish the importance that the evaluator assigns to a criterion over the rest.
- As the number of alternatives increases, PBEC-2013 is more user-friendly since it requires only direct assessment, adding one more input to the Fuzzy Interface System. In PBEC-2016, for each extra alternative to be added, the number of pairwise comparison increases (e.g. 2 alternatives: 5 comparisons, 3 alternatives: 15 comparisons, 4 alternatives: 30 comparisons...) making it harder to use. This can be solved by making a selection per tournament [16] between pairs to obtain the best alternative in a more practical manner.

Table 6 and Table 7 show participants' evaluation of Effort, Difficulty, Satisfaction, and Recommendation for PBEC-2013 and PBEC-2016.

Summarizing:

- Effort: PBEC-2016 takes less effort than PBEC-2013, averaging approximately 16 minutes less.
- Difficulty: PBEC-2016 seems harder to use than PBEC-2013, although the graphical display of assessments (as a spider chart) should have made differences more noticeable.

- Satisfaction: both versions had similar satisfaction rate (3.8 vs 3.6); we venture (but couldn't prove) that the use of AHP sensitivity analysis to determine recommendation stability had a small positive impact.
- Recommendation: PBEC-2016 was recommended by 80% of 9 participants, whereas PBEC-2013 had been recommended by 100% of 6 participants.

Table 6. Subjects evaluations of PBEC-2016

Aspect	**P1**	**P2**	**P3**	**P4**	**P5**	**P6**	**P7**	**P8**	**P9**	**Exp**
Duration (min)	50	30	40	30	60	40	50	30	60	40
Difficulty (1-5)	4	4	5	3	4	4	3	2	4	4
Satisfaction (1-5)	5	4	3	4	2	3	4	4	5	5
Recommend? (Y,N)	Y	Y	Y	Y	Y	Y	Y	Y	Y	Y

Table 7. Subjects evaluations of PBEC-2013

Aspect	**P1**	**P2**	**P3**	**P4**	**P5**	**P6**
Effort (min)	52	60	68	60	40	61
Difficulty (1-5)	4	3	4	3	4	4
Satisfaction (1-5)	4	5	3	3	3	3
Recommend? (Y,N)	Y	Y	Y	Y	Y	Y

7 Conclusions and future work

This article describes an improved version (here called PBEC-2016) of the OTSS Process-Based Evaluation and Comparison (PBEC-OTSS, here called PBEC-2013) software assessment technique, a systematic approach to assess and compare alternative OTSS that focuses on measuring contribution to a specific organization rather than using general evaluation criteria. PBEC-OTSS proposes 5 assessment criteria (Coverage, Automation, Interoperability, Integration, and Fraction of Users with automated tasks).

PBEC-2016 uses AHP for pairwise comparison of alternatives in each criterion, allowing sensitivity analysis even if the alternatives' scores are similar. An interactive tool has been prototyped and its results grace these pages.

PBEC-2016 was compared in an experimental study against PBEC-2013 and ESA (Enterprise Software Analyzer), an existing assessment technique, regarding effort, evaluator's satisfaction, and recommendation quality measured against an expert's ground truth.

Comparing PBEC-2016 with ESA yield that assessment effort was similar, but PBEC-2016 had higher evaluator satisfaction and slightly better results; thus, PBEC-2016 seems to be a generally better technique than ESA.

Comparing PBEC-2016 with PBEC-2013 found it to take less effort but be harder to use; this may explain why satisfaction in both versions was similar but PBEC-2016 had a lower was recommendation rate (80% of 9) than PBEC-2013 (100% of 6 participants); thus, the introduction of AHP-based sensitivity analysis seems to reduce effort but make it

Although the comparison was conducted with a specific software, PBEC seems applicable to any type of OTSS and in any kind of organization, since its emphasis is on the relation between business processes and technological choices.

References

1. Lundell, B. & Lings, B. (2004). "Changing perceptions of CASE technology." *Journal of Systems and Software*, 7(2), pp. 271-280.
2. Jadhav, A. & Sonar, R. (2011). "Framework for evaluation and selection of the software packages: A hybrid knowledge based system approach." *Journal of Systems and Software*, 84 (8), 1394-1407
3. Keil, M. & Tiwana, A. (2006). "Relative importance of evaluation criteria for enterprise systems: a cojoint study." *Information Systems Journal, 16* (3), 237-262.
4. Saen, R. (2006). "A decision model for selecting slightly non-homogeneous technologies." *Applied Mathematics and Computation*, 177 (1), 149-158.
5. Shehabuddeen, N., Probert, D., & Phaal, R. (2006). "From theory to practice: challenges in operationalizing a technology selection framework." *Technovation*, 26, 324-335.
6. Shyur, H. (2006). "COTS evaluation using modified TOPSIS and ANP." *Applied Mathematics and Computation*, 177 (1), 251-259.
7. Şen, C., Baraçlı, H., Şen, S., & Başlıgil, H. (2009). "An integrated decision support system dealing with qualitative and quantitative objectives for enterprise software selection." *Expert Systems with Applications*, 36 (3), 5272-5283.
8. Chatzoglou, P., Diamantidis, A., Vraimaki, E., Vranakis, S., & Kourtidis, D. (2011). "Aligning IT, strategic orientation and organizational structure." *Business Process Management Journal*, 17 (4), 663-687.
9. Brynjolfson, E. (1993). "The productivity paradox of information technology." *Communications of the ACM*, 36 (12), 67-77.
10. Saaty, T. L. (1980). *The analytic hierarchy process*. New York: McGraw Hill.
11. Bernroider, E., & Koch, S. (2001). "ERP selection process in midsize and large organizations." *Business Process Management Journal, 7* (3), 251-257.
12. Lin, H., Hsu, P., & Sheen, G. (2007). "A fuzzy-based decision-making procedure for data warehouse system selection." *Expert Systems with Applications, 32* (3), 939-953.
13. Erdoğğğmuş, Ş., Kapanoglu, M., & Koç, E. (2005). "Evaluating high-tech alternatives by using analytic network process with BOCR and multiactors." *Evaluation and Program Planning, 28* (4), 391-399.
14. Faundes, M., & Astudillo, H., & Hitpass, B. (2013). "Process-based evaluation and comparison of OTS software alternatives." *FedCSIS 2013:* 1087-1094
15. Comella-Dorda, S., Dean, J., Morris, E., Oberndorf, P. (2002). "A Process for COTS Software Product Evaluation." *1st International Conference on COTS-Based Software System*, pp. 86-96. NRC 44925. (LNCS 2255, Springer)
16. Miller, B. L., Goldberg, D. E. (1995). "Genetic algorithms, tournament selection, and the effects of noise." *Complex Systems*, 9(3), 193-212.
17. Triantaphyllou, E., & Lin, C. T. (1996). *Development and evaluation of five fuzzy multiattribute decision-making.*
18. Duran, O., & Aguilo, J. (2007). "Computer-aided machine-tool selection based on a fuzzy-AHP approach." *Expert Systems with Applications*, 34(3), 1787–1794.

Continuous Integration in Chile: Knowledge, Perception, and Interest

Tomás Vargas[1], Henrique Chevreux[1], Valeria Henríquez[1], and Harlley Lima[2]

[1] Universidad Austral de Chile, General Lagos 2086, Valdivia, Chile
{tomas.vargas, henrique.chevreux, valeria.henriquez}@inf.uach.cl
[2] Universidade Federal de Minas Gerais, Av. Antônio Carlos, 6627 - 31270-901, Belo Horizonte, Brazil
harlley@dcc.ufmg.br

Abstract. In agile methodologies, Continuous Integration (CI) is the technique that requires all development team members to integrate their progress frequently in a common repository through an automated build. The main contribution of CI is fixing errors early and mitigating many common problems when developing software. In this work, we conducted a survey to measure the current state of knowledge, perception, and interest about CI by Chilean developers. Even though they show an explicit interest in CI and believe it may improve the quality of their projects, our findings demonstrate that it is necessary to leverage the knowledge of these practices in Chilean industry.

Keywords: Continuous Integration - software engineering - agile methodologies

1 Introducción

La terminología Integración Continua (IC) fue introducida en el contexto de diseño orientado a objetos en 1991 por Grady Brooch [3], luego adaptada como una de las prácticas de eXtreme Programming (XP) por Kent Beck [1]. Posteriormente el concepto fue sistematizado y popularizado en entrada del blog de Martin Fowler [8], actualizada y extendida en 2006 [5].

La noción básica es que todo el trabajo de los desarrolladores en un equipo es continuamente compilado, construido y probado, por tanto se comprueba que el software sigue funcionando a cada nuevo cambio [17].

Según Hilton et al. [11] IC no es una moda pasajera, su utilización es amplia y está aumentando. Sin embargo, el mismo artículo [11] revela que hay relativa escasez de publicaciones al respecto y realiza un llamado a investigadores.

Este trabajo indaga los niveles de conocimiento, percepción e interés sobre IC en el mercado profesional chileno. Esto se realiza mediante encuesta que evalúa: el actual conocimiento sobre IC de profesionales informáticos; donde lo adquieren; cual es su percepción sobre sus eventuales beneficios; si tienen interés en seguir empleando las prácticas que ya conocen y en aprender más al respecto.

A continuación se resumen los principales hallazgos de este trabajo:

- En general, el grado de conocimiento sobre IC en Chile es moderado, similar a niveles internacionales.
- El grado de conocimiento de IC aumenta según la cantidad de años de experiencia profesional.
- La mayoría de los profesionales aprende sobre IC en el mercado de trabajo o de forma autodidacta; pocos han aprendido sobre las prácticas asociadas a esta técnica en el lugar de educación formal.
- La percepción sobre IC es muy positiva así como el interés en seguir utilizando y/o aprender más sobre sus prácticas.

Las secciones restantes del artículo están organizadas conforme descrito a continuación. La sección 2 aborda los Trabajos Relacionados, agrupados en estudios sobre (i) beneficios e importancia de IC y (ii) uso y percepción de desarrolladores sobre IC. La sección 3 detalla la Metodología de esta investigación, incluyendo las bases para el diseño de la encuesta utilizada y las características de los encuestados. En la sección 4 se realiza el Análisis de los Datos obtenidos a partir de las respuestas a la encuesta aplicada. La sección 5 presenta las Conclusiones de esta investigación.

2 Trabajos Relacionados

A continuación, los trabajos relacionados son agrupados en dos áreas: (i) Beneficios e importancia de IC y (ii) Uso y percepción de IC.

2.1 Beneficios e importancia de IC

Un estudio de Vasilescu et al. [17] muestra que IC ayuda a aumentar la productividad de los desarrolladores y Humble [12] ha reportado impacto de IC en reducción de costos de desarrollo. Nuestra investigación afianza estos hallazgos, pues más de dos tercios de los profesionales reporta que *"IC optimiza tiempos, al automatizar procesos"*.

En relación a las capacidades de comunicación, la literatura muestra que IC ayuda a mejorarla entre equipos de desarrollo [14] y de estos con sus clientes [4]. Nuestro estudio confirma este beneficio, pues la mayoría de los profesionales reporta que IC *"ayuda a mejorar la comunicación y perspectiva del equipo frente a fallos"*.

Entrega Continua (metodología relacionada *"construida sobre IC"* [13, 6]) es tan importante que, según Fowler [7], está efectivamente escrita en el primer principio ágil: *"Nuestra mayor prioridad es satisfacer al cliente mediante la entrega temprana y continua de software con valor"* [9]. En contraste con otras tendencias que se popularizan y desvanecen rápidamente, IC representa una historia consolidada de éxito en ingeniería de software. Sin embargo, Hilton et al. [11] destacan que *"nosotros no tenemos respuestas a muchas preguntas relacionadas con IC"*. Esto refuerza la motivación a investigar sobre IC en distintos contextos. Según el conocimiento de los autores, esta es la primera investigación sobre IC con profesionales de múltiples empresas en el contexto profesional chileno.

2.2 Uso y percepción sobre IC

En la encuesta State of Agile Industry 2017 [16], 61% de las empresas participantes reportó IC como una de sus prácticas de ingeniería de software. Estudios han indicado amplia utilización en proyectos de código abierto [17, 11]. Según Hilton et al. [11] 94% de los desarrolladores reportan que usarán IC en su siguiente proyecto, inclusive 53% de los que no lo están utilizando actualmente. Nuestro estudio confirma esta percepción positiva e interés en aumentar la utilización de IC en el futuro próximo: 80% de los profesionales encuestados prefieren desarrollar software utilizando las prácticas IC que conocen; el 96% encuentra que IC ayuda a asegurar la calidad del software.

Sin embargo, estos trabajos previos [11, 16, 17] tratan el uso de IC de forma booleana (*"nuestra primera pregunta cuestionó si el participante usa o no IC"* [11]). En este trabajo se optó por abordar este tema consultando a los participantes por su conocimiento respecto a cada una de las prácticas esenciales de IC [5] de forma separada. La alta variabilidad entre el grado de conocimiento entre distintas prácticas (hasta 50 puntos porcentuales) sugiere la necesidad de más estudios en esta línea. Así como Beller et al. [2] han detectado que los desarrolladores reportan realizar pruebas tres veces más de lo que realmente hacen, es posible que esos estudios indagando el uso de IC de forma binaria [11, 16, 17] sufran de incongruencia similar. Según el conocimiento de los autores, esta es la primera investigación sobre el conocimiento, percepción e interés respecto a IC de forma no-booleana, mediante desglose de cada una de las once prácticas esenciales sistematizadas por Fowler [5].

3 Metodología

Para el desarrollo de este trabajo se realizó una encuesta, de la cual a continuación se detalla la metodología utilizada para su diseño, aplicación y posterior análisis de los datos obtenidos.

3.1 Diseño de Encuesta

Aunque otros autores [11,16] hayan elaborado encuestas que averiguan el uso de IC, éstas tratan la técnica de forma binaria. Este trabajo optó por diseñar una encuesta que indaga el conocimiento, percepción e interés sobre IC mediante las prácticas que efectivamente la conforman. Por tanto, la encuesta pide al participante indicar el nivel de conocimiento en cada una de las once prácticas clave que conforman IC, según expuesto por Fowler [5] y explicitadas en la Tabla 1.

Tabla 1: Las once prácticas esenciales de Integración Continua [5]

Práctica de Integración Continua
1. Mantener un único repositorio del código fuente por cada proyecto.
2. Automatizar el 'build' o compilación.
3. Hacer que el 'build' sea autotesteable.
4. Hacer que todo el equipo realice 'commits' todos los días.
5. Hacer que cada 'commit' ejecute el 'build' en una máquina de integración.
6. Corregir 'builds' fallidos rápido.
7. Mantener un 'build' rápido.
8. Ejecutar tests en un clon de la máquina de producción.
9. Entregar fácilmente a todos los stakeholders el último ejecutable.
10. Hacer que todos puedan ver el estado del 'build'.
11. Automatizar el despliegue.

La encuesta permite al participante seleccionar cuatro opciones (en escala Likert [15] sin punto medio para evitar sesgo de deseabilidad social [10]) para su grado de conocimiento en cada práctica: *conocimiento alto*, *medianamente alto*, *medianamente bajo* y *bajo*. A continuación, se preguntó al encuestado dónde aprendió esos conocimientos, siendo las opciones: *lugar de trabajo*, *autodidacta* y *lugar de formación profesional*. Por último, se formularon preguntas relacionadas con la percepción de la metodología, como por ejemplo sobre el éxito e impacto al implementar IC y si habría interés en aumentar el conocimiento en las prácticas de IC. En total, la encuesta desarrollada contiene 16 preguntas, las cuales se pueden revisar en: https://goo.gl/Bd8AMd

3.2 Aplicación de Encuesta

En el mes de junio de 2017 se aplicó la encuesta a 60 profesionales informáticos de 46 empresas chilenas, desde el área educacional hasta empresas netamente de desarrollo de software, de los cuales 30 encuestados fueron contactados vía correo electrónico y los otros 30 respondieron voluntariamente la encuesta en línea. La Tabla 2 muestra la cantidad de encuestados agrupados según sus años de experiencia laboral. En total 13 instituciones de formación profesional fueron indicadas por los encuestados, contando con el 65% de la Universidad Austral de Chile.

3.3 Amenazas a la Validez

Puesto que la aplicación de esta encuesta se realizó en línea, se necesitó de un mecanismo para prevenir un sesgo de deseabilidad social o de obtener demasiadas respuestas neutrales. Este mecanismo fue eliminar el punto medio en las opciones de respuesta a preguntas de opinión de selección múltiple. De esta forma se logró obtener de mejor manera la opinión real de los encuestados.

Como se menciona anteriormente, el 65% de los encuestados realizó sus estudios profesionales en la Universidad Austral de Chile. Si bien este último dato podría considerarse una amenaza a la validez debido a un eventual sesgo en la muestra, los resultados del trabajo arrojaron que los encuestados que realizaron su formación profesional en dicha universidad declararon un promedio de autopercepción de conocimiento sobre IC del 67%, muy cercano al 64% que declararon los demás encuestados. Este promedio se analiza de forma general en la sección 4.

Tabla 2: Años de experiencia laboral de los encuestados

Rango de años de experiencia	Cantidad de personas	%
1 a 5	28	47,7%
6 a 10	16	26,7%
11 a 15	5	8,3%
16 a 20	6	10%
21 a 25	4	6,7%
26 o más	1	1,7%

4 Análisis de los Datos

Con la elaboración de la encuesta con 16 preguntas y su aplicación a 60 profesionales, se obtuvo un total de 960 respuestas. Esta sección presenta el análisis de los datos obtenidos respecto a los niveles de conocimiento, percepción e interés en IC. En particular, las subsecciones a continuación responden a las siguientes preguntas de investigación:

Q1. ¿Cuál es el grado de conocimiento sobre IC
- **(a)** general en las empresas?
- **(b)** según los años de experiencia profesional?

Q2. ¿Dónde los profesionales aprenden sobre IC?

Q3. ¿Qué percepción se tiene sobre IC?

4.1 Grado de conocimiento sobre IC

Conforme a lo descrito en la subsección 3.1, se investigó el grado de conocimiento sobre IC mediante cada una de sus once prácticas esenciales. Con base en esto, se contestan las preguntas de investigación Q1(a) y (b).

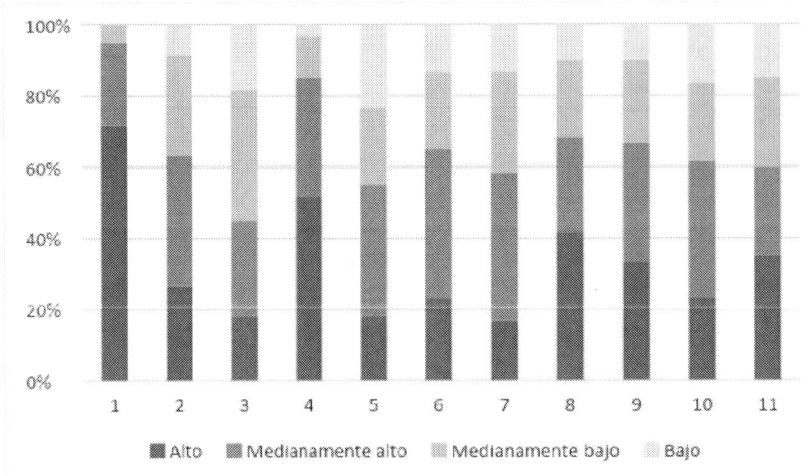

Fig. 1. Gráfico de conocimiento general sobre prácticas.

Conocimiento general de IC Para responder la pregunta de investigación Q1(a), la Fig. 1 muestra el resultado de la declaración de conocimiento de los encuestados sobre cada una de las prácticas. Se obtuvo un promedio de autopercepción de conocimiento (alto y medianamente alto) de las prácticas de aproximadamente el 66%.

Además, se aprecia alta variabilidad dependiendo de la práctica considerada. Por ejemplo, mientras el 95% de las respuestas respecto a la práctica 1 (*Mantener un único repositorio del código fuente por cada proyecto*) posee un nivel alto o medianamente alto de conocimiento, la práctica 3 (*Hacer que el 'build' sea auto-testeable*) presenta un nivel de conocimiento alto o medianamente alto en solo 45% de las respuestas.

Para evaluar como el conocimiento en las prácticas de IC puede cambiar a lo largo de la experiencia laboral, en la siguiente sección se hace el análisis del conocimiento de IC de acuerdo con el tiempo de trabajo.

Grado de conocimiento en IC según los años de experiencia En general, el 66% de los encuestados presenta un promedio de autopercepción alto y medianamente alto sobre las prácticas IC. Sin embargo, para dar una respuesta a la pregunta de investigación Q1(b), se hizo el análisis del conocimiento de IC según los años de experiencia laboral. Así, se dividieron los resultados relacionados con el conocimiento de las prácticas según los años de trabajo en grupos de hasta un año, dos años, entre dos y cinco años y con más de cinco años de experiencia laboral, como se ve en la Fig. 2.

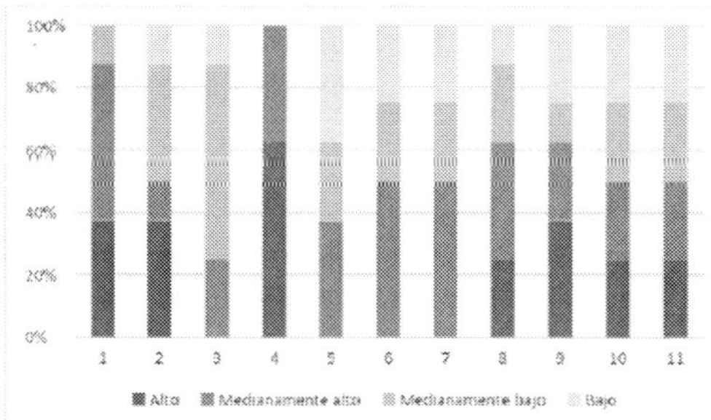

(a) Hasta un año de experiencia.

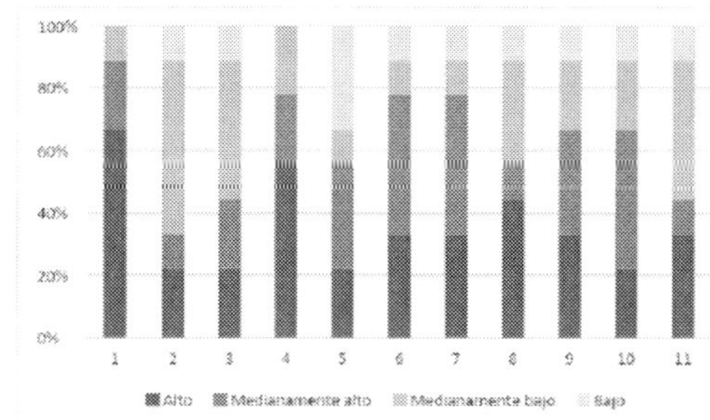

(b) Hasta dos años de experiencia.

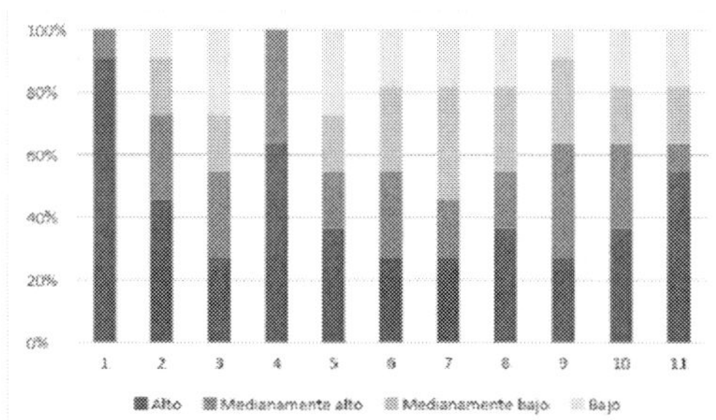

(c) Entre 2 y 5 años de experiencia.

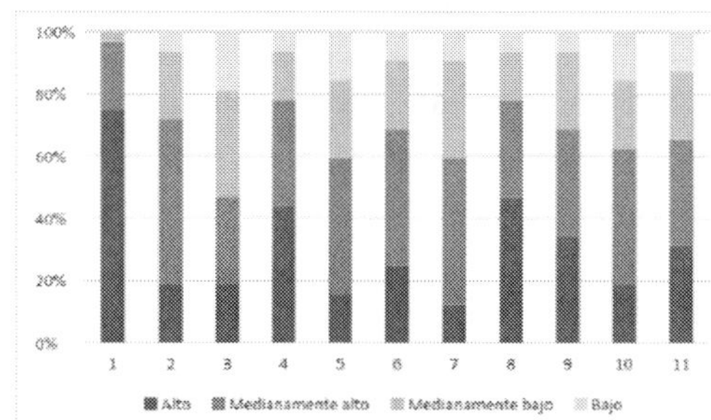

(d) Más de 5 años de experiencia.

Fig. 2. Grado de conocimiento en las once prácticas de IC a lo largo de los años de experiencia profesional.

En la Fig. 2(a) se muestra el grado de conocimiento de ocho encuestados con hasta un año de experiencia. Se observa una disminución en el conocimiento de las prácticas en comparación al grado de conocimiento general presentado en la Fig. 1, obteniendo un promedio de autopercepción de conocimiento del 57%. Aunque, el grado de conocimiento en la práctica 4 no ha presentado valores como "Bajo" o "Medianamente bajo", en las prácticas 3, 5, 6 y 7 no hay encuestados con alto conocimiento.

Luego, en la Fig. 2(b) se muestra el grado de conocimiento de nueve encuestados que tenían hasta dos años de experiencia laboral, en que se puede apreciar un aumento de este grado de conocimiento en comparación con los datos obtenidos de los encuestados con hasta un año de experiencia, obteniendo un promedio de autopercepción de conocimiento del 63%. En relación a los encuestados con hasta un año de experiencia, hubo una disminución de profesionales con bajo conocimiento en las prácticas 6 hasta 11, aumentando el promedio de conocimiento de los encuestados con dos años de experiencia.

El siguiente grupo analizado fueron los 11 encuestados que tenían entre dos y cinco años de experiencia laboral. De la Fig. 2(c) se obtiene que existe un aumento en el promedio de autopercepción de conocimiento sobre las prácticas, llegando al 66%. Aquí se destaca que en las prácticas 1 y 4 todos tienen conocimiento alto o medianamente alto. Por último, se analizaron los datos de los 32 encuestados que tenían más de cinco años de experiencia laboral. Se aprecia en la Fig. 2(d) una disminución en encuestados con bajo y medianamente bajo nivel de conocimiento en IC, obteniendo un promedio de autopercepción de conocimiento del 69%.

En conclusión, el grado de conocimiento en las prácticas de Integración Continua va aumentando según los años de experiencia laboral, contestando la pregunta de investigación Q1(b). Aunque esté claro el aumento del conocimiento en IC a lo largo de años de trabajo, solo esta pregunta no respondería si el aprendizaje ocurre en el ambiente de trabajo, en lugar de formación profesional o con iniciativas autodidactas de los profesionales. En la siguiente sección se discute ese punto.

4.2 Lugar de aprendizaje de IC

En esta sección son analizados los resultados relacionados al lugar de aprendizaje de Integración Continua declarado por los profesionales, pertinentes a la pregunta de investigación Q2. En particular, son presentados los resultados de la pregunta: '*¿Dónde diría usted que adquirió mayormente estos conocimientos?*'.

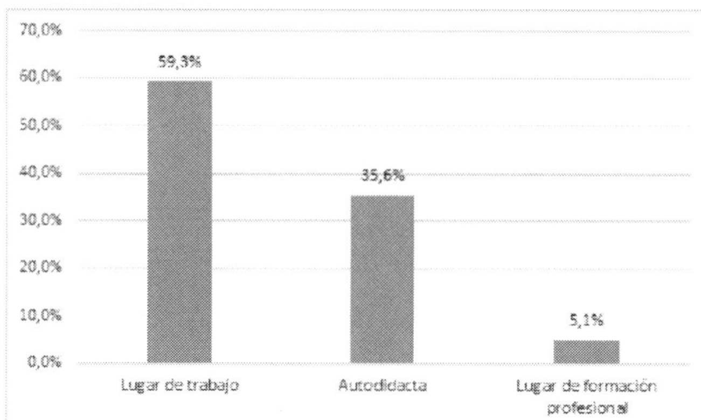

Fig. 3. Lugar de aprendizaje sobre las prácticas de IC.

La Fig. 3 muestra estos resultados, en que se destaca la poca participación de los lugares de formación profesional en la enseñanza sobre estos temas, siendo que la mayoría de los desarrolladores aprendieron los conceptos de IC en el lugar de trabajo o de forma autodidacta.

4.3 Percepción sobre IC

En esta sección, se analiza la percepción de los encuestados en relación a la Integración Continua. Para responder a la pregunta de investigación Q3, fue preguntado (en escala Likert) a los encuestados cuál es su nivel de conformidad con las siguientes afirmaciones:

- *"Prefiero desarrollar un producto software utilizando las prácticas que indiqué anteriormente"*
- *"La implantación de estas prácticas ayudan a asegurar el éxito del producto software"*

- *"Me gustaría tomar algún tipo de asesoramiento o perfeccionamiento en la utilización de estas prácticas"*

Fue preguntado también a los encuestados cuáles son los impactos más importantes de la incorporación de la mayoría de las prácticas de IC en sus proyectos.

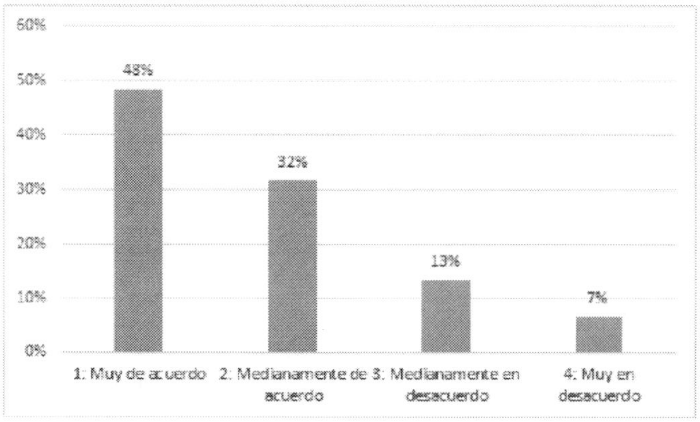

Fig. 4. Preferencia por utilizar prácticas de IC.

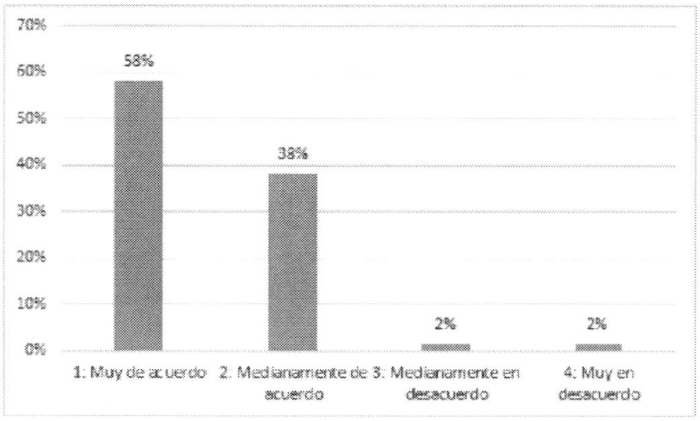

Fig. 5. Percepción sobre éxito al implantar IC.

En la Fig. 4 se observa que aproximadamente el 80% de los encuestados declaró estar 'Muy de acuerdo' o 'Medianamente de acuerdo' con la afirmación *'Prefiero desarrollar un producto software utilizando las prácticas que indiqué conocer anteriormente'*. Los encuestados prefieren desarrollar utilizando las prácticas de IC por que creen que estas prácticas aseguran la calidad del producto software, como se muestra en la Fig. 5, en que el 96% de los encuestados declaró estar *'Muy de acuerdo'* o *'Medianamente de acuerdo'* con la afirmación *'La implantación de estas prácticas ayuda a asegurar el éxito del producto software'*. Finalmente, en la Fig. 6 se muestra la cantidad de encuestados que declararon estar de acuerdo con uno o más de los impactos listados. Se destaca que el 90% de los encuestados cree que la implantación de las prácticas de Integración Continua ayuda a *'Mejorar la calidad del producto software'*.

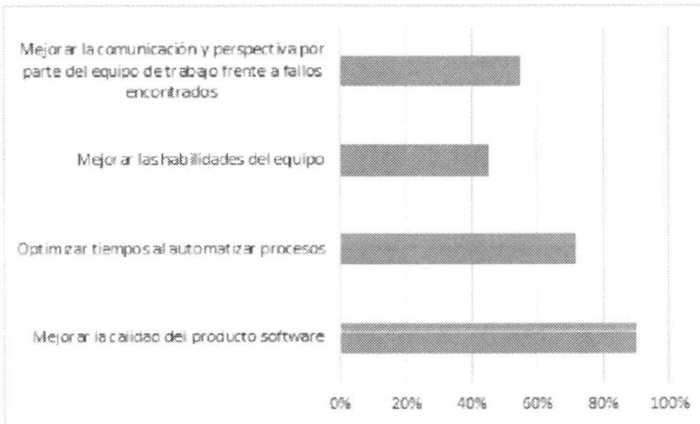

Fig. 6. Percepción sobre impactos al implantar prácticas de IC.

Además, a continuación se mencionan los impactos más frecuentes declarados por parte de los encuestados en pregunta abierta del cuestionario:

- *Minimizar impacto de errores.*
- *Lograr un producto acorde a las expectativas.*
- *Cumplir con alcance, tiempo y presupuestos de un proyecto, además de garantizar el cumplimiento de los procesos de trabajo.*
- *Facilitar la incorporación de un nuevo desarrollador al equipo.*
- *Aumenta la felicidad.*

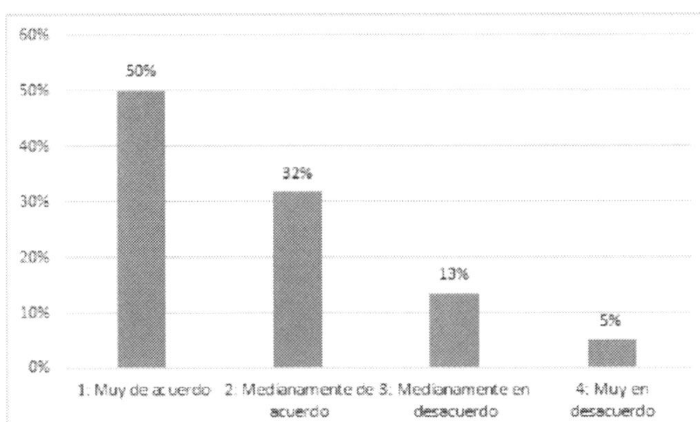

Fig. 7. Interés sobre aumentar conocimiento en prácticas de IC.

Finalmente, se puede considerar que existe un alto interés de parte de los encuestados por aumentar sus conocimientos sobre este tema, tal como se muestra en la Fig. 7, donde el 82% de los encuestados declararon estar *'Medianamente de acuerdo'* o *'Muy de acuerdo'* con la afirmación *'Me gustaría tomar algún tipo de asesoramiento o perfeccionamiento en la utilización de estas prácticas'*. En conclusión, los profesionales creen que la incorporación de IC mejora la calidad del proyecto y estarían dispuestos a recibir asesoramiento para la implementación de sus prácticas, contestando la pregunta de investigación Q3.

Por tanto, la percepción sobre IC es mayoritariamente positiva. Los profesionales prefieren desarrollar empleando las prácticas IC que ya conocen y también demuestran alto interés en aprender más al respecto.

5 Conclusiones

IC constituye una de las principales técnicas del desarrollo ágil desde sus inicios. En contraste con otras tendencias que se popularizan y desvanecen rápidamente, representa una historia consolidada de éxito en ingeniería de software. Este trabajo estudió los niveles de conocimiento, percepción e interés sobre prácticas de IC entre desarrolladores chilenos. Como innovación, en vez de tratar el conocimiento de IC de forma booleana, se investiga mediante preguntas sobre las prácticas que efectivamente conforman esta técnica.

Los principales resultados de investigación se pueden resumir como:

1. Se muestra similitud entre el contexto del mercado profesional chileno versus demás estudios en otros contextos [11, 16, 17, 14]. En particular, sobre la metodología introducida por este trabajo (según la cual se averigua cada una de las once prácticas esenciales de IC), se requieren más estudios para averiguar eventuales diferencias según el contexto.
2. En general, el nivel de conocimiento de las prácticas IC es moderado (66%) y similar a niveles internacionales (61% según [16]).
3. El nivel de conocimiento puede variar significativamente entre las distintas prácticas IC.
4. Existe una percepción muy positiva sobre IC entre los desarrolladores chilenos, 80% demuestran interés en seguir usando las prácticas que ya conocen, 90% cree que la implantación de sus prácticas ayuda a "Mejorar la calidad del producto software" y 82% les gustaría aprender más al respecto.
5. Mientras más años de experiencia, mayor el conocimiento sobre las prácticas IC.
6. La mayoría de los profesionales adquiere los conocimientos sobre IC en el lugar de trabajo o de forma autodidacta.
7. Considerando la baja participación de los lugares de educación formal como medio de aprendizaje de IC, existe la oportunidad de enriquecer las mallas curriculares donde se imparten materias relacionadas con Ingeniería de Software.

Se sugieren como trabajos futuros: realización de más estudios sobre IC en contextos fuera de los grandes centros mundiales de desarrollo; replicar en otros contextos la metodología de investigación no-binaria del conocimiento y uso IC, a partir de sus prácticas constituyentes separadamente; analizar en mayor profundidad la variabilidad de la difusión entre las distintas prácticas IC.

Referencias

1. Beck, K.: Embracing change with extreme programming. Computer **32**(10), 70–77 (1999)
2. Beller, M., Gousios, G., Zaidman, A.: How (much) do developers test? In: Proceedings of the 37th International Conference on Software Engineering - Volume 2. pp. 559–562. ICSE '15, IEEE Press, Piscataway, NJ, USA (2015), http://dl.acm.org/citation.cfm?id=2819009.2819101
3. Booch, G.: Object Oriented Design with Applications. Benjamin-Cummings Publishing Co., Inc., Redwood City, CA, USA (1991)
4. Fitzgerald, B., Stol, K.J.: Continuous software engineering and beyond: Trends and challenges. In: Proceedings of the 1st International Workshop on Rapid Continuous Software Engineering. pp. 1–9. RCoSE 2014, ACM, New York, NY, USA (2014)
5. Fowler, M.: Continuous integration (2006), http://martinfowler.com/articles/continuousIntegration.html, consultado en: 2018-03-21
6. Fowler, M.: Continuous delivery (2013), https://martinfowler.com/bliki/ContinuousDelivery.html, consultado en: 2018-03-21
7. Fowler, M.: Continuous delivery (2015), https://youtu.be/aoMfbgF2D_4, consultado en: 2018-03-21
8. Fowler, M., Foemmel, M.: Continuous integration (2000), https://www.martinfowler.com/articles/originalContinuousIntegration.html, consultado en: 2018-03-21
9. Fowler, M., Highsmith, J.: The agile manifesto. Software Development **9**(8), 28–35 (2001)
10. Garland, R.: The mid-point on a rating scale: Is it desirable. Marketing Bulletin pp. 66–70 (1991)
11. Hilton, M., Tunnell, T., Huang, K., Marinov, D., Dig, D.: Usage, costs, and benefits of continuous integration in open-source projects. In: Proceedings of the 31st IEEE/ACM International Conference on Automated Software Engineering. pp. 426–437. ASE 2016, ACM, New York, NY, USA (2016)
12. Humble, J.: Evidence and case studies (2000), https://continuousdelivery.com/evidence-case-studies/, consultado en: 2018-03-21
13. Humble, J., Farley, D.: Continuous Delivery: Reliable Software Releases through Build, Test, and Deployment Automation (Adobe Reader). Pearson Education (2010)
14. Janus, A., Schmietendorf, A., Dumke, R., Jäger, J.: The 3c approach for agile quality assurance. In: Proceedings of the 3rd International Workshop on Emerging Trends in Software Metrics. pp. 9–13. WETSoM '12 (2012)
15. Likert, R.: A technique for the measurement of attitudes. Archives of Psychology **22**(140), 1–55 (1932)
16. One, V.: 11th annual state of agile report. Tech. rep. (2017), http://www.agile247.pl/wp-content/uploads/2017/04/versionone-11th-annual-state-of-agile-report.pdf, consultado en: 2018-03-21
17. Vasilescu, B., Yu, Y., Wang, H., Devanbu, P., Filkov, V.: Quality and productivity outcomes relating to continuous integration in github. In: Proceedings of the 2015 10th Joint Meeting on Foundations of Software Engineering. pp. 805–816. ACM, New York, NY, USA (2015)

Escuela Superior Politecnica de Chimborazo
Panamericana Sur km 1 1/2
Riobamba - Ecuador
Postal Code: EC060155

Universidad de Atacama
Copiapo, Chile
Copayapu 485, Copiapo
Region de Atacama, Chile

ISBN 978-1-5108-6325-5

CURRAN ASSOCIATES INC.
proceedings.com

9 781510 863255